The Official® Price Guide

OLD
BOOKS

The Official® Price Guide to

OLD
BOOKS

Marie Tedford
and
Pat Goudey

FIRST EDITION
House of Collectibles · New York

This is a registered trademark of Random House, Inc.

Published by: House of Collectibles
201 East 50th Street
New York, NY 10022

Distributed by Ballantine Books, a division of Random House, Inc., New York, and simultaneously in Canada by Random House of Canada Limited, Toronto.

Manufactured in the United States of America

ISSN: 1073-8614

ISBN: 0-876-37915-3

Text design by Holly Johnson
Cover design by Kristine V. Mills
Cover photo by George Kerrigan

First Edition: June 1994

10 9 8 7 6 5 4 3

To Marie's mother, and Pat's grandmother, Jenny, who could neither read nor write. She thought books were a frivolous pastime, but would have thoroughly enjoyed the irony of this book.

CONTENTS

Acknowledgments ix
Introduction 1
Market Review 3
A Closer Look at the Book Trade 7
The Care and Repair of Old Books 20
How to Use This Book 28
Glossary 31
List of Abbreviations 71
Old Books Listing 75
Bibles 360
Recommended Periodicals and Research Sources 364

ACKNOWLEDGMENTS

During the months we have been preparing this book, a number of special folks have given us their time and expertise. Our sincerest appreciation goes to Connell Gallagher and his staff—Kevin Graffagnino, Nadia Smith, and Ingrid Bower—at the Bailey-Howe Library in Burlington, Vermont, for allowing us to photograph their books. Thanks to booksellers Terry Harper; Helen Tudhope; Ben Koenig; Ken Anderson; the folks at Bygone Books; Michael Ginzberg; Colleen Urbanek; Patterson Smith; Vincent Gulotta; John Zubal; and the staff at Christie's, Sotheby's, and California Book Auction for their invaluable information and comments. And to all the many dealers and collectors we talked to across the country who gave us the benefit of their time and thoughts on the many facets of this fascinating business.

Thanks also to Pat's friend, Marilyn Green, who photographed some of the bookplates, and to Lucy Wells, the darkroom wizard.

Finally, a special thanks to Bill, Rob, and Ted, and to the rest of our families for accepting us back into the fold after our delinquent absence and for the summer we put you all through.

The Official® Price Guide to

OLD
BOOKS

INTRODUCTION

Bibliophiles have gone about the business of amassing book collections since man first penned his thoughts on paper. Never doubting the value and joy of books, they were comfortable with their benign vice and content to browse the book mart with kindred spirits in a somewhat elite specialty.

During the past twenty years, interest in used books has taken a quantum leap. Of course, the market for antiquarian books has always been brisk. Now, a new breed of collector and dealer has exploded onto the scene. Perhaps more people can afford to buy books, or perhaps the mania for collecting everything from old fountain pens to political pins has spilled over into books as these collectibles find their way to the marketplace.

Whatever the reason, the drive is propelling collectors to search for their favorite authors of the nineteenth century, pristine first editions barely ten or twenty years old, and any and all things Americana or illustrated.

Twenty years ago, when Marie met bookseller John Westerberg at a wedding reception across the road from her home in Underhill Center, Vermont, they began chatting about old books. She had a few around the house that she'd picked up over the years; books have always been an important part of her life.

When she showed John her treasures, he said Marie had an eye for old books and would she like to scout for his Rochester, New

York, bookstore. John gave her a few pointers on what to look for, told her how to quote a book, and she was on her own. Marie had a good eye for books, John said, but over the twenty years she has been in the business, she learned a bookseller needs more than a talent for spotting a good book. She could have used a guide like this one—basic, to the point, with enough background to get a book scout started, plus pointers on where to look for additional information.

If you're interested in old books and the book trade, you need to go into that world equipped to deal competently with whatever you find there. This guide is one tool to that end.

No one book can have all the answers to the myriad questions the public has about old and used books. We suggest you use the information we've provided and consult many other sources, the best of which we have listed at the back of this book.

Marie learned the hard way, by trial and error—and not just a few errors, either—until she got the hang of it. That's not all bad. Experience is, after all, a pretty good teacher. But a good book is a good friend.

We want this book to do more than tell you the going rate for a particular title. Books are much more than just a commodity with a price tag. Our intention is to inform you, pique your interest, and even entertain you a bit. Because the best reason we discovered for developing an interest in books, and you may agree, is for the sheer fun of it.

MARKET REVIEW

The used book trade held steady during several years of economic slowdown in the United States. But the business is not immune to market forces and a continued sluggish economy is showing its effects as we enter the mid-'90s.

When we began working on this market review, we put our ears to the ground, button-holed dealers, interrogated collectors, and sent out requests for information from some of the leading auction houses. We'd be Pollyannas if we reported that the collectible book business is flourishing and bookmen are making piles of money. In fact, the consensus is that "flush times" are behind us and belt-tightening is the order of the day. But not to despair. Bookmen who modified their expectations and held the line on prices are getting by and even doing well.

Feedback from the field was mixed, with the high-end businesses and auction houses finding a stable market while middle- and low-end dealers were often feeling the pinch. Browsing bookstores like Bygone Books in Burlington, Vermont, reported an active summer with good returns selling an eclectic assortment of moderate and lower priced reading books. John Mayo of Tuttle's Bookstore in Rutland, Vermont, said business was slower than usual but wasn't standing still.

On the opposite coast, Rick Boyles, proprietor of My Book Heaven in Alameda, California, said his business had been pretty solid. But, he believes California as a rule does a strong business in antiquarian books.

In Philadelphia, the Petersons reported their ad responses were down and show activity had dropped off. The couple, in the business for twenty years, specializes in children's and illustrated books through mail order and shows. On the other hand, Selma Peterson said that their son, Montreal bookseller S.W. Welch, reported a very good year by the summer of '93.

Gerrie at The Book Exchange in the college town of Missoula, Montana, said: "Business is booming!" And Judy Brothers of Elkhart, Indiana, said The Bookstack Bookstore recorded higher sales in the first six months of 1993 than they'd enjoyed previously. General sales were increasing, and book fairs were good. They attributed some of this positive activity to affordable pricing.

In Chicago, Illinois, Tony Polito and Thomas J. Joyce agreed that their business was "very tight and tentative." They deal heavily in modern first editions and that market is more speculative than the antiquarian markets, with more of a tendency to experience fads of short duration. They predict the bubble will burst on some of the "hot" contemporary authors currently commanding premium prices.

Colleen Urbanek of Colleen's Books in Houston, Texas, said she's always careful to buy books she knows will move off her shelves quickly. She has one of the largest used bookstores in the Houston area with an extensive collection of Texana she keeps well stocked. In the spring of '93, Colleen's customer base was stable, with active trade in collectible books, but the researchers and college professors were cutting down on their purchases.

Patterson Smith of Montclair, New Jersey, has specialized in books on crime, criminology, and related fields for thirty-six years. He noticed a drop in activity from institutions and libraries over the past few years in favor of increased sales to private collectors. He theorizes that institutions have less money for special collections during tight times. Topics he found moving well include serial killers and gangsters of the 1920s and '30s.

A couple new to the business from South Carolina visited our shop in Vermont in August. They said book-selling was slow in their part of the country.

Many voices cried out during the early '90s, "Where have all the customers gone?" Bookman after bookman praised the quality of goods available, saying perhaps some collectors are selling treasures during tough times to raise cash and some dealers are releasing good books for similar reasons. But the customers just aren't there to take advantage of the largesse.

One dealer from Massachusetts who works primarily through mail order said his typical catalog response was $13,000 four years ago, down to $1,000 by 1993. "I should be calling it a hobby at this point," he lamented. Still, he reported business at the Vermont Antiquarian Bookseller's show in Pomfret, Vermont, on August 1 was one of his best shows ever in the state. Several other exhibitors said they did well, too, all reporting they were holding the line on their prices, having bought very carefully and marked up with restraint. Reason for hope.

Auctions give another perspective. Sotheby's reported at the end of 1992 (the last year for which we could collect full data) sales of genres other than Americana showed an increasingly selective buyer. In December of '92, Sotheby's New York sale of Americana realized a hefty $4,864,000 against a top estimate of $2,660,000, with much manuscript and holographic material included.

The company's aggregate sale for the year in books and manuscripts was $11,056,012. A 1493 German *Nuremberg Chronicle*, in contemporary binding, fetched $254,000, a record price. A 1462 illuminated vellum bible in chained binding brought $286,000. A copy of Yeats's "Mosada" with provenance and inscription brought $66,000 during only light bidding on the modern English collection of Dr. Morton McMichael of which the volume was a part.

John Zubal of Zubal Auction Company, Cleveland, Ohio, a midrange house, said science and medicine were hot genres during 1993. Zubal said books on the history of science and the military, battles, and wars were especially strong, as were military regimentals. Science fiction and fantasy have gone crazy, Zubal said. Sports were very strong and anything on golf always sells.

In San Francisco, the auction book market weathered the height of the recession well, although sales of intermediately priced goods (under $500) were off, according to Laurie J. Thompson of the California Book Auction, now a division of Butterfield & Butterfield. Rising prices were still the order of the day for holographic and manuscript materials, she said, while prices held firm for children's books, modern first editions (especially if signed), travel and exploration books, and Americana. All genres, of course, assume excellent condition, she said.

Thompson echoed the booksellers' observation that private collectors and dealers, rather than institutions, were currently bidding for the more significant offerings on the block.

Swann Galleries reported that during late 1992, the market was strong in Americana, the demand for magic was "insatiable," while modern illustrated books, especially those by stars of the School of Paris, were in high demand. At a November 12 auction, a Limited Editions Club volume of *Ulysses*, illustrated by Matisse and signed by both author and artist, went for $7,150.

Photographic books were an up-and-coming field, as well, especially early works using photo illustrations. In October 1992, Swann sold a photo-illustrated volume of *The North American Indian* for $9,350.

A CLOSER LOOK
AT THE BOOK TRADE

Whenever we mention that we're used and rare book dealers, we're met with raised eyebrows and a host of questions about books people have tucked away in an attic or closet. We suspect the world contains many would-be bookmen needing only a little nudge to get them started. Below, we'll offer a nudge, try to dispel some of the mystery surrounding old books, and answer the questions we're often asked.

WHAT IS OLD IN OLD BOOKS?

This seems like a reasonable question, but it's not relevant to the bookman. We don't think anybody knows what the cut-off date is for "antiquarian" books. Is it nineteenth century? Early twentieth?

Unless you are a rare book dealer focusing on the earliest printed material—incunabula or the first printed books in the new world—you need to put actual age out of your mind and learn which books are sought by dealers and other collectors. You'll discover a busy trade in books from past centuries and books from last year—from the antiquarian to the modern first editions.

Rather than age, think about content: What is the book about and who wrote it? If you must choose between two books in good condition, one printed in London in 1632 by an obscure British

A typical generalist's bookstall holds a little something for each collector. The stall pictured is run by bookseller Terry Harper in the Middlebury Antique Center in Middlebury, Vermont.

poet no one has ever heard of, and the other a nineteenth-century tome on the American Indian published in New York, choose the one on the American Indian. There's a lively market for Native Americana and you'll likely find a customer for the book. The poetry is merely fun to have on the shelf because it's old. It isn't automatically a collector's item.

Instead of thinking in terms of "old," consider your books used, out-of-print, or rare. These descriptions apply to collectible books of all ages from earliest printing to modern first editions.

WHERE WILL I FIND GOOD BOOKS?

The first source that comes to mind is the antiquarian and collectible book dealer. For many genres, used book stores will yield exactly what you're after, often at bargain prices. Throw in a little conversation with the bookseller and you've found your book and learned something about your subject, too. Bought from a reputable dealer, the book has been pre-screened and you won't have to do further research to verify your find.

Booksellers consider other dealers a prime source of good stock. You can buy direct from dealers through bookstores, dealer catalogs, advertisements, industry periodicals, and at book fairs. As a beginner, attend the smaller regional fairs and shows that are popular all over the country. They're an education unto themselves.

"I think it's a very good place to be if you're a novice," advised Victor Gulotta, former sales director for a rare book house in Boston. "In one place, you'll find a lot of dealers and a lot of books. They have good books with prices at the lower end."

Other excellent sources are flea markets, estate sales, auctions, the Salvation Army, antique stores, and garage sales. These are the places that professionals go to find books.

HOW GOOD ARE AUCTIONS FOR BUYING AND SELLING BOOKS?

Books at local auctions are plentiful and they're a fine source of collectibles, but you can't be sure of picking up a bargain any longer. In too many cases, except perhaps at exclusive rare book and collectible houses like Swann's, Christie's, and Sotheby's, the popularity of auctions has brought with it a kind of recreational bidder. In the heat of competition for an item, bidding may be driven much higher than a careful buyer would be willing to pay in a bookstore or in a private transaction.

Great books can still be had for excellent prices if buyers exercise caution, know how much they are willing to pay ahead of time, and sit on their hands when the bidding gets rowdy.

If you're selling books, auctions and dealers are on a par, each having their strong and weak points. On a particular day, if an auction attracts a spirited audience, you could do well. On an off day, you risk your books selling for less than you hoped. Selling through dealers requires more of your time and effort, but dealers have pipelines to collectors who may be looking for just the book you're selling.

In the final analysis, we can only tell you what is available. You must choose what's right for you.

WHAT BOOKS SHOULD I PICK UP?

There's no one answer to this question. Before you ask it, you have some decisions to make, and then the question will begin to answer itself. Are you buying books for investment or fun? Will you be a collector? Or a dealer? Will you specialize or be a generalist?

Carefully bought collectible books hold their value well and grow in value at a steady rate of up to 10 percent per year. They're a safe investment, but with rare exceptions, they're not speculative and most likely won't make you a killing.

Swann Auction Galleries put the eclectic Raymond Epstein collection on the block in April 1992. Mr. Epstein had carefully recorded the purchase prices of his books, which were maintained in excellent condition, providing a fine opportunity to compare market price, then and now. A copy of *Dracula* bought in 1965 for $46 was maintained in a specially made case costing $38. The book realized $11,000 at auction in 1992. A copy of *Ulysses* bought for $400 in 1965 and maintained in a $350 case sold for $19,800. Mr.

A charming copy of Kate Greenaway's Almanack from 1888, *held in the Bailey-Howe Library Special Collections at the University of Vermont, was printed by George Routledge & Sons, Great Britain.*

Epstein acquired *Tom Sawyer* in 1966 for $1,250 and it sold for $9,350. An $885 *Wizard of Oz* acquired in 1972 sold for $20,900.

As often as not, even those who collect as an investment wind up excited by the hunt and end up collecting for fun, too.

If you decide to specialize, whether bookseller or collector, learn all you can about your subject. Don't neglect allied subjects that broaden and flesh out your knowledge. Visit bookstores, talk to dealers, read dealer catalogs to see what's being offered and what someone else wants. Visit libraries.

Michael Ginsberg, a bookseller from Massachusetts and past president of the Antiquarian Booksellers Association of America (ABAA) recommends that you read the bibliographies of books related to your speciality; you'll discover other books to read and some you'll want to collect or stock in your store.

Fifteen years ago, the late Elizabeth Woodburn, a specialist in horticulture, advised Marie to specialize after Marie had offered her some very nice herbals and catalogs. Marie would probably be an expert on one subject by now had she taken the New Jersey

Ever popular, The Complete Angler *(sometimes spelled Compleat Angler), by Isaac Walton (sometimes spelled Izaak Walton), in several incarnations, along with other books of the genre, are held in Special Collections at the University of Vermont's Bailey-Howe Library. Shown are (l. to r.) Izaak Walton and Charles Cotton,* The Complete Angler, *William Pickering, London, 1836; John Williamson,* The British Angler, or a Pocket Companion for Gentlemen Fishers, *1740; Walton and Cotton,* The Complete Angler, *London, 1824; and Izaak Walton,* The Complete Angler, *illustrated by E.J. Sullivan, J.M. Dent Co., London, 1896.*

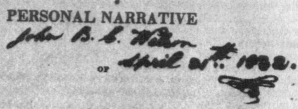

THE

PERSONAL NARRATIVE

OF

JAMES O. PATTIE,

OF

KENTUCKY,

DURING AN EXPEDITION FROM ST. LOUIS, THROUGH THE VAST REGIONS
BETWEEN THAT PLACE AND THE PACIFIC OCEAN, AND THENCE BACK
THROUGH THE CITY OF MEXICO TO VERA CRUZ, DURING JOURNEY-
INGS OF SIX YEARS; IN WHICH HE AND HIS FATHER, WHO
ACCOMPANIED HIM, SUFFERED UNHEARD OF HARDSHIPS
AND DANGERS, HAD VARIOUS CONFLICTS WITH THE IN-
DIANS, AND WERE MADE CAPTIVES, IN WHICH
CAPTIVITY HIS FATHER DIED; TOGETHER
WITH A DESCRIPTION OF THE COUNTRY,
AND THE VARIOUS NATIONS THROUGH
WHICH THEY PASSED.

EDITED BY TIMOTHY FLINT.

CINCINNATI:
PRINTED AND PUBLISHED BY JOHN H. WOOD,
1831.

Overland journey narratives (as this type of book is known to collectors) are always in demand, and the early ones—such as Pattie's—can go for really prodigious prices. In this case a well-preserved specimen would run about $10,000.

bookseller's advice, but that decision is a matter of temperament. Marie knew that she wouldn't be able to resist picking up books outside her specialty and she'd be right back where she started—a generalist.

CATEGORIES OR ANA

When you get more involved in books as a dealer or collector, you'll become familiar with references to the common genres and specialties, sometimes called "ana" (*see* Glossary). These will include topics from books on the settling of the Americas, native peoples, black studies, maritime trades, foreign countries, children's books, medicine, science, sporting books, zoology, anthropology, magic, antiques, the military, cooking, poetry, railroads, billiards, the radical labor movement, and on and on. Add to that limited editions, fine presses, fine bindings, illustrated books; the list doesn't end. And each genre has subgenres, ad infinitum.

These categories help people to communicate. Dealers use them to describe their specialities and collectors use them to define their area of interest. But genres are not mutually exclusive; there is enormous overlapping, and they are just one tool for evaluating books.

AMERICANA VERSUS US-IANA

A very popular specialty is Americana, but what do bookmen mean by that term? Do they refer to books on the discovery, exploration, and political and cultural development of the United States? Or do they adopt the broader and truer meaning of the term and include all the Americas from Canada to Argentina?

In modern vernacular, the meaning of Americana has narrowed to refer to the United States and its territories though some dealers use it in the more inclusive form. To be technically correct when referring to the United States, the term US-iana was coined by bibliographer Wright Howes, author of *Howes USIANA* issued in 1954, but that term is less widely used.

Instruction with Delight.

A LITTLE PRETTY
POCKET-BOOK,
INTENDED FOR THE
INSTRUCTION and AMUSEMENT
OF
LITTLE MASTER TOMMY,
AND
PRETTY MISS POLLY.
With Two LETTERS from
JACK the GIANT-KILLER;
AS ALSO
A BALL and PINCUSHION;
The Use of which will infallibly make TOMMY
a good Boy, and POLLY a good Girl.
To which is added,
A LITTLE SONG-BOOK,
BEING
A NEW ATTEMPT to teach CHILDREN
the Use of the English Alphabet, by Way
of Diversion.

THE FIRST *WORCESTER* EDITION.

PRINTED at WORCESTER, *Massachusetts.*
By ISAIAH THOMAS,
And SOLD, Wholesale and Retail, at his Book
Store. MDCCLXXXVII.

This charming little children's book would be a highly desirable collector's item even if it carried a foreign imprint. But as it was printed in Worchester, Massachusetts, by the very celebrated Isaiah Thomas, it carries far greater impact. Thomas was not only a printer/publisher but a pioneer antiquary who preserved many relics of the local New England history. No author is verified for this book.

WHAT ABOUT CONDITION?

This is probably the most important judgment you will make about a book you're buying or selling. Depending on its condition, a book can be a collector's item or just a nice book to read. We often see the same look of perplexity on the faces of people not in the trade when we reject the old book in their hand. "But it's old!"

No matter.

Unless the book is an Eliot Bible, or another great rarity, it must be in good condition—bindings attached, pages all there, illustrations accounted for, no underlining, no tears, and clean covers. If the book was issued with a dust jacket, the jacket must be present and in good condition, especially for modern first editions. The absence of the jacket radically reduces the value.

Sounds cranky, doesn't it? But we can't stress enough the importance of condition in collectible books. But don't throw away that intact book in less than good condition. Scholars, researchers, and recreational readers are another market for inexpensive reading copies.

SPEAKING OF BIBLES ...

So many bible owners think their old family bible is a collectible item. Sadly, this is not so. Most old bibles have no value to any but the family that has its own history listed on the flyleaves.

Of course, if the family name is Lincoln and they have the dates of Old Abe's birth, marriage, children, death, and maybe a laundry list laid in, they may actually have something. Otherwise, a bible must be special to be collectible—very early printings (the Gutenberg comes to mind, printed in 1446 in Germany; and, in America, the "Eliot" or "Natick Bible" from 1663) or bibles translated into aboriginal languages are often highly sought after. Those printed by noteworthy pressmen or illustrated by notable artists also attain collectibility. (See our listings under Bibles at the end of the general book listings.)

HOW IMPORTANT ARE FIRST EDITIONS?

Rare book collectors want first editions because they reflect the first time these particular thoughts of an author appeared in print. They are perceived to be closest to the author's true intent. As further editions are issued, the supply of books is increased, thereby diminishing the value of succeeding editions. But relative scarcity of firsts remains constant.

As often as not, collectors don't read their first editions, but buy them to enjoy the possession of something rare and special, something others don't have. Scholars and readers will pay a price for later editions, but it will be a mere shadow of the price paid for a first edition.

Now, after having said that, let us confuse you further. Popular titles are often reissued in limited editions. Printed on high quality papers, with fine bindings and slipcases, these commonly include illustrations by noted artists. Limited editions may command higher prices than first editions, since most are numbered and signed by the author, the artist, or both.

WHAT'S THE STORY ON MODERN FIRST EDITIONS?

If any area of book collecting is in danger of falling victim to fads, this is it. Modern first editions attest to the fact that a book can be published in the past year or two and already have a collectible price affixed, which nullifies the idea that age determines price.

Tom Clancy's book *The Hunt for Red October*, published in 1984, has been offered by some dealers at $150 to $750. Clancy is currently popular and his books are being made into movies, this one a box-office hit starring Sean Connery. Has the attention increased the value of the book?

A first edition of Raymond Chandler's 1939 mystery, *The Big Sleep*, in a near-perfect dust jacket, sold for $7,150 in 1992, more than twice what experts had estimated it would bring in. Considered a classic in the genre, it, too, was dramatized in a movie starring Humphrey Bogart. Is it exposure that brings these prices up?

What really sets the pace for what a book is worth? We suspect that whimsy has a lot to do with modern books trading.

Percy Muir had a wonderful discussion on the subject in his delightful publication *Book Collecting as a Hobby*. He says when a contemporary author is "hot" the demand for first editions will drive up the price. When the demand is satisfied, prices decline. If the author's work has lasting substance, collectors will rediscover him and prices will rise again.

Muir cautions, "Never, never collect an author when he is in the height of fashion." He advises anticipating who will be the next to rise, or waiting until authors have weathered the test of time.

The bottom line is, take care in buying and pricing. Watch trends, understand them, plan for them, but don't be swept up in them.

HOW DO I PRICE A BOOK?

The plain truth is, there is no right price for a used book. It's all subjective. The law of supply and demand is in play. During flush times, price and sales soar, and in a lagging economy, they come back down. Market correction.

With a book in your hand, you'll do the research and then settle on a number. In the end, the value of a book is only what you or your customer are willing to pay. You will notice for some books we've listed, the price range is narrow. According to our sources, including dealers' pricing and auction records, folks agree on the current value of those books. For others, the range is hundreds or even thousands of dollars. These are actual prices people have asked for and paid. They reflect differing opinions from one dealer to another, or from one part of the country to another, and such disparities are common.

We've listed some titles more than once to show the difference in price between, for instance, trade and limited editions, the first edition and a later edition, a first edition with dust jacket and one without, or a signed copy and an unsigned one. We've assigned our prices assuming very good to fine condition, with the rare exception noted. Where you don't find the actual title you're after, but we list other titles by the same author, you've verified the author as collectible. You have more research to do, however, before you can price the book in your hand. Some authors have many titles to their credit, not all prized. The whole subject is fraught with cautions.

Talk to people in the business, consult price guides and dealer catalogs, visit antiquarian book stores. Learn as much as you can and then learn some more.

Pricing stock for a shop begins when you buy the books. Will your initial investment be tied up for months or a year, or do you have a ready customer for the book? Do you have a shop with overhead costs or do you mail order?

As dealers, when we know exactly what book we're looking for, the quickest way to find it is through other professionals. That means we dealers often buy from each other and the price goes up as a book passes from hand to hand before it ever reaches the public. How many times can that happen? You must make these judgments based upon your growing knowledge of the business.

In the end, you're bound to make some mistakes. It's that kind of business. But you'll learn from them. We all do.

THE CARE AND REPAIR
OF OLD BOOKS

AVOIDING DAMAGE

Though paper may be fragile, books are surprisingly durable if they are treated well. Proof of this is in the considerable number of incunabula that have survived from the Middle Ages in sturdy enough shape to delight collectors and continue serving as reference materials for serious scholars today.

Our own examination of a 300-year-old Eliot's *Natick Indian Bible* at the Boston Public Library revealed a book with pages solid enough to withstand the careful attentions of readers and researchers for many more years.

Even ignored and uncared for, an ancient tome left undisturbed and dry may survive without serious damage, as did a Gutenberg Bible found in a church belltower in Germany. A leather binding will certainly dry out and crack without proper dressing, but the pages of old books are stubbornly durable.

Unfortunately, newer books may not last as long. Modern paper manufacture produces a lot of paper quickly, but the quality of the paper is inferior and it has a far shorter lifespan. The common product today has a high acid content that causes it to degrade, discolor, become brittle, and fall apart over a few decades. Pulp paper used in newspapers and cheap magazines shows this defect in the extreme, as newspapers yellow and become brittle afer a mere few days. Unless the industry corrects this problem, older books will be in better shape a hundred years from now than books printed last year.

Some chief enemies of books are:

Fire. Fire has totally or partially destroyed many important libraries, often during war (for example, the burning of the Alexandrian Library by Caesar's troops, and the destruction of the Library of Congress in Washington by the British in the War of 1812), and sometimes by accident. The Jenkins Company of Austin, Texas, lost an extensive inventory to fire in December 1985. Fortunately some of the more valuable items—many acquired from other collections' dispersal sales through the years—were stored in a large walk-in vault and survived the blaze.

Light or moderate fire damage to a book may be repaired. The binding can be replaced and page ends, if scorched, may be trimmed. If a badly scorched book is still worth the trouble, the leaves may be unbound and mounted by a professional bookbinder.

Some precautions can be taken to minimize the threat of fire damage to a collection. A book room should have fire retardant carpets; draperies and curtains should be kept at a minimum; upholstered and overstuffed furniture should be avoided. Glass-enclosed bookshelves are safer than open shelves where fires are a risk. A fire extinguisher should be kept handy and the door kept shut when the room is not in use.

Water. Books can be water damaged by floods, fire fighting efforts, plumbing problems, storms, or any occasion when water comes into contact with covers and leaves.

Whether or not a soaked book can be salvaged depends on the paper quality. Vellum can often take a soaking and be reconditioned. A good rag paper has the best chance, but the book must be dismantled and each leaf dried separately. Modern books on coated paper, such as art books, however, are a loss. The coating disintegrates and you're left with sticky goo and incomplete images on the pages.

Newspapers, too, cannot take moisture. They absorb water and return to the pulp they started from.

Properly drying out a book is a delicate process and should be done by a professional. Restoration is an expensive procedure, so a book should be evaluated carefully to determine whether it is worth the cost.

Some steps to take to guard against water damage include avoiding rooms with overhead water pipes for book rooms. (Be aware of kitchens and bathrooms on the floor above. Those pipes are not always visible, but they can still leak down onto your books if they burst.) Avoid basement rooms that may leak or be damp at best. Cover books carefully when transporting them, especially when there is a risk of bad weather.

Excessive Humidity or Excessive Dryness. Dry air damages leather bindings. Humid air breeds mold and mildew, curls paper, and loosens bindings. The ideal humidity for books is around 50 percent, give or take ten points. In a humid environment, without a dehumidifier, it's best to store books on open shelves rather than in glass cases where moisture can build up inside.

To help leather remain supple in all environments, but especially in dry air, treat regularly with a leather dressing. This will be taken up at greater length when we discuss leather care.

Rough Handling. Books that are improperly handled do not remain long in collectible condition. Be gentle when handling all books, not just those that appear fragile. Even a big, brawny folio can be easily damaged—sometimes by the weight of its own pages pulling on the spine—if it's not handled well.

Don't open any book too wide, this cracks the hinges. Don't press a book flat on a table to copy from it for the same reason.

Older books with metal clasps require special handling. If the clasps are tight, don't tug at them to open them. Instead, gently squeeze the outer edges of the book until the clasps pop open easily. To close them, squeeze again and gently fit the clasps in place. If they won't close, don't force them. Over time these books, especially vellum, may have swelled and the clasps no longer fit. Leave them open or risk damaging the binding with too much squeezing.

Improper Storage. A book can be damaged by improper shelving, though the harm is often done over time, almost imperceptibly, so you may not notice it's happening until it's too late. Common mistakes are wedging books too tightly on a shelf or letting books flop about on unfilled shelves, stacking books flat on their sides, one atop another, or shelving books on their fore-edge.

Most spine problems of folio books and larger are caused by shelving on the fore-edge, causing the books to develop loose sections or covers, bent edges and corners, and possible damaged pages. While it's tempting to place a book that's too large for a shelf on its edge, you should resist the impulse. The weight of the pages will pull them away from the spine and you'll end up with a broken book.

If you can, stand large books on top of the bookcase supported by bookends. If you can't do this, place them flat on the bookshelf, but don't put other books on top of them.

Light. Especially sunlight. Direct sunlight, the ultraviolet component, degrades many kinds of paper and fades the color—or "mellows" the bindings—of books that stand for long periods in the sun. Nothing is more discouraging than to see a table full of books at a flea market warping and wilting unprotected from a hot summer sun.

Bookcases shouldn't receive direct sunlight if it can be avoided, though indirect sunlight to brighten a room is okay. Interior lighting should be incandescent. Flourescent light damages books.

Insects and Pests. A particularly nasty enemy of books is the bookworm. Not the bookish person devoted to reading, but insect larvae that feast on the binding and paste of books. Bugs, too, can wreak havoc on books. Some bugs, like silverfish, love a meal of sizing and starches used in the manufacture of paper. Some like the dyes and materials used in bindings like buckram.

The best recourse, if worms or insects are attacking your collection, is to call in a professional and have the entire house treated, but don't spray insecticide directly on your volumes. You may cause more damage than the bugs.

DISPLAYING YOUR BOOKS

Bookshelves. You'd think it would be simple to figure out how to store and display your books. Put them on a bookshelf, of course. But, it's not as simple as it sounds. Many book enthusiasts think that old books belong in old bookcases and they will go out to an antique shop or auction and buy the first old bookcase they see. Wrong.

It's important to look past the brass trimming and the darling carved gargoyles to see how the bookcase is constructed. Are the shelves adjustable in height? Are they sagging, cracked, or splintered? Are all the shelf supports present? Are they sturdy enough to carry the weight of heavy books?

Whether or not your bookcase should have glass doors depends of several factors. Do you want the books handled? Are there children in the house too young to appreciate the delicacy of your treasures? Do you have pets who like to sit on top of a shelf of books? (Cats do.)

Glass doors are a great protection from dust and they cut down on the work you must do, as well as wear and tear on your books, keeping the books clean. But they are bulky and stand between you and your collection in a way that open, inviting shelves don't.

Bookends. Many bookends are collectible, from the Art Nouveau and the Arts and Crafts movements, stunning in brass, copper, and bronze. But do they do the job?

Bookends should keep your books from tumbling around and should support heavy volumes. If your find you're constantly repositioning and straightening or tightening them up, they aren't working and should be replaced. For the best service, and at a fraction of the cost of the fancy bookend, we recommend the metal L-shaped or t-shaped models in which the lower portion slides beneath the first several books. Be sure the edges are smooth and won't scuff your books.

BOOK REPAIR

We cannot emphasize too strongly leaving the repair of a rare book to a competent bookbinder. For those more common or moderately priced books, learning a few pointers on how to repair them yourself is worthwhile.

Professional Bookbinding. A good bookbinder is a valuable resource, and anyone interested in used and old books should know one. He's first-aid for books, rescuing broken and defective volumes from oblivion, making suggestions and offering alternatives you may not realize you had.

Do not order a complete new binding if the old, loose one is in fairly sound condition. A loose cover can be rehinged, and missing leather can be replaced. New bindings can be created in which usable portions of the old leather are inlaid into a leather of similar grain and color. The old spine—or what's left of it—can be reset into a new spine.

These procedures are expensive and probably not worth the cost unless your book has some special appeal or is particularly ancient or rare.

When pages or gatherings are loose, the book may need resewing. If the paper is too fragile to permit this, the book can be dismantled and the inner edges of the leaves can be attached to guards that are then sewn together. When guard are used, it is generally not possible to recase the volume—that is, return it to the original binding—because the page ends will protrude from the fore-edge. A new binding is necessary.

You may try some home repair on mildly damaged books that are not so rare or expensive that a mistake would be a disaster. Some of the more common repairs are:

• *Loose bindings.* Loose cloth bindings can usually be repaired by opening the book midway, laying it face downward, and brushing glue along the inner side of the spine. Do not use cement-type glues; polyvinyl acetate, such as Elmer's Glue-All, does the job best. Use it sparingly. When completed, place rubber bands around the book and allow it to dry for several hours.

• *Cracked inner hinges.* Inner hinges can be strengthened by folding a narrow strip of paper and pasting it along the hinge. The paper should be about as heavy as an index card for best results. Make sure it is neither too long nor too short.

• *Torn spines.* Spines are best treated by simply brushing a small quantity of glue on the torn sections, pressing them firmly into place, and allowing them to dry under the pressure of a rubber band.

• *Notations or underlinings.* Markings done in pencil are easily—but gently!—erased. When the marks are in ink, nothing removes them satisfactorily, and it is probably wise not to make the effort. The paper could be damaged by using strong cleansers or by scraping. Besides, the notations might be of interest and could even possibly provide evidence on the book's previous ownership (called provenance).

• *Moisture*. Treat the book before the pages dry. Once stains are set by drying, they won't come out. Now the treatment we recommend may seem a little strange, but, if the book doesn't warrant professional attention, try this anyway.

First, mop any surface water by patting gently with soft paper towels. Place an oversized sheet of wax paper between all leaves that have gotten wet. In a wooden box about twice the size of the book, place an inch-thick layer of pipe tobacco and lay the book in it. Sprinkle a few more tobacco leaves over the book and seal the box tightly. Store the box in a dry place for several weeks. Some stains will probably remain, but they'll be less visible than if treatment had not been tried.

CARE OF LEATHER BOOKBINDINGS

Leather bindings, though more attractive than cloth, require more upkeep. Leather, an animal substance, has natural oils when new. As it grows old the oil dries out and the leather brittles. Red dust on your bookshelves is a sure sign that your bindings are dry. At that point, emergency treatment is necessary. It won't cure damage that has already occurred but it will halt further deterioration.

Leather bindings must be dressed. This may not be the most pleasant chore, but it can be rewarding. Be sure to get a good leather care preparation, and use it intelligently. Too much will the the binding sticky.

For best results, use a dressing made expressly for bindings such as the British Museum Leather Dressing. This old standby was once hard to get in America and collectors sent to London for it and paid the price. Today, it can generally be purchased in the states. Abide by the directions and don't be disappointed if the leather doesn't look polished. The aim in dressing leather is to give it a drink, not a shine.

Most old leathers will not polish and should not be expect to.

Give your leather-bound books a dressing about every six months. With regular care, any leather binding bought in good condition should remain so. But don't buy a shabby binding in the belief that it can be easily refurbished, as this is impossible.

HOW TO USE THIS BOOK

The books in the listing section are arranged alphabetically by author's last name, or, if no author, then by the first important word in the title (with "The" and "A" or "An" eliminated in most cases).

Categories of books such as Americana, Travel, Sporting, etc., have been dispensed with since many, if not the vast majority, of books can be assigned to more than one category. We believe that in our system of listing books you will find a simpler and more "user friendly" guide. We discuss genres and categories in the Glossary and in our chapter on "A Closer Look at the Book Trade," and a careful reader will soon be able to determine the proper categories for whatever book is in question.

In most listings, the author's name is followed by the title, the place of publication, and a date. Dates have been taken from the title page *or* the copyright page. In preferred listing format, which we endorse and use in our own business, dates taken from the copyright page would be bracketed. Not having all these books in hand, we relied on sources, some of whom did not bracket dates taken from copyright pages. Rather than misinform the reader, we reluctantly dispensed with brackets altogether. The dates we provide may denote the year in which the edition was printed (title page date), or it may tell the year in which the work was copyrighted (copyright page date).

We have not limited ourselves to listing first editions, but we have identified first editions where that information was available to us. Where a question remains as to whether or not you have a first edition in hand, further research in reference bibliographies is called for. Several excellent research sources are listed at the back of the book.

In most cases, the number of pages in a volume is not given, but where identification of a rare pamphlet or small work requires it, we have included page counts. Similarly, where illustrations include colored or engraved plates, the number of plates has been included where identification of an important book is dependent on that information. When examining any volume, check the table of contents or list of illustrations against the plates present to be sure they are all accounted for, since some people remove plates from old books, framing and selling the illustrations separately.

Readers will notice that many books listed are not first editions. Some titles are rare and valuable in whatever editions they appear. Later editions may contain signatures, provenance, or other attributes of note or may be illustrated by artists of great renown, making those editions more valuable than the first.

Unless otherwise stated, the prices given are for books in their original bindings except for those dating to the seventeenth century or earlier, in which case a good period binding is assumed.

Our prices reflect fair retail value based on a concensus of asking prices and realized prices of books on the open market over the past three years.

Dealers typically offer a 10 percent discount to other bookmen. A dealer may pay about 50 percent of retail for a book bought from a private individual if a customer is waiting in the wings for that book. For stock, a dealer will offer from 20 to 35 percent of a book's retail value. If you should offer a dealer an extremely rare and sought-after book, the dealer may act as an agent to market the book and take only a commission on the sale.

Pricing antiquarian and collectible books is a highly subjective process, but realized prices at auctions, reports of booksellers, and twenty years experience in the business have combined to give you the best possible estimates on the retail value of the books listed.

At times, the variation in our price listings reflects slight differences in the condition of books offered by different dealers. At times, it reflects the vicissitudes of the market, where a book may fetch a smart price in the mountains of New England and go far more cheaply in the deserts of Arizona. Or a dealer may offer a book at one price in his shop, while patrons of an auction house bought it at a far different price. We have not shied away from listing these broad ranges so the reader can see clearly the idiosyncrasies of the antiquarian book trade.

In all cases, books are assumed to be in at least very good condition, and where modern first editions are concerned, excellent condition. To realize their best price, modern firsts must have their dust jackets intact, but some listings clearly do not state dust jacket. These books have been offered or sold for a lower price than they would have fetched with the jacket. Still, many modern firsts even without their jackets are worth more than the $.50 charged at library sales, so we've included them here.

At all times, remember that this price guide is only a guide and not a guarantee of prices. The final determinant of the real value of used and old books is the marketplace, which is forever in flux, although the value of collectible books has proved to remain constant, with a comfortable yearly rise, for many years.

We have endeavored to verify the statistics for each listing, but no book of this type can guarantee freedom from error. The serious bibliophile will not depend on any one source, but will use multiple research tools to verify data on important books.

A list of abbreviations used in the listings appears on page 71. A glossary of terms for the antiquarian book trade begins on page 31, a section answering common questions about the business starts on page 7, and advice on the care and repair of old and used books begins on page 20.

GLOSSARY

ADDENDA (or **ADDENDUM**). Supplemental material inserted at the end of a book.

ADVANCE COPY. Copies of a book issued ahead of schedule to gain final approval from the author or to send to reviewers before the edition is released. Sometimes the advance copies will be identical to the regular edition, but often they are not, at least to the extent that they are labeled advance copies. If the only difference is in style or color of binding, it may be difficult to determine later if the copies are an advance issue or simply a binding variant, which could be part of a normal trade run.

Collectors often value advance copies since they represent an early state of the text and, however rare the case, they may contain notations by the author.

ALL EDGES GILT. Indicates that all three edges of the leaves (top, bottom, and fore-edge) have been gilded. The term is abbreviated a.e.g. or, if only the top edge is gilded, t.e.g.

AMERICANA. In the strict sense, refers to material dealing with the American hemisphere. But today, the term more often refers narrowly and loosely to books, documents, pamphlets, and other printed material that shows why, how, when, and by whom the United States was developed.

ANA (or **IANA**). Suffix denoting items related to a particular subject, be it a person, a time, or place in history, or some such. For instance,

Joyceiana is material relating in some way to James Joyce, even if the connection is remote. The heading covers such things as pamphlets, books, newspaper accounts, artifacts, and letters by, about, or to the subject.

Collecting ana (or iana) is widespread among those interested in a particular author or historical time or personality. Even those who have written only one book (or none) can be the subject of an extensive collection of written and artifact items. Institutions and libraries are notable collectors of ana.

ANTHOLOGY. A collection of short works, by one or more writers, in one book or set of volumes. Anthologies are most often collections of work that has appeared elsewhere.

ANTIQUARIAN BOOKSELLING. Sale of used, old, and rare books; printed fare; and related items; usually refers to trade in books out of print.

Until about the twelfth century, most books were handcrafted in monasteries and churches and remained their property. Except to those who owned them and valued the information they contained, books had no intrinsic value unless they contained gold gilt or were inlaid with precious stones. Not until sometime around the thirteenth century, when craftspeople in the secular world began to make and sell books, adding topics like philosophy and literature, did books take on a broader commercial value.

Michael Olmert, author of the *Smithsonian Book of Books* (1992) remarks, "An intriguing question is when did books become valuable enough to steal?" Olmert says that thieves profited from stealing books once a commercial market for them was established. As proof that books were taking on value, he reports book owners of the twelfth century began writing curses on their flyleaves to discourage theft, warning that whoever steals the books would be damned to hellfire.

Even as the first commercial markets were growing, bookmaking was done slowly by hand, comparatively few books were produced, and those were often custom-made for specific buyers. Bookselling was primarily a second-hand business but was not yet antiquarian bookselling. Since bound books were still in their infancy, you wouldn't term their trade antiquarian.

By the seventeenth century, enough time had elapsed, printing had become mechanized, and enough books were in circulation for true antiquarian bookselling to arise in England, France, and elsewhere.

Few catalogs were issued at first. Most early shops gathered in clusters, such as those that sprang up in St. Paul's Churchyard, London. Most shopkeepers located in large cities, primarily in stalls with much of their material displayed on the sidewalk and very little within. The PENNY BOXES that became such a favorite of the bargain hunters in later years were probably not present early on. Prints, engravings, maps, and such were sold by at least some dealers.

The emergence of the scholar-dealer—the collector at heart who studied his merchandise with interest—did not occur until the early part of the nineteenth century. By this time, bookselling was big business. The Bohn brothers of London are generally credited with giving birth to modern rare-book dealing. By 1900, at least a half dozen English dealers boasted inventories in excess of half-a-million volumes. Several German booksellers by this time had stocks even larger.

APPRAISAL. Estimation of the value of a book or a collection. An appraisal should be made by a qualified professional in the antiquarian book trade with the tools and the experience to do the job right. Some appraisers will offer an opinion based on a mere list and description of volumes, but that is not recommended. The value of a book depends on many factors, not the least of which is its condition. The best appraisals are done by experts who can hold the books in their hands and examine them in fine detail. This can't be done with a list.

AQUATINT. A method of etching that stresses soft tones and shades, resembling wash paintings. The French artist LePrince is generally credited with perfecting the process during the late eighteenth century. The technique became popular in Britain during the eighteenth and nineteenth centuries.

Sometimes aquatint printing was done in color and sometimes the coloring was added by hand later. When printing in colored aquatint, a separate plate for each color is necessary. A few famous artists such as Goya and Picasso experimented with the process.

ART PAPER. Shiny, coated stock on which most art books (or at least the illustrations) are printed. The paper ages badly and is easily damaged by moisture. Also, dirt stains cannot be removed without damaging the surface of the paper.

AS NEW. Showing no signs of wear; the book doesn't look used. Basically a British expression, Americans prefer MINT, which carries the same meaning.

ASSOCIATION COPY. A book that was part of the author's own library or was associated in one way or another with a famous person. It may be that the author inscribed the book to a friend, or the book may contain an inscription by another famous owner, perhaps a dedication or a presentation, or the book was merely included— without any inscriptions—in a famous person's library. But the point is, there must be proof that the book has been in the possession of someone famous.

The value of association copies to the collector derives from the book's connection to history, or in modern times, to people who are perceived as larger than life. If we were to learn that Abraham Lincoln had a favorite book of sonnets that he daily carried with him, we would love to have that book. It would be an association copy.

Association copies should be distinguished from signed copies, which proliferate these days with the popularity of book tours and autograph signings. And beware the forgeries! Experts in the trade can help you weed them out.

AUTHORIZED EDITION. Usually refers to biographies written with the approval or even help of the subject. The term is intended to draw attention and interest, but a drawback to the authorized editions is the public perception that if the subject of a biography authorized the work, it wouldn't tell tales of the subject's secret life.

B.A.L. The *Bibliography of American Literature*, authored by Jacob Nathaniel Blanck and published in 1955 by the Yale University Press for the Bibliographical Society of America. Virginia Smyers and Michael Winship edited the work and later added a final volume. The seven-volume work is a detailed bibliography of important American literature through much of the twentieth century and an indispensable research tool for the serious book person.

BASTARD TITLE. Another name for the HALF-TITLE PAGE, the leaf preceding the title page that carries the title in small print but no other information. Use of this page is a holdover from the incunabula days when the title page consisted of only this. It has no other real purpose and is retained in many volumes merely because old habits die hard. With a nod to decorum, many bibliographers referred to this as the "bas. title."

BAY PSALM BOOK. The first full-length American-printed book. Issued at Cambridge, Massachusetts, in 1640 by Stephen Daye, the name derives from the Massachusetts Bay Colony. Only eleven volumes are known to remain, all but one in public or institutional collections. The total number of copies printed isn't known, but is guessed to be from 100 to 300. Though the usual press run at the time was considerably more, experts theorize that Daye would not have had a large market for books printed locally and would have printed less than the usual number. The book was collected as a rarity as early as the mid-1700s. The actual title of Daye's volume is *The Whole Booke of Psalmes Faithfully Translated into English Metre*, but printers in Europe had produced works with similar titles, and therefore *Bay Psalm Book* more clearly distinguishes Daye's work from the others.

BEVELED EDGES. Angle-cut edges on wooden boards once used in bookbindings. They're of little consequence when judging the value of an antiquarian book.

BIBLIOGRAPHY. Commonly, a list of books organized by subject or author. For instance, libraries consider an author bibliography to be a list, as complete as possible, of all specimens of an author's work that have appeared in print.

The term has taken on an alternate meaning coming into its own now as the study of books themselves, including their origins, history, development, physical appearance, construction, and value.

BIBLIOMANIA. A preoccupation with books, a compulsion to be around them, learn about them, and own them. Booksellers and collectors are prone to this disease. The malady can be observed at library sales, auctions, and house sales.

BIBLIOPHILE. An ardent and avid book collector. One who loves books. A mild, benign form of bibliomania.

BIBLIOTHECA AMERICANA. A comprehensive directory of books on Americana, twenty-nine volumes in all, dating from the coming of the Europeans to the twentieth century. Begun by Joseph Sabin, who completed the first thirteen volumes, the work was continued by Wilberforce Eames and completed by R.W.G. Vail.

A bookseller's display of fine bindings illustrates the workmanship and appeal of these leatherbound volumes. These books are displayed in Terry Harper's bookstall at the Middlebury Antique Center in Middlebury, Vermont.

BINDING COPY. A book in need of a new binding. A British term.

BINDINGS. The permanent cover of a book, not to be confused with a dust jacket. As soon as books were made of folded leaves instead of scrolls, they needed a proper covering. The earliest bindings were probably uncovered wooden boards with a hide spine—what we call today a "half-leather" binding. This evolved into a full-leather binding. Early ornamentation on books consisted of painting and encrusting with jewels and bone carvings. In time, these gave way to **BLINDSTAMPING** and finally goldstamping.

Materials used over the centuries for binding books are numerous and even macabre. Most common were vellum, pigskin, calf, morocco, and various types of cloth or muslin. A practice arose during the Middle Ages of occasionally stripping the skin of slain

On this VERY old binding—early seventeenth century—a bishop's hat and crozier adorn the coat of arms in the center. Research through heraldry books would tell you that these are the bearings of Antoine deSeve, the Abbot of Isle-le-Barrois, France. The book was printed in Venice in 1604 but bound in France. Later it popped up in an English collection and its location is presently unknown. $1,300–$1,500.

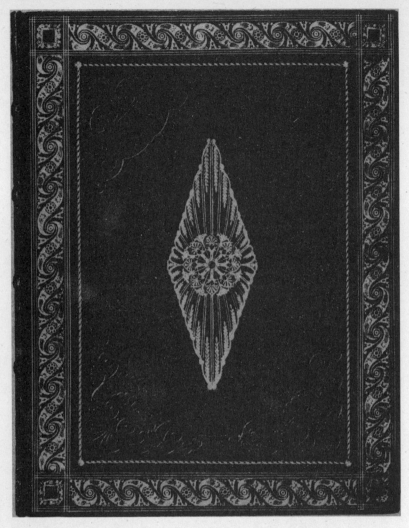

The above binding which features blindstamping and gilt tooling is French and dates from the second quarter of the nineteenth century. $325–$400.

enemy soldiers. One use of the leather made out of these skins: book bindings. (In some cathedrals in Europe one can still see doors covered in these human hides. Tour guides often hesitate to mention this fact.)

Collecting fine bindings is a major area of book collecting.

BLINDSTAMPING. Recessed or raised impressions on the bindings of books that are not inked or colored. Blindstamping did not originate with bookbinding but was long a popular means of hand-decorating leather. As a decoration for bindings, the process did not appear until the twelfth century.

BOARDS. Uncovered hard cardboard, wooden boards, or boards covered with thin paper, linen, buckrum, etc., used as front and back covers in bindings. The term is a holdover from the early days of printing when books were bound with actual wooden boards held together by leather or buckram at the spine. In the bookselling trade today, "boards" refers to stiff bindings covered in paper instead of the more common cloth or even leather.

BOOK OF HOURS. Illuminated medieval prayer books. During the Middle Ages, wealthy patrons commissioned these stunning books for their personal use. They were prized for their calendars, which frequently featured pictures of month-by-month activities— planting in spring, harvesting in fall, etc.—providing historians with valuable insights into medieval society and habits. Small in size, handy to carry to church services, the books included psalms, litanies, and various offices of the church. The organization of these books was based on the church's prescribed daily schedule for devotions, hence the name "Book of Hours."

BOOK OF KELLS. An Irish manuscript of Christian scripture from the eighth century. The opening page of each Gospel is lavishly illustrated with brightly colored designs and images of saints and religious persons and events. Depictions of nature, such as animals, fish, and trees, abound throughout. The art of the monks and their use of color and whimsey shows the attainment of the Irish artists of the early Middle Ages. By the way figures are depicted in the hand illuminations, it is obvious artists of the day had not perfected the study of anatomy, but that deficiency was made up for in their exquisite concepts of color and design. The folio manuscript is housed in the Library of Trinity College, Dublin, Ireland.

BOOKPLATES. A label identifying ownership usually pasted on the inside of a book cover. Older, intricately designed and executed bookplates are collector's items in their own right. Some are delightful examples of art. Their use dates from the fifteenth century. If a modern bookplate is inserted by a person of no particular renown, the plate does not detract from the book; when properly applied, they do no harm, but they should not be affixed over existing plates or in such a way that they obscure important inscriptions or writings.

Plates of antiquity, either engraved by some famous craftsman or showing possession by some notable person, are highly sought after by collectors of bookplates but they really should not be removed from the books. Contrary to common belief, this practice damages the books and destroys evidence of a book's **PROVE-NANCE**, or history, an important phase of bibliography.

BOOK SCOUT. A person who beats the bushes looking for saleable books who then markets these finds to booksellers. Since a bookseller is often tied down with a shop, scheduling time for a buying trip can be a problem. Enter the book scout. With no overhead and unfettered by the minutiae of a bookseller's store, scouts have time to ferret out books sitting on somebody's shelf in an attic or the eternal Friends of the Library book sale.

A bookseller might have several scouts scattered in different parts of the country haunting the flea markets, Salvation Army stores, and garage sales. But for the most part, scouts work independently, seeking out the bookseller with the strongest interest in their finds.

Often a person starting out as a scout develops into a fulltime bookseller. Scouts of the seedy, unsavory ilk described by John Dunning in his mystery novel, *Booked to Die* (1992), may exist somewhere, but our experience of scouts in New England (Marie started out as one twenty years ago) reveals a type of person who loves books to begin with and is delighted to chase them for booksellers.

BOOK SIZES. Industry terms loosely inferring the size of volumes. The terms describe books according to their **FORMAT** (the way they are printed and bound, rather than actual measurements), giving the practiced professional only an indication of how big the books really are.

The common book size formats are folio, quarto, octavo, and duodecimo, indicating the manner in which the printer folds the paper sheets on which a book is printed to create leaves (pages). Regardless of the planned format, all sheets are fed through a press in full size and folded later into "quires." These are collected and bound together, the closed edges of the folded sheets are slit, and, presto, you have a book.

If each printed sheet is folded once to create two leaves, the book becomes a folio, the largest format. If folded twice, we get four leaves, or a quarto, written "4to." Fold again and there are eight leaves, an octavo, or "8vo"; twelve leaves are duodecimo, "12mo." Keep going and you have progressively smaller sizes and larger numbers: 16mo, 24mo, 32mo, and 64mo. A 128mo format exists, but it's only seen in the very tiniest of miniature volumes.

You can't divine the actual measure of a book from the format, but it isn't a useless convention. What you can reliably ascertain from a statement of format is something about the shape of a volume. Octavos tend to be sleek, at least 1½ times tall as they are wide. Quartos tend to be squarish and dumpy. Folios are tall and well proportioned. The Gutenberg Bible is a folio. Most modern novels are 8vo's. Coffee table art books are folios and large quartos.

BOOKWORMS. The larval stage of a beetle that likes to eat books, a pesty little worm that feeds upon the bindings and leaves. They've been preying on libraries since the very earliest times. These maggots were the scourge of monastic libraries in the Middle Ages. No area of Europe was free of the bookworm, and contrary to some beliefs, they did not seek out only filthy habitations but ate books in fine homes and libraries as well. Modern chemicals have virtually exterminated them.

BREAKER. Someone who takes books apart and then sells the parts separately, especially the illustrations. Breaking a book may bring a higher price for the parts than the book would fetch as a whole. When a book is so badly damaged that it cannot be repaired or recovered as a book, breaking is a way of preserving the plates and putting them into circulation.

Breaking books that are not otherwise damaged is looked down on by serious antiquarian booksellers and collectors as a horrendous practice.

BROADSIDE. A poster, announcement, or proclamation, usually

printed on one side of a sheet and meant to be posted on a wall. Many a political statement was brought to the people's attention in this manner even after the advent of newspapers. Old auction posters, especially horse auctions, might be adorned with an illustrated display of wares adding to the value and desirability of the artifact.

Broadsides are popular with collectors today.

BUCKRAM. A modern binding material very much like cloth but tougher and somewhat more attractive. Libraries most always have their books rebound in buckram. Inexpensive, buckram can be dyed all the colors of the rainbow, as well as goldstamped. The natural shade, which is rather like a cross between straw and wheat, is preferred by many.

Buckram bindings are often described in catalogs as cloth and vice versa, a fact of life that collectors must endure.

CALF. Leather used for bookbindings.

CALLED FOR. Points mentioned in bibliographies that determine the edition of a book. For instance, if a handbook written by Smith says that a blank leaf follows the title in a certain edition of a certain book, then the blank leaf is "called for" for that edition and must be there for the book to be complete.

CALLIGRAPHY. The art of handwriting, dating back to the clay tiles of Egypt and Sumeria. Writing, as with anything else, passed through various modes, but today, the calligraphic specimens of the nineteenth century are the most familiar. Letter writers of the time were dutifully faithful to the style of Platt Roger Spenser, in the 1800s an important influence in American penmanship. Who hasn't marveled at the dazzling script of the Spencerian pen our forefathers so beautifully executed?

The term calligraphy includes reference to drawing, as well, though the flourished works we refer to as calligraphic drawings were in use before Spencer. Rather than a likeness executed by drawing in a single line, the best exercised calligraphic drawings were made with repetitive scallops. The method was taught in the schools using standard texts, not surprisingly resulting in drawings that exhibited similar likenesses of popular subjects—the deer, lion, eagle and other birds, and the horse.

Most collectors now prefer samples of the drawings to penmanship, but handwriting books of the time are not overlooked. Earlier eighteenth-century books were published in small numbers and so are difficult to find. Even more than the booklets of instruction, finished works of calligraphy are sought by the avid collector.

CAXTON, WILLIAM. The first English printer. Born at Kent, he started his business life as a mercer, or dealer in yarn goods, a trade he followed for most of his life, showing no particular mechanical skills or flair for literature. Around 1441, Caxton went to Burgundy. He spent most of his adult life on the continent. In 1471, he entered the service of the Duchess of Burgundy and, under her influence, he performed his first effort with books, translating the *Recuyell of the Historyes of Troye.*

On a visit to Cologne that year, he was apparently introduced to the art of printing, which he brought back to Bruges, setting about to give the city a printing press. Together with a Flemish calligrapher, Colard Mansion, Caxton issued the first English language book, the same *Recuyell.* After printing two more books with Mansion, Caxton returned alone to England and founded a printing office in the parish of Westminster.

Compared to the best French and Italian printing of the time, Caxton's books come off a sorry second. His fame has led many to assume that his talent as a craftsman and type designer must have been extraordinary, but this was not the case. He did, however, exert much influence upon his contemporaries and followers. He began with types modeled on German gothic and stuck with them to the end. This set the trend for English printers and it was not until a century after his death that the types were replaced by the more graceful Roman.

A craze for Caxtons among collectors began in the early part of the nineteenth century and has gathered steam ever since. The finest collections are at the British Museum and John Rylands Library. In the United States, the Morgan and Huntington libraries are notable for their Caxtons.

CHAPBOOK. A small pamphlet or booklet usually associated with children's stories or rhymes. Most are diminutive in size and illustrated with woodcuts. In the eighteenth century, itinerant peddlers, or "chapmen," hawked the booklets door to door. Because they were cheaply made, many of the books have not survived in very good condition, but those that have are highly prized and collectible.

CHEAP COPY. A defective copy which is being offered at a dis-

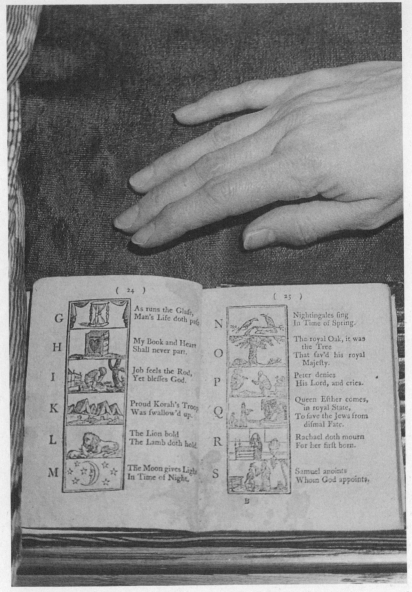

Two pages of The Boston Primer, *a popular chapbook (this one printed in 1811, with engravings to illustrate the alphabet for young learners), are typical examples of the style used on these popular little books.* (Courtesy of the Trustees of the Boston Public Library. Photographed by Marilyn Green.)

Chapbooks are popular fare during the nineteenth century, often sold door-to-door by traveling salesmen commonly called chapmen. The collection is included in Special Collections at the Bailey-Howe Library at the University of Vermont. Shown are (top row) The Farm House, *Mahlon Day printer, early 1800s;* The Red Squirrel, *A. Phelps, Greenfield, 1846;* Cinderella or The Glass Slipper, *H & E Phinney, Cooperstown, 1834; (bottom row)* Stories for Children about Whales, *Rufus Merrill, Concord, NH, 1843;* Cock Robin's Courtship and Marriage, *Sidney's Press, New Haven, 1824;* The Young Sailor, or The Sea Life of Tom Bowline, *Kiggins & Kellogg, NY, 1840s.*

count. The dealer wants the prospective buyer to be aware of the poor condition.

CLOTH BINDING. The ideal binding substance—cheap, durable, easy to apply, and comes in a variety of colors. For modern books, cloth has replaced leather as the binding of choice. True, the disappearance of leather is lamentable, but the cost of leather binding would prohibit ownership of books to all but a limited class of collectors.

In the first years of cloth binding, publishers let their imaginations run wild. Every effort was made to ornament the bindings lavishly. The books were gilded and blindstamped using patterns copied from notable bindings of earlier ages. But unlike the books of old, gilding was done with large panel stamps impressed by machine rather than with tools worked by hand. The purpose was to make the public forget leather. It succeeded; out of sight, out of mind. In time, only connoisseurs who kept fine libraries retained any affection for leather. That is not to say, however, that we have become so undiscriminating that we cannot still appreciate a book bound in fine, soft leather.

CODEX. Applies to leaves bound in book form—this book you are holding, for example—as opposed to scrolls or tablets. The invention is generally credited to Roman legal clerics who grew weary of cumbersome scrolls and cut them down to convenient size. The practice made sense at a time when the whole process of managing information was time-consuming and laborious.

COLLATED. Inspected from cover to cover to be sure all pages, plates, maps, and the like are present, intact, and in their proper place. In the case of earlier books, a perfect copy—or comprehensive knowledge of one—is necessary to make a comparison when collating.

A good practice when purchasing a book is to check out the list of illustrations numbered in the table of contents and confirm that they are all there. If maps should be present, check them out. Nothing is more frustrating when you get home than to discover pages missing from a book you were all excited about purchasing.

And never, never send out a book to a dealer or customer before collating it. Selling a book with missing pages could be cause for manslaughter, or, more seriously, labeling yourself unprofessional.

COLOPHON. The "finishing touch." The tradition of medieval scribes when completing their manuscripts was to record, on the last page, their name and place of residence and, sometimes, the day on which the book was finished.

At times, the addition of a colophon was done out of vanity but, more often than not, such information was necessary. Without it, a printer or publisher could not identify an edition as his own, which might result in legal difficulties if the book were pirated or stolen by another printer.

The average colophon was a model of simplicity, one sentence or so, giving the essential facts. Colophons were replaced after the sixteenth century by information included on the title page. Some modern books, usually limited editions, still add a colophon, perhaps out of respect for tradition. You might find one that starts out: "This book was set on the monotype in Fournier . . ."

CONDITION. The general state of a book. This singularly most important point cannot be overemphasized when considering whether to buy or sell a collectible book.

Like people, books are either in fine shape, very good shape, bad shape, or various states in between. As no hard and fast definitions exist, the terms used to designate a book's condition are subject to personal opinion. Having said that, we hasten to add that there is some agreement in the book trade as to what the terms mean.

Mint. As new. Right off the press.

Fine. Nearly new. Sometimes a dealer might overlap this with mint.

Very good. Definitely showing wear, but not damaged. Usually a clean, tight copy. Most collectible books fit this category.

Good. Obviously read. Perhaps the covers show moderate wear, a hinge is cracked in front or back, some minor spine fading might be present, the binding scuffed. Perhaps the book is even a little shaken, not quite as tight as it used to be. All in all, the condition shows the book has been around for a while and used. No really major defects.

Fair. Worn and used. Cover soiled, scuffed, evidence of repairs, shaken, perhaps a page torn here or there. The book has definitely been around the barn.

Reading copy. About all it is good for. Or, it may interest collectors of modern first editions who keep their pristine copies on a shelf safe from prying hands but who may still want to read Hemingway or Faulkner. Reading copies come in handy for research.

Now when all is said and done, should a disheveled rare book come up at auction, you can bet your bottom dollar—and you might have to—that such a book will not lack for spirited bidding. So extenuating circumstances call for common sense. If a book is being purchased for investment, then by all means, abide by the most rigid rules of condition.

COPPER PLATE ENGRAVING. A process for producing prints and book illustrations. Plates were prepared by a battery-hammer method, then smoothed by rubbing with pumice and oilstone. Though costly and time-consuming, this method gave the best possible surface for engraving. The majority of English illustrated books of the eighteenth century used copper plates.

COPYRIGHT. The equivalent of a patent on a work of literature. A copyright prohibits anyone from reproducing the work, either in whole or in part, without consent of the copyright holder.

CURIOSA. In today's market, books that deal with off-beat subjects like a monograph on foot fetishes or the psychology of wearing hats. During the Victorian age, anything of a sexual nature was hidden under the heading of Curiosa. Today's bookseller has no problem with that subject and classifies erotic material where it belongs, under Erotica.

C.W.O. Cash with order. Most booksellers append this to their ads, safeguarding their interests, choosing not to send a book out to a customer before they have payment in hand. But through the years, we have never encountered a deadbeat customer or bookseller. We have sent out books before the check arrives, in particular, a $5,000 sporting book to a dealer with a fine reputation.

At times, we need to have a little faith in our fellow human beings. Of course, in this case, it was easy as we knew the man's character.

DAMP STAINS. Damage caused by excessive humidity, but not water as is sometimes thought. Books damaged by damp are ragged and musty rather than crisp.

Improper ventilation can cause as much damage as water. Humidity constantly above 70 percent can damage a book as it stands untouched in a bookcase. In a book with lovely plates, dampness can cause the pages to stick together. Pulling them apart damages the plates, thus greatly altering the value and aesthetics of the book.

DAYE, STEPHEN. An important individual, the first man to print mechanically in America. Daye, a British locksmith, came to the Massachusetts Bay Colony in 1633. He and his son, Matthew, a printer's apprentice, set up a printing shop in Cambridge at Harvard College. The earliest surviving book of the Daye's press is commonly known as the *Bay Psalm Book*, after the colony where it was printed.

DELUXE EDITION. Meant to imply extraordinary production qualities; those books which, by superior design, type, paper, binding, or other factors, are set above the pale.

DISBOUND. Refers to a pamphlet or other brief work that once was part of a larger work and has been separated. Purists look down on this practice of removing the piece from the larger collection much as they look down on breaking a book.

DISCARD STAMP. A mark used by libraries when they are culling their collections to show the books have been released for sale or distribution. This is a matter of procedure to guard against theft and to show the book is legitimately no longer a part of the library collection. How nice when a librarian thinks like a book collector and carefully selects an inobtrusive place for the stamp.

DOG-EARED. Originally referred to the corners of pages that have become ragged or creased. Now, it applies to any pages that have the appearance of heavy use. One of the causes of dog-earing is the regrettable habit many readers have of turning down the corner of a page to mark their place. Thank goodness not all readers are guilty of this barbaric practice, choosing instead to use bookmarks.

DOS-A-DOS BINDING. A type of late medieval binding in which two books of equal size are bound together, joined like a loveseat. The two back covers are attached so that the fore-edges face in opposite directions. The practice originated in monasteries as a convenience for monks who carried books attached to a chain around their waist. If they wished to carry two books, they would require two chains. With a dos-a-dos binding, two books became one. Examples of dos-a-dos are very rare but we're mentioning them here because the thought of them is intriguing.

DURER, ALBRECHT. A German artist, painter, and book illustrator at the turn of the sixteenth century. He was famous and in great demand for quality woodcuts used in book illustrations. Among his early works are the woodcuts for Sebastian Brant's famous *Ship of Fools*.

Most of Durer's fame came after 1500 when he was prolific in his output not only in book illustration but working in oils, watercolor, silverpoint, and other artistic media.

DUST JACKET (or DUST WRAPPER). The decorative paper cover that protects the binding from soil and wear. Jackets were

A page with a woodcut illustration is shown from The History of Reynard the Fox, *printed in 1894 by David Nutt, London. It is included in Special Collections at the Bailey-Howe Library, University of Vermont.*

sometimes used during the nineteenth century and if you found a volume with a jacket of such antiquity, hooray for you. Jackets for books dating back to the early part of the twentieth century, too, are like icing on the cake. They're desirable, but hard to come by. For newer books, however—the MODERN FIRST EDITIONS—jackets are a must.

If a book such as William Faulkner's *Light in August* has no dust jacket, it can lose half its value. Even reprints of Zane Grey or Edgar Rice Burroughs command higher prices when accompanied by dust jackets. A modern book with its jacket missing can be likened to an antique table without its legs.

To avoid confusion with WRAPPERS—a paper binding and essential part of a book—the term dust jacket is preferred.

EDGES. Refers to the three outer edges of the leaves. Style of edges is a very important part of a book's makeup, especially in fine or rare editions. New books are delivered to the binder in folded but uncut sheets, or gatherings, and the binder must separate the leaves by cutting the folds. The edges are usually trimmed to make them perfectly even. Books bound without trimming the edges, showing the original state of the paper with all its irregularities, are valued by some collectors. But then there is a collector for just about anything.

ELSE FINE. A term used after a recitation of a book's faults indicating that, otherwise, something is right with the book. The phrase "o/w very good," is more common.

ENGRAVING. Illustrations printed from a metal plate or woodblock. Engravings on steel were developed in the fifteenth century, an improvement over wood that permitted more fine detail and delicate shading.

Collectors of engravings seek the early impressions in a print run, those among the first taken from a plate, as the fine lines of the engraved image sometimes wear down with repeated use.

EPHEMERA. Items that were meant to last a short time. Some booksellers abhor the myriad post cards, sheet music, and advertising paper that appear at book shows under this heading. But many of these items are extensions of book collecting that we accept as not only legitimate but desirable. Say you are putting together a collection of P.G. Wodehouse. Why would you reject the sheet music he wrote? Or the Christmas cards by Robert Frost to round out a collection of his books of poetry? Or the screen scripts written by now famous authors when they were down on their luck and needed to eat?

Ephemera is fun and exciting and some very famous artists like Maxfield Parrish produced beautiful ads as well as book illustrations for some of the most sought-after children's books. Tucked into old volumes, many ephemera treasures have come to light. A stevensgraph or a hollow-cut silhouette, even a letter with historical information, are some of the bonuses possible when turning the pages of an old book.

A Vermont bookseller was a little chagrined when she learned she'd sold a book on Calvin Coolidge with a holograph letter tucked unnoticed among the leaves. The next day the customer returned and asked did she have any more of those books with letters of the president inside?

ERASURES. Removal of underlining or notations with an eraser, discussed further under Notations and Underlining in the section on "Care and Repair of Books."

A bookseller may resort to erasing pencil or pen markings made by former owners of a book, generally by use of a wad of art gum or pencil eraser. Collectors have mixed feelings about notations and whether or not they should be removed. The value and rarity of a book will influence whether a book is rejected due to the presence of notations or purchased and lived with as is. For the bibliophile, a notation might suggest some continuity with the former owners and be cherished.

The erasures themselves should be clean and not leave unsightly blotches or destroy the print.

ERRATA. Mistakes in printing. Regardless of the amount of proofreading, errors are common to most books. Some are the fault of the printer, others of the author, and still others of the publisher. Several practices provide all parties concerned a chance to wash their hands of errata. The "errata leaf" is still used in cases where a blooper was spotted too late to correct the print run but early enough to bind a note into the book stating the error and correction. More frequently seen is the "errata slip," a small strip of paper containing the correction which may be pasted in the book, or laid-in loosely, after the book has been bound.

EX-LIBRARY (EX-LIB). Indicates the book belonged to a library or bears evidence of having been in a library collection, e.g., the library stamp, card pockets, or identifying marks on the spine. These books, unless they are exceedingly rare, are not often sought by collectors as they usually show considerable wear and damage due to use and library mutilation.

Ex-lib books are almost as difficult to sell as Book of the Month Club or Reader's Digest editions.

FINE PRINTING. Any book in which the quality of type and layout are a main consideration. Books printed by individuals or presses which design their own type may rate as fine printing if the type is well designed. Such books do not necessarily have to be limited editions or kept from public sale. All the products of early typographers were sold on the general market, yet some represent excellent presswork. Had these men bought their types from foundries rather than having a hand in their design, their books might not be so respected.

FIRST EDITION. The first appearance of a book in print. Collectors refer to the first impression (print run) of the book as a true first edition. Identification of true first editions can be an art and even the most experienced booksellers and collectors run the risk of making an error.

The way printers specify the edition somewhere inside the book—or fail to give any indication at all of which edition it is— varies widely from printer to printer, era to era, and country to country. Best to go prepared with a pocket guide on the subject when browsing through bookstores, for you could not possibly keep in mind the vast number of codes that publishers have used or the legions of points that identify specific titles. Unfortunately, if a book does not readily admit in print to being a second or a third or a fifteen-thousandth edition, the uninformed public automatically assumes the book is a first. The collector or bookseller cannot afford this casual assumption as most collectors acquire first editions for many reasons, not least among them, investment.

FIRST IMPRESSION. The first time a set of plates has been used to print a book. Also called a "printing."

All impressions using the same set of plates constitute one edition, thus each edition can include more than one impression. Most sellers and collectors are speaking of the first impression of the first edition when discussing collectible FIRST EDITIONS.

FIRST THUS. Not the first edition, but you may see this used to describe an altered edition of an old book. Since the revised book is an edition unlike the original, perhaps issued by a different publishing house or illustrated by some other artist, the book can be presented as first thus. Like a distant cousin to the first edition.

FLYLEAF. Blank leaf after the front free endpaper, not always present. The term is often misapplied to the front endpaper.

FOLDING PLATES. Plates which fold out to a larger size than the book leaves. Volumes published by the Government Printing Office during the nineteenth century have many folding maps and color illustrations bound into the books. Guide books are designed with folding illustrations and maps, too. Through the years, unfortunately, folding plates begin to show wear and tear from handling.

FOLIO. A standard book size, measuring from about 12″ tall on up. An atlas folio is 24″, and an elephant folio is 20″ or more. Audubon's *Birds of America* is a most valued natural history book measuring 37″ tall.

FORE-EDGE. The outer edge of a book, opposite the spine.

FORE-EDGE PAINTING. Painting the edges of a book's leaves with a scene or other picture. The book must be held in a special press and while the leaves are slightly fanned out the artist paints or decorates the exposed fore-edges of the leaves. When the book is fully closed, the edge is gilded to conceal traces of the painting. But lightly fan out the edges, and the fore-edge painting can be a lovely surprise. Because the painting is hidden, a book with a fore-edge painting can go undetected, even by a knowledgeable bookseller, until the book is opened.

FORMAT. The size of a book determined by the specific number of times the original printed sheet of paper has been folded to form the leaves. For standard format sizes used in the book trade, see BOOK SIZES.

FOXED. Discoloration with brown spots and blotches caused by microorganisms that find the paper in certain books appetizing.

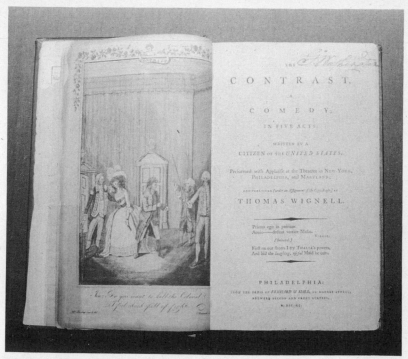

Frontis and title page of "Contrast, a Comedy, in Five Acts" from the private library of George Washington, containing Washington's signature in the upper righthand corner of the title page. The play, written by the Vermont author of A Citizen of the United States, *Royal Tyler, was the first American play written by an American and produced on the American stage. This rare copy, bound in red leather with gold tooling, is in Special Collections at the Bailey-Howe Library of the University of Vermont.*

Dampness can encourage the problem. The spots are often dark and, when the foxing is heavy, can seriously detract from the value of an otherwise good book.

FRAKTUR. A German style of gothic or black-letter type. Fraktur was most prevalent at Augsburg and Nuremburg in the post-incunabula period when gothic had been almost totally dropped by French and Italian printers. Popular with the Pennsylvania Dutch, early birth certificates decorated and embellished with fraktur are becoming harder to find and more expensive to buy.

FRONTISPIECE. An illustration appearing opposite the title page. More often than not, the frontis (as abbreviated) is a portrait of the author, but in many books, the frontis is a lovely color plate or a steel engraving.

GILT EDGES. Gold applied to all three edges of a book's leaves. In book parlance, t.e.g. means top edge gilt, and a.e.g. means all edges gilt.

GROLIER, JEAN. A French bibliophile of the sixteenth century noted for the beauty of the bindings he ordered for his books. Although described as haughty and dull, his taste in fine bindings was anything but quiet and dignified, as were some English bindings of the time. Rather, Grolier's bindings, in the French style, leaned toward busyness and extravagance, intricate and lavish design. During his lifetime, which spanned some eighty-six years, Grolier built a private library of about 3,000 volumes.

The Victorian age saw a profusion of bogus Groliers foisted upon an unsuspecting and gullible collecting public. The danger of such fraud remains because genuine Groliers, even though more than four centuries old, often look much newer. The usual signs of age one would expect—scratches, abrasions in the leather, dryness or pieces of leather worn away—are seldom found. Fortunately, held in such high esteem, the books have been meticulously cared for through the centuries.

GUTTA-PERCHA BINDING. A method of book binding substituting a tough rubberlike substance for stitching to hold the leaves together. The inner edges of the leaves are trimmed to eliminate the gathering fold and then glued together to the inside of the spine. The process, used as early as 1840 and continued through the nineteenth century, was unsuccessful with large, weighty books whose pages quickly pulled away from the spine. Cost effectiveness notwithstanding, the experiment finally petered out, though its cheapness made publishers hesitate to give it up.

HALF-BOUND. A book with leather extending over the spine and about an inch or so along the front and back covers. The rest of the binding is either cloth or paper. If the spine is leather and the four corners of the book are covered in leather triangles, you have a book which is called three-quarter leather. Thought to be an English custom, the practice goes back to the seventeenth century, but did not become popular until the eighteenth century.

HALF-TITLE. Usually the first appearance of print in a volume, the title printed on an otherwise blank sheet before the title page. This is a holdover from the days of early printing when the title was the only information given on the title page.

The half-title is also known as **BASTARD TITLE.** Grant Uden, in his book *Understanding Book Collecting*, puts this appellation down to the insensitivity of Americans who he says often adopt their own bibliographical terminology. But whosoever puts these terms together, all you have to remember is that the half-title is most often the first appearance of print in a volume.

In the past, when restoring a book, binders often discarded the half-title page. They may have considered it superfluous, and well it might be, unless you are a collector, and then that half-title page had better be there.

HEADBAND. A (usually) colorful band inside of the spine, sewn across the top of the leaves. In modern bindery, it has no function and is primarily decorative, if it is present at all. Headbands are more often seen in older books. The term is used to include the tailband (sewn across the bottom inside of the spine) as well.

HINGE. The ridge where the front or back cover meets the spine. When a book has a hinge crack, the cover is intact but loose. It definitely needs attention before worse can happen, which is separation of the covers from the book.

HOLOGRAPH. A document written wholly in the hand of the author. Although autograph collectors use the term more frequently, booksellers find it helpful to indicate more than mere inscription or presentation material on the flyleaf of a book; specifically, a laid-in letter or a **MANUSCRIPT.**

HORNBOOK. A sheet of paper, printed on one side with the alphabet or some other rudiments of school work, pasted onto a handled piece of wood then covered with transparent horn. In colonial America, these were a child's first school books. Used from the sixteenth to the eighteenth century, genuine hornbooks are rare, but imitation copies turn up now and then, no doubt prompted by the high price an original would command.

ILLUMINATED MANUSCRIPT. A work containing dazzling letters, initials and sentence openings, hand decorated in bold colors and finished off with gold and silver. Spectacular and colorful, the art work did, in essense, brilliantly shed light upon the text. Manuscript illumination is known to have been practiced as early as the fifth century. Monks in the seventh and eighth centuries produced specimens of great artistry in Ireland, including the awe-inspiring **BOOK OF KELLS.**

Illuminating manuscripts remained the province of monastic scribes until the end of the fourteenth century when the commercial manuscript industry came into its own and the secular world took a serious interest in book ownership. Unfortunately, the invention of printing, which literally set the book business on its head, also contributed to the demise of the manuscript trade. By 1470, the German manuscript industry had virtually ceased to function; those of Italy and Spain gave way soon after. France was the last stronghold of illuminated manuscripts, turning out specimens of quality even after the age of **INCUNABULA.** But in the end, the writing was on the wall and manuscripts were only hand illuminated by special request.

IMPRESSION. In the strictest sense, a run of copies, large or small, ordered by a publisher from the printer at one time. After the first impression, other runs may be printed from the same setting of type, and are usually so noted. Collectors of first editions are actually looking for the first impression of the first edition of a volume, as all impressions taken from one setting of type constitute an edition.

In days past, when type was set in metal and was ungainly and difficult to store for long periods, a book that remained in demand after its first edition sold out was likely to need resetting before it could be reissued. Printings from the new set of type then constituted impressions of a second edition.

IMPRINT. The information at the foot of the title page that refers to the publisher or the place of publication. The book industry includes collectors who specialize in imprints. Those of the Revolutionary period and the Confederacy are especially prized.

INCUNABULA (INCUNABLE). Books printed on presses in the fifteenth century. The word is derived from the Latin root meaning "in the cradle," and indicates printing in its infancy. Incunabula is automatically valuable and collectible.

INDIAN BIBLE. The name commonly given to an edition of the bible in a Native American language, an Algonquin dialect, translated and compiled by the Rev. John Eliot and published at Cambridge, Massachusetts, in 1663. The bible is also known as the Natick Bible and the Eliot Bible.

INSCRIBED COPY. A book carrying a signed inscription, usually saying something like "with regards to" or "for a special friend." Should the author of the inscription be famous, the book's value is enhanced. However, simply an inscription by the former owner, who may be a nice person, does not constitute an inscribed copy.

ISSUE. A term applied to a second printing (impression) of an edition that includes a change or correction—but not a complete resetting of type—made *after* the first impression is printed. Adding to the confusion are "states," or printings in which changes have been made *during* the print run. The terms are technical but important to the identification of older first editions. Many booksellers use "issue" and "state" interchangeably.

LAID IN. Refers to a piece of paper, such as a letter or a photo, placed in the book but not attached.

LEAF. A single sheet of paper, with a RECTO (front) page and a VERSO (back) page. Many people confuse pages and leaves. Pages are just one side of a leaf.

LIBRARY OF CONGRESS. America's largest library, located in Washington, D.C. Once founded as a working library for members of Congress, the library now holds not only government documents, but one of the largest collections of incunabula in the United States.

LIMITED EDITION. Special printing of a limited number of books. Printing and binding are often of a higher quality than the usual trade books or may be the product of a PRIVATE PRESS. The books are often numbered and signed by the author and illustrator, if there is one.

LIMP. Refers to bookbindings made of material that is not supported by boards. The cover is literally hanging limp. Limp vellum was first used as a trade binding for printed books almost since the beginning of typography and remained popular in Italian, Spanish, and Portuguese bindery during the fifteenth to seventeenth centuries. Limp bindings were often fitted with leather thong ties in place of clasps.

In the nineteenth century, limp leather was often used as a binding for bibles, giving way to imitation leather in later years.

LITHOGRAPHY. A principal method of printing developed in the nineteenth and twentieth centuries, especially suited to reproducing drawings and illustrations. The process consists of printing from an impression drawn on smooth lithographic limestone using chemical inks. Many artists came to use the process to replace engraving, including the renowned Currier and Ives. Lithography is now a prominent art form.

LOOSE. A book that is in danger of separating from its binding. No longer held tight by the spine, the joints cannot support the weight of the book.

MANUSCRIPT. In the book world, refers to a handwritten document. Technically, a work written by hand, but in the modern world, a manuscript can be typewritten and still be considered a manuscript. The distinction is that it was not typeset or printed. If the writing is in the author's hand, it's termed a **HOLOGRAPH** manuscript. In the Middle Ages, monks copying sacred texts created **ILLUMINATED** (illustrated) manuscripts of great beauty, but with the invention and proliferation of mechanical printing, the practice died out.

MARBLED. A technique of decorating paper to create the effect of marble, mostly used for endpapers. Some examples have intriguing patterns that craftspeople today are duplicating to frame or to function as book covers.

MEZZOTINT. The process of engraving on copper plates.

MINIATURE. Actually not what you'd think; derived from "miniate," which means to paint with vermilion. The ancient artists who used this red paint were called miniators. Originally, miniatures referred to the colored drawings in early manuscripts.

MINT CONDITION. Like new. Right off the press.

MISPRINT. An error in printing, very important when identifying first editions. For instance, in the first American edition of Mark Twain's *Adventures of Huckleberry Finn* the word "saw" was printed incorrectly as "was" on line 23, page 57. Misprints are of-

The English were the masters of panel binding. It is very symmetrical and orderly. The material is black morocco, the tooling is in gold, and the spine has extra embellishing, c. 1690. $1,200–$1,500.

A

THANKSGIVING SERMON,

PREACHED JANUARY 1, 1808,

*In St. Thomas's, or the African Episcopal, Church,
Philadelphia:*

ON ACCOUNT OF

THE ABOLITION

OF THE

AFRICAN SLAVE TRADE,

ON THAT DAY,

BY THE CONGRESS OF THE UNITED STATES

BY ABSALOM JONES,
RECTOR OF THE SAID CHURCH.

————

PHILADELPHIA:
PRINTED FOR THE USE OF THE CONGREGATION.
FRY AND KAMMERER, PRINTERS.
1808.

This tract, laying out the position of abolitionists decades before the Civil War made their arguments moot, has survived in excellent shape for a pamphet in wraps. (Courtesy of the Trustees of the Boston Public Library. Photographed by Marilyn Green.)

ten among the important POINTS which must be present if a book is a true first edition.

MODERN FIRST EDITIONS. Includes books published since the turn of the twentieth century. Here again in book parlance, phrases are evolving with time and most people use the term in reference to books from the 1920s on.

MOROCCO. Leather made from goatskin.

ND. No date of publication is given.

NP. No place of publication is given.

OCTAVO. The most common size/format of books. Usually seen expressed as "8vo," the most common octavos measure approximately 8″ high.

OUT OF PRINT. No longer obtainable from the publisher.

PAMPHLET. A small work, issued unbound or in wraps, and usually sewn or stapled together.

PAPERBACK. Softcovered books, primarily books bound in heavy paper, published from the 1930s on. Today, early paperbacks are collectible and sought after, especially the Horror and Science Fiction genres.

The term is not to be confused with WRAPS, a thin paper cover.

PARTS. Books released in serial form or in installments. Many books started out this way and were only later published in book form. The works of Dickens followed this pattern—his *Dombey and Son* was printed in parts, nineteen of the twenty parts in green pictorial wrappers, as were several of his other works. Amassing all the parts can be a daunting task since unprotected paper is fragile and many did not survive.

PENNY BOXES. Trays or boxes outside antiquarian bookshops where the bookseller puts cheap, miscellaneous stock to attract browsers. A century ago, larger dealers doing a brisk business often carelessly consigned books to the penny boxes, sometimes leaving gems among the chaff. Collectors willing to cull through the boxes could travel from shop to shop and build reputable libraries without ever leaving the street. Today's penny boxes are more mundane, usually holding only left-overs from large collections or dead stock that has already stood too long on the shelves.

The modern version may not be as charming as the penny boxes of old, they may not offer up the same rewards, but booksellers still use them, and bibliophiles still have trouble passing one by without stopping to see what's in there.

PLATE. A full page devoted to an illustration, separate from the text pages of the book. The verso is blank.

POINTS. Characteristics which determine whether or not a book is a first edition. For instance, the first edition of a book may contain a specific spelling or other publishing mistake on a certain page that was corrected in later editions. The presence of the mistake is a point.

PRESENTATION COPY. Inscribed by the author as a gift. Not to be confused with a signature acquired by a total stranger who asked for the author's autograph in the book.

PRESS BOOK. A finely produced book, published by a private press, an individual, or established publisher for the sake of excellence in printing and binding and not necessarily for the book's literary value. Prices run high on these specialties—from the outset, not just as collectibles—again for the high manufacturing standard, not because the book is wonderful literature, though it might be.

PRINT RUN. The number of volumes of a book run off the press at one time.

PRIVATELY PRINTED. Not produced by a publisher. The author pays for the publication out of his own pocket. Quite often the privately printed book was compiled for a select group of people, family, or friends. Some very collectible books have been privately published, not the least of which was Edgar Allan Poe's *Tamerlane*. A copy recently sold at auction for a quarter of a million dollars.

PRIVATE PRESS. Publishers of limited editions or, simply, a single person producing (publishing) books.

PROVENANCE. The history of a book's ownership. Provenance may add to value if it shows prized associations. Many bibliophiles like information on the provenance of a book for its own sake. A love of old books and their history seem to go hand in hand.

QUARTER BOUND. Only the spine of a book is leather. The rest is boards or cloth.

QUOTES. The backbone of the bookseller's trade, a written description of a book with the asking price of the book stated. When quoting, use a 3″ × 5″ index card for each book quoted. Print the title, author, publisher, date, edition, number of pages, whether or not illustrations or maps are present, and the type of binding. Then carefully describe the condition. It is here a bookseller appreciates full disclosure of the defects. Even if you are as accurate as you know how to be, sometimes a dealer will envision something different and find the quote wanting. Include your name, address, and sale requirements and state whether the transaction is CWO (Cash With Order) or future billing.

READING COPY. A book that has seen better days, worn from use and in less than good condition. They're appreciated by scholars for research, but not by collectors unless the volume is exceedingly rare.

REBACKED. Fitted with a new spine and hinges. When considering such repairs, be prepared to pay well for a competent job. Unless you have a personal affinity for the book, before ordering any restoration by a professional book binder, have your volume appraised to see if it is worth the preservation cost.

REBOUND. Fitted with a new binding. Here again, as in the rebacked book, we are talking restoration and expensive repairs. Whenever this route is undertaken, opt for reattaching the original covers, if that is possible. Again, if you are selling the book, value should be there to justify the expense.

RECTO. In a book, the right-hand page, the front of the leaf.

REMAINDER. Selling book stock to a distributor at a considerable discount when the publisher believes the title has sold as many copies as it is likely to sell at full price in bookstores.

REPRINT. A reissue of a book previously published. A.L. Burt and Grosset & Dunlap reissued and made available many famous works to those who otherwise could not afford the first editions. In an elderly farm woman's house we visited in Vermont, the shelves in an upstairs bedroom were lined with books, reprints by Zane Grey, E.R. Burroughs, Dixon, Henty, Horatio Alger, and more. And proud she was that she had read them all.

REVIEW COPY. Complimentary copies of books sent to editors, journalists, and institutions, hoping for a review or at least a mention in their publications or programs.

RUBBED. Scratches or wear spots on leather bindings.

FANSHAWE,

A TALE.

"Wilt thou go on with me?"-- Southey.

BOSTON:
MARSH & CAPEN, 362 WASHINGTON STREET.

PRESS OF PUTNAM AND HUNT.

1828.

Facsimile Title Page

T A M E R L A N E

AND

OTHER POEMS

BY A BOSTONIAN

Young heads are giddy and young hearts are warm
and make mistakes for manhood to reform.

Cowper

BOSTON:

CALVIN F. S. THOMAS . . PRINTER

~~~~~~~~~~~~~~~

1827

Facsimile Title Page

SABIN, JOSEPH. An English bookseller who emigrated to the United States and became one of the foremost authorities on Americana, setting about to publish a comprehensive bibliography of the genre. Unfortunately, Sabin lived to see only the first thirteen volumes realized. Wilberforce Eames and R.W.G. Vail completed the monumental work, finishing with a total of twenty-nine volumes.

SCUFFED. Worn, scratched, nicked.

SEARCH SERVICE. Precisely what the term implies, initiating a search for a title through dealership and trade channels. Let's say you want a particular book, and you cannot find it in a used bookstore. If you know the title and author, a bookseller will print an inquiry in the trade journals welcoming quotes from other dealers. Since these journals have wide exposure among booksellers, the likelihood of finding your book is strong.

Most booksellers now charge a basic fee for the service whether or not a book is found. Back in the good old days, Wright Howes noted in his fall 1933 catalog "out of print and scarce books sought for and reported free of charge." The times, they are a changing.

SPINE. The backstrip of a book.

STATE. Changes or corrections made during a print run. Sometimes used interchangeably with "issue," which indicates changes or corrections, but not a full resetting of the type, made between impressions.

SUNNED. Faded. The original color of the book loses brightness and freshness when exposed to direct bright light, especially sunlight.

THREE-QUARTER LEATHER. Leather on the spine and about an inch beyond, along with triangles of leather at the corners of the book. The rest of the binding could be cloth or boards.

TIPPED-IN. Glued in, as when illustrations are not bound into a book but glued in after binding. The technique is most often used to add glossy pictures or maps, with glue applied to the back of the illustration at the top only. Tipping-in was used to incorporate illustrations that would have been too expensive to print and bind into the book.

TISSUE GUARDS. Tissue paper bound into the book that protects the plates.

TITLE PAGE. The page at the front of each book which gives the title, author, publisher and, sometimes, the printing date. In most books, this information is on a recto page. Always consult the title page for pertinent information about a book; never depend upon what is printed on the spine or cover. (*See* facsimile illustrations)

TOOLING. Impressing a design by hand in leather.

TRADE CATALOG. Printed pamphlets, booklets, or books that list items for sale. Catalogs fully describe the merchandise offered, and many are embellished with detailed illustrations. A popular method of merchandising in rural areas, catalogs gave farmers and others living far from towns and commercial centers a chance to see items such as clothing, farm equipment, guns and ammunition, seeds, and horticultural goods that they considered buying. A catalog had to take the place of a good salesperson, interest the customer, and sell the product on the basis of the pictures and information included in the catalog. Old catalogs are like a page out of history.

UNCUT. Untrimmed leaves. When sheets are printed, folded, and bound, the trimming process to open the leaves can miss some folds, leaving the pages uncut and unopened.

UNOPENED. Uncut leaves. Tearing can open them, but they would remain "uncut."

VELLUM. Calfskin binding. Also sometimes called parchment. Vellum and other leather bindings should be carefully cared for to keep them from drying and cracking (*see* "Care and Repair of Books").

VERSO. Left-hand page of a book, the back side of a leaf.

WANT LIST. A listing of books needed either to fill a dealer's bookshelves or to accommodate customers looking for particular works. Booksellers periodically send out want lists to other dealers. Often the bookseller will include a "permanent want list" in which case there is no cut-off date for acquiring those books, and duplicates may even be welcome.

WESTERN AMERICANA. The genre covering the settling of the American West and American western culture, including indigenous peoples. Everyone seems to want this category, and the prices are high for the really good stuff. The collector, of course, is looking for pioneer imprints, broadsides, handbills, documents, handwritten journey narratives, or ledgers. Books on Indians, explorations, outlaws, mining, and whatever else attested to the westward push are collectible.

WRAPPERS. Paper binding. This does not refer to modern paperbacks, which are bound in stiff paper with illustrations. The term refers to simple paper covering, sometimes plain paper serving also as a title page. Before modern bindings, books were often published with plain paper covers. Customers brought the works to their own binderies to have custom leather or cloth covers put on. Older pamphlets were often published with thin paper covers, or wrappers.

WRAPS. Same as wrappers.

LIST OF ABBREVIATIONS

Advanced reading copy	ARC	Editor(s)	(ed)
Albany	Alb	English	Eng
All edges gilded	aeg	Engravings	engr
American Museum of Natural		Ex libris	xlib
History	AMNH	Facsimile	facs
Association books	asso copy	First edition	1st ed
Atlanta	Atl	Folding	fldg
Backed	bkd	Frontispiece	frontis
Baltimore	Balt	Government Printing	
Boards	bds	Office	GPO
Boston	Bos	Illustrated	illus
Black and white	b/w	Impression	imp
Cambridge	Camb	Indianapolis	Ind
Catalog	cat	Inscribed	inscrb
Chicago	Chi	Leather	lea
Cincinnati	Cinc	Limited edition	ltd
Cleveland	Cleve	Lithographs	litho
Color	clr	London	Lon
Copies	cc	Marbled	mar
Dust jacket/dust wrapper	dj	Milwaukee	Milw
Edinburgh	Edin	Minneapolis	Minn
Edition	ed	Morocco	mor

Museum of Modern Art	MOMA	Revised	rev
National Geographic Society	NGS	Richmond	Rich
		Sacramento	Sac
No place	np	Salt Lake City	SLC
Oxford	Ox	San Francisco	SF
Pages	pp	Signed (by author)	sgn
Philadelphia	Phila	Top edge gilded	teg
Pittsburgh	Pitts	Tipped-in	tip-in
Photographs	photos	Title has been abbreviated	...
Printing	prntg	Toronto	Tor
Providence	Prov	United Kingdom	UK
Rebacked	rbkd	University	Univ
Rebound	rbnd	Volumes	vols
Reprint	rprnt	Wrappers, soft paper cover	wrps

The Official® Price Guide to

OLD

BOOKS

OLD BOOKS LISTING

5th Reader. Cinc/NY, 1885. ....$25–$40

A Century of Achievement. MA, 1949, illus. ....$10–$14

A.A. Mark's Artificial Limbs. NY, 1891, wrps, illus. .....$38–$45

Act for the Making of Bread. Lon, 1758. ....$50–$75

Aesop's Fables. Winston Co., 1928, illus by John Fitz, Jr.
....$14–$20

Alaska Our Frontier Wonderland. Seattle, 1913, wrps, fldg map.
....$22–$30

Alaska Via McKinley Park Route. Alaska Railroad, 1924, illus,
fldg timetable. ....$20–$28

Alcoholics Anonymous. 1st ed, 14th prntg, dj. ....$350–$600

Alphabetical List of Currier & Ives Prints. NY, private prntg,
1930, ltd #282, 1,000 cc. ....$30–$45

American Heritage Picture History of Civil War. NY, 1960,
2 vols, slipcase. ....$15–$20

American Pioneer in Science ... William James Beal. Amherst,
MA, 1925, 1st ed, illus. ....$50–$75

American Type Founders Co. Specimen Book. 1923. ....$25–$45

American War Songs. Phila, 1925, illus. ....$14–$18

Antarctic Bibliography, Vol. I. GPO, 1965. ....$30–$40

Arabian Nights. 1924, illus by Frances Brundage, clr plates. ....*$30–$40*

Architectural Review Congress Number. Lon, 1906, illus. ....*$40–$55*

Art of Cookery Made Plain and Easy . . . by a Lady. Lon, 1774, calf, rbkd. ....*$275–$395*

Art Work of the Mohawk River and Valley, Its Cities and Towns. Chi, 1902, 9 vols. .... *$75–$90*

Artemus Ward's Panorama. NY, 1860, 1st ed. ....*$20–$22*

Atchison City Directory for 1880. Atchison, KS, 1880. .*$52–$64*

Atlas and Index of Historic Sites in Montgomery County, Md. 1977, folio. ....*$55–$90*

Atmospheric System Developed. Hartford, self-published, 1870, 1st ed. ....*$14–$20*

Baby Bunting ABC. NY, McLaughlin Bros., 12 pp, illus, soft linen. ....*$15–$20*

Baby's Opera. Lon/NY, Warne & Co., Ltd., 1968, illus by Walter Crane, dj. ....*$28–$35*

Barn Plans and Outbuildings. NY, 1883, illus. ....*$40–$65*

Battleground Korea: The Story of the 25th Infantry Division. Arlington, 1951, 1st ed, dj. ....*$50–$85*

Beauford Delaney: A Retrospective. Harlem, 1978, wrps, illus. ....*$20–$25*

Belgian Congo. Oxford Univ. Press, 1944, illus, geographical handbook, maps, charts, photos. ....*$30–$45*

Berra: Behind the Plate. Argonaut, 1962. ....*$18–$20*

Biography of Our Baby. Illus by Bessie Collins Pease, boxed. ....*$45–$65*

Black Arrow. Scribner's, 1916, illus by N.C. Wyeth, 14 clr plates. ....*$40–$55*

Black Book: The Nazi Crime against the Jewish People. NY, 1946, 1st ed, dj. ....*$25–$40*

Boar's Head and Yule Log as Celebrated at Hoosac School. NY, 1930, illus. ....*$25–$35*

Book of Baseball. NY, 1911. ....*$115–$150*

Book of Birds. NGS, 1932–39, vols 1 and 2, dj. ....*$30–$40*

Book of Fishes. NGC, illus, dj. ....*$15–$20*

Book of Kells. Lon/NY, 1933, illus, 4th ed, tip-in clr pl. .*$50–$95*

Book of Pirates by Henry K. Brooke. . . . Phila, 1847, illus. ....*$100–$175*

Borough of the Bronx. 1913, illus, presentation copy. ...*$25–$45*

Boy Scouts of America: Handbook for Boys. 1928, wrps, Norman Rockwell cover. ....*$20–$35*

Boy's Book of Shipwrecks and Ocean Stories. Phila, 1860, illus, rbkd. ....*$40–$75*

Brae-Burn Country Club. 1905. ....*$35–$45*

Brattleboro Country Club. 1926, pamphlet. ....*$20–$30*

Bricks without Straw. OH, 1944, 45 pp, bds, illus. ....*$14–$30*

Brown Derby Cookbook. NY, 1949, 1st ed. ....*$37–$40*

Buckaroo Ballads. NY, Paull-Pioneer Music Co., 1940, wrps. *$14–30*

By-laws of the Chicago and Rock Island Rail Road Co. NY, 1858, 10 pp, wrps. ....*$85–$100*

Calendar of the American Fur Company's Papers. DC, 1945, 2 vols, 1st ed. ....*$50–$85*

Cambridge of 1776. Camb, 1876. ....*$22–$30*

Campfire Chats. Chi, 1887, illus. ....*$40–$60*

Catalogue of Parts. Jeffrey Mfg. Co., 1918, wrps. ....*$25–$32*

Catalogue of an Exhibition of Angling Book Plates. . . . NY, 1918. ....*$35–$50*

Centennial Souvenier Cookbook. 1966. ....*$10–$14*

Chicago School of Architecture. Random House, 1964, dj. ....*$60–$75*

Chrysalis. 1916. ....*$30–$35*

Church Psalmist. NY, 1855, 40th ed, lea. ....*$25–$35*

Collector's Book of Railroadiana. ....*$18–$20*

Collier's New Photographic History of the World's War. NY, 1918, 1st ed. ....$45–$90

Colorado Outings. 1898, 47 pp, wrps, illus, fldg map. ..$22–$35

Colt's Police Revolver Handbook. Hartford, 1942, illus cat. ....$18–$28

Combat History of 2nd Infantry Division. Baton Rouge, 1946. ....$55–$65

Come to Alaska. 1926, illus, tourist booklet. ....$22–$25

Complete Course of Jiu-jitsu and Physical Culture. Bos, 1905, illus. ....$22–$30

Complete Dog Book. NY, American Kennel Club, 1947, illus, photos. ....$15–$25

Conquerers of the Sky. McLaughlin Bros., 1932, illus. ..$10–$15

Contributions to Medical and Biological Research. NY, 1919, 2 vols, illus, ltd #20/1,600 cc. ....$75–$125

Cook's Tourist's Handbook for Egypt, the Nile, and the Desert. 1897, 1st ed, pocket map. ....$37–$55

Cook's Tourist's Handbook for Palestine and Syria. Lon, 1900, maps. ....$18–$25

Cooning with Cooners. Hunter-Trader, 1924, illus, 2nd ed. ....$12–$24

Cottage Physician. Springfield, 1895. ....$22–$30

Cram's Universal Atlas.... Chi, 1889, ¾ lea. ....$95–$125

Cruise of the Revenue Steamer Corwin in Alaska.... GPO, 1883, illus, clr and b/w plates. ....$95–$135

Currier & Ives Prints: The Red Indian. Lon/NY, 1931, intro by W.S. Hall, sgn by Hall, dj. ....$35–$45

Davey's Illustrated Guide to Niagara Falls. 58 pp, illus, photos. ....$18–$30

Description of the New York Central Park. NY, 1869. ..$50–$95

Doctrines and Discipline of Methodist Episcopal Church ... 1872. NY, 1872. ....$12–$19

Dr. Chase's Recipes.... Ann Arbor, 1866. ....$22–$25

Dr. Daniels Horse Book: Home Treatment for Horse and Cattle. Bos, 1911. ....$24–$35

Dress Regulations for the Army. Tuttle, 1970. ....$15–$25

EROS Magazine, Vol. 1, #1. ....$30–$35

Earth Photographs from Gemini III, IV, and V. DC, 1967. ....$25–$28

East of the Sun and West of the Moon. NY, 1922, illus by Kay Nielson, tip-in clr plates, dj. ....$150–$300

Economic Trends of War and Reconstruction 1860–1870. NY, 1918, 1st ed. ....$45–$75

El Museo Del Oro. Bogota, Colombia, 1948, wrps, clr plates. ....$65–$90

Electric Railway Dictionary. McGraw-Hill, 1911, 1st ed, illus. ....$95–$125

Epworth Hymnal. NY, 1885. ....$5–$11

Evangelical Rambler, Vol. 2. NY, 1837. ....$10–$14

F. Weber Co. Guide to Tapestry, Painting, and Stenciling.... Phila, 1915, wrps, illus. ....$20–$30

Feed My Sheep. Anchorage, nd. ....$10–$14

Felix S. Cohen's Handbook of Federal Indian Law. Albuquerque, 1958. ....$28–$35

Fifth Rpt. of Senate Fact Finding Comm. on Un-Amer. Activities. Sac, 1949, wrps, illus. ....$20–$25

First Ann. Rep. of the Bd. of Pharmacy of the St. of Washington. Olympia, 1892, 1st ed, wrps. ....$40–$50

First Annual Sports and Bicycle Races. PA, 1896, 8 pp, wrps. ....$19–$30

First Editions of Famous American Songs. Scribner's, nd, wrps, cat. ....$10–$15

Five Thousand Miles ... on the South African Railways. 1934, 1st ed, wrps, illus. ....$32–$45

Flags of Army of U.S. during the War of Rebellion 1861–65. Phila, 1887, 1st ed, illus, clr lithos, folio. ....$275–$450

Frank Leslie's Illustrated History of the Civil War. NY, 1895, 1st ed, small folio. ....$85–$125

Fugitives: The Story of Clyde Barrow and Bonnie Parker. Dallas, 1934, 1st ed. ....$47–$65

Gambling, Gaming Supplies. Chi, H.C. Evans Co., 1929. ....$85–$125

Gambling World by Rouge et Noir. Dodd Mead, 1898. .$50–$65

Georgia Scenes by a Native Georgian. NY, 1840, illus, 2nd ed. ....$100–$195

Girl Scout Equipment Catalog. 1948, wrps. ....$15–$18

Golfers Year-book. 1938, illus. ....$27–$35

Grand Union Grille Works. Chi, 1911, wrps, architectural cat. ....$38–$45

Great Northwest: A Guide Book and Itinerary. St. Paul, 1889, illus, fldg map, engr. ....$37–$45

Guardian of Liberty. Auburn, NY, 1855. ....$15–$22

Guide in the Wilderness ... First Settlements in W. New York. Cooperstown, 1936, wrps, 3rd prntg. ....$15–$20

Gulliver's Travels. E.P. Dutton, 1909, 1st ed, illus by Arthur Rackham. ....$125–$150

Gun Cotton and Its Uses. Lon, illus. ....$25–$45

Handbook for Scout Masters—Boy Scouts of America. NY, Boy Scouts of America, 1914, 1st ed, illus. ....$20–$28

Handbook of Tobacco Culture for Planters in So. Rhodesia. Salisbury, 1913, 1st ed, illus. ....$75–$115

Harpers Bazaar. 1872, 2 vols, illus, folio, plates. ....$150–$225

Herbalist and Herb Doctor. Ind, 1932, illus. ....$15–$22

Hiss Case: A Lesson for the American People. DC, GPO, 1950, Nixon speech. ....$35–$40

Historical Sketch of the Town of Brookfield, Ct. Danbury, 1896, wrps. ....$22.50–$25

History 2nd Infantry Division. 1953. ....$45–$75

History of Iowa County, Wisconsin. Chi, 1881, ¼ lea. ....$75–$110

History of Ireland from Earliest Times.... NY, 1885, 2 vols. ....$22–$30

History of the 14th Armored Division. Atlanta, nd. ....$55–$65

History of the 157th Infantry Regiment, 4 June, '43–8 May, '45. Baton Rouge, 1946, 1st ed, illus, photos, fldg maps. ....$95–$130

History of the 413 Infantry. Los Angeles, 1946. ....$57-$75

History of the Delaware and Hudson Company, 1823–1923. Albany, 1925, illus. ....$40–$60

History of the Fire and Police Depts. of Paterson, NJ. Paterson, 1893, 1st ed, illus, plates. ....$48–$60

History of the Jews. Lon, 1829, 3 vols, maps, calf, mar bds. ....$150–$175

Hymns for the Use of Methodist Episcopal Church. Cinc, 1863, rev ed, lea. ....$25–$40

Illustrated Catalogue of Railway and Contractors Supplies. Buda Foundry & Mfg. Co., 1902, illus, cat. ....$75–$125

In Memoriam: John Booth ... Died in Austin, Nevada, 1884. Austin, 1884, 8 pp, softbound. ....$22–$32

Indian Costumes of Guatemala. Osborne, Australia, 1966, wrps. ....$35–$65

Indian Narratives. Containing a Correct and Interesting History of the Indian Wars. Claremont, 1854. ....$55–$75

Iowa, A Guide to the Hawkeye State. WPA, 1938, 1st ed, map. ....$28–$40

Iron Toys. PA, Dent Hardware, wrps, illus, cat. ....$48–$55

J.S. Lothrop's Champaign County Directory 1870–71.... Chi, 1871, illus, fldg map. ....$55–$75

Jane's Fighting Ships. 1971. ....$20–$30

Jane's Fighting Ships. 1920. ....$85–$100

Jane's Weapons Systems. 1970, dj. ....$20–$35

Japan: The Pocket Guide. Tokyo, Japan Travel Bureau, 1947, illus, maps. ....$10–$15

Jesse James, My Father. Cleve, 1906, 2nd ed. ....$28–$34

Johnson's New Illustrated Family Atlas. NY, 1865, folio, mor, maps. ....$600–$750

Johnson's New Illustrated Family Atlas. NY, 1863, folio ....$385–$425

Johnson's New Illustrated Family Atlas. NY, 1862. ..$300–$650

Journal of a Prisoner of War in Richmond. NY, 1862. .$40–$50

Journal of American-Irish Historical Society. NY, 1919. ....$15–$25

Journal of Indian Textile History. India, 1960, wrps, illus. ....$25–$35

Journal of a Young Lady of Virginia, 1782. Balt, 1871. .$20–$25

Klansman's Manual. Atlanta, 1924, 1st ed, wrps. ....$75–$125

Knights of the Ku Klux Klan.... Atlanta, 1926, wrps. .$55–$75

Kodak Milestones. Eastman Kodak Co., 1967, wrps. ......$15–$20

La Mode Feminine de 1720 a 1775. Paris, Editions Nilsson, illus, hand-clr plates. ....$25–$35

Labrador Retriever Club 1931–1956. 25th Anniversary ed. ....$20–$25

Lands in Alabama.... GPO, 1828, 1st ed. ....$18–$25

Last Journals of David L. Livingstone. Hartford, 1875, illus, maps. ....$35–$40

Legend of the Shasta Spring of California. SF, nd, 1st ed, 16 pp, wrps. ....$50–$75

Lessons in Furcraft. Omaha, 1932. ....$18–$27.50

Letters of John James Audubon, 1826–1840. 1930, 2 vols, ltd 225 cc, slipcase. ....$250–$275

Life and Adventures of Sam Bass the Notorious ... Train Robber. Dallas, 1878, wrps. ....$75–$125

Life in the Woods. Chi, nd. ....$12–$22

Life of Miss Anne Catley: Celebrated Singing Performer.... Lon, 1888. ....$30–$40

Life's Picture History of WWII. NY, 1950, slipcase. .....$15–$20

Literary Outlaw: The Life and Times of William S. Burroughs. 1988, wrps. ....$24–$30

Little Folks' Mother Goose. NY, 1931, illus by Chris Rule and Mary Royt, dj. ....*$14-$18*

Little Miss Muffet and Other Stories. NY, 1902. ....*$15-$20*

Loss of the United States Steamer Oneida. U.S. Gov Doc, HED #236, 1870, fldg map. ....*$25-$35*

Louisa's Tenderness to the Little Birds in Winter. Portland, Bailey & Noyes, nd, wrps. ....*$37-$45*

Magician's Own Book. . . . NY, 1857, 1st ed. ....*$150-$200*

Magnetic Physician: Vital Magnetic Cure. . . . Bos, 1871. ....*$35-$60*

Manual for the Legislature of New York. Albany, 1858, lea. ....*$25-$35*

Manual of Homeopathic Veterinary Practice . . . Domestic Animals. NY, 1874, ½ lea. ....*$45-$55*

Manufacture of Optical Glass and of Optical Systems. GPO, 1921, illus. ....*$18-$25*

Marie Burroughs Art Portfolio of Stage Celebrities. Chi, 1894, 14 parts, bound. ....*$50-$75*

Maritime History of New York. NY, WPA Writers Project, 1941, illus, dj. ....*$35-$50*

Maternal Physician . . . by an American Matron. Phila, 1818, 2nd ed, lea. ....*$175-$225*

Matthew Brady and His World. Time-Life, 1977, 1st ed. ..*$16-$20*

McDougall on Dice and Cards. 1944, 1st ed. ....*$12-$15*

Mem. Concerning Several Ministers . . . Society of Friends. Lon, 1816. ....*$22-$28*

Memoirs by Harry S. Truman, Vol I, Year of Decision. NY, 1955, 1st ed, dj. ....*$15-$20*

Memoirs of Colonel Sebastian Beauman and Descendants. np, 1900. ....*$22-$25*

Memoirs of the Late Mrs. Robinson, Written by Herself. Phila, 1802, calf. ....*$25-$35*

Memoirs of the Life of the Late Charles Lee, Esq. NY, 1792. ....*$45-$55*

Memorial Volume of the Town of Windham, Conn. Hartford, 1893, illus. ....$18–$20

Mickey Mouse Waddle Book. NY, 1934, bds. ....$85–$110

Miscellany of Arms and Armor: Presented to Bashford Dean. np, 1927, illus, ltd #127/ 150 cc, presentation copy from Hugh Smiley. ....$125–$200

Miss Beecher's Domestic Receipt-book. NY, 1867, 5th ed. ....$30–$45

Mitchell's Modern Geography of the World. Phila, 1856, illus, woodcuts. ....$25–$35

Mitchell's New General Atlas. Phila, 1864, folio, maps. ....$300–$400

Modern Way in Picture Making. Rochester, 1905, illus. .$27–$35

More Waterfowl. NY, 1931. ....$8–$12

Mother Goose Panorama, Ten Feet Long. Platt & Munk, 1950. ....$25–$35

Mother Goose Rhymes. Saalfield, illus by Frances Brundage. ....$20–$25

Mrs. Putnam's Receipt Book. Bos, 1858. ....$33–$40

Multiplication Table in Rhyme for Young Arithmeticians. NY, nd, 16 pp, wrps. ....$22–$40

Musselhorn's Pencil Sketches of Missouri. St. Louis, 1974. ....$18–$25

Narrative of Capt. James Cook's Voyages Round the World. Lon, 1848. ....$58–$70

Narrative of Five Youths from the Sandwich Islands. . . . NY, 1816, wrps. ....$50–$100

New Japanese Photography. MOMA, 1974, wrps. ....$15–$22

New System of Domestic Cookery . . . by a Lady. Edin, 1843, illus, rbnd, ¾ calf, marb bds. ....$95–$110

New Treatise on Surveying and Navigation. NY, 1864. .$18–$25

Nyasaland Road Guide . . . through . . . British Central Africa. 1951, wrps. ....$27–$45

Official Guide of the National Asso. of Pro. Baseball Leagues. NY, Spalding, 1903, wrps, illus, photos. ....$100–$125

Old Cabin Home Minstrels. Lorenz, 1921, wrps. ....*$6–$12*

Old Dame Trot and Her Comical Cat. Lon, nd, illus. ..*$350–$450*

Old Sol. Lamps and Lighting. 1919, illus. ....*$12–$22*

Old Woman and Her Pig. Lon, Warne & Co., nd, 12 pp, wrps, illus, clr panels. ....*$35–$50*

Olympia 1936. Germany, 1936, 2 vols, illus, photos. ...*$160–$195*

Orwell Reader, George Orwell. NY, 1956, 1st ed. ....*$50–$75*

Our New Friends. Dick and Jane Reader. 1946. ....*$25–$30*

Outdoor Visits. Don and Nan Reader. 1934. ....*$15–$20*

Pages from the Gutenberg Bible of 42 Lines. NY, 1940, ltd 2,000 cc, folio. ....*$100–$125*

Parlour Magic. Phila. 1938, 1st U.S. ed. ....*$50–$60*

People from Dickens. NY, Scribner's Classic, 1935, illus by Thomas Fogarty. ....*$25–$35*

Peter Rabbit Story Book. Platt & Munk, 1935, illus. .....*$15–$25*

Pictographic History of the Oglala Sioux. Lincoln, 1967, illus by Amos Bad Heart Bull, boxed. ....*$37–$45*

Pictorial History of the Second World War. NY, 1944–65, 5 vols, illus, photos. ....*$45–$60*

Picturesque Cuba, Puerto Rico, Hawaii, and The Philippines. Springfield, 1898, wrps. ....*$30–$35*

Pipe and Pouch: The Smoker's Own Book of Poetry. Bos, 1895. ....*$18–$25*

Poisonous Snakes of the World. DC, GPO, nd, illus, b/w and clr plates. ....*$40–$55*

Pop-up Minnie Mouse. 1933, illus, 3 pop-ups. ....*$100–$200*

Pop-up Mickey Mouse. Blue Ribbon Books, 1933, illus, 3 pop-ups. ....*$200–$300*

Prison Life during the Rebellion. VA, 1869, wrps. ....*$65–$150*

Probable Termination of Mormon Troubles in the Utah Territory. GPO, 1858. ....*$45–$55*

Proceedings of Grand Lodge of . . . Masons of Virginia. 1923. ....*$20–$25*

Proceedings of Grand Royal Arch Chapter of the State of Va.
Rich, 1867, wrps. ....$28–$35

Proceedings of the Exec. of the U.S. Respecting . . . Insurgents.
Phila, 1795, (Whiskey Rebellion). ....$125–$175

Public Documents of Legislature of Mass. Bos, 1813, 1st ed,
wrps, sewn. ....$60–$90

Question of Color. NY, 1895. ....$33–$38

Radio Amateur's Handbook. 1927, 2nd ed, softcover. ...$25–$35

Radioactivity in America. Balt/Lon, 1976, 1st ed. ....$35–$40

Rand McNally & Co.'s New Dollar Atlas of the U.S. and Canada.
Chi, 1884, cloth bds. ....$40–$60

Randolph Caldecott Graphic Pictures. Lon, 1883, illus, folio.
....$85–$115

Receipt Book of Melvina Poe. Augusta, GA, 1833, handwritten,
lea, marb bds. ....$275–$315

Red Detachment of Women . . . Ballet. Peking, China Ballet
Troupe, 1972, illus, red silk dj. ....$12–$18

Reflections on Salt Lake City and Vicinity. 1885, view book.
....$18–$24

Regulations for the Care of Camels. Cairo, War Office Printing
Press, 1896, wrps. ....$55–$75

Reminiscences of Winfield Scott Hancock by His Wife. NY, 1887.
....$20–$25

Rep. of Regents of N.Y. on Longitudes of Dudley Observatory.
NY, 1862, wrps. ....$30–$50

Report of the Secretary of the Navy . . . Nov. 5, 1864. Rich, 1864,
52 pp, 1st ed, wrps. Confederate imprint. ....$250–$350

Report on Japanese Research on Radio Wave Propagation. U.S.
Army, 1946, 1st ed. ....$50–$65

Report on the Census of Cuba, 1899. DC, GPO, 1900, illus, pho-
tos. ....$48–$60

*Report on U.S. Geographical Surveys West of 100th Merid-
ian. . . .* DC, GPO, 1877, illus. ....$80–$120

Report on the Control of the Aborigines of Formosa. 1911, illus,
maps. ....$75–$100

Reports of Explorations and Surveys to the Pacific Ocean. illus, plates. ....$150–$250

Reports . . . Joint Palestine Survey Commission, October 1, 1928. Bos, 1928, illus. ....$95–$125

Revised Regulations for the Army of the United States. Phila, Lippincott, 1862. ....$75–$95

Rhinegold and the Valkyrie. Lon/NY, 1914, illus by Arthur Rackham, tip-in plates. ....$60–$75

Rock 'n Roll Star Art. 1979. ....$20–$25

Rocky Mountain Country Club. 1905. ....$45–$60

Rocky Mountain Views. . . . Denver, 1917, wrps, photos. .$15–$25

Rollicking Rhymes for Youngsters. Fleming Revell Co., 1902, 1st ed, illus. ....$27–$55

Rubaiyat of Omar Khayyam. NY, Doran, nd, illus by Edmund Dulac. ....$45–$65

Rugs from the Handlooms of the Far Orient. Kansas City, 1909, wrps, illus, postcard laid in. ....$22–$35

Sacred Melodies. NH, Free Will Baptist, 1870. ....$15–$25

Savage Arms and Ammo. 1920s, 24 pp, cat #65. ....$20–$30

Sketch of the 126th Regiment Pennsylvania Volunteers. PA, 1869, 1st ed. ....$95–$125

Skier's Song Book. CA, 1950, illus, dj. ....$12–$15

Slang Dictionary. Lon, 1864, 2nd ed. ....$40–$60

Smokeless Powders for Rifles and Revolvers. Dupont, 1908, 45 pp, cat. ....$18–$27

Some Accounts . . . Soc. of Friends towards Indian Tribes (NJ and Pa). Lon, 1844, fldg map. ....$200–$350

Some Poems of Friedrich Holderlin. Norfolk, 1943, wrps. ....$30–$50

Songs of the Glenwood Mission Inn, Riverside, Cal. 1910, wrps, illus, photos. ....$15–$20

Songs of the Range. Chi, 1938, wrps. ....$12–$15

Sons of the Sires. . . . Phila, 1855. ....$22–$28

Specimen Book of Monotype, Linotype and Foundry Type Faces, Etc. Bos, 1941, 1st ed. ....$28–$35

Star Trek Technical Manual. 1975, 1st ed. ....$20–$25

Stoddard's Lectures (John L.). Bos, 1909, 15 vols, lea, mar bds. ....$30–$50

Story of Dark Plot or Tyranny on the Frontier. Warren Press, 1903. ....$28–$35

Story of King Arthur and His Knights. Scribner's, 1903, 1st ed, illus by Howard Pyle. ....$85–$115

Telephone Appeals—1887. 1887, 1st ed, softcover. ....$125–$165

Tell It All: The Story of a Life's Experience in Mormonism. Hartford, 1874. ....$15–$20

The Southern Songster.... Liverpool, 1864, 82 pp, wrps. ....$175–$225

The Three Kittens. Lon, nd, wrps. ....$50–$75

Theory of the Universe. NY, 1868. ....$50–$65

Third Marine Division. DC, 1948, 1st ed. ....$42–$50

Three Little Pigs. McKay, nd, illus by J.R. Neill. ....$16–$22

Tiffany Table Settings. Crowell, 1960, 1st ed. ....$14–$18

Trial of Andrew Johnson, President of the U.S. .... DC, GPO, 1868, 3 vols. ....$65–$100

Trip around the World in an Automobile. McLaughlin Bros., 1907, wrps, illus, lithos. ....$50–$80

Two Soldiers: The Campaign Diaries of Key and Campbell. Chapel Hill, 1938. ....$20–$27

Universal Indian Sign Language. Boy Scouts, 1929. ....$32–$45

U.S. Camera. 1950, 1st ed, dj. ....$20–$25

U.S. Camera. 1947, 1st ed, dj. ....$25–$30

U.S. Camera Annual. 1935. ....$25–$40

U.S. Cartridge Company's Collection of Firearms. U.S. Cartridge Co., nd, cat. ....$35–$50

Van Loan's Catskill Mountain Guide and Bird's-eye View.... NY, 1879, illus, maps. ....$175–$225

Walter Browning or the Slave's Protector. Cinc, 1856. .*$15–$20*

Walter Camp's Book of College Sports. NY, 1893, 1st ed. ....*$145–$175*

Warren's Common School Geography. Phila, 1881. ....*$45–$75*

Westward the Way. St. Louis, 1954, illus. ....*$18–$25*

What Made Ireland Sinn Fein. . . . np, 1921. ....*$20–$30*

What They Said about the 4th Armored. Germany, 1945. ....*$22–$25*

Where to Hunt American Game. MA, 1898, 1st ed, illus. ....*$50–$75*

Woman's Kingdom. NY, 1869, illus, 1st American ed. ...*$22–$30*

Wonderful Adventures of a Lady of French Nobility. . . . NY, 1852, 4th ed. ....*$18–$25*

Wright and Ditson's Lawn Tennis Guide for 1895. wrps. .*$25–$45*

Young Lady's Friend. By a Lady. Bos, 1837. ....*$35–$40*

Zebulon Pike's Arkansaw Journal. Stewart Commission, 1932. ....*$52–$60*

* * *

Abbot, W.J. *Panama and the Canal.* Syndicate Pub. Co., 1913, 414 pp, illus. ....*$12–$15*

Abbott, J.S.C. *Life of General U.S. Grant.* Bos, 1868, illus. ....*$20–$25*

Abbott, Jacob. *Cousin Lucy on the Sea Shore.* Derby & Miller, 1850. ....*$15–$22*

Abbott, Jacob. *The Little Philosopher.* Hickling, Swan, 1855. ....*$18–$22*

Abele, Hyacinth. *The Violin and Its Story.* Lon, 1905, illus. ....*$20–$30*

Abelow, Samuel P. *History of Brooklyn Jewry.* Brooklyn, 1937, 1st ed. ....*$115–$175*

Abercrombie, John. *Pathological and Practical Researches on Diseases of . . . Abdomen.* Edin, 1828. ....*$35–$50*

Abernethy, John. *Surgical Observations ... Treatment of Local Diseases.* . . . Lon, 1825, bds. ....$25–$35

Abernethy, John. *The Surgical Works.* Lon, 1816, 2 vols, new ed 1 plate, calf. ....$40–$50

Abrahams, Israel. *Jewish Life in the Middle Ages.* Phila, 1896, 1st ed. ....$18–$30

Academy of Motion Picture Arts and Sciences. *Motion Picture Sound Engineering.* 1938, 1st ed, illus. ....$30–$45

Ackerman, Irving C. *The Wire-haired Fox Terrier.* NY, 1928, illus. ....$15–$18

Ackley, Edith F. *Marionettes.* NY, Stokes, 1929, dj. ......$25–$45

Adair, J. *Navajo and Pueblo Silversmiths.* Norman, OK, 1944, 1st ed, dj. ....$35–$45

Adams, Andy. *A Texas Matchmaker.* Bos, 1904, 1st ed. ..$15–$20

Adams, Andy. *The Log of a Cowboy.* Bos, 1903, 1st ed, illus by E. Boyd Smith, 2nd issue. ....$40–$72

Adams, Ansel and Nancy Newhall. *The Tetons and the Yellowstone.* Redwood City, CA, 1970, wrps. ....$25–$35

Adams, Ansel. *An Autobiography.* 1985, wrps, dj. ....$15–$20

Adams, Ansel. *Born Free and Equal.* US Camera 1944, wrps. ....$95–$150

Adams, Ansel. *Camera and Lens Studio.* Morgan & Lester, 1948, 1st ed. ....$18–$25

Adams, Ansel. *The Negative.* 1964, sgn, dj. ....$30–$60

Adams, Ansel. *Yosemite and the Range of Light.* Bos, 1979, illus, dj. ....$50–$80

Adams, Emma H. *To and Fro, Up and Down in Southern California.* Cinc, 1888, 1st ed. ....$38–$50

Adams, Harrison. *Pioneer Boys of the Mississippi.* Bos, 1913, 1st ed, illus. ....$10–$20

Adams, Harrison. *Pioneers of the Great Lakes.* Bos, 1912, 1st ed, illus. ....$10–$15

Adams, John D. *Arts-Crafts Lamps: How to Make Them.* Chi, 1911, illus. ....$65–$85

Adams, John. *The Adams-Jefferson Letters.* Univ. of North Carolina, 1959, 2 vols, 1st ed, boxed. ....$22–$35

Adams, Joseph. *Observations on Morbid Poisons.* ... Lon, 1795, bds. ....$130–$185

Adams, Paul M. *When Wagon Trails Were Dim.* ... MT, 1957. ....$12–$15

Adams, Ramon F. *More Burrs under the Saddle: Books and Histories of the West.* Norman, OK, 1979, 1st ed. ....$35–$65

Adams, Richard. *Watership Down.* Macmillan, 1972, sgn, dj. ....$75–$140

Addams, Charles. *Black Maria.* NY, 1960, 1st ed, dj. ..$20–$30

Addams, Jane. *The Spirit of Youth and the City Streets.* NY, 1909, 1st ed, author inscrb. ....$18–$25

Adler, Felix. *An Ethical Philosophy of Life.* NY, 1925. ..$30–$45

Adney, Edwin Tappan. *The Bark Canoes and Skin Boats of North America.* DC, 1964, illus. ....$30–$45

Agassiz, Louis. *The Structure of Animal Life: Six Lectures.* Scribner's, Armstrong, 1874, 3rd ed. ....$15–$22

Agassiz, Louis and A.A. Gould. *Outlines of Comparative Physiology.* Lon, 1855, illus. ....$35–$40

Aguilar, Grace. *Women of Israel.* NY, 1870, 2 vols, illus..$20–$35

Ahlstrom, L.J. *Eighty Years of Swedish Baptist Work in Iowa, 1835–1933.* Des Moines, 1933, 1st ed, illus. ....$45–$75

Akin, Otis F. *Reminiscences of the Klondike Rush of 1898.* 8 pp, 1st ed, wrps. ....$75–$100

Albee, Edward. *Malcolm.* NY, 1966, 1st ed, dj. ....$20–$30

Albee, Edward. *Who's Afraid of Virginia Woolf?* NY, 1962, 1st ed, dj. ....$65–$75

Albert, Lillian Smith and Jane Ford Adams. *The Button Sampler.* NY, illus, dj. ....$18–$25

Albion, Robert Greenhalgh and Robert Howe Connery. *Forestal and the Navy.* NY, 1962, illus, dj. ....$16–$25

Albrecht, Arthur Amil. *International Seaman's Union of America.* ... GPO, 1923, wrps. ....$16–$25

Alcoholics Anonymous. *The Little Red Book.* Minn, 1949.
....*$55–$75*

Alcott, Louisa May. *An Old Fashioned Girl.* Bos, 1870, 1st ed.
....*$65–$100*

Aldrich, L.C. *History of Ontario County.* Syracuse, 1893.
....*$85–$120*

Aldrich, Thomas Bailey. *Poems.* NY, 1863. ....*$35–$50*

Alexander, E.P. *Military Memoirs of a Confederate.* NY, 1907, 1st ed, illus, fldg map. ....*$30–$50*

Alger, Horatio. *Silas Snobden's Office Boy.* Garden City, 1973, dj.
....*$14–$25*

Alger, Horatio. *Strive and Succeed.* Bos, 1872. ....*$75–$95*

Algren, Nelson. *A Walk on the Wild Side.* Farrar, Straus & Cudahy, 1956, 1st ed, dj. ....*$25–$37*

Algren, Nelson. *The Man with the Golden Arm.* NY, 1949, 1st ed, dj. ....*$15–$20*

Alken, Henry. *Scraps from the Sketch Book.* Lon, 1823, illus, hand-clr plates, folio. ....*$500–$650*

Allen, Charles Dexter. *American Book-plates.* NY, 1905, illus, rprnt. ....*$18–$35*

Allen, Doug. *Facing Danger in the Last Wilderness.* NY, 1962, 1st ed, photos. ....*$10–$20*

Allen, Edward H. *Violin Making As It Was and Is.* 1885, illus, 2nd ed, dj. ....*$40–$50*

Allen, Gardner Weld. *Our Navy and the Barbary Corsairs.* Bos/NY/Chi, 1905, 1st ed, illus, 16 plates. ....*$30–$50*

Allen, H. Rowland. *The New England Tragedies in Prose.* Bos, 1869. ....*$20–$25*

Allen, James Lane. *The Reign of Law.* Macmillan, 1900, illus.
....*$6–$12*

Allen, Lewis. *American Herd Book Containing Pedigrees of Short Horn Cattle. . . .* Buffalo, 1946, 1st ed. ....*$67–$90*

Allen, Miss A.J. *Ten Years in Oregon.* Ithaca, 1848, 2nd issue.
....*$100–$150*

Allen, Woody. *Side Effects.* 1980. ....*$12–$20*

Allsop, F.C. *Practical Electrical Light Fitting.* 1923, illus, 9th ed. ....*$18–$25*

Alpatov, M.W. *Art Treasuries in Russia.* NY, 1967, illus, clr plates. ....*$40–$60*

Alvarez, A. *Biggest Game in Town.* Bos, 1983, dj. ....*$12–$15*

Ambler, Charles H. *Washington and the West.* 1936, dj. .*$25–$33*

Ambler, Henry Lovejoy. *Facts, Fads, and Fancies about Teeth.* Cleve, 1900, illus by W.L. Evans. ....*$16–$45*

Amory, Thomas C. *The Life of Admiral Sir Isaac Coffin, Baronet....* Bos, 1886, 1st ed, illus. ....*$50–$75*

Amsden, Charles Avery. *Navaho Weaving, Its Technique and History.* Albuquerque, 1949. ....*$30–$50*

Amsden, Charles Avery. *Navaho Weaving....* Glorietta, NM, 1974, illus, rprnt of 1934 ed. ....*$15–$25*

Amsden, Charles Avery. *Prehistoric Southwesterners from Basketmaker to Pueblo.* Los Angeles, 1949, wrps, illus. .*$25–$35*

Andersen, Hans Christian. *A Picture Book without Pictures.* NY, 1848, 1st U.S. ed. ....*$50–$60*

Andersen, Hans Christian. *The Nightingale and Other Stories.* NY/Lon, nd, 1st ed, illus by Edmund Dulac, tip-in clr pls. ....*$150–$200*

Anderson. *The Tiger Roars, Hunting Man-eaters of India.* NY, 1967, dj. ....*$13–$18*

Anderson, Charles C. *Fighting by Southern Federals.* NY, 1912, 1st ed. ....*$75–$100*

Anderson, E.W. *The Machinery Used in the Manufacture of Cordite.* 1898, ½ lea, mar bds. ....*$18–$25*

Anderson, Eva Greenslit. *Chief Seattle.* Caldwell, IN, 1943, 1st ed, map. ....*$75–$115*

Anderson, John. *Last Survivors in Sail.* Lon, nd, illus. ....*$18–$28*

Anderson, Marian. *My Lord, What a Morning.* NY, 1958, illus. ....*$18–$28*

Anderson, Marian. *My Lord, What a Morning.* NY, 1941, 1st ed, dj. ....*$35–$45*

Anderson, Poul. *Flandry of Terra.* Phila, 1965, 1st ed, dj. ....$25–$35

Anderson, R.C. *The Rigging of the Ships in the Days of the Spritsail Topmast.* . . . Salem, 1927, illus, plates. ....$65–$110

Anderson, Sherwood. *Tar.* NY, 1926. ....$18–$28

Andrade, E.N. *The Structure of the Atom.* Lon, 1924, illus, 2nd prntg. ....$12–$20

Andrews, Allen. *The Pig Plantagenet.* Viking, 1980, illus by Michael Foreman. ....$10–$18

Andrews, Clarence L. *The Story of Alaska.* Caxton, Caldwell, 1938, 1st ed, dj. ....$18–$30

Andrews, Eliza Frances. *The War-time Journal of a Georgia Girl, 1864–1865.* NY, 1908, 1st ed. ....$55–$85

Andrews, Roy Chapman. *All about Whales.* NY, 1954, illus. ....$15–$22

Andrews, Wayne. *Architecture in New York.* NY, 1969, wrps. ....$35–$45

Angelou, Maya. *Gather Together in My Name.* Random House, 1974, 1st ed, dj. ....$30–$40

Angelou, Maya. *Gather Together in My Name.* Random House, 1974, 1st ed, sgn dj. ....$42–$50

Angelou, Maya. *Just Give Me a Cool Drink of Water 'Fore I Die.* NY, Random House, 1971, 1st ed, sgn, dj. ....$45–$65

Angolia, John R. *For Fuhrer and Fatherland, Vol. 1,* San Jose, 1976. ....$20–$30

Anno, Mitsumasa. *Anno's Flea Market.* Philomel Books, 1984, 1st U.S. ed, dj. ....$15–$20

Anthony, Edgar Waterman. *A History of Mosaics.* Bos, 1935, ltd #21/ 50 cc, sgn, vellum. ....$95–$110

Appender, Grace. *The Women of Israel.* NY, 1853, 2 vols, 1st ed. ....$50–$75

Appleton, L.H. *Indian Art of the Americas.* NY, 1950, illus. ....$75–$150

Appleton, Victor. *Don Sturdy in the Land of Giants.* Grossett & Dunlap, 1930, dj. ....$3–$6

Appleton, Victor. *Tom Swift among the Fire Fighters.* Grosset & Dunlap, 1921. ....*$5–$9*

Appleton, Victor. *Tom Swift and His Television Detector.* 1933, 1st ed. ....*$12–$18*

Aptheker, Herbert. *The Labor Movement in the South during Slavery.* NY, International Publishers. ....*$12–$18*

Archdeacon, W. *Archdeacon's Kitchen Cabinet.* Chi, 1876. ....*$18–$25*

Archer, Gleason. *Big Business and Radio.* 1939, 1st ed, illus, dj. ....*$45–$65*

Arctander, J. *Apostle of Alaska.* NY, 1909, illus. ....*$25–$35*

Arendt, Hannah. *Eichman in Jerusalem. . . .* NY, 1979, wrps. ....*$10–$15*

Armes, Ethel. *The Story of Coal and Iron in Alabama.* AL, 1910, 1st ed, illus. ....*$45–$60*

Armitage, Angus. *William Herschel.* Lon. ....*$5–$10*

Armour, J. Ogden. *The Packers, the Private Car Lines, and the People.* Phila, 1906, 1st ed, illus. ....*$65–$125*

Armstrong, Benjamin G. *Early Life among the Indians.* 1892, 1st ed, plates. ....*$22–$30*

Armstrong, Harry G. *Principles and Practice of Aviation Medicine.* Balt, 1939, illus, charts, dj. ....*$65–$100*

Armstrong, John. *The Young Woman's Guide to Virtue, Economy, and Happiness. . . .* Newcastle, nd, illus. ....*$100–$140*

Armstrong, Thomas R. *My First and Last Buffalo Hunt.* np, 1918, wrps, illus. ....*$60–$75*

Arnold, Augustus C.L. *Rationale and Ethics of Freemasonry. . . .* NY, 1858, 1st ed. ....*$45–$75*

Arnold, Isaac N. *Lincoln and Slavery.* Chi, 1866, 1st ed, illus. ....*$45–$60*

Arnold, Issac N. *Sketch of the Life of Abraham Lincoln.* NY, 1869. ....*$35–$40*

Arnold, W.H. *Ventures in Book-collecting.* NY, 1923, 1st ed. ....*$45–$60*

Arundel, Louis. *Motorboat Boys among the Florida Keys.* Donohue. ....$12–$17

Asbury, Herbert. *A Methodist Saint: The Life of Bishop Asbury.* NY, 1927. ....$12–$16

Asch, Sholem. *The Nazarene.* Putnam, 1939, ltd 500 cc, presentation. ....$30–$40

Asch, Sholem. *The Nazarene.* NY, 1939, sgn, dj. ....$12–$20

Ash, Cay Van. *The Fires of Fu Manchu.* NY, 1987, 1st ed, dj. ....$15–$25

Ash, Christopher. *Whaler's Eye.* NY, 1962, illus, 1st American ed, dj. ....$20–$25

Ashbrook, F.G. and E.N. Sater. *Cooking Wild Game.* NY, 1945, illus, dj. ....$25–$50

Ashby, Thomas. *The Valley Campaigns.* NY, 1914, 1st ed. ....$150–$225

Ashley, Clifford W. *The Yankee Whaler. . . .* Bos, 1938, illus, 2nd ed, dj. ....$75–$100

Ashley, George T. *Reminiscences of a Circuit Rider.* Hollywood, 1941, 1st ed. ....$10–$20

Ashton, James. *The Book of Nature Containing Information for Young People. . . .* NY, 1870, flexible cloth. ....$95–$130

Ashton, John. *Chap-books of the Eighteenth Century.* Lon, 1882. ....$48–$55

Asimov, Isaac. *Extraterrestrial Civilizations.* NY, 1979, 1st ed, dj. ....$15–$25

Asimov, Isaac. *Extraterrestrial Civilizations.* NY, 2nd prntg, sgn, dj. ....$25–$30

Asimov, Isaac. *In Memory Yet Green.* 1979, inscr. ....$25–$35

Asimov, Isaac. *The End of Eternity.* Garden City, 1955, 1st ed, dj. ....$85–$200

Asimov, Isaac (ed). *The Hugo Winners.* 1985, ARC, dj. .$30–$50

Asimov, Isaac. *The Intelligent Man's Guide to Science.* NY, 1960, 2 vols, 1st ed. ....$25–$35

Asimov, Isaac. *The Subatomic Monster.* 1985, ARC, dj. .....$25–$32

Asimov, Isaac. *Understanding Physics.* NY. ....*$12–$20*

Askins, Charles. *Game Bird Shooting.* NY, 1931, 1st ed, dj. ....*$22–$37*

Assoc. of Edison Illuminating Co. *Edisonia.* 1904, 1st ed, illus. ....*$55–$75*

Astaire, Fred. *Steps in Time.* NY, 1959, 1st ed, wrps.....*$20–$30*

Atherton, Gertrude. *California: An Intimate History.* NY, 1927. ....*$10–$15*

Atherton, Gertrude. *Life in the War Zone.* NY, 1916, sgn. ....*$25–$35*

Atherton, Gertrude. *The Foghorn.* SF, 1937, ltd 600 cc, sgn. ....*$25–$30*

Atkins, Arthur. *Letters with Notes on Painting.* SF, 1908. ....*$18–$20*

Atwater, Caleb. *A History of the State of Ohio.* Cinc, 1838, 2nd ed, lea. ....*$48–$65*

Atwater, Kent. *Atwater Kent Service Manual.* 1929, 1st ed. ....*$40–$55*

Atwood, Margaret. *Power Politics.* NY, 1973, 1st ed, dj..*$28–$37*

Atwood, Margaret. *The Handmaid's Tale.* sgn. ....*$40–$60*

Auchincloss, Louis. *The Injustice Collectors.* Bos, 1950, 1st ed, dj. ....*$75–$95*

Auden, W.H. *The Age of Anxiety.* NY, 1947, 1st ed, dj..*$45–$125*

Auden, W.H. *On This Island.* NY, 1937, 1st U.S. ed, dj..*$30–$50*

Audsley, George A. *Artistic and Decorative Stencilling.* Lon, 1911, illus. ....*$95–$145*

Audsley, W. and G. Audsley. *Outlines of Ornament in the Leading Styles.* Lon, 1881. ....*$55–$75*

Audubon, John J. *The Birds of America.* NY/Phila, 1840–44, 7 vols, illus, 500 hand-clr plates. ....*$18,000–$25,000*

Audubon, John J. *The Birds of America.* Lon, 1827–38, 4 vols, illus, elephant folio, 435 hand-clr aquatints. ...*$425,000–$550,000*

Audubon, John J. *The Birds of America.* NY, 1937, illus, clr plates. ....*$35–$50*

Audubon, John W. *Audubon's Western Journal, 1849–1850.* Cleve, 1906, 1st ed. ....$150–$195

Audubon, Maria. *Audubon and His Journals.* 1900, 2 vols. ....$85–$125

Auel, Jean. *Clan of the Cave Bear.* NY, 1980, 1st ed, sgn, dj. ....$50–$65

Auel, Jean. *Mammoth Hunters.* 1985, 1st ed, dj. ....$17–$25

Auel, Jean. *Plains of Passage.* 1990, 1st ed, sgn, dj. ......$25–$50

Aunt Louisa's Big Picture Books. *Nursery Rhymes.* McLaughlin, nd, wrps, illus. ....$50–$75

Austen, Jane. *Pride and Prejudice.* Heritage, 1940, Limited Edition Club, dj, slipcase. ....$22–$30

Austen Jane. *Pride and Prejudice.* Lon, 1813, 3 vols, 1st ed. .... $6,500–$11,000

Austin, Mary. *The Flock.* Houghton Mifflin, 1906, 1st ed, illus by Smith. ....$100–$175

Austin, Mary. *The Land of Little Rain.* Bos/NY, 1903, 1st ed. ....$125–$200

Averill, Mary. *Japanese Flower Arrangement.* 1933. ......$14–$20

Averill, Mary. *The Flower Art of Japan.* 1st ed. ....$25–$35

Ayers, James T. *The Diary of James T. Ayers, Civil War Recruiter.* S. Springfield, IL, 1947, 1st ed. ....$30–$45

Babington, S.H. *Navajo Gods and Tom-toms.* NY, 1950, illus, dj. ....$30–$40

Bach, Capt. F.W. *How to Judge a Horse.* NY, 1893, 1st ed. ....$37–$50

Bach, Carl Philipp Emanuel. *Essay on the True Art of Playing Keyboard Instruments.* NY, 1949, 1st ed, dj. ....$15–$23

Bacheller, Irving. *Man for the Ages.* Bobbs-Merrill, 1919, illus. ....$7–$15

Bachrach, Max. *Fur—A Practical Treatise.* NY, 1953. ....$18–$25

Badeau, Adam. *Grant in Peace . . . A Personal Memoir.* Phila, 1888, 1st ed. ....$45–$85

Baden-Powell, Lord. *Memories of India.* nd, clr illus. ...$50–$80

Baden-Powell, Lord. *Scouting for Boys.* nd, Canadian ed. ....*$30–$45*

Baedeker, Karl. *Belgium and Holland.* Leipzig, 1905, 14th ed. ....*$14–$20*

Baedeker, Karl. *Berlin and Its Environs.* 1923, 6th ed, dj. ....*$14–$18*

Baedeker, Karl. *Central Italy.* 1914, 14th ed. ....*$15–$25*

Baedeker, Karl. *Egypt.* 1914, 7th ed. ....*$110–$130*

Baedeker, Karl. *Etats-Unis.* 1894. ....*$35–$50*

Baedeker, Karl. *Great Britain.* 1901. ....*$10–$25*

Baedeker, Karl. *Israel.* Englewood, NJ, nd, wrps, illus, map laid in. ....*$10–$15*

Baedeker, Karl. *Italy.* 1909. ....*$10–$20*

Baedeker, Karl. *London and Its Environs.* Leipzig, 1908, 1st ed. ....*$15–$25*

Baedeker, Karl. *Northern France.* 1889, 1st ed, dj. ....*$35–$75*

Baedeker, Karl. *Rhine.* Leipzig, 1906, 16th rev ed. ....*$25–$35*

Baedeker, Karl. *Southern Germany.* Leipzig, 1907, 10th ed. ....*$14–$20*

Baedeker, Karl. *Spain and Portugal.* 1912, in German. .....*$25–$35*

Baedeker, Karl. *Switzerland.* 1907. ....*$10–$22*

Baedeker, Karl. *United States.* 1909, 4th ed. ....*$40–$75*

Bagnasco, Erminio. *Submarines of World War Two.* Annapolis, 1978, illus, photos, dj. ....*$15–$25*

Bailey. *The Birds of Florida.* Balt, 1925, illus, private prntg, ltd ed. ....*$115–$150*

Bailey, L.H. *Standard Cyclopedia of Horticulture.* 1953, 3 vols. ....*$85–$100*

Bain, John Jr. *Tobacco in Song and Story.* NY, 1896, suede, teg. ....*$25–$40*

Bainbridge, Henry Charles. *Peter Carl Faberge: Goldsmith and Jeweller.* . . . Lon, 1949, 1st ed, illus, dj. ....*$95–$120*

Baines, Thomas. *Greenhouse and Stove Plants, Flowering and Fine Leaved.* . . . Lon, 1894, illus. ....*$30–$45*

Baird, P.D. *Expeditions to the Canadian Arctic.* 1949, 1st ed. ....*$24–$32*

Baker, Gen. L.C. *History of the U.S. Secret Service.* Phila, 1867, 1st ed. ....*$32–$40*

Baker, J.C. *Baptist History of the North Pacific Coast.* . . . Phila, 1912, 1st ed. ....*$30–$60*

Baker, Marcus. *Geographic Dictionary of Alaska.* GPO, 1906, 2nd ed. ....*$70–$85*

Baker, Mary and William Bridges. *Wild Animals of the World.* Garden City, 1948, illus, clr and b/w. ....*$15–$25*

Baker, N. *Cyclone in Calico.* Bos, 1952, 1st ed, dj. ....*$16–$24*

Baker, Pearl. *The Wild Bunch.* NY, 1971, 1st ed, dj. .....*$20–$30*

Baker, Richard St. Barbe. *Men of the Trees.* NY, 1931, illus, photos. ....*$10–$15*

Balcom, Mary G. *Ketchikan Alaska's Totemland.* Chi, 1961, illus, softcover, sgn. ....*$18–$25*

Baldwin, James. *Going to Meet the Man.* Dial, 1965, 1st ed, dj. ....*$25–$30*

Baldwin, James. *If Beale Street Could Talk.* NY, 1974, 1st ed, dj. ....*$35–$40*

Baldwin, James. *Just Above My Head.* dj. ....*$20–$25*

Baldwin, James. *Nobody Knows My Name.* Dial, 1961, 1st ed, dj. ....*$30–$40*

Baldwin, James. *The Fire Next Time.* Dial, 1963, 1st ed, dj. ....*$25–$50*

Baldwin, Leland. *Pittsburgh: The Story of a City.* Pitts, 1938. clothbound. ....*$10–$15*

Baldwin, W.J. *An Outline of Ventilation and Warming.* NY, nd. ....*$18–$20*

Baldwin, William C. *African Hunting from Natal to the Zambesi.* NY, 1863, illus, fldg map. ....*$75–$125*

Balfour, Henry. *The Evolution of Decorative Art.* NY, 1893, illus, 1st American ed. ....*$18–$25*

Ball, Robert. *Time and Tide: A Romance of the Moon.* Lon, 1909. ....*$14–$22*

Ball, Sir Robert, et al. *Notes on Mars.* GPO, 1901, pamphlet. ....*$5–$10*

Ballantine, Stuart. *Radio Telephony for Amateurs.* Mckay, 1923, 2nd ed. ....*$15–$25*

Ballou, Maturin M. *Pearl of India.* Bos, 1895, 2nd ed. .*$10–$20*

Baly, E.C.C. *Spectroscopy.* Lon, 1912. ....*$10–$16*

Balzac, Honore de. *Droll Stories.* Boni & Liveright, 1928, 2 vols, illus by Ralph Barton. ....*$20–$45*

Balzer, R. *Street Times.* NY, 1972, illus, dj. ....*$14–$18*

Bamford, Georgia Loring. *The Mystery of Jack London.* Oakland, 1931, 1st ed, dj. ....*$95–$125*

Bancroft, Caroline. *Six Racy Madams of Colorado.* Johnson, 1965, 1st ed, illus. ....*$10–$15*

Bancroft, George. *In Memoriam of Abraham Lincoln.* . . . DC, 1866, wrps. ....*$65–$75*

Bancroft, George. *Oration on the Life and Character of Abraham Lincoln.* DC, GPO, 1866, 1st ed. ....*$75–$125*

Bancroft, Hubert Howe. *History of Alaska, 1730–1886.* SF, 1886, map. ....*$150–$225*

Bancroft, Hubert Howe. *History of the Northwest Coast.* SF, 1886, 2 vols. ....*$150–$175*

Bancroft, Hubert Howe. *History of Utah.* SF, 1890. ...*$50–$120*

Bancroft, Hubert Howe. *The New Pacific.* NY, 1900, teg, frontis, map. ....*$35–$50*

Banergi, P. *Snake-bite with a System of Treatment and Reported Cases and Notes.* Calcutta, 1956, illus. ....*$40–$50*

Bangay, R.D. *Wireless Telephony.* 1923, 1st ed, illus. ....*$18–$25*

Bangs, John Kendrick. *A House-boat on the Styx.* NY, 1896, 1st ed. ....*$40–$55*

Bangs, John Kendrick. *Ghosts I Have Met.* 1898, 1st ed..*$25–$45*

Bangs, John Kendrick. *Mr. Munchausen.* Bos, 1901, 1st ed, 4th state. ....*$18–$25*

Bangs, John Kendrick. *Mrs. Raffles.* 1905, 1st ed. ....$60–$75

Bangs, John Kendrick. *Olympian Nights.* 1902, 1st ed. .....$25–$35

Bangs, John Kendrick. *Peeps at People.* NY, 1899, illus by Penfield. ....$25–$30

Bangs, John Kendrick. *The Enchanted Typewriter.* NY, 1899, 1st ed, illus by Peter Newell. ....$45–$55

Banks, Nathaniel P. *Purchase of Alaska.* DC, 1868, 1st ed. ....$50–$75

Bannerman, Helen. *Historie du Petit Negre Sambo.* Stokes, 1921, 1st ed, French, dj. ....$55–$110

Bannerman, Helen. *Little Black Sambo.* 1931, illus by Fern Bisel Peat. ....$50–$80

Bannerman, Helen. *Little Black Sambo.* Platt & Munk, 1928, dj. ....$45–$60

Bannerman, Helen. *Little Black Sambo.* NY, Little Golden Book, 1948. ....$40–$55

Bannerman, Helen. *Sambo and the Twins.* Phila, 1946, illus by Helen Bannerman. ....$45–$60

Bannerman, Helen. *The Story of Little Black Sambo.* Lon, 1899, 1st ed, illus by Bannerman. ....$750–$2,500

Banning, K. *West Point Today.* 1937, dj. ....$16–$20

Barbeau, M. *Haida Myths Illustrated in Argillite Carvings.* Ottawa, 1953, 1st ed, wrps. ....$55–$65

Barbeau, M. *Totem Poles.* National Museum of Canada, 1950, illus. ....$150–$250

Barbeau, Marius. *Ancient France Lingers.* 1936, illus, softcover. ....$20–$30

Barbeau, Marius. *Jongleur Songs of Old Quebec.* NJ, 1962. ....$15–$20

Barbeau, Marius. *The Downfall of Temlaham.* Tor, 1928, 1st ed, illus, dj. ....$75–$145

Barber, Edwin A. *Lead Glazed Pottery.* Phila, 1907, 1st ed, illus. ....$25–$35

Barber, Edwin A. *Majolica of Mexico.* Phila, 1908. ......$40–$60

Barber, Joel. *Wild Fowl Decoys.* NY, 1934, illus, dj. .....$48–$65

Barbour, T. *Sphaerodactylus.* Camb, 1921. ....$25–$40

Barde, Frederick. *Life and Adventures of Billy Dixon.* OK, 1914, 1st ed. ....$68–$75

Barger, E.H. and L.E. Card. *Diseases and Parasites of Poultry.* Phila, 1935, illus. ....$27–$37

Barker, Clive. *The Books of Blood.* 1984, 6 vols, sgn. .$175–$400

Barker, Clive. *The Damnation Game.* Ace-Putnam, 1987, 1st American ed, sgn. ....$25–$45

Barker, Clive. *The Great and Secret Show.* Lon, 1989. .$20–$25

Barnard, Charles. *First Steps in Electricity.* NY, 1888, 1st ed, illus. ....$40–$60

Barnard, Frederick A.P. *The Metric System of Weights and Measures.* Bos, 1879, 3rd ed. ....$40–$55

Barneby, Henry W. *Life and Labour in the Far, Far West.* . . . Lon, 1884, 1st ed. ....$150–$250

Barnes, A.R. *The South African Household Guide.* Cape Town, 1907, 4th ed. ....$25–$55

Barnes, Fancourt. *A Manual of Midwifery.* Lon, 1891. .$25–$40

Barnes, R.M. *Military Uniforms of Britain and the Empire.* Lon, 1972, wrps. ....$10–$18

Barnes, Robert. *United States Submarines.* New Haven, 1944. ....$75–$112

Barnhart, John D. *The Impact of the Civil War on Indiana.* Ind, 1962, 1st ed. ....$18–$23

Barnum, P.T. *Struggles and Triumphs.* Hartford, 1876. .$25–$30

Barnum, P.T. *Struggles and Triumphs.* Warren Johnson & Co., 1872. ....$45–$65

Baron, Salo. *A Social and Religious History of the Jews.* Columbia Univ. Press, 1939, 3 vols. ....$30–$40

Barrett, Edwin S. *What I Saw at Bull Run.* Bos, Beacon Press, 1886, 48 pp. ....$72–$95

Barrie, J.M. *Peter Pan in Kensington Gardens.* NY, 1940, illus by Arthur Rackham. ....$25–$35

Barrie, J.M. *Peter Pan in Kensington Gardens.* 1907, illus by Arthur Rackham. ....*$150–$200*

Barrie, James Matthew. *Quality Street: A Comedy in Four Acts.* Lon, 1913, illus by Hugh Thomson, 21 tip-in clr plates. .*$85–$175*

Barron, Archibald F. *Vines and Vine Culture.* Lon, 1900, 4th ed. ....*$40–$50*

Barrows, W.B. *Michigan Bird Life.* Lansing, 1912, illus..*$50–$85*

Barth, John. *Giles Goat-boy.* Doubleday, 1966, sgn, dj..*$35–$75*

Barth, John. *Lost in the Funhouse.* Garden City, 1968. .*$15–$20*

Barth, John. *The Floating Opera.* Garden City, 1967, 1st ed, dj. ....*$25–$35*

Barth, John. *The Sot-weed Factor.* Garden City, 1960, 1st ed, dj. ....*$125–$150*

Barthelme, Donald. *Come Back, Dr. Caligari.* Bos, 1964, 1st ed, dj. ....*$55–$95*

Barthelme, Donald. *Guilty Pleasures.* NY, 1974, 1st ed, dj. ....*$20–$30*

Barthelme, Donald. *Sunny Marge.* Minn/St. Paul, 1980, ltd, 125 cc, sgn. ....*$45–$50*

Barthelme, Donald. *Unspeakable Practices, Unnatural Acts.* NY, 1968, 1st ed, dj. ....*$45–$55*

Bartholomew, Ed. *Wild Bill Longley, a Texas Hard-case.* Houston, 1953, illus. ....*$30–$40*

Bartlett, W. *An Elementary Treatise on Optics. . . .* NY, 1839, 1st ed, illus, fldg plates. ....*$30–$40*

Barton, Lucy. *Historic Costume for the Stage.* Bos, 1935, illus. ....*$18–$25*

Barton, William E. *Hero in Homespun.* Bos, 1897, 1st ed, illus by Dan Beard. ....*$18–$25*

Baskerville, Rosetta. *Flame Tree and Other Folk-lore Stories from Uganda.* Lon, nd, illus. ....*$10–$15*

Baskin, Esther. *The Poppy and Other Deadly Plants.* NY, 1967, 1st ed, illus by Leonard Baskin, dj. ....*$35–$50*

Batchelder, Marjorie. *The Puppet Theatre Handbook.* NY, 1947, 1st ed, dj. ....*$15–$25*

Bate, H. Maclear. *Report from the Rhodesias.* 1953, 1st ed, dj. ....*$22–$35*

Battersby, Martin. *The World of Art Nouveau.* 1968. ....*$24–$35*

Batty, J.H. *Practical Taxidermy and Home Decoration.* NY, 1883, illus. ....*$27–$35*

Baughman, A.J. *History of Huron County, Ohio.* Chi, 1909, 2 vols, illus. ....*$90–$115*

Baum, L. Frank. *Glinda of Oz.* Tor, 1920, 1st ed. ....*$175–$300*

Baum, L. Frank. *Ozma of Oz.* Chi, Reilly & Britton, 1907, 1st ed, illus. ....*$75–$90*

Baum, L. Frank. *Rinkitink in Oz.* Reilly & Lee, illus by J.R. Neill, clr plates. ....*$60–$75*

Baum, L. Frank. *The Land of Oz.* Reilly & Lee, illus by J.R. Neill. ....*$45–$60*

Baum, L. Frank. *The Lost Princess of Oz.* Chi, 1939, illus by J.R. Neill, Junior Ed. ....*$18–$27*

Baum, L. Frank. *The Magical Monarch of Mo.* 1947, illus, dj. ....*$18–$25*

Baum, L. Frank. *The Marvelous Land of Oz.* Reilly & Britton, 1904, 1st ed, illus by J.R. Neill, 2nd state. ....*$245–$275*

Baum, L. Frank. *The New Wizard of Oz.* Ind, 1903, illus by Denslow, 2nd ed, 2nd state. ....*$75–$110*

Baum, L. Frank. *The Patchwork Girl of Oz.* Reilly & Britton, 1913, 1st ed, illus, 1st state. ....*$150–$195*

Baum, L. Frank. *The Tin Woodsman of Oz.* Reilly & Lee, illus by J.R. Neill, clr plates. ....*$65–$75*

Baum, L. Frank. *The Wizard of Oz.* 1982, ltd 500 cc, slipcase. ....*$50–$65*

Baum, L. Frank. *Tik-Tok of Oz.* Reilly & Lee, illus by J.R. Neill, clr plates. ....*$65–$75*

Baxter, James P. *The Trelawny Papers.* Portland, 1884, fldg maps. ....*$30–$45*

Baxter, W.T. *The House of Hancock: Business in Boston.* Harvard Univ. Press, 1945. ....$25–$40

Bayard, Samuel J. *A Sketch of the Life of Commodore Robert F. Stockton.* NY, 1856. ....$35–$50

Baylies, Nicholas. *Eleazor Wheelock Ripley of the War of 1812.* Des Moines, 1890. ....$24–$30

Beach, Rex. *The Ne'er-do-well.* Harper, 1911, illus by Howard Chandler Christy, dj. ....$20–$35

Beach, S.A. *The Apples of New York.* Alb, 1905, 2 vols, illus, plates. ....$65–$120

Beadle, J.H. *Life in Utah.* Phila, 1870, map, plates. ......$70–$85

Beadle, J.H. *Polygamy or the Mysteries and Crimes of Mormonism.* 1904, illus. ....$22–$30

Beadle, J.H. *Polygamy or the Mysteries and Crimes of Mormonism.* National Publishing Co., 1882. ....$35–$85

Beale, Lionel S. *How to Work with the Microscope.* Lon, 1868, illus, 4th ed. ....$45–$65

Bealer, Alex W. *The Art of Blacksmithing.* NY, 1969, dj..$20–$25

Beamish, Richard J. *The Boy's Story of Lindbergh the Lone Eagle.* John Winston, 1928, illus. ....$12–$18

Bean, L.L. *Hunting, Fishing, and Camping.* 1942, 3rd ed. ....$15–$18

Beard, D. *American Boys Handy Book of Camplore and Woodcraft.* Lippincraft, 1920. ....$15–$18

Beard, George M. *A Practical Treatise on Nervous Exhaustion.* NY, 1880. ....$42–$50

Beard, James Melville. *K.K.K. Sketches, Humorous and Didactic.* . . . Phila, 1877, 1st ed. ....$95–$175

Beard, James. *Delights and Prejudices.* NY, 1964, 1st ed, dj. ....$18–$25

Beard, O.T. *Bristling with Thorns.* Detroit, 1884, illus. ......$10–$15

Beardsley, E. Edwards. *Life and Times of William S. Johnson . . . from Connecticut.* Bos, 1886. ....$33–$45

Beaton, Cecil and Gail Buckland. *The Magic Image.* NY, 1975, illus, 1st U.S. ed, dj. ....*$22–$35*

Beattie, Ann. *Alex Katz.* Abrams, 1987, 1st ed, dj. ....*$30–$40*

Beattie, Ann. *Falling in Place.* 1980, 1st ed. ....*$10–$22*

Beattie, Ann. *Love Always.* Random House, 1985, 1st ed, dj. ....*$18–$20*

Beatty, Clyde and Earl Wilson. *Jungle Performers.* NY, 1941, 1st ed, sgn, dj. ....*$25–$90*

Beaver, C. Masten. *Fort Yukon Trader—Three Years in an Alaskan Wilderness.* NY, 1955, 1st ed, illus, dj. ....*$25–$40*

Bechstein, J.M. *The Natural History of Cage Birds.* Lon, 1885, illus, engr. ....*$30–$45*

Beddie, M.K. (ed). *Bibliography of Captain James Cook.* Sydney, 1970, 2nd ed. ....*$40–$60*

Bedford-Joncs, H.B. *D'Artagnan's Letter.* Covici Friede, 1931, 1st ed, dj. ....*$20–$40*

Bedford-Jones, H.B. *Saint Michael's Gold.* NY, 1926, 1st ed. ....*$14–$17*

Bedford-Jones, H.B. *The Mardi Gras Mystery.* NY, 1921, 1st ed. ....*$18–$25*

Beebe, Lucius. *American West.* 1955, 1st ed. ....*$30–$35*

Beebe, William. *Half Mile Down.* NY, 1934, 1st ed, illus, dj. ....*$25–$45*

Beebe, William. *Nonsuch Land of Water.* 1st ed, sgn, dj..*$45–$60*

Beebe, William. *Pheasants—Their Lives and Homes.* Garden City, 1936, illus, clr and b/w. ....*$75–$100*

Beebe, William. *The Arcturus Adventure.* NY, 1926, 1st ed, illus, clr and b/w. ....*$50–$70*

Beebee, William. *Book of Bays.* 1942, 1st ed. ....*$10–$18*

Beecher, Catherine E. *A Treatise on Domestic Economy.* NY, 1850, illus, rev ed. ....*$35–$65*

Beecher, Catherine E. *Miss Beecher's Domestic Receipt Book.* NY, 1849, 3rd ed. ....*$60–$85*

Beecher, Henry Ward. *Norwood or Village Life in New England.* NY, 1868. ....$25–$35

Beede, A. McG. *Sitting Bull–Custer.* Bismark, ND, 1913, 1st ed, illus. ....$125–$150

Beehler, W.H. *The Cruise of the Brooklyn.* Phila, 1885, illus. ....$50–$95

Beer, George Louis. *The Origins of the British Colonial System 1578–1660.* NY, 1908. ....$32–$47

Beerbohm, Max. *Fifty Caricatures.* NY, 1913, 1st ed. ...$50–$65

Beerbohm, Max. *Mainly on the Air.* NY, 1947, 1st ed, dj..$30–$45

Beerbohm, Max. *Observations.* Lon, 1923, 1st ed, dj. ..$125–$200

Beerbohm, Max. *Things New and Old.* Lon, 1923, 1st ed, dj. ....$60–$85

Beers, D.B. *Atlas of Luzerne County, Pa.* Phila, 1873, illus, hand-clr maps. ....$210–$300

Beers, F.W. *Atlas of Delaware County, NY.* NY, 1869. .$150–$200

Begin, Menachem. *White Nights: The Story of a Prisoner in Russia.* NY, 1977, 1st U.S. ed, dj. ....$35–$45

Behan, Brendan. *Confessions of an Irish Rebel.* NY, 1965, dj. ....$10–$15

Behan, Brendan. *Hold Your Hour and Have Another.* Little Brown, 1954, 1st American ed, dj. ....$25–$30

Behan, Brendan. *Richard's Cork Leg.* Grove Press, 1974, 1st U.S. ed, dj. ....$15–$25

Behan, Brendan. *The Scarperer.* NY, 1964, 1st ed, dj. ..$25–$35

Beirne, F. *The War of 1812.* NY, 1949, 1st ed, maps. ...$20–$28

Belasco, David. *Plays Produced under the Stage Direction of David Belasco.* NY, 1925. ....$35–$45

Belasco, David. *The Return of Peter Grimm.* 1912, illus by John Rae. ....$20–$25

Belknap, Jeremy. *A Sermon Preached at the Installation of Rev. Jedidiah Morse.* Bos, 1789, 1st ed, wrps, sewn. ....$75–$100

Bell Telephone Laboratories. *A History of Engineering and Science in the Bell System.* 1975, 1st ed, illus, dj. ....$20–$30

Bell, Edward I. *The Political Shame of Mexico.* NY, 1914, 1st ed. ....*$22–$28*

Bell, Ernest A. *Fighting the Traffic in Young Girls.* np, nd, illus. ....*$20–$30*

Bell, Helen G. *Winning the King's Cup.* NY, 1928, illus, fldg charts and plans. ....*$24–$30*

Bell, Louis. *The Telescope.* NY/Lon, 1922, 1st ed, illus..*$35–$50*

Bell, Maj. *Reminiscences of a Ranger . . . in Southern California.* 1927. ....*$18–$25*

Bell, W.O.M. *Karamojo Safari.* NY, 1949, 1st ed. ....*$30–$65*

Bell, Walter D.M. *Bell of Africa.* Bos, 1961, 1st American ed, dj. ....*$18–$40*

Belle, Francis P. *Life and Adventures of Bandit Joaquin Murrieta. . . .* Chi, 1925, 1st ed, ltd 975 cc. ....*$50–$75*

Bellow, Saul. *Great Jewish Short Stories.* Dell, 1963, 1st ed, pb. ....*$18–$25*

Bellow, Saul. *Henderson the Rain King.* NY, 1959, 1st ed, dj. ....*$80–$110*

Bellow, Saul. *Herzog.* NY, 1964, 1st ed, dj. ....*$30–$40*

Bellow, Saul. *Humboldt's Gift.* Viking, 1975, 1st ed, dj..*$35–$65*

Bellow, Saul. *The Adventures of Augie March.* Viking, 1953, 1st ed, dj. ....*$90–$120*

Bellow, Saul. *The Dean's December.* NY, 1982, 1st ed, dj. ....*$25–$35*

Bellow, Saul. *The Last Analysis.* NY, 1965, 1st ed, dj. ...*$40–$54*

Bemelmans, Ludwig. *Hansi.* NY, 1934, 1st ed. ....*$75–$175*

Bemelmans, Ludwig. *Madeline and the Gypsies.* Viking, 1959. ....*$20–$35*

Bemelmans, Ludwig. *The Eye of God.* NY, 1949, dj. .*$12.50–$30*

Benchley, Nathaniel. *A Winter's Tale.* NY, 1964, 1st ed, dj. ....*$25–$35*

Benchley, Nathaniel. *Robert Benchley.* NY, 1955, dj. .*$12.50–$15*

Benchley, Robert. *Benchley or Else.* NY, 1947, 1st ed. ......*$18–$25*

Benedict, George Grenville. *Vermont in the Civil War....* Burlington, VT, 1886–88, 2 vols, 1st ed. ....$75–$125

Benet, Stephen Vincent. *Thirteen O'Clock.* NY, 1937, 1st ed, dj. ....$25–$35

Benet, Stephen Vincent. *Burning City.* Farrar & Rinehart, 1936, 1st ed, dj. ....$40–$50

Benet, Stephen Vincent. *John Brown's Body.* 1930, illus by J. Daugherty, dj. ....$15–$20

Benet, Stephen Vincent. *John Brown's Body.* Garden City, 1928, 1st ed. ....$20–$50

Benjamin, Marcus. *Washington during War Time.* DC, nd. ....$15–$25

Bennett, Colin N. *The Guide to Kinematography.* 1917, 1st ed, illus. ....$75–$85

Bennett, Frank M. *The Monitor and the Navy under Steam.* NY, 1900. ....$14–$18

Bennett, Ira C. *History of the Panama Canal....* DC, 1915, illus, plates. ....$18–$24

Bennett, James. *Overland Journey to California....* NY, 1932, ltd 200 cc, dj. ....$45–$50

Bennett, Russell H. *The Complete Rancher.* NY, 1946, 1st ed, illus by Ross Santee, dj. ....$120–$150

Bennett, W.P. *The First Baby in Camp.* SLC, 1893, softbound. ....$50–$75

Benson, Joseph. *The Life of the Rev. John W. Flechere.* NY, 1820, lea. ....$27–$45

Benson, William S. *The Merchant Marine.* NY, 1923. ...$14–$20

Bent, Arthur Cleveland. *Life Histories of North American Thrushes....* DC, 1949, wrps, plates. ....$28–$35

Benton, Jesse J. *Cow by the Tail.* Bos, 1943. ....$18–$25

Benton, Josiah Hart. *Voting in the Field.* ltd 100 cc. ....$50–$75

Benton, Thomas Hart. *Artist in America.* NY, 1937, 1st ed, illus. ....$18–$24

Beny, Roloff. *To Everything There is a Season.* Lon, 1969, illus, photos, dj. ....$45–$50

Berger, John A. *The Franciscan Missions of California.* Garden City, 1948, dj. ....$16–$20

Berman, Bruce D. *Encyclopedia of American Shipwrecks.* Bos, 1973, dj. ....$22–$38

Berrigan, Daniel. *Prison Poems.* Greensboro, NC, 1973, dj. ....$10–$14

Berry, A.J. *Henry Cavendish—His Life and Scientific Work.* Lon, 1960. ....$28–$40

Berry, F.A. Jr., et al. (eds). *Handbook of Meteorology.* NY, 1945, 1st ed, dj. ....$35–$60

Berry, Robert Elton. *Yankee Stargazer: The Life of Nathaniel Bowditch.* NY, 1941, 1st ed. ....$16–$20

Berson, L. *The Negroes and the Jews.* 1971. ....$10–$15

Bertram, James M. *Crisis in China.* Lon, 1937, illus. ..$10–$15

Best, F. *The Maori As He Was . . . in Pre-European Days.* New Zealand, 1934, 2nd issue. ....$15–$20

Bester, Alfred. *The Demolished Man.* 1953, dj. ....$40–$50

Beston, Henry. *Fairy Tales.* 1952, 1st ed, illus. ....$18–$25

Bethe, H.A. *Elementary Nuclear Theory.* NY, 1947, dj. .$18–$25

Betten, H.L. *Upland Game Shooting.* Phila, 1940, 1st ed, illus by Lynn Bogue Hunt. ....$40–$60

Bhushan, Jamila Brij. *Indian Jewelry, Ornaments, and Decorative Designs.* Bombay, nd, 1st ed, illus. ....$75–$140

Bick, Edgar. *History and Source Book of Orthopaedic Surgery.* 1933. ....$14–$25

Biddle, Ellen. *Reminiscences of a Soldier's Wife.* Phila, 1907. ....$32–$40

Biden, C.L. *Sea-angling Fishes of the Cape (South Africa).* Lon, 1930, illus. ....$30–$40

Bidwell, John. *Echoes of the Past.* Chico, CA, nd, softbound. ....$35–$50

Bierce, Ambrose. *Ten Tales.* Lon, 1925. ....$28–$35

Bierce, Ambrose. *The Shadow on the Dial.* SF, 1909. ...*$34–$40*

Bierce, Ambrose. *Write it Right: A Little Blacklist of Literary Faults.* NY, 1909, dj. ....*$20–$35*

Bierhorst, John. *Songs of the Chippewa.* NY, 1974, illus. ....*$10–$15*

Bigelow. *Borderland of Czar and Kaiser.* NY, 1895, illus by F. Remington. ....*$20–$40*

Bigelow, John. *Memoir of the Life and Public Services of John Charles Fremont.* NY, 1856. ....*$40–$60*

Bigelow, John. *The Peach Orchard.* Minn, 1910, 1st ed, illus, fldg maps. ....*$55–$75*

Bigelow, Poultney. *White Man's Africa.* Harper, 1898.....*$20–$25*

Biggers, Earl Derr. *Keeper of the Keys.* Bobbs-Merrill, 1932, 1st ed. ....*$60–$75*

Biggers, Earl Derr. *Keeper of the Keys.* NY, Grosset & Dunlap. ....*$7–$12*

Biggers, Earl Derr. *Love Insurance.* Bobbs-Merrill, 1914, 1st ed. ....*$35–$75*

Biggers, Earl Derr. *The Chinese Parrot.* NY, 1926, rprnt, dj. ....*$25–$35*

Billings, John D. *Hardtack and Coffee . . . Unwritten Story of Army Life.* Bos, 1887, 1st ed, illus, plates. ....*$200–$275*

Bingham, Caleb. *The Columbian Orator.* Bos, 1817. .....*$10–$15*

Bingham, Capt. *The Bastille.* NY, 1901, 2 vols, illus, ltd 150 cc, plates, djs. ....*$75–$90*

Bingham, Hiram. *A Residence of 21 Years in the Sandwich Islands.* Hartford, 1847, ½ lea. ....*$100–$325*

Bingham, John. *Trial of Conspirators . . . Assassination of President Lincoln.* DC, GPO, 1865, wrps. ....*$65–$75*

Binkerd, Adam D. *The Mammoth Cave and Its Denizens.* Cinc, 1869, 1st ed, 95 pp, wrps. ....*$65–$90*

Binkley, William C. *The Texas Revolution.* Baton Rouge, 1952, 1st ed, dj. ....*$25–$50*

Bird, Annie Laurie. *Boise, the Peace Valley.* ID, 1934. ......*$32–$40*

Bird, H.E. *Chess: A Manual for Beginners.* Lon, nd, illus. ....*$14–$20*

Bird, Isabella. *A Lady's Life in the Rocky Mountains.* 1885, illus, 5th ed. ....*$65–$75*

Bird, Isabelle. *A Lady's Life in the Rocky Mountains.* Lon, 1910, 7th ed. ....*$55–$65*

Bird, William. *A Practical Guide to French Wines.* Paris, nd, wrps, maps. ....*$14–$19*

Birdsong, James C. *Brief Sketch of the North Carolina State Troops. . . .* Raleigh, 1894. ....*$42–$60*

Birkett, John. *The Diseases of the Breast and Their Treatment.* Lon, 1850, 11 plates. ....*$250–$450*

Bishop, Abraham. *Oration Delivered in Wallingford . . . Before Republicans of Ct.* New Haven, 1801. ....*$32–$45*

Bishop, Ebenezer. *Farewell Address of Elder Ebenezer Bishop of New Lebanon. . . .* Canterbury, 1850, 15 pp, wrps. ......*$135–$170*

Bishop, Harriet E. *Floral Home.* NY, 1857, plates. ....*$33–$55*

Bishop, Nathaniel. *A 1,000 Mile Walk across South America.* Bos, 1869. ....*$40–$65*

Bishop, Richard E. *Bishop's Wildfowl.* St. Paul, 1948, 1st ed, lea. ....*$125–$200*

Bishop, Richard E. *The Ways of Wildfowl.* Chi, 1971, deluxe ed, lea. ....*$75–$200*

Bissell, Richard. *The Monongahela.* Rinehart & Co., 1952, illus, dj. ....*$5–$10*

Bixby, William. *South Street.* NY, 1972, illus, dj. ....*$15–$25*

Black, Jeremiah S. *Eulogy on the Life and Character of General Andrew Jackson.* Chambersburg, 1845, 1st ed. ....*$45–$75*

Blackburn, I. *Illus. of Gross Morbid Anatomy of the Brain in the Insane.* GPO, 1908, 1st ed. ....*$45–$65*

Blacker, J.F. *Chats on Oriental China.* Lon, 1919, illus, 4th imp. ....*$12–$20*

Blackford, William Willis. *War Years with Jeb Stuart.* NY, 1945, 1st ed, dj. ....*$35–$50*

Blackmore, Howard L. *British Military Firearms, 1650–1850.* Lon, 1961, illus. ....$20–$30

Blackwell, Sarah Ellen. *A Military Genius . . . Life of Anna Ella Carroll of Maryland.* DC, 1891, 1st ed. ....$40–$50

Blackwood, Algernon. *The Centaur.* Lon, 1911, 1st ed. ..$45–$50

Blackwood, Algernon. *The Centaur.* Lon, 1916, rprnt. ..$25–$35

Blackwood, Algernon. *The Doll and One Other.* Arkham House, 1946, 1st ed, dj. ....$40–$70

Blades, William F. *Fishing Flies and Fly Tying.* Harrisburg, 1962, 2nd ed, dj. ....$35–$60

Blair, Walter A. *A Raft Pilot's Log.* Cleve, 1930. ....$33–$45

Blake, John L. *A Geographical, Chronological, and Historical Atlas. . . .* NY, 1826, illus, charts, engr. ....$75–$80

Blake, Sallie E. *Tallahassee of Yesterday.* Tallahassee, 1924, 1st ed. ....$37–$45

Blake, W.O. *History of Slavery and the Slave Trade.* Columbus, 1858. ....$55–$75

Blanch, H.J. *A Century of Guns. . . .* Lon, 1909, illus, index. ....$35–$40

Blanchan, Neltje. *Birds That Hunt and Are Hunted.* NY, 1898, illus, clr plates. ....$30–$65

Blanchan, Neltje. *The Nature Library.* NY, 1926, 6 vols, illus. ....$32–$45

Blanchard, Leola H. *Conquest of Southwest Kansas.* Wichita, 1931. ....$30–$45

Blanchard, Rufus. *The Discovery and Conquests of the Northwest.* Chi, 1880. ....$65–$125

Bland, J.O. and E. Backhouse. *China under the Empress Dowager.* Phila/Lon, 1912. ....$25–$65

Bland, W. *Hints on the Principles . . . of Ships and Boats. . . .* Lon, 1856, 2nd ed. ....$65–$85

Bland-Sutton, J. *Tumors, Innocent and Malignant.* Chi, nd. ....$15–$25

Blandford, G.F. *Insanity and Its Treatment.* Phila, 1871, 1st ed. ....*$36–$45*

Bledsoe, Albert T. *An Essay on Liberty and Slavery.* Phila, 1856. ....*$65–$75*

Bleeker, S. *The Delaware Indians.* NY, 1953, dj. ....*$25–$35*

Blinn, Henry Clay. *The Life and Gospel Experience of Mother Ann Lee.* Canterbury, Shakers, 1842, 15 pp, wrps. ....*$65–$85*

Bliss, Percy. *A History of Wood Engraving.* Lon, 1928. ....*$125–$195*

Bloch, Robert. *Cold Chills.* 1977, wrps. ....*$18–$30*

Bloch, Robert. *Terror.* NY, 1962, 1st ed, paperback. ......*$15–$20*

Block, Herbert. *Special Report.* 1st ed, sgn. ....*$16–$20*

Block, Lawrence. *Like a Lamb to Slaughter.* Arbor House, 1984, 1st ed, sgn, dj. ....*$30–$45*

Blond, Georges. *The Great Whale Game.* Lon, 1954, illus, 1st English ed. ....*$15–$22*

Blot, Pierre. *Hand-book of Practical Cookery.* NY, 1868..*$18–$25*

Bly, Robert. *Jumping out of Bed.* Barre Publishers, 1973, 1st ed, wrps, sgn. ....*$30–$45*

Bly, Robert. *Morning Gloria.* SF, 1969, wrps, illus by Tommie De Paloa, ltd 800 cc. ....*$25–$30*

Bly, Robert. *The Man in the Black Coat Turns.* Dial, 1981, 1st ed, dj. ....*$20–$28*

Bodfish, Capt. Hartson. *Chasing the Bowhead.* Harvard Univ. Press, 1936, 1st ed, dj. ....*$28–$37*

Bodine, A. *Chesapeake Bay and Tidewater.* NY, 1979, rprnt, dj. ....*$16–$20*

Bodine, *Chesapake Bay and Tidewater.* 1954, 1st ed. ......*$24–$35*

Boerhaave, Hermann. *De Viribus Medicamentorum, The Virtue and Energy of Medicines.* Lon, 1720, illus, calf. ....*$150–$275*

Bolles, Albert S. *The Financial History of the U.S. from 1774–1789.* NY, 1879. ....*$48–$65*

Bond, James H. *From out of the Yukon.* Portland, OR, 1948, illus, dj. ....*$35–$50*

Bond, James H. *From out of the Yukon.* Portland, OR, 1948, illus, sgn, dj. ....$50–$75

Boni, M.B. *Fireside Book of Folk Songs.* NY, 1947. ......$35–$55

Bonney, Edward. *The Banditti of the Prairies....* Chi, 1856, wrps, illus, 3rd ed, woodcuts. ....$3,500–$4,500

Bonnin, Gertrude. *Oklahoma's Poor Rich Indians: An Orgy of Grafting and Exploitation.* Phila, 1924, softbound. ....$65–$95

Bontemps, Arna. *Free at Last.* Dodd Mead, 1971, illus, dj. ....$5–$10

Bonwick, James. *The Mormons and the Silver Mines.* Lon, 1872. ....$95–$125

Boomer and Boschert. *Cider and Wine Presses.* Syracuse, NY, 1876, wrps. ....$65–$90

Booth, Mary. *History of the City of New York.* NY, 1867, 2 vols, lea. ....$50–$85

Booth, Maud Ballington. *After Prison—What?* NY, 1903, rprnt, sgn. ....$28–$45

Borden, Mrs. John. *The Cruise of the Northern Light....* NY, 1928, 1st ed, illus. ....$28–$35

Borges, Jorge Luis. *A Personal Anthology.* NY, Grove Press, 1967, 1st ed, dj. ....$35–$50

Born, Max. *Atomic Physics.* NY, 1946, 4th ed. ....$28–$36

Born, Max. *La Constitution de la Matiere.* Paris, 1922, wrps, illus, Nobel Prize–winning author. ....$37–$45

Bosse, Sara and Onoto Watanna. *Chinese-Japanese Cook Book.* Chi/NY, 1914. ....$14–$20

Bostock, Frank C. *The Training of Wild Animals.* NY, 1903, illus. ....$37–$45

Botkin, B.A. *A Civil War Treasury of Tales, Legends, and Folklore.* NY, Promontory Press, dj. ....$20–$30

Botkin, B.A. *A Treasury of American Folklore.* 1944. .....$15–$22

Botkin, B.A. *A Treasury of Southern Folklore.* 1949. ......$17–$22

Botkin, B.A. *Lay My Burden Down....* Univ. of Chicago Press, 1957, 3rd ed, dj. ....$12–$20

Botta, Charles. *History of the War of Independence of the U.S.A.* New Haven, 1834, 2 vols, translated from Italian. ....*$35–$50*

Bouchard, Georges. *Other Days, Other Ways ... in French Canada.* Montreal, 1928, illus, wood engr, dj. ....*$14–$20*

Boucher, Jonathan. *Reminiscences of an American Loyalist, 1783–1789.* Bos, 1925, bds, boxed. ....*$35–$50*

Bourjaily, Vance. *Now Playing at Canterbury.* NY, 1976, 1st ed, dj. ....*$12–$20*

Bourke-White, M. *Say, Is This the USA?* Duell, Sloan, 1941. ....*$45–$65*

Bourke-White, M. *Shooting the Russian War.* NY, 1942. .*$15–$22*

Bourke-White, Margaret. *Dear Fatherland Rest Quietly.* NY, 1946, 1st ed, sgn. ....*$200–$300*

Bourke-White, Margaret. *They Called it Purple Heart Valley: A Combat Chronicle....* NY, 1944, illus, 2nd prtng. ....*$20–$65*

Boutell, H.S. *Fist Editions of To-day and How to Tell Them.* 1929, 1st ed. ....*$35–$42*

Boutwell, George S. *Reminiscences of Sixty Years in Public Affairs.* NY, 1902, 2 vols, 1st ed, illus. ....*$30–$50*

Bova, Ben. *The Star Conquerors.* Phila, 1959, 1st ed, dj..*$75–$130*

Bovey, Martin. *The Saga of the Waterfowl.* DC, 1949, 1st ed, illus, presentation copy, dj. ....*$40–$50*

Bovey, Martin. *The Saga of the Waterfowl.* DC, 1949, illus. ....*$18–$25*

Bovey, Martin. *The Saga of the Waterfowl.* DC, 1949, 1st ed, dj. ....*$25–$30*

Bowditch, Henry I. *Life and Correspondence of Henry I. Bowditch.* Bos, 1902, 2 vols. ....*$24–$30*

Bowen, Eliza A. *Astronomy by Observation.* NY, 1886, 1st ed, illus. ....*$25–$35*

Bowen, Elizabeth. *Afterthought.* Lon, 1962. ....*$20–$30*

Bowen, Elizabeth. *The Demon Lover and Other Stories.* Lon, 1945, 1st ed. ....*$35–$45*

Bower, B.M. *Cow Country.* Bos. 1921. ....*$26–$45*

Boy Scouts of America. *The Official Handbook for Boys.* NY, 1913, 4th ed. ....*$35–$50* ·

Boyce, William D. *Illustrated Africa, North Tropical South.* NY, 1935, 1st ed, illus, sgn, maps. ....*$25–$30*

Boyd, Brendan and Fred Harris. *The Great American Baseball Card.* . . . 1973, 1st ed, dj. ....*$20–$28*

Boyd, James. *Drums.* NY, 1929, illus by N.C. Wyeth. ...*$35–$45*

Boyd, William. *An Ice Cream War.* Morrow, 1983, 1st ed, dj. ....*$15–$20*

Bozman, John Leeds. *A Sketch of the History of Maryland.* Balt, 1811, 1st ed, lea. ....*$60–$75*

Brackenridge, Henry M. *History of the Late War between the U.S. and Great Britain.* Phila, 1839, illus, calf. ....*$65–$95*

Bradburn, Samuel. *The Question, Are Methodists Dissenters?* Lon, 1792, pamphlet. ....*$8–$14*

Bradbury, Ray. *Martian Chronicles.* Limited Edition Club, illus, sgn, boxed. ....*$35–$150*

Bradbury, Ray. *Something Wicked This Way Comes.* Simon & Schuster, 1962, 1st ed, dj. ....*$120–$150*

Bradbury, Ray. *The Golden Apples of the Sun.* Garden City, 1953, 1st ed, illus, dj. ....*$50–$75*

Bradbury, Ray. *The Toynbee Convector.* Knopf, 1988, 1st ed, dj. ....*$25–$40*

Bradbury, Ray. *Zen and the Art of Writing.* 1st ed, sgn..*$50–$60*

Bradford, E. *Four Centuries of European Jewelry.* Eng, 1967, illus, dj. ....*$32–$40*

Bradford, R. *John Henry.* NY, 1931, 1st ed, dj. ....*$22–$30*

Bradley, A.G. *Sketches from Old Virginia.* Lon, 1897. ...*$25–$32*

Bradley, David. *No Place to Hide.* 1948, 1st ed. ....*$14–$20*

Bradley, Marion Zimmer. *The Mists of Avalon.* Knopf, 1982, 1st ed, dj. ....*$35–$45*

Brady, James F. *Modern Turkey Hunting.* NY, 1973, 1st ed, illus, dj. ....*$12–$20*

Brady, Joseph P. *The Trial of Aaron Burr.* NY, 1913, 89 pp.
....*$28–$35*

Bragdon, O.D. *Facts and Figures . . . Information for the People of Louisiana.* New Orleans, 1872, charts, softbound. ......*$42–$50*

Braid, James and Harry Vardon. *How to Play Golf.* NY, nd, illus. ....*$45–$58*

Brake, Hezekiah. *On Two Continents.* KS, 1896, 1st ed. ....*$85–$100*

Brand, Max. *Happy Jack.* Dodd Mead, 1936, 1st ed, dj. .*$47–$65*

Brand, Max. *Lost Wolf.* Dodd Mead, 1953, dj. ....*$10–$18*

Brand, Max. *The Gun Tamer.* Dodd Mead, 1929, 1st ed, dj. ....*$200–$250*

Brand, Max. *The Seventh Man.* NY, 1921, 1st ed, dj. ...*$25–$35*

Brand, Max. *The Thunderer.* Derrydale Press, 1933, illus by Paul Brown. ....*$45–$50*

Brandt, Herbert. *Arizona and Its Bird Life.* 1951, illus, dj. ....*$150–$195*

Brant. *True Story of the Lindbergh Kidnapping.* NY, 1932, 1st ed. ....*$30–$35*

Brebner, John B. *North Atlantic Triangle.* New Haven, 1945, maps. ....*$28–$45*

Brehme, H. *Picturesque Mexico,* NY, 1925, illus, folio. .*$22–$25*

Breilhan, Carl W. *Badmen of the Frontier Days.* NY, 1957. ....*$25–$35*

Brennan, Joseph Payne. *Nine Horrors and a Dream.* Arkham House, 1958, 1st ed, dj. ....*$75–$100*

Bresson, Henri Cartier. *The People of Moscow.* NY, 1955, 1st ed, dj. ....*$50–$135*

Brewer, A.T. *History of the Sixty-first Regiment, Pennsylvania Volunteers, 1861–65.* Pitts, 1911. ....*$65–$90*

Brewer, Samuel Child. *Every Man His Own Brewer: A Small Treatise. . . .* Lon, nd, 3rd ed, half calf. ....*$75–$115*

Brewster. *A Treatise on Magnetism.* Edin, 1838, 1st ed. ......*$50–$67*

Brewster, Charles W. *Rambles about Portsmouth.* Portsmouth, 1859, 1st ed. ....$75–$95

Brewster, William. *Concord River.* Harvard, 1937, 1st ed. ....$15–$20

Bricker, Charles. *Landmarks of Mapmaking.* NY, 1976, illus, maps, dj. ....$55–$100

Bridges, C. *Thin Air, a Himalayan Interlude.* 1930, 1st ed. ....$15–$20

Briggs, Richard. *The English Art of Cookery....* Lon, 1794, illus, 3rd ed, engr plates. ....$95–$150

Bright, Charles. *The Story of the Atlantic Cable.* NY, 1903, 1st ed, illus. ....$20–$30

Bright, John. *Speeches of John Bright, M.P.* Bos, 1865..$25–$45

Brininstool, E.A. *Fighting Red Cloud's Warriors: True Tales of Indian Days....* Columbus, OH, 1926, 1st ed, illus. ....$55–$75

Brininstool, E.A. *Trooper with Custer and ... Battle of the Little Bighorn.* Columbus, OH, 1925, 1st ed, illus. ....$55–$75

Brisbin, Gen. James. *Belden, the White Chief ... among the Wild Indians of the Plains.* 1870, 1st issue. ....$95–$125

Briscoe, T.W. *Orchids for Amateurs.* Lon, nd, illus. ....$14–$20

Bristol, Sherlock. *The Pioneer Preacher, an Autobiography.* NY, 1887. ....$12–$20

Bristow, Alec. *The Sex Life of Plants.* NY, 1978, dj. .....$18–$25

Broder, Patricia Janis. *Bronzes of the American West.* NY, nd, illus, dj. ....$75–$125

Brogile, Louis. *Matter and Light.* NY, 1st American ed, dj. ....$22–$35

Bromfield, Louis. *Mr. Smith.* NY, 1951, ltd 650 cc, sgn, dj. ....$18–$25

Bromfield, Louis. *The Farm.* NY, 1946, 1st ed, illus. ......$5–$10

Bronte, Charlotte. *Villette.* NY, 1855. ....$37–$50

Bronte, Emily. *Wuthering Heights.* Lon. ....$50–$75

Brooke, Arthur. *The Way of a Man with a Horse.* Lon, 1929, illus. ....$12–$15

Brooke, Geoffrey. *Horse Lovers.* NY, 1928, illus by Snaffles. ....*$12–$15*

Brooks, N. *The Boy Emigrants.* 1929. ....*$22–$30*

Brooks, R.O. *Vinegars and Catsup.* NY, 1912. ....*$8–$15*

Brooks, Van Wyck. *New England Indian Summer.* NY, 1940, 1st ed, dj. ....*$12–$20*

Brooks, Van Wyck. *New England: Indian Summer, 1865–1915.* NY, 1940, 1st ed, slipcase, ltd #151/997 cc, sgn. ....*$50–$65*

Brooks, Van Wyck. *The World of Washington Irving.* NY, 1944. ....*$15–$18*

Broomhall, Marshall (ed). *Martyred Missionaries of the China Inland Mission.* Lon, nd, illus, fldg maps, photos. ....*$20–$30*

Brown, Bernard. *Amateur Talking Pictures and Recording.* 1933, 1st ed, illus. ....*$18–$22*

Brown, Capt. Thomas. *Taxidermist's Manual.* Lon, 1874, illus, 25th ed. ....*$25–$65*

Brown, D.W. *Salt Dishes.* MA, 1937, illus. ....*$30–$45*

Brown, Dee. *Bury My Heart at Wounded Knee.* 1971. ...*$14–$25*

Brown, Dee. *The Gentle Tamers: Women of the Old West.* NY, 1958, 1st ed, illus. ....*$18–$30*

Brown, G.S. *First Steps to Golf.* Bos, Small Maynard, nd. ....*$60–$75*

Brown, George M. *Ponce De Leon Land and Florida War Record.* St. Augustine, 1901, 3rd ed. ....*$23–$38*

Brown, Helen E. *A Good Catch, or, Mrs. Emerson's Whaling Cruise.* Phila, 1884, 1st ed, illus. ....*$75–$125*

Brown, Henry Collins. *The City of New York.* NY, Old Colony Press, 1915, 1st ed, illus, limp lea. ....*$35–$50*

Brown, Innis (ed). *How to Play Golf.* NY, 1930, illus, Spalding's Athletic Library. ....*$45–$50*

Brown, John. *Twenty Five Years a Parson in the Wild West.* Fall River, MA, 1896, published by author. ....*$150–$175*

Brown, L. *African Birds of Prey.* Lon, 1970, illus. ....*$30–$40*

Brown, M.M. *Nature Underground, The Endless Caverns.* New Market, 1921, illus. ....*$18–$25*

Brown, Mark H. and W.R. Felton. *The Frontier Years.* NY, 1955. ....*$40–$50*

Brown, Riley. *Men, Wind, and Sea.* NY, 1943, illus, rprnt. ....*$10–$20*

Brown, Susan A. *The Invalid's Tea Tray.* Bos, 1885. .....*$30–$45*

Brown, Warren. *The Chicago Cubs.* NY, 1946, illus. ....*$30–$40*

Brown, William E. *How to Train Hunting Dogs.* NY, 1942, 1st ed, illus, dj. ....*$12–$20*

Browne, John Ross. *Crusoe's Island.* 1864. ....*$130–$150*

Browne, Lewis. *The Graphic Bible.* Macmillan, 1928, 1st ed, illus. ....*$16–$20*

Browne, M. *Artistic and Scientific Taxidermy and Modeling.* Black, 1896. ....*$48–$60*

Browning, E.B. *Sonnets from the Portuguese.* NY, Crowell, nd, wrps, illus by Pogany, tip-in clr plates, dj. ....*$75–$125*

Browning, Robert. *The Pied Piper of Hamelin.* 1939, illus by Rackham. ....*$30–$40*

Brownlow, W.G. *Sketches of the Rise, Progress and Decline of Secession.* Phila, 1862, 1st ed, illus. ....*$25–$35*

Bruccoli, M. Raymond Chandler. *A Bibliography.* Pitts, 1979. ....*$50–$60*

Bruce. *Along Hudson with Washington Irving.* Poughkeepsie, 1913. ....*$15–$20*

Bruce, George A. *The Capture and Occupation of Richmond.* np, nd, 1st ed, illus, presentation copy, sgn. ....*$55–$75*

Bruce, William C. *Benjamin Franklin, Self-revealed.* NY, 1917, 2 vols. ....*$60–$80*

Bruette, William. *American Duck, Goose and Brant Shooting.* NY, 1945. ....*$14–$25*

Bruette, William. *The Cocker Spaniel: Breeding, Breaking and Handling.* NY, 1937, 1st ed. ....*$25–$40*

Brummitt, Stella W. *Brother Van.* NY, 1919, 1st ed. .....*$50–$75*

Bryan, Thomas Conn. *Confederate Georgia.* Athens, 1953, 1st ed. ....$48–$65

Bryant, William Cullen. *Picturesque America.* NY, 1874, 2 vols, illus, small folio, steel plates, woodcuts, ½ lea. ....$150–$250

Bryant, William Cullen. *Picturesque America.* NY, 1872, 2 vols. ....$175–$250

Bryant, William Cullen. *The Flood of Years.* NY, 1878, 1st ed, full mor, raised bands. ....$100–$145

Bryce, Viscount. *Treatment of Armenians in the Ottoman Empire, 1915–16.* Lon, 1916, 1st ed, fldg map. ....$50–$75

Bryk, F. *Circumcision in Man and Woman.* 1934, ltd ed. .$30–$35

Brynner, Irena. *Modern Jewelry—Design and Technique.* NY, 1968, illus. ....$45–$60

Buber, Martin. *Israel and Palestine.* Lon, 1952, dj. ......$25–$45

Bubolz, Gordon A. *Land of the Fox.* Appleton, WI, 1949, illus, sgn. ....$12–$20

Buchanan, James. *Message of the Pres. of the U.S. . . . Massacre at Mountain Meadows.* DC, 1860, softbound. ....$75–$100

Buchanan, Lamont. *Ships of Steam.* NY, 1956, illus, dj..$22–$30

Buck, Frank. *All in a Lifetime.* 1943. ....$20–$24

Buck, Frank. *Bring 'em Back Alive.* NY, 1930, 1st ed, illus, photos. ....$30–$45

Buck, Franklin. *A Yankee Trader in the Gold Rush.* Bos, 1930, dj. ....$50–$65

Buck, James. *The Modern Japanese Military System.* Lon, 1975. ....$18–$25

Buck, M.S. *Book Repair and Restoration.* 1918, illus. ...$25–$30

Buck, Pearl. *Fighting Angel.* 1936, 1st ed, dj. ....$24–$30

Buck, Pearl. *Imperial Woman.* 1956, 1st ed, dj. ....$17–$20

Buck, Pearl. *The Patriot.* 1939, 1st ed, dj. ....$16–$20

Buck, Pearl S. *The Kennedy Women.* NY, 1970, 1st ed, illus, dj, sgn. ....$16–$20

Buckingham, Nash. *Game Bag.* NY, 1945, 1st ed, illus by Hoecker, dj. ....$22–$30

Buckingham, Nash. *Mark Right!* Derrydale Press, ltd 1,250 cc. ....*$175–$225*

Buckingham, Nash. *Tattered Coat.* Putnam, 1944, ltd #279/995 cc, sgn. ....*$140–$165*

Buckland, C.E. *Dictionary of Indian Biography.* NY, 1968, rprnt. ....*$14–$20*

Buckley, William. *Buckley's History of the Great Reunion of the North and South.* np, 1923, illus. ....*$20–$35*

Budge, Sir A.E.W. *The Divine Origin of the Craft of the Herbalist.* Lon, 1928. ....*$25–$35*

Buechner, Thomas S. *Norman Rockwell, Artist and Illustrator.* NY, 1970. ....*$55–$100*

Buist, Robert. *The Family Kitchen Gardener. . . .* Judd, 1866. ....*$35–$60*

Buist, Robert. *The Rose Manual.* Phila, 1847, 7th ed. ...*$47–$65*

Bukowski, Charles. *The Movie: "Barfly."* 1987, ltd 400 cc, sgn. ....*$55–$70*

Buley, R. Carlyle. *The Old Northwest.* Indiana Univ. Press, 1962, 2 vols, illus, maps, plates. ....*$30–$45*

Bulfinch, Thomas. *Oregon and Eldorado.* Bos, 1866. ...*$57–$65*

Bull, J. *Birds of New York State.* NY, 1974, illus. ....*$45–$60*

Bull, Rice C. *Soldiering: The Civil War Diary of Rice C. Bull, 123rd Vol. Inf. . . . .* CA, 1977, 1st ed, dj. ....*$32–$45*

Bullard, Robert L. *Personalities and Reminiscences of the War.* NY, 1925, 1st ed. ....*$45–$75*

Bullen, Frank. *Cruise of the Cachalot.* NY, 1926, illus by Mead Schaeffer. ....*$25–$35*

Bullen, Frank T. *Denizens of the Deep.* NY, 1904, illus..*$30–$50*

Bulley, Margaret H. *Ancient and Medieval Art: A Short History.* NY, 1914, illus, clr chart. ....*$18–$25*

Bullock, Shan F. *A "Titanic" Hero: Thomas Andrews, Shipbuilder.* Riverside, CT, 1973, illus, rprnt, dj. ....*$18–$30*

Bulpin, T.V. *The Hunter Is Death.* Johannesburg, 1962, 1st ed, illus. ....*$22–$30*

Bumstead, John. *On the Wing.* Bos, 1869, illus. ....$30–$50

Burack, Benjamin. *Ivory and Its Uses.* Rutland, VT, 1984, illus, dj. ....$12–$18

Burbank, Nelson L. *House Construction Details.* NY, 1942, 2nd ed. ....$22–$30

Burch, John P. and Charles W. Burch. *Quantrell: A True History of His Guerrilla Warfare. . . .* TX, published by author, 1923, illus. ....$18–$25

Burckhardt, John Lewis. *Notes on the Bedouins and Wahabys.* Cinc, 1968, rprnt. ....$20–$35

Burder, George. *The Welch Indians.* NY, 1922, softbound. ....$24–$35

Burdett. *The Life and Adventures of Christopher Carson.* Phila, 1861. ....$28–$45

Burdett, Charles. *The Life of Kit Carson.* 1902. ....$25–$35

Burdick, Usher. *The Last Battle of the Sioux Nation.* Fargo, 1929, 1st ed, dj. ....$35–$50

Burgess, Anthony. *A Clockwork Orange.* 1963, 1st American ed, dj. ....$100–$125

Burgess, Anthony. *But Do Blondes Always Prefer Gentlemen?* McGraw-Hill, 1986, 1st ed, dj. ....$12–$25

Burgess, Anthony. *The Devil's Mode.* Random House, 1989, 1st American ed, dj. ....$20–$40

Burgess, Anthony. *The Kingdom of the Wicked.* Franklin Library, 1985, illus, 1st U.S. ed, lea, sgn. ....$48–$60

Burgess, Fred W. *Chats on Old Copper and Brass.* Lon, 1914. ....$25–$35

Burgess, Gelett. *The White Cat.* IN, 1906, illus by Will Grefe. ....$30–$40

Burgess, Thornton W. *Billy Mink.* 1924, 1st ed, dj. ......$45–$85

Burgess, Thornton W. *How Unc' Billy Possum Met Buster Bear.* Cole & Winthrop Press, 1914. ....$20–$30

Burgess, Thornton W. *Old Mother Westwind.* Little Brown, 1919, illus. ....$20–$30

Burgess, Thornton W. *The Advent of Prickly Porky.* Bos, 1916. ....*$12–$15*

Burgess, Thornton W. *The Adventures of Ol' Mister Buzzard.* Little Brown, illus by Harrison Cady. ....*$15–$22*

Burke, Emma Maxwell. *A Perfect Course in Millinery.* NY, 1925, illus. ....*$30–$40*

Burness, Tad. *Cars of Early Twenties.* NY. ....*$10–$14*

Burnet, J.A. *Treatise on Painting.* Lon, 1850, plates. ..*$85–$100*

Burnett, Frances Hodgson. *Editha's Burglar.* Dana Estes, illus by H. Sandham, dj. ....*$30–$40*

Burnett, Frances Hodgson. *Giovanni and the Other.* Scribner's, 1892, 1st ed. ....*$50–$60*

Burnett, Frances Hodgson. *Hawworth's.* NY, 1879, 1st ed. ....*$20–$30*

Burnett, Frances Hodgson. *Little Lord Fauntleroy.* NY, 1886, illus by Reginald Birch. ....*$30–$45*

Burnett, Frances Hodgson. *Sara Crewe, or What Happened at Miss Minchin's.* NY, 1888, illus by Reginald Birch. ....*$30–$45*

Burnett, Frances Hodgson. *Two Little Pilgrim's Progress.* Scribner's, 1895, 1st ed. ....*$30–$45*

Burnham, Major Frederick. *Scouting on Two Continents.* Garden City, 1926, 1st ed, sgn. ....*$25–$35*

Burns, Eugene. *Advanced Fly Fishing.* Harrisburg, 1953, illus. ....*$120–$150*

Burns, Walter Noble. *A Year with a Whaler.* NY, 1913, 1st ed, illus. ....*$80–$100*

Burns, Walter Noble. *Saga of Billy the Kid.* NY, 1926. $22–$30

Burns, Walter Noble. *Tombstone: An Illiad of the Southwest.* NY, 1927. ....*$35–$50.*

Burpee, Lawrence, J. *The Search for the Western Sea. . . .* Lon, 1908, 1st ed, illus, maps, plates. ....*$125–$200*

Burr, F. *The Life of General Philip Sheridan.* Prov, 1888..*$15–$20*

Burris-Meyer, Elizabeth. *Decorating Livable Houses.* NY, 1937, 1st ed, illus. ....*$20–$25*

Burroughs, Edgar Rice. *At the Earth's Core.* Canaveral, dj.
....*$50–$80*

Burroughs, Edgar Rice. *At the Earth's Core.* McClurg, 1922, 1st ed, dj. ....*$275–$350*

Burroughs, Edgar Rice. *Beasts of Tarzan.* A.L. Burt, 1916.
....*$10–$25*

Burroughs, Edgar Rice. *Escape on Venus.* 1946, 1st ed, dj.
....*$90–$150*

Burroughs, Edgar Rice. *Jungle Tales of Tarzan.* McClurg, 1st ed, dj. ....*$60–$80*

Burroughs, Edgar Rice. *Tarzan and the Foreign Legion.* Tarzana, 1948, 1st ed, dj. ....*$55–$110*

Burroughs, Edgar Rice. *Tarzan of the Apes.* A.L. Burt, 1915, dj.
....*$75–$150*

Burroughs, Edgar Rice. *Tarzan the Untamed.* McClurg, 1920, 1st ed, dj. ....*$60–$180*

Burroughs, Edgar Rice. *Tarzan's Quest.* Tarzana, 1st ed, dj.
....*$110–$450*

Burroughs, Edgar Rice. *The Chessmen of Mars.* Chi, 1922, 1st ed. ....*$75–$150*

Burroughs, Edgar Rice. *The Chessmen of Mars.* NY, 1922, rprnt.
....*$10–$18*

Burroughs, Edgar Rice. *The Gods of Mars.* NY, 1918, rprnt.
....*$10–$14*

Burroughs, Edgar Rice. *The Land That Time Forgot.* Grosset & Dunlap, 1925, dj. ....*$25–$30*

Burroughs, Edgar Rice. *The Moon Maid.* NY, 1926, rprnt.
....*$10–$18*

Burroughs, Edgar Rice. *The Return of Tarzan.* McClurg, 1915, 1st ed, dj. ....*$45–$65*

Burroughs, John. *Bird Stories.* Bos, 1911, 1st ed, illus by L.A. Fuertes. ....*$18–$25*

Burroughs, John. *Camping and Tramping with Roosevelt.* Bos, 1907, 1st ed, illus, photos. ....*$24–$35*

Burroughs, John (ed). *Songs of Nature.* NY, 1901. ......*$5–$6.50*

Burroughs, William S. *Naked Lunch.* NY, 1959, dj. ......$75–$95

Burroughs, William S. *Queer.* NY, 1986, dj. ....$20–$30

Burroughs, William S. *Soft Machine.* NY, Grove Press, 1966, dj. ....$75–$90

Burroughs, William S. *Third Mind.* NY, 1978, dj. ....$35–$40

Burroughs, William S. *Tornado Alley.* Cherry Valley Editions, 1989, 1st ed, ltd 100 cc. ....$75–$150

Bursey, Jack. *Antarctic Night.* Lon, 1958, illus, dj. ....$25–$35

Burton, Frederick R. *American Primitive Music . . . Songs of the Ojibways.* NY, 1909. ....$55–$65

Burton, Richard. *Lake Regions of Central Africa.* NY, 1860. ....$50–$75

Burton, Richard F. *The City of Saints, and across the Rocky Mts. to California.* NY, 1862, 1st American ed, map, plates. .$125–$275

Burton, Richard F. *The City of the Saints, and across the Rocky Mts. to Calif.* Lon, 1861. ....$150–$300

Busch, Wilhelm. *Max and Moritz.* Munich, 1939, illus. .$25–$45

Bush, Walter L. *A Saga of Duck and Goose Shooting.* Minn, 1979, illus by Kouba, 2nd prntg. ....$25–$40

Bushnan, J.S. *The Naturalist's Library, Ichthyology. Vol II.* Edin, 1840, illus. ....$58–$75

Bushnell, Charles I. *A Narrative of the Life and Adventures of Levi Hanford. . . .* NY, private prntg. 1863, 1st ed, illus, bds. ....$95–$150

Busk, Hans. *The Navies of the World.* Lon, 1859. ....$55–$68

Butler, Benjamin F. *Autobiography . . . of Major General Benjamin F. Butler.* Bos, 1892, 1st ed, illus. ....$27–$35

Butler, T. Harrison. *Cruising Yachts.* Southampton, 1958, 3rd ed, dj. ....$22–$35

Butts, I.R. *The Merchant and Shipmaster's Manual. . . .* Bos, 1867, illus, 4th ed, plates. ....$95–$135

By a Free-will Baptist. *The Church Member's Book . . . in Three Parts.* NH, 1847. ....$28–$30

By a Lady of Boston. *Stories of Gen. Warren.* 1835, lea..$12–$25

By a Practical Housekeeper. *The Good Cook.* NY, 1853.
....$55–$65

By Himself. *The Fall of Prince Florestan of Monaco.* Lon, 1874.
....$15–$25

Byrd, R.E. *Little America.* NY, 1930, 1st ed, illus, sgn, dj.
....$35–$70

Byrd, Richard E. *Alone.* Putnam, 1938, sgn, dj. ....$30–$40

Byrd, Richard Evelyn. *Little America.* Putnam, 1930, 1st ed,
illus, photos, maps. ....$30–$45

Byrd, William. *The Secret Diary of William Byrd of Westover,
1709–1712.* Rich, 1941, dj. ....$18–$24

Byrne, R. *McGoorty Story of a Billiard Bum.* Secaucus, 1972, 1st
ed, dj. ....$16–$20

Cabell, Granch. *The St. Johns: A Parade of Universities.* Farrar &
Rinehart, 1943, 1st ed, illus. ....$20–$30

Cabell, James Branch. *Cream of the Jest: A Comedy of Evasions.*
NY, 1927. ....$35–$40

Cable, George. *Old Creole Days.* NY, 1890, 1st ed, illus, Moran
etching, teg. ....$30–$40

Cable, George. *The Creoles of Louisiana.* Lon, 1885. ..$145–$200

Cable, George W. *Gideon's Band.* NY, 1914, 1st ed. .....$25–$30

Cable, George W. *Old Creole Days.* NY, 1897. ....$25–$35

Cable, George W. *The Negro Question.* NY, 1888, softbound.
....$45–$60

Cabot, Sebastian. *A Memoir of Sebastian Cabot.* Lon, 1831, illus.
....$40–$50

Cabot, W.B. *In Northern Labrador.* Bos, 1912, 1st ed. ..$32–$40

Caiger, G. *Dolls on Display.* Tokyo, 1933, illus, silk brocade with
silk ties. ....$45–$65

Cain, James M. *The Moth.* NY, 1948, 1st ed, dj. ....$25–$60

Calasanctius, M.J. *The Voice of Alaska: A Missioner's Memories.*
Lachine, 1935, illus, 1st English ed, mar bds. ....$30–$45

Caldecott, R. *Caldecott's Collection of Pictures and Songs.* Lon,
nd, clr engr. ....$35–$45

Caldecott, R. *Picture Book.* Lon, 1st ed, illus, clr plates..*$25–$38*

Calderwood, W.L. *The Life of the Salmon.* Lon, 1907, illus.
....*$25–$50*

Caldwell, Erskine. *Claudelle Inglish.* Bos, 1958, 1st ed, dj.
....*$20–$30*

Caldwell, Erskine. *God's Little Acre.* NY, 1933, 1st ed..*$50–$60*

Caldwell, Erskine. *Place Called Estherville.* NY, 1949, 1st ed, dj.
....*$25–$30*

Caldwell, Erskine. *Tobacco Road.* NY, 1940, 1st ed, dj, illus by
Fredenthal, boxed. ....*$65–$75*

Calisher, Hortense. *Queenie.* Arbor, 1971, 1st ed, dj. ....*$20–$25*

Callow, Edward. *Old London Taverns.* NY, 1901. ....*$20–$25*

Calvert, Roy E. *The Death Penalty Enquiry.* Lon, 1931, softcover.
....*$10–$14*

Camehl, A.W. *The Blue China Book.* NY, 1916. ....*$22–$30*

Cameron, James R. *Motion Picture Projection.* 1922, illus, 3rd
ed. ....*$22–$30*

Cameron, Will. *From Cape Town. . . .* Belgian Congo, 1929.
....*$10–$20*

Camp, R. *Duck Boats: Blinds, Decoys.* NY, 1952, 1st ed..*$40–$50*

Camp, R. *Game Cookery.* NY, 1958. ....*$12–$15*

Camp, Walter (ed). *Official Football Rules—1914.* NY, 1914,
wrps, illus. ....*$18–$25*

Campbell. *Beauty, History, Romance, and Mystery of Canadian
Lake Region.* Tor, 1910, clr plates. ....*$35–$50*

Campbell, Ernest Q. and Thomas F. Pettigrew. *Christians in
Racial Crisis . . . Study of Little Rock's Ministry. . . .* DC, 1959, 1st
ed. ....*$30–$45*

Campbell, John F. *A Short American Tramp in the Fall of 1864.*
Edin, 1865. ....*$45–$65*

Campbell, Mary Emily. *The Attitude of Tennesseans toward the
Union 1847–1861.* NY, 1961, 1st ed. ....*$30–$45*

Campbell, Patrick. *Travels in the Interior Inhabited Parts of
North America.* Tor, 1937, 1st American ed, ltd 550 cc. .*$95–$150*

Campbell, Ruth. *Small Fry and Winged Horse.* Volland, 1927, illus by Tenggren. ....*$30–$35*

Campbell, W.W. *Lecture on the Life and Military Service of Gen. James Clinton.* NY, 1839, sgn, pamphlet. ....*$32–$45*

Camus, Albert. *The Plague.* Knopf, 1950, 5th U.S. translation, dj. ....*$14–$18*

Camus, Albert. *The Stranger.* NY, 1946, 1st U.S. ed, dj..*$75–$100*

Candee, Helen C. *The Tapestry Book.* NY, 1935. ....*$28–$35*

Candee, Helen C. *Weaves and Draperies.* NY, 1930, 1st ed, illus. ....*$40–$50*

Canfield, D. *Seasoned Timber.* NY, 1939, 1st ed, boxed..*$16–$22*

Canfield, Dorothy. *Home Fires in France.* NY, 1918, 1st ed. ....*$20–$25*

Cannon, James. *History of Southern Methodist Missions.* Nashville, 1926, sgn. ....*$14–$20*

Capa, R. *Images of War.* NY, 1964, 1st ed, dj. ....*$75–$95*

Capote, Truman. *A Christmas Memory.* NY, 1956, ltd 600 cc, sgn, slipcase. ....*$40–$50*

Capote, Truman. *In Cold Blood.* 1965, 1st ed, dj. ....*$25–$75*

Capote, Truman. *Other Voices, Other Rooms.* NY, 1948, 1st ed. ....*$125–$300*

Capote, Truman. *The Grass Harp.* NY, 1951, 1st ed, dj. .*$50–$95*

Capote, Truman. *The Muses Are Heard.* Random House, 1956, 1st ed, dj. ....*$75–$85*

Capote, Truman. *The Thanksgiving Visitor.* Random House, 1967. ....*$24–$35*

Capote, Truman. *The Thanksgiving Visitor.* Random House, 1967, 1st ed, slipcase. ....*$60–$100*

Capp, Al. *The Return of the Schmoo.* NY, 1959, 1st ed, wrps. ....*$28–$35*

Caras, Roger. *Monarch of Deadman Bay—The Life and Death of a Kodiak Bear.* Bos, 1969, 1st ed, dj. ....*$10–$15*

Carey, A.M. *American Firearms Makers.* NY, 1953, illus, dj. ....*$20–$25*

Carey, H.C. *The Slave Trade, Domestic and Foreign....* Phila, 1853, 1st ed. ....*$55–$75*

Carleton, Will. *Farm Ballads.* Harper, 1882, illus. ....*$10–$14*

Carleton, Will. *Farm Festivals.* NY, 1881. ....*$20–$40*

Carleton, Will. *Farm Legends.* NY, 1875. ....*$20–$45*

Carleton, William. *Traits and Stories of the Irish Peasantry.* Dublin, 1843–44, 2 vols. ....*$115–$150*

Carlisle, D. *The Belvedere Hounds.* Derrydale Press, 1935, ltd 1,250 cc. ....*$35–$45*

Carmer, Carl. *Deep South.* NY, 1930, 1st ed, sgn. ....*$18–$24*

Carmer, Carl. *Rivers of America: The Hudson.* Lon, 1951, illus, dj. ....*$15–$20*

Carmer, Carl. *Rivers of America: The Hudson.* NY, 1939, illus, sgn. ....*$50–$75*

Carmichael, John P. *Who's Who in the Major Leagues.* 1950. ....*$18–$25*

Carnegie, Andrew. *Round the World.* NY, 1884, 1st American trade ed. ....*$35–$50*

Carnochan, F.G. and H.S. Adamson. *The Empire of the Snakes.* NY, 1935, illus. ....*$15–$25*

Caron, Pierre. *French Dishes for American Tables.* NY, 1886, 1st ed. ....*$25–$35*

Carpenter, R. *Game Trails from Alaska to Africa, 1938.* Private prntg, 1938, ltd 850 cc, sgn. ....*$125–$150*

Carpenter, W. *Elements of Physiology.* Phila, 1846, illus, 1st American ed, lea. ....*$25–$35*

Carpenter, W. *The Microscope and Its Revelations.* Lon, 1862, illus, 3rd ed. ....*$40–$50*

Carpenter, W. *The Microscope and Its Revelations.* Phila, 1856, 1st American ed. ....*$60–$85*

Carr, Harry. *The West is Still Wild.* Bos, 1932, 1st ed, illus. ....*$25–$35*

Carrick, Alice Van Leer. *A History of American Silhouettes ... 1790–1840.* Rutland, 1968, dj. ....*$30–$50*

Carrick, Alice Van Leer. *Collector's Luck in England.* Bos, 1926, illus. ....$25–$30

Carrington, Frances C. *Army Life on the Plains.* Phila, 1911, 2nd ed. ....$45–$65

Carrington, Henry B. *Military Movements in Indiana in 1864.* np, nd, wrps. ....$50–$75

Carroll Lewis. *Alice's Adventures in Wonderland.* Doubleday, illus by Arthur Rackham. ....$70–$100

Carroll, Lewis. *Alice's Adventures in Wonderland.* NY/Lon, 1901, illus by Peter Newell. ....$75–$130

Carroll, Lewis. *Alice's Adventures in Wonderland and Through the Looking Glass.* Random House, 1946, 2 vols. ....$18–$25

Carroll, Lewis. *Sylvie and Bruno.* Lon, 1889, 1st ed. .....$25–$35

Carroll, Lewis. *The Annotated Alice.* NY, illus by Tenniel, dj. ....$18–$25

Carroll, Lewis. *The Hunting of the Snark.* Lon, 1876, 1st ed. ....$185–$225

Carrol, Lewis. *The Hunting of the Snark and Other Poems.* Harper, 1903, illus by P. Newell. ....$90–$120

Carroll, M. *Ten Years in Paradise: Leaves from a Society Reporter's Notebook.* San Jose, 1903, illus. ....$25–$35

Carruth, Hayden. *The Crow and the Heart.* Macmillan, 1959, 1st ed, dj. ....$30–$45

Carruth, Hayden. *Tracks End.* NY, 1911, 1st ed. ....$15–$25

Carson, Rachel. *Silent Spring.* Houghton Mifflin, 1962..$10–$18

Carson, Rachel. *Under the Sea Wind.* NY, 1952, illus, 2nd ed, dj. ....$15–$20

Carson, Rachel L. *The Sea around Us.* Oxford Univ. Press, 1951, 1st ed. ....$18–$22

Carter, Jimmy and Rosalynn. *Everything to Gain.* 1987, 1st ed, 2nd prntg, sgn by both. ....$40–$50

Cartier-Bresson, Henri. *The Face of Asia.* NY, 1972, illus, photos, dj. ....$30–$60

Carvalho, S.N. *Incidents of Travel and Adventure in the Far West.* NY, 1857. ....$45–$50

Carver, Jonathan. *Travels through the Interior Parts of No. America . . . 1766, '67, '68.* Lon, 1781, 3rd ed, lea, mor bkd clamshell case, hand-clr maps and plates. ....$900–$1,500

Carver, Jonathan. *Voyage de M. Carver dans l'Interierur de l'Amerique. . . .* Paris, 1784. ....$80–$100

Carver, Raymond. *Cathedral.* NY, 1983, 1st ed, dj. ......$14–$25

Carver, Raymond. *Early for the Dance.* Firefly Press, 1986, 1st ed, ltd #1/100 cc, sgn. ....$95–$125

Carver, Raymond. *If It Pleases You.* Lord John Press, 1984, 1st ed, ltd #1/200 cc, sgn. ....$125–$150

Carver, Raymond. *The Toes.* Ewert, 1988, 1st ed, wrps, ltd 26 cc. ....$125–$175

Carver, Raymond. *What We Talk about When We Talk about Love.* NY, 1981. ....$35–$40

Cary, Alan L. *Famous Liners and Their Stories.* NY, 1937, illus. ....$37–$45

Casey, Robert J. *The Black Hills and Their Incredible Characters.* Ind, 1949. ....$25–$35

Casey, Robert J. *The Texas Border.* Bobbs-Merrill, 1950, 1st ed, illus, photos, ltd, sgn, dj. ....$25–$35

Casserly, Gordon. *The Jungle Girl.* NY, 1922, 1st U.S. ed. ....$12–$18

Cassill, R.V. *The Goss Women.* Doubleday, 1974, 1st ed, dj. ....$22–$27

Castaneda, Carlos E. *The Mexican Side of the Texan Revolution.* Dallas, 1928. ....$95–$120

Castle, Henry A. *The Army Mule and Other War Sketches.* IN, 1898, illus. ....$20–$40

Castleman, Alfred. *Army of the Potomac.* Milw, 1863. ..$83–$95

Caswell, J. *Sporting Rifles and Rifle Shooting.* 1920, 1st ed, illus, photos. ....$24–$35

Cate, Wirt Armistead. *Lucius Q.C. Lamar: Secession and Reunion.* Chapel Hill, 1935, 1st ed, illus. ....$45–$75

Cather, Willa. *A Lost Lady.* NY, 1923, 1st ed, dj. ....$50–$175

Cather, Willa. *Death Comes for the Archbishop.* Knopf, 1927, 1st ed, dj. ....$65–$75

Cather, Willa. *Sapphira and the Slave Girl.* NY, 1940, 1st ed, dj. ....$35–$75

Cather, Willa. *Shadows on the Rock.* Knopf, 1931, 1st ed, dj. ....$35–$60

Cather, Willa. *The Old Beauty and Others.* NY, 1948, 1st ed, dj. ....$23–$40

Cather, Willa. *The Professor's House.* NY, 1925, 1st ed..$50–$200

Catherwood, Frederick. *Views of Ancient Monuments in Central America.* Barre, MA, 1965, illus, ltd 500 cc, plates. ...$300–$500

Cattelle, W.R. *The Pearl.* Phila, 1907, 1st ed. ....$30–$40

Catton, Bruce. *Grant Moves South.* Bos/Tor, 1960, 1st ed, illus, presentation copy, sgn, dj. ....$27–$40

Catton, Bruce. *This Hallowed Ground.* Garden City, 1956, 1st ed, dj. ....$25–$37

Century Company War Book. *Battles and Leaders of the Civil War.* NY, 1884–87, 4 vols. ....$75–$100

Cescinsky, Herbert and Ernest Gribble. *Early English Furniture and Woodwork.* Lon, 1927, 2 vols, illus, folio, lea. .....$135–$200

Chadwick, Lee. *Lighthouses and Lightships.* Lon, 1971, illus, photos, dj. ....$25–$33

Chalfant. *Gold, Guns, and Ghost Towns.* Stanford, 1947..$25–$35

Chamberlain. *Open House in New England.* NH, 1939, sgn. ....$18–$20

Chamberlain, Esther and Lucia. *The Coast of Chance.* Bobbs-Merrill, 1908, illus by Clarence F. Underwood. ....$9–$18

Chamberlain, George A. *African Hunting among the Thongas.* NY, 1923, 1st ed, illus. ....$45–$65

Chamberlain, Samuel. *Rockefeller Center.* 1947, photos, dj. ....$10–$18

Chandler, Raymond. *The Big Sleep.* NY, 1939, 1st ed, dj. ....$1,800–$2,200

Chandler, Raymond. *The Little Sister.* Houghton Mifflin, 1949, 1st American ed, dj. ....*$150–$350*

Channing, William Ellery. *Slavery.* Bos, 1835, 1st ed. .*$68–$79*

Chapel, C.E. *Boy's Book of Rifles.* 1948. ....*$18–$25*

Chapelle, Howard I. *History of American Sailing Ships.* NY, illus, rprnt, photos, plates, dj. ....*$20–$25*

Chapin. *The Heart of Music.* Tor, 1906, illus. ....*$14–$20*

Chaplin, R. *Wobbly.* Chi, 1948, presentation copy, dj. ...*$30–$50*

Chapman, A. *On Safari.* Lon, 1908, illus, photos. .....*$100–$140*

Chapman, Charles E. *A History of California: The Spanish Period.* NY, 1921, illus, maps. ....*$40–$50*

Chapman, F. Spencer. *Northern Lights.* NY, 1933, illus, 1st American ed, fldg map. ....*$60–$75*

Chapman, Frank M. *Bird Life.* Appleton, 1900, wrps. .*$20–$35*

Chapman, Frank M. *Bird Life: A Guide to Study of Our Common Birds.* NY/Lon, 1915, illus, clr plates. ....*$45–$55*

Chapman, Frank M. *Camps and Cruises of an Ornithologist.* NY, 1908, 1st ed, illus. ....*$35–$45*

Chapman, Olive Murray. *Across Iceland, the Land of Frost and Fire.* Lon/NY, 1930, 1st ed, illus. ....*$40–$95*

Chapple, H. Barton. *Popular Television.* 1935, 1st ed, illus, dj. ....*$45–$60*

Chardin, Sir John. *Travels in Persia.* Lon, 1927, illus, ltd 927 cc. ....*$175–$225*

Charters, Ann. *Jack Kerouac: A Bibliography.* NY, 1975. ....*$40–$60*

Chase, A. *Dr. Chase's Recipes.* Ann Arbor, 1867. ....*$25–$35*

Chase, Edward. *The Memorial Life of General William Tecumseh Sherman.* Chi, 1891, 1st ed. ....*$40–$85*

Chase, J. *California Desert Trails.* 1919, 1st ed. ....*$18–$25*

Chase, Mary Ellen. *The Fishing Fleets of New England.* Bos, 1961, illus. ....*$22–$35*

Chatelain, Verne. *Defenses of Spanish Florida, 1565 to 1763.* DC, 1941, 1st ed, illus, fldg maps and plates. ....*$85–$125*

Chatterton, E. Keble. *Sailing Ships and Their Story.* Lon, 1909, illus, fldg plates, ¾ black mor, cloth bds. ....$60–$75

Chatterton, E. Keble. *Ships and Ways of Other Days.* Lon, 1913, illus. ....$18–$28

Chatterton, E. Keble. *The Mercantile Marine.* Bos, 1923, illus, plates. ....$25–$35

Chayefsky, Paddy. *Altered States.* NY, 1978, 1st ed, dj..$28–$35

Cheever, John. *Oh, What a Paradise It Seems.* NY, 1982, 1st ed, dj. ....$20–$25

Cheever, John. *The Brigadier and the Golf Widow.* NY, 1964, 1st ed, dj. ....$35–$40

Cheever, John. *The Enormous Radio.* NY, 1963. ....$35–$45

Cheever, John. *The Enormous Radio.* NY, 1953, 1st ed, dj. ....$75–$195

Cheever, John. *The Wapshot Scandal.* Harper, 1964, 1st ed. ....$15–$25

Cheiro. *Palmistry for All.* NY, 1916. ....$10–$18

Chekov, Anton. *Two Plays: Cherry Orchard and Two Sisters.* Heritage Books, 1966, sandglass, slipcase. ....$10–$14

Chennault, Clair. *Way of a Fighter.* NY, 1949, 1st ed, dj..$25–$45

Chesterton, G.K. *The Ballad of the White Horse.* 1911. .$30–$37

Chevalier, Haakon. *Oppenheimer: The Story of a Friendship.* NY, 1965. ....$10–$16

Chief Standing Bear. *My People, the Sioux.* Bos, 1928, 2nd prntg, dj. ....$35–$40

Child, Hamilton. *Gazetteer and Bus. Directory of Rensselaer County, NY, 1870–71.* ....$45–$55

Child, L. Maria. *The Right Way, the Safe Way. . . .* NY, 1860, wrps. ....$25–$35

Child, Mrs. Lydia M. *An Appeal in Favor of That Class of Americans Called Africans.* NY, 1836. ....$90–$115

Child, William. *A History of the Fifth Regiment, N.H. Vol., in Amer. Civ. War.* Bristol, 1893. ....$40–$65

Childress, Alice. *A Hero Ain't Nothin' But a Sandwich.* NY, 1973, sgn. ....*$45–$50*

Childs, Gladys. *A Little Bit of Florida.* NY, 1970, 1st ed, illus, dj. ....*$12–$20*

Childs, Mary Fairfax. *De Namin' Ob De Twins and Other Sketches from the Cotton Land.* NY, 1908, 1st ed. ....*$85–$125*

Chipman, Elizabeth. *Women on the Ice.* np, 1986, 1st ed, illus, map, dj. ....*$20–$30*

Chipman, N.P. *The Tragedy of Andersonville, Trial of Captain Henry Wirz.* . . . Sac, 1911, 2nd ed. ....*$50–$65*

Chittenden, Hiram M. *A History of the American Fur Trade of the Far West.* Stanford, 1959, 2 vols, maps, djs. ....*$45–$65*

Chittenden, Hiram M. *American Fur Trade of the Far West.* NY, Harper, 1902, 3 vols. ....*$575–$675*

Chittenden, Hiram M. *History of Early Steamboat Navigation on the Missouri River.* . . . NY, 1903, 2 vols, ltd 950 cc. .*$275–$350*

Chittenden, Hiram M. and A.T. Richardson. *Life, Letters, and Travels of Father Pierre-Jean De Smet.* NY, 1905, 4 vols. ....*$325–$400*

Chrichton, Michael. *Jurassic Park.* NY, 1990, 1st ed, dj..*$65–$95*

Christie, Agatha. *Curtain.* 1975, dj. ....*$15–$20*

Christie, Agatha. *N OR M?* NY, 1941, 1st U.S. ed. ....*$40–$100*

Christie, Agatha. *Nemesis.* NY, 1971, 1st U.S. ed, dj. ..*$22–$25*

Christie, Agatha. *Postern of Fate.* 1973, 1st American ed, dj. ....*$14–$22*

Christie, Agatha. *Sleeping Murder.* 1976, dj. ....*$15–$20*

Christie, Agatha. *The Murder of Roger Ackroyd.* 1926, 1st ed. ....*$45–$65*

Christie, Agatha. *The Pale Horse.* NY, 1962, 1st U.S. ed, dj. ....*$20–$30*

Christy, Howard Chandler. *The Christy Girl.* Bobbs-Merrill, 1906, illus by Christy, clr plates. ....*$50–$85*

Chu, Arthur and Grace Chu. *The Collector's Book of Jade.* NY, 1978, illus, dj. ....*$14–$18*

Churchill, Winston. *A History of the English-speaking Peoples.* Lon, 1956–58, 4 vols, 1st ed, djs. ....$175–$200

Churchill, Winston. *Great Contemporaries.* NY, 1937, 1st U.S. ed. ....$35–$40

Churchill, Winston. *The Second World War.* Lon, 1948–54, 6 vols, 1st ed, djs. ....$125–$300

Churchill, Winston. *The Unrelenting Struggle.* Lon, 1942, 1st ed. ....$35–$110

Churchill, Winston S. *The End of the Beginning War Speeches.* Bos, 1943, 1st ed, 2nd prntg, dj. ....$40–$50

Churchill, Winston S. *The Sinews of Peace.* Lon, 1948, 1st ed, dj. ....$75–$100

Chute, Carolyn. *Letourneau's Used Auto Parts.* Ticknor & Fields, 1988, 1st ed, dj. ....$25–$35

Clancy, P.A. *Gamebirds of Southern Africa.* NY, 1967, illus. ....$37–$45

Clancy, Tom. *Cardinal of the Kremlin.* Putnam, 1988, 1st ed, dj. ....$10–$12

Clancy, Tom. *Patriot Games.* Putnam, 1987, 1st ed, dj. .$25–$45

Clancy, Tom. *Red Storm Rising.* Putnam, 1986, 1st ed, dj. ....$30–$45

Clancy, Tom. *The Hunt for Red October.* Naval Inst. Press, 1984, 1st ed, sgn, dj. ....$650–$750

Clancy, Tom. *The Hunt for Red October.* 1984, 7th prntg, dj. ....$15–$18

Clark, Arthur H. *The Clipper Ship Era.* NY, 1910, 1st ed, illus. ....$25–$35

Clark, Emmons. *History of the Seventh Regiment of New York.* NY, 1890, 2 vols, 1st ed. ....$65–$95

Clark, George W. *Liberty Minstrel.* NY, 1845, 4th ed. ..$14–$20

Clark, Hugh and Thomas Wormull. *Short and Easy Introduction to Heraldry in Two Parts.* Lon, 1781, illus, ½ calf, bds. .$75–$100

Clark, Imogen. *Rhymed Receipts for Any Occasion.* Bos, 1912. ....$12–$20

Clark, Kenneth. *Rembrandt and the Italian Renaissance.* New York Univ./Appleton, 1966, dj. ....$16–$20

Clark, Ronald W. *Edison: The Man Who Made the Future.* 1977, 1st ed, illus, dj. ....$14–$20

Clark, Walter Van Tilburg. *The Track of the Cat.* NY, 1949, dj. ....$35–$46

Clarke, Arthur C. *2001: A Space Odyssey.* NY, 1968, 1st ed, dj. ....$95–$125

Clarke, Arthur C. *The Exploration of Space.* 1951, 1st ed, illus. ....$15–$20

Clarke, Arthur C. *The Wind from the Sun.* NY, 1972, 1st ed, dj. ....$30–$35

Clarke, Asia. *Unlocked Book: A Memoir of John Wilkes Booth.* NY, 1938, 1st ed. ....$18–$25

Clarke, J.B.B. *An Account of the Religious Literary Life of Adam Clarke.* NY, 1839, lea. ....$25–$45

Clarke, John, M.D. *Diseases of the Heart and Arteries.* Lon, 1895. ....$25–$30

Clarke, Lewis. *Narr. of the Sufferings of Lewis and Milton Clarke. . . .* Bos, 1846. ....$85–$95

Clarke, T.W. *Emigres in the Wilderness.* NY, 1941, sgn, dj. ....$35–$55

Clay, John. *My Life on the Range.* NY, 1861, rprnt. ......$35–$45

Clay, R.S. and T.H. Court. *History of the Microscope.* Lon, 1975, rprnt, dj. ....$18–$25

Clayton, Victoria V. *White and Black under the Old Regime.* Milw, 1899, 1st ed. ....$125–$150

Cleater, P.E. *Rockets through Space.* NY, 1936, 1st ed, illus. ....$35–$50

Cleaver, Eldridge. *Eldridge Cleaver: Post Prison Writings and Speeches.* NY, 1969, dj. ....$20–$22

Cleaver, Eldridge. *Soul on Ice.* NY, 1968, 1st ed, dj. ....$22–$27

Cleland, John. *The Life of Fanny Hill.* Hoboken, NJ, illus. ....$16–$20

Clement, Arthur W. *Our Pioneer Potters.* NY, 1947, illus, ltd 500 cc, slipcase. ....*$85–$100*

Clerk, Dugald. *The Gas Engine.* Wiley, 1893. ....*$20–$35*

Cleveland, Grover. *Fishing and Shooting Sketches.* NY, 1906, illus. ....*$20–$25*

Clifford, F. *Romance of Perfume Lands.* Bos, 1881. ......*$32–$45*

Clift, Virgil A. (ed). *Negro Education in America, Its Adequacy, Problems, and Needs.* NY, 1962, 1st ed. ....*$28–$37*

Clougher, T.R. (ed). *Golf Clubs of the Empire: The Golfing Annual.* Lon, 1931, 5th issue. ....*$45–$50*

Coakley. *Diseases of the Nose and Throat.* 1901, illus, 2nd ed. ....*$22–$30*

Coan, T. *Life in Hawaii: An Autobiographic Sketch.* NY, 1882. ....*$35–$47*

Coates, Robert. *The Outlaw Years.* NY, 1930, 1st ed. ...*$17–$30*

Coatsworth, Eliz. *The Sun's Diary.* 1929, 1st ed, dj. .....*$35–$55*

Cobb, E. Elijah. *A Cape Cod Skipper: 1768–1848.* New Haven, 1925, 1st ed, illus. ....*$18–$25*

Cobb, Irvin S. *Fibble.* NY, 1916, 1st ed. ....*$20–$30*

Cobb, Lyman. *Cobb's Juvenile Reader, No. 3.* Ind, 1837..*$12–$15*

Cobb, Ty. *My Life in Baseball.* NY, 1962, 1st ed, dj. ....*$30–$40*

Cobb, W. Mantague. *The First Negro Medical Society . . . Dist. of Columbia, 1884–1939.* DC, 1939. ....*$35–$45*

Coblentz, Stantion A. *Villains and Vigilantes.* NY, 1936..*$30–$45*

Cochran, D.M. *Frogs of Southeastern Brazil.* DC, 1955, illus. ....*$25–$45*

Cochran, D.M. and C.J. Goin. *Frogs of Columbia.* DC, 1970, illus. ....*$30–$45*

Cockburn, A.P. *Political Anals of Canada.* Lon, 1909. .*$20–$40*

Cody, William F. *Buffalo Bill's Wild West and Cong. of Rough Riders of the World.* Chi, 1893, 64 pp wrps. ....*$50–$60*

Cody, William F. *Story of the Wild West and Camp Fire Chats by Buffalo Bill.* Phila, 1889, 1st ed, illus. ....*$35–$60*

Cody, William F. *True Tales of the Plains.* NY, 1908. .*$50–$100*

Coffey, Leora S. *Wilds of Alaska Big-game Hunting.* NY, 1963, 1st ed. ....$18–$30

Coffin, Charles C. *Boys of 1861.* Bos, 1885. ....$25–$35

Coffin, Charles C. *Life of Abraham Lincoln.* NY, 1893. .$40–$50

Coffin, Charles "Carleton." *Stories of Our Soldiers.* Bos, 1893, 1st ed, illus. ....$22–$35

Coffin, Joseph. *Vector Analysis.* Wiley, NY, 1911. ....$20–$25

Coffin, Robert P. Tristram. *Captain Abby and Captain John.* NY, 1939, illus. ....$15–$22

Coffin, Robert P. Tristram. *Mainstays of Maine.* NY, 1933. ....$14–$20

Cohen, I.B. *Introduction to Newton's "Principia."* Harvard Univ. Press, 1971, dj. ....$35–$50

Cohen, J.X. *Jewish Life in South America.* Block, 1941..$22–$30

Cohen, M. *Pathways through the Bible.* 1955, illus by Arthur Szyk. ....$18–$30

Cohen, Octavus Roy. *Bigger and Blacker.* Bos, 1925, 1st ed, sgn. ....$50–$85

Colbert, E. *Chicago and the Great Conflagration.* Cinc, 1872, 1st ed, illus. ....$28–$45

Colcord, Joanna C. *Songs of American Sailormen.* NY, 1938, illus. ....$35–$60

Cole, George E. *Early Oregon: Jottings . . . of a Pioneer, 1850.* np, 1905, 1st ed. ....$25–$30

Colgrave, Bruce. *How to Fly Fish for Salmon.* Sidney, B.C., 1971, 1st ed. ....$5–$12

Collins. *The FBI in Peace and War.* NY, 1943, inscrb by Hoover. ....$50–$65

Collins, A. Frederick. *Experimental Television.* 1932, 1st ed, illus, dj. ....$95–$175

Collins, A. Frederick. *The Book of Wireless.* 1922, illus, 2nd ed. ....$18–$27

Collins, Hubert E. *Warpath and Cattle Trail.* NY, 1928..$50–$85

Collins, John S. *Across the Plains in '64.* Omaha, 1904, 1st ed. ....*$25–$37*

Collins, Wilke. *No Name.* NY, 1863, 1st ed, illus. ....*$85–$100*

Collins, Wilkie. *Armadale.* NY, 1866, 1st American ed. ..*$60–$75*

Collins, Wilkie. *Poor Miss Finch.* NY, 1872. ....*$25–$30*

Collis, Septima M. *A Woman's Trip to Alaska.* NY, 1890, illus, clr map. ....*$55–$70*

Collodi, Carlo. *Pinnochio.* Garden City, illus by Maude and Miska Petersham. ....*$15–$35*

Collodi, Carlo. *Pinocchio.* Donohue, nd. ....*$10–$14*

Colson, Percy. *Melba: An Unconventional Biography.* Lon, 1932, illus. ....*$40–$50*

Colton, H.S. and F.C. Baxter. *Days in the Painted Desert and the San Francisco Mountains.* Flagstaff, 1932, illus. ....*$30–$45*

Colton, J.H. *Colton's Railroad and Township Map of the State of Ohio.* NY, 1864. ....*$65–$75*

Colton, Julia M. *Annals of Old Manhattan, 1609–1664.* NY, 1901. ....*$20–$25*

Colton, Walter. *Deck and Port....* A.S. Barnes & Co., 1854, illus. ....*$35–$50*

Colum, Padraic. *Crossroads in Ireland.* NY, 1930, 1st ed, illus. ....*$8–$12*

Colum, Padraic. *Dramatic Legends and Other Poems.* NY, 1922, 1st ed, sgn. ....*$75–$90*

Colum, Padraic. *The Boy Who Knew What the Birds Said.* NY, 1930, illus. ....*$12–$18*

Colum, Padraic. *The Road Round Ireland.* 1926, 1st U.S. ed. ....*$35–$40*

Combe, George. *Elements of Phrenology.* Lon, 1825, 2nd ed, 2 plates. ....*$20–$25*

Combs, Trey. *The Steelhead Trout.* Portland, 1971, 1st ed, dj. ....*$50–$85*

Comstock, J.L. *An Introduction to the Study of Botany....* NY, 1846, calf. ....*$18–$20*

Comstock, J.L. *Natural History of Quadrupeds.* Robinson, 1829.
....*$22–$35*

Comstock, John H. *How to Know the Butterflys: A Manual of Butterflys of East. U.S.* NY, 1904, illus, clr plates. ....*$25–$35*

Condon, E.U. and G.H. Shortly. *The Theory of Atomic Spectra.* Macmillan, 1935, 1st ed. ....*$45–$60*

Condon, Eddie. *We Called It Music.* NY, 1927, 1st ed, dj.
....*$20–$30*

Conkey, W.B. *The Official Guide to the Klondyke Country....* Chi, 1897, softbound. ....*$200–$350*

Conklin, E. *Picturesque Arizona.* NY, 1878. ....*$250–$300*

Conlan, P.J. *On the Threshold of Home Rule.* 1913, 1st U.S. ed.
....*$30–$45*

Connelley, William E. *John Brown.* Topeka, 1900, 1st ed.
....*$50–$65*

Connelley, William E. *Quantrill and the Border Wars.* IA, Torch Press, 1910, 1st ed, illus, maps. ....*$85–$125*

Connelley, William. *Wild Bill and His Era: The Life and Adventures of James Hickok.* NY, 1933. ....*$40–$150*

Connett, E. *Duck Decoys.* VT, 1953, illus, clr and b/w, dj.
....*$14–$22*

Connett, E. (ed). *Duck Shooting along the Atlantic Tidewater.* NY, 1947, illus, dj. ....*$55–$100*

Connett, E. *Wildfowling in the Mississippi Flyway.* Van Nostrand, 1949, 1st ed, illus. ....*$125–$195*

Connolly, James B. *On Tybee Knoll: A Story of the Georgia Coast.* NY, 1905, 1st ed, illus. ....*$28–$40*

Connor, Ralph. *Black Rock.* NY, 1900, illus by Louis Rhead.
....*$10–$15*

Conrad, Joseph. *A Conrad Argosy.* NY, 1942, illus, woodcuts, dj.
....*$30–$45*

Conrad, Joseph. *Lord Jim: A Romance.* NY, 1900, 1st American ed. ....*$95–$135*

Conrad, Joseph. *Tales of Hearsay.* NY, 1925, 1st American ed, dj.
....*$30–$60*

Conrad, Joseph. *The Nigger of the Narcissus.* Lon, 1898, 1st ed. ....$200–$225

Conroy, Pat. *Prince of Tides.* Bos, 1986, 1st ed, dj. ......$35–$50

Conroy, Pat. *The Great Santini.* Bos, 1976, 1st ed, sgn, dj. ....$75–$125

Considine, Bob. *The Remarkable Life of Dr. Armand Hammer.* Harper & Row, 1975, 1st ed. ....$20–$30

Conway, M.D. *Testimonies Concerning Slavery.* Lon, 1864. ....$50–$95

Conwell, R.H. *History of the Great Boston Fire, Nov. 9th and 10th, 1872.* Bos, 1873, 1st ed, illus. ....$15–$30

Cook, C. *Observations of Fox Hunting and Management of Hounds.* Lon, 1826. ....$175–$250

Cook, Frederick A. *My Attainment of the Pole.* NY, 1911, 1st ed. ....$50–$90

Cook, Frederick A. *To the Top of the Continent.* NY, 1908, 1st ed. ....$75–$100

Cook, Harry. *Borough of the Bronx.* 1913, illus, presentation copy. ....$15–$18

Cook, Joel. *America Picturesque and Descriptive.* Phila, 1900, 3 vols, slipcase. ....$25–$35

Cook, Joel. *Switzerland Picturesque and Descriptive.* Henry Coates, 1904, 1st ed, illus, tissued photos, dj. ....$30–$45

Cook, Roy Bird. *The Family and Early Life of Stonewall Jackson.* VA, 1925, 1st ed. ....$45–$65

Cook, William W. *Around the World in Eighty Hours.* NY, 1925, 1st ed, dj. ....$40–$65

Cooke, E.W. *Shipping and Craft.* San Remo, 1979, illus by E.W. Cooke, ltd 500 cc, rprnt of 1829 ed, 65 etched plates, boxed. ....$225–$300

Cooke, Philip St. George. *Cavalry Tactics.* NY, 1862. .....$85–$125

Cooke, T.G. *Finger Prints, Secret Service, Crime Detection.* Chi, 1936, illus. ....$15–$28

Coombs, Sarah B. *South African Plants for American Gardens.* NY, 1936, illus. ....$12–$17

Coon, Carleton S. *Riffian.* Bos, 1933, illus by Paul Wenk, sgn, dj.
....*$15–$25*

Cooper, A. *The Complete Distiller.* . . . Lon, 1757. .....*$225–$300*

Cooper, Courtney R. *Lions 'n' Tigers 'n' Everything.* Bos, 1925.
....*$10–$20*

Cooper, J. Wesley. *Natchez: Treasury of Antebellum Homes.* Phila,
1957, 1st ed, dj. ....*$16–$20*

Cooper, James Fenimore. *Deerslayer.* Scribner's, 1929, illus by
N.C. Wyeth, 9 clr plates. ....*$35–$55*

Cooper, James Fenimore. *The Crater or Vulcan's Peak.* MA,
Belknap Press, 1962, Thomas Philbrick (ed), dj. ....*$15–$25*

Cooper, John M. *Analytical and Critical Biblio. of Tribes of
Tierra del Fuego.* GPO, 1917, fldg map. ....*$35–$50*

Cooper, Lt. A. *In and Out of Rebel Prisons.* Oswego, NY, 1888,
illus. ....*$40–$55*

Cooper, Matthew. *The German Army, 1933–1945.* NY, 1978, 1st
ed, illus. ....*$14–$18*

Coover, Robert. *The Universal Baseball Association, Inc.* Lon,
1970, 1st ed, dj. ....*$75–$175*

Cope, Gilbert. *Genealogy of the Smedley Family.* Lancaster, 1901.
....*$35–$45*

Copeland, Thomas. *Observations on the Principal Diseases of the
Rectum and Anus.* Lon, 1814, 2nd ed, bds. ....*$150–$200*

Coppard, A.E. *Fearful Pleasures.* Arkham House, 1946, 1st U.S.
ed, dj. ....*$45–$55*

Copway, George. *The Life, History, and Travels of Kah-Ge-Ga-
Gak-Bowk* . . . *Ojibway.* . . . PA, 1847, 2nd ed, presentation copy,
sgn. ....*$200–$225*

Corbett, Jim. *Man-eaters of Kumaon.* NY/Bombay, 1946, 1st U.S.
ed, dj. ....*$25–$35*

Corbett, Jim. *Man-eaters of Kumaon.* Ox, 1946, 1st ed, dj.
....*$15–$20*

Cornelius, Mrs. *The Young Housekeeper's Friend.* Bos/NY, 1846.
....*$100–$175*

Cornell, K. *I Wanted to Be an Actress.* NY, 1939, 1st ed, sgn, dj. ....*$20–$25*

Corner, George W. *Doctor Kane of the Arctic Seas.* Phila, 1972, 1st ed, illus, dj, maps. ....*$28–$35*

Cornish, Dudley Taylor. *The Sable Arm Negro Troops in the Union Army, 1861–1865.* NY, 1956, 1st ed. ....*$48–$65*

Correll and Gosden. *All about Amos 'n' Andy and Their Creators Correll and Gosden.* NY, 1930, illus, 2nd ed. ....*$22–$35*

Corrigan, D. *That's My Story.* NY, 1938, 1st ed, dj. ......*$16–$20*

Corso, Gregory. *The Happy Birthday of Death.* New Directions, 1960, 1st ed. ....*$20–$35*

Costain, Thomas B. *The Silver Chalice.* Garden City, 1952, 1st ed, slipcase, ltd #146/750 cc, sgn. ....*$45–$65*

Costello, A. *Our Police Protectors: Hist. of N.Y. Police.* 1885. ....*$50–$85*

Cotsell, George. *A Treatise on Ships' Anchors.* Lon, 1856, 1st ed, illus. ....*$125–$185*

Cotton, Josiah. *Vocabulary of the Massachusetts (or Natick) Indian Language.* Camb, 1829. ....*$45–$60*

Coues, Elliott. *Birds of the Northwest.* DC, GPO, 1874..*$65–$95*

Coues, Elliott. *Birds of the Northwest. . . .* Bos, 1877. .....*$30–$40*

Coues, Elliott. *Key to North American Birds.* Salem, 1872, 1st ed, plates. ....*$75–$80*

Coues, Elliott (ed). *New Light on the Early History of the Greater Northwest. . . .* NY, 1897, 3 vols. ....*$250–$300*

Coues, Elliott. *The Expeditions of Zebulon Montgomery Pike.* Minn, 1962, 2 vols, ltd 2,000 cc, boxed. ....*$35–$45*

Coulter, Ellis Merton. *William G. Brownlow: Fighting Parson of the Southern Highlands.* Chapel Hill, 1937, 1st ed. ....*$60–$85*

Coulter, Ellis Merton. *Civil War and Readjustment in Kentucky.* Chapel Hill, 1926, 1st ed. ....*$65–$85*

Courcy, Henry de. *The Catholic Church in the United States.* NY, 1856. ....*$25–$35*

Courlander, Harold. *Negro Folk Music, U.S.A.* NY, 1963, illus by James and Ruth McCrea. ....$20–$24

Coward, Noel. *Conversation Piece.* NY, 1934, 1st ed, dj..$10–$15

Cox, Charles E. *John Tobias, Sportsman.* NY, Derrydale Press, 1937, illus by Aiden L. Ripley, ltd #97/950 cc. ....$35–$50

Cox, Earnest Sevier. *Let My People Go.* Rich, 1925, 1st ed. ....$55–$75

Cox, Florence Tinsley. *The Epic of Ebenezer.* Dodd Mead, 1912, 1st ed. ....$18–$25

Cox, Jacob D. *Military Reminiscences of The Civil War.* NY, 1900, 2 vols. ....$65–$85

Cox, Warren. *The Book of Pottery and Porcelain.* NY, 1973, 2 vols. ....$35–$40

Cox, Warren. *Chinese Ivory Sculpture.* NY, 1946. ....$38–$45

Cozzens, James Gould. *Morning, Noon, and Night.* Harcourt, 1968, 1st ed, dj. ....$35–$45

Crabb, Alfred. *Nashville, Personality of a City.* Ind, 1960. ....$10–$15

Craig, Maurice. *Psychological Medicine.* Lon, 1905, plates. ....$20–$27

Craig, William N. *Lillies and Their Culture in North America.* Chi, 1928, 1st ed, illus. ....$16–$20

Crandall, Julie V. *The Story of Pacific Salmon.* Portland, 1946. ....$12–$20

Crane, Stephen. *Maggie: A Girl of the Streets.* NY, 1896, 1st ed. ....$55–$75

Crane, Stephen. *The Little Regiment.* NY, 1896, 1st ed..$38–$50

Crane, Stephen. *The Open Boat and Other Stories.* NY, 1898, 1st ed. ....$215–$250

Crane, Stephen. *The Red Badge of Courage.* NY, 1896, 2nd ed. ....$95–$100

Crane, Walter. *Flora's Feast of Flowers.* Lon, 1889, 1st ed, illus by Walter Crane. ....$135–$150

Crane, Walter. *Decorative Illustration of Books.* Lon, 1916, illus. ....$45–$75

Crane, Walter B. *Odd Tales.* NY, 1900, 1st ed, wrps, illus. ....$75–$85

Craven, Thomas. *Modern Art.* NY, 1934. ....$18–$25

Craven, Thomas. *Treasury of American Prints . . . Living American Artists.* NY, 1939, slipcase. ....$70–$85

Crawford, F. Marion. *Adam Johnstone's Son.* Macmillan, 1896, 1st ed, illus. ....$27–$45

Crawford, Samuel W. *The Genesis of the Civil War: The Story of Sumter, 1860–1861.* NY, 1887. ....$35–$45

Creel, George. *Ireland's Fight for Freedom.* 1919, 1st U.S. ed. ....$22–$25

Crew, Henry and Alfonso De Salvio (eds). *Dialogues Concerning Two New Sciences.* Macmillian, 1914. ....$18–$22

Crews, Harry. *A Childhood.* NY, 1978, 1st ed, dj. ....$20–$25

Crews, Harry. *Florida Frenzy.* Gainesville, 1982, 1st ed. ....$30–$45

Crichton, Michael. *Andromeda Strain.* Knopf, 1969, 1st ed, dj. ....$20–$30

Crisler, Lois. *Arctic Wild.* Lon, 1959, illus, dj. ....$15–$22

Crocker, A. *The Elements of Land Surveying.* Lon, 1813, illus, plates, presentation copy, lea. ....$55–$75

Croff, G.B. *Progressive American Architecture.* DC, 1875, illus, folio, plates. ....$1,200–$1,450

Croffut, W.A., et al. *The Military and Civil History of Conn. . . . during War of 1861–65.* NY, 1868. ....$30–$75

Croly, Mrs. J.C. *Jennie June's American Cookery Book.* NY, 1870. ....$45–$62

Cromie, R. *Dillinger: A Short and Violent Life.* NY, 1962, 1st ed, sgn, dj. ....$22–$28

Cross & Dunlop. *Bibliography of Yeats.* NY, 1975, dj. .$15–$20

Cross, John Keir. *The Red Journey Back.* NY, 1954, 1st ed, dj. ....$25–$45

Cross, Wilbur. *The History of Henry Fielding.* Yale, 1918, 3 vols, 1st ed. ....*$50–$75*

Crossman, E.C. *Military and Sporting Rifle Shooting.* NC, 1932. ....*$32–$45*

Crowninshield, Mary Bradford. *All among the Lighthouses.* Bos, 1886. ....*$42–$50*

Cullen, Countee. *Color.* NY, nd. ....*$18–$30*

Cullen, Countee. *Copper Sun.* 1927, 1st ed. ....*$25–$32*

Culleton, James. *Indians and Pioneers of Old Monterey.* Fresno, 1950, dj. ....*$18–$24*

Culver, H.B. and Gordon Grant. *The Book of Old Ships.* Garden City, 1935, illus, dj. ....*$30–$37*

Culver, Henry B. *The Book of Old Ships.* NY, 1928, illus, drawings, mor, mar bds. ....*$35–$55*

Culverwell, Robert J. *How to Live 100 Years.* Lon, 1847, stiff paper. ....*$30–$45*

Cumbers, Frank. *The Book Room.* Lon, 1956. ....*$10–$12*

Cummings, e.e. *Eimi.* Covici & Friede, 1933, 1st ed, sgn. ....*$155–$200*

Cummings, e.e. *Puella Mea.* Golden Eagle Press, 1923, 1st ed. ....*$45–$65*

Cunningham, Peter. *Hand-book of London.* Lon, 1850. ..*$30–$45*

Curie, Eve. *Madam Curie.* 1937, 1st ed, illus, dj. ....*$15–$20*

Curran and Kauffeld. *Snakes and Their Ways.* 1937, 1st ed. ....*$20–$25*

Curry, Manfred. *Yacht Racing. . . .* NY, 1927. ....*$25–$35*

Curtis, George William. *Howadji in Syria.* NY, 1877. ..*$22–$30*

Curtis, John H. *An Essay on the Deaf and Dumb.* Lon, 1834, 2nd ed, 2 plates. ....*$40–$50*

Curtis, Mattoon. *The Story of Snuff and Snuff Boxes.* NY, 1935, illus, dj. ....*$35–$50*

Curtis, Newton. *From Bull Run to Chancellorsville.* NY, 1906. ....*$65–$85*

Curtis, Paul A. Jr. *American Game Shooting.* NY, 1927, dj. ....$48–$62

Curtis, W.H. *The Elements of Wood Ship Construction.* NY, 1919, 1st ed, illus. ....$65–$95

Curts, F. George, M.D. *A Book on Diseases of the Eye, Ear, Nose, Throat....* Kansas City, MO, nd. ....$25–$30

Curwood, James Oliver. *The Flaming Forest.* NY, 1921. ....$10–$15

Cushing, Caleb. *Outlines of the Life and Public Services ... Wm. H. Harrison.* Bos, 1840, softbound. ....$25–$35

Cushing, Harvey. *Consecratio Medici.* 1928, 1st ed. ...$40–$150

Cushing, Harvey. *From a Surgeon's Journal 1915–1918.* Bos, 1936, 1st ed. ....$35–$75

Cushing, Harvey. *Life of Sir William Osler.* Ox, 1940. .$40–$80

Cushing, Harvey. *The Life of William Osler.* Ox, 1926, 2 vols, 4th imp. ....$100–$250

Cushman, Dan. *Tall Wyoming.* NY, 1957, 1st ed, paperback. ....$5–$12

Cushman, Dan. *The Great North Trail.* NY, 1966, 1st ed, dj. ....$10–$18

Cushman, H.B. *History of the Choctaw, Chickasaw, and Natchez Indians.* Greenville, 1899. ....$160–$250

Custead, E. Rose and Elza. *Songs and Stories of Bygone Days in Fayette County.* NY, 1882, 1st ed. ....$17–$25

Custer, Elizabeth. *Boots and Saddles.* NY, 1885, 1st ed..$75–$125

Custer, Elizabeth. *Boots and Saddles.* NY, 1885, 1st ed, illus, 2nd issue, map. ....$60–$80

Custer, Elizabeth. *Following the Guidon.* NY, 1890, 1st ed. ....$45–$110

Custer, Elizabeth. *Tenting on the Plains.* Norman, OK, 1971. ....$15–$25

Custer, Elizabeth. *Tenting on the Plains.* NY, 1893. ......$25–$35

Custer, Gen. G.A. *Life on the Plains.* NY, 1874, 1st ed..$75–$100

Cutler, Carl C. *Greyhounds of the Sea.* NY, 1930. ....$30–$40

Cutler, Carl C. *Queens of the Western Ocean.* U.S. Naval Institute, 1967, illus. ....*$30–$40*

D'Aulaire, Ingri and Edgar Parin. *Leif the Lucky.* NY, 1941, illus, dj. ....*$25–$40*

D'Ewes, J. *Sporting in Both Hemispheres.* Lon, 1858, 2nd ed. ....*$95–$125*

Dabney, R.L. *Life and Campaigns of Lieut.-Gen. T.J. Jackson.* NY, 1866, 1st ed, fldg map. ....*$27–$35*

Dabney, Wendell Phillips. *Cincinnati's Colored Citizens. . . .* Cinc, 1926, 1st ed, presentation copy. ....*$195–$285*

Dahl, Roald. *Ah, Sweet Mysteries of Life.* Knopf, 1989, illus, 1st U.S. ed, dj. ....*$20–$30*

Dahl, Roald. *Fantastic Mr. Fox.* NY, 1970, 1st ed, dj. ..*$16–$20*

Dahl, Roald. *Switch Bitch.* NY, 1974, 1st ed, dj. ....*$15–$30*

Dailey, A. *Mollie Fancher, The Brooklyn Enigma.* NY, 1894, illus. ....*$18–$28*

Dale, Harrison C. (ed). *The Ashley-Smith Explor. and Disc. of Route to Pacific, 1822–1829.* Cleve, 1918, 1st ed, maps, plates. ....*$125–$200*

Dalgliesh, Alice. *The Enchanted Book.* 1947, 1st ed, dj..*$20–$35*

Dali, Salvador. *Hidden Faces.* 1944, illus, 1st U.S. ed, dj. ....*$65–$75*

Dali, Salvador. *Les Diners de Gala Felicie.* NY, 1973, dj. ....*$100–$135*

Dalton. *Swimming Scientifically Taught.* 1912. ....*$18–$28*

Daly. *Daly's Billiard Book.* Chi, 1923, illus, rev. ....*$18–$25*

Dana, Charles. *The Life of Ulysses S. Grant.* 1868. ......*$20–$25*

Dana, Charles L. *The Peaks of Medical History: Outline of Evolution of Medicine.* NY, 1926, 1st ed, illus, plates. ....*$50–$75*

Dana, Richard H. *To Cuba and Back.* Bos, 1859, 1st ed. .*$50–$75*

Dana, Richard Henry Jr. *Two Years Before the Mast.* LA, 1964, 2 vols, illus by R.A. Weinstein, slipcase. ....*$25–$40*

Dana, Richard Henry Jr. *Two Years Before the Mast.* NY, Grabhorn Press, 1936, ltd 1,000 cc. ....*$60–$77*

Dana, Richard Henry Jr. *Two Years Before the Mast.* Riverside Press, 1911, illus by E. Boyd Smith. ....$30–$40

Darby, Charles. *Bacchanalia, or, A Description of a Drunken Club.* Lon, 1680, folio, calf. ....$325–$425

Dark, Sidney. *London.* NY, 1936, 1st ed, illus by J. Pennell. ....$16–$25

Darrow, Clarence S. *Farmington.* Chi, 1904, 2nd ed, sgn. ....$250–$325

Darrow, George M. *The Strawberry: History, Breeding, and Physiology.* NY, 1966, 1st ed, illus, dj. ....$15–$23

Darwin, C. *Journal of Researches ... Countries Visited by HMS Beagle.* Hafner, 1952, rprnt, dj. ....$40–$50

Darwin, Charles. *Expression of the Emotions: Man and Animals.* Appleton, 1873. ....$75–$125

Darwin, Charles. *Insectivorous Plants.* NY, 1875, 1st U.S. ed. ....$95–$125

Darwin, Charles. *On the Origin of Species.* NY, 1963, illus by Paul Landacre, Limited Edition Club, lea, slipcase. .....$150–$200

Darwin, Charles. *On the Origin of Species by Means of Natural Selection.* Harvard Univ. Press, 1964, facs. ....$18–$25

Darwin, Charles. *On the Origin of Species by Means of Natural Selection.* Appleton, 1871, 5th ed. ....$30–$50

Darwin, Charles. *On the Origin of Species by Means of Natural Selection.* Lon, 1860, 2nd ed. ....$150–$235

Darwin, Charles. *The Descent of Man.* Lon, 1871, 2 vols. ....$400–$600

Darwin, Charles. *The Descent of Man. . . .* NY, 1871, 2 vols, 1st American ed. ....$125–$150

Darwin, Charles. *The Effects of Cross and Self-fertilization. . . .* NY, 1889. ....$38–$45

Darwin, Charles. *The Power of Movement in Plants.* Da Capo Press, 1966, facs of 1881 ed, vinyl dj. ....$25–$35

Darwin, Charles. *The Various Contrivances by Which Orchids Are Fertilized.* Univ. Chicago Press, 1984, facs of 1877 ed. ....$10–$15

Darwin, Francis (ed). *Charles Darwin's Autobiography.* Schuman, 1959. ....$15–$25

Darwin, G.H. *The Evolution of Satellites.* GPO, 1898, pamphlet. ....$5–$10

Datrell, G. *The Flight from the Flag.* Chapel Hill, 1940, 1st ed, dj. ....$20–$25

Daumas, M. *Scientific Instruments of the 17th and 18th Centuries....* Lon, 1989, rprnt of 1972 ed, dj. ....$25–$30

Davenport, Alfred. *Camp and Field Life of the Fifth New York Volunteer Infantry.* NY, 1879. ....$40–$65

Davenport, John. *Aphrodisiacs and Anti-aphrodisiacs.* Lon, 1869, buckram. ....$30–$45

David, Henry. *The History of the Haymarket Affair.* NY, 1936, 1st ed, dj. ....$18–$25

Davidoff, Zeno. *The Connoisseur's Book of the Cigar.* Paris, 1967. ....$18–$25

Davidson, Ellis. *A Practical Manual of House Painting....* Lon, 1884. ....$45–$50

Davidson, Gordon Charles. *The North West Company.* Berkeley, 1918, 1st ed, illus, maps, plates. ....$95–$145

Davidson, J.N. *Muh-he-ka-ne-ok. A History of the Stockbridge Nation.* Milw, 1893. ....$45–$55

Davies, Thomas. *The Preparation and Mounting of Microscopic Objects.* Lon, 1896, illus. ....$18–$25

Davis. *Jamestown and Her Neighbors.* Rich, 1929, 2d prntg. ....$15–$20

Davis, Brian L. *German Army Uniforms and Insignia, 1933–1940.* NY, 1972, wrps. ....$22–$30

Davis, Burke. *Grey Fox: Robert E. Lee and The Civil War.* NY, 1956, illus, maps, dj. ....$10–$18

Davis, Clyde Brion. *The Arkansas.* Farrar & Rinehart, 1940, illus by Donald McKay, dj. ....$12–$20

Davis, Daniel. *A Practical Treatise ... Justices of the Peace....* Bos, 1824, 1st ed. ....$50–$75

Davis, Jefferson. *The Purchase of Camels for Military Transportation.* DC, 1857, illus. ....$150–$200

Davis, John P. *The Union Pacific Railway: A Study in Railway Politics.* Chi, 1894. ....$48–$60

Davis, M.L. *Memoirs of Aaron Burr.* NY, 1936, 2 vols, slipcase. ....$150–$175

Davis, R.H. *The Congo and Coasts of Africa.* Lon, 1908, illus. ....$47–$65

Davis, Richard H. *The West from a Car Window.* NY/Lon, 1892, 1st ed, illus by Frederick Remington. ....$50–$65

Davis, Richard Harding. *About Paris.* NY, 1895, 1st ed, illus by Gibson. ....$14–$20

Davis, Richard Harding. *Captain Macklin, His Memoirs.* Scribner's, 1902, 1st ed. ....$14–$18

Davis, Richard Harding. *Soldiers of Fortune.* NY, 1897, 1st ed, illus. ....$20–$32

Davis, Richard Harding. *The Cuban and Porto Rican Campaigns.* NY, 1898, 1st ed, illus. ....$30–$75

Davis, Richard Harding. *The Deserter.* Scribner's, 1917, illus by Valentine. ....$25–$35

Davis, Richard Harding. *Van Bibber and Others.* NY, 1892, 1st ed. ....$35–$40

Davis, Susan Lawrence. *Authentic History of the Ku Klux Klan 1865–1877.* NY, private prntg, 1924. ....$140–$225

Davis W. *El Gringo, or New Mexico and Her People.* NY, 1857. ....$95–$150

Davis, W. *The Spanish Conquest of New Mexico.* Doylestown, PA, 1869, 1st ed. ....$450–$575

Dawson, Mrs. Nelson (Edith B.) *Enamels.* Chi, 1910, illus. ....$25–$35

Dawson, Sarah M. *A Confederate Girl's Diary.* Bos, 1913, 1st ed. ....$35–$65

Day, Clarence. *Life with Mother.* Knopf, 1937, dj. ....$12–$15

Day, Donald. *Big Country Texas.* 1st ed, dj. ....$20–$30

Day, Jeremiah. *Introduction to Algebra.* New Haven, 1814, 1st ed. ....$45–$65

Day, L.W. *Story of the One Hundred and First Ohio Infantry.* Cleve, 1894, 1st ed, illus. ....$48–$60

Day, Lal Behari. *Bengal Peasant Life.* Lon, 1892. ....$22–$30

Day, Lewis. *Art Nouveau Embroidery.* 1974, illus. ....$12–$15

Dayan, Moshe. *The Story of My Life.* NY, 1976, 1st ed, illus, photos, sgn, dj. ....$30–$45

Dayton, Ruth Woods. *Pioneers and Their Homes on Upper Kanawha.* 1947. ....$18–$32

De Beauvoir, Simone. *The Long March.* Cleve/NY, 1958, 1st ed, dj. ....$47–$60

De Beauvoir, Simone. *The Mandarins.* NY, 1956, 1st American ed, dj. ....$22–$30

De Brunhoff, Jean. *Histoire De Babar.* Paris, 1931, 1st ed. illus. ....$375–$900

De Camp, Etta. *The Return of Frank Stockton.* NY, 1913, 1st ed. ....$75–$85

De Carle, Donald. *Practical Clock Repairing.* Lon, 1968, 2d ed. ....$10–$15

De Clifford, N.F. *Egypt, the Cradle of Ancient Masonry.* NY, 1907, 2 vols. ....$65–$85

De Groat, Robert W. *Totem Poles—A Happy Hobby for Boys.* NY, Boy Scouts of America, 1930, 1st ed, wrps, illus. ...$28–$35

De La Mare, Walter. *Memoirs of a Midget.* Lon, 1921, 1st ed. ....$28–$35

De La Mare, Walter. *The Listeners.* NY, 1916, 1st U.S. ed, dj. ....$18–$30

De La Mare, Walter. *The Riddle and Other Stories.* Lon, 1923, 1st ed, dj. ....$35–$45

De La Mare, Walter. *The Veil.* NY, 1922. ....$22–$30

De Leon, T. C. (ed). *South Songs: From the Lays of Later Days.* NY, 1866, 1st ed. ....$95–$125

De Monfried, Henri. *Pearls, Arms, and Hashish.* NY, 1930, illus. ....*$18–$25*

De Monvel, M. Boutet. *Joan of Arc.* NY, nd. ....*$25–$37*

De Poncins, Gontran. *From a Chinese City.* Garden City, 1957, 1st ed, dj. ....*$50–$65*

De Quille, Dan. *Snow-shoe Thompson.* LA, 1954. .....*$325–$385*

De Roos, Frederick. *Personal Narrative of Travels in the U.S. and Canada in 1826.* Lon, 1827, illus, 2nd ed, lithos, maps. ....*$125–$165*

De Shields, James T. *Border Wars of Texas.* Tioga, TX, 1912, 1st ed, illus. ....*$125–$175*

De Smet, P.J. *Western Missions and Missionaries.* NY, 1859, 1st ed. ....*$105–$195*

De Smet, Pierre-Jean. *Oregon Missions and Travels Over the Rocky Mountains.* NY, 1847, 1st ed, plates, fldg map. ..*$225–$350*

De Voto, Bernard. *Across the Wide Missouri.* Bos, 1947, illus. ....*$30–$40*

De Voto, Bernard. *Mark Twain at Work.* 1942, 1st ed, dj..*$22–$35*

De Voto, Bernard. *The Year of Decision, 1846.* Bos, 1943, 1st ed, dj. ....*$24–$32*

De Vries, Hugo. *Species and Varieties: Their Origin by Mutation.* Chi, 1906, 2nd ed. ....*$75–$95*

De Vries, Peter. *I Hear America Singing.* Little Brown, 1976, 1st ed, dj. ....*$24–$30*

De Vries, Peter. *Slouching towards Kalamazoo.* Bos, 1983. ....*$10–$14*

De Vries, Peter. *The Handsome Heart.* NY, 1943, 1st ed, dj. ....*$175–$250*

Dean, Beryl. *Ideas for Church Embroidery.* C. Branford, 1968, illus. ....*$11–$16*

Dean, Helen. *Four and Twenty Black Birds.* Stokes, 1937, 2nd prntg. ....*$14–$20*

Dearborn, Henry. *Revolutionary War Journals of . . . , 1775–1783.* Chi, 1939, 1st ed, illus, ltd 350 cc, bds. ..*$125–$150*

Dearborn, R.F. *Saratoga Illustrated.* Troy, NY, 1872, 1st ed, illus, fldg map, clr lithos. ....*$96–$125*

Deason, Wilborn J. *Nature's Silent Call.* Waukegan, 1925, 1st ed, photos. ....*$12–$20*

Decker, John W. *Cheese Making.* WI, 1909. ....*$30–$45*

Defoe, Daniel. *Robinson Crusoe.* Phila, 1916, illus by John Williamson, teg. ....*$15–$20*

Defoe, Daniel. *The Life and Surprising Adventures of Robinson Crusoe.* Lon, 1856, illus, ½ calf, mar bds. ....*$75–$85*

Deforest, Lee. *Television—Today and Tomorrow.* 1942, 1st ed, illus. ....*$30–$50*

Deighton, Len. *Only When I Laugh.* NY, 1987, ltd 250 cc, sgn, slipcase. ....*$30–$40*

Deighton, Len. *The Berlin Game.* NY, 1983, wrps, ARC, 1st U.S. ed. ....*$20–$25*

Deite, C. *Practical Treatise on Manufacture of Perfumery.* Phila, 1892, illus, 1st American ed. ....*$40–$55*

Del Rey, Lester. *Prisoners of Space.* Presentation copy. .*$18–$25*

Delany, Samuel R. *The Einstein Intersection.* NY, 1967, 1st ed, paperback. ....*$12–$17*

Deming, Henry C. *The Life of Ulysses S. Grant.* CT, 1868. ....*$15–$20*

Dempsey, Hugh. *History in Their Blood: The Indian Portraits of N. Grandmaison.* Hudson Hills, NY, dj. ....*$32–$45*

Dempsey, Jack. *Dempsey: By the Man Himself.* 1960, 1st ed, sgn. ....*$50–$65*

Dempsey, Jack. *Round by Round.* 1940, 1st ed. ....*$28–$35*

Denison, Merrill. *Klondike Mike.* 1948, photos, dj. ....*$16–$20*

Dennys, Rodney. *The Heraldic Imagination.* NY, 1975. ....*$25–$35*

Densmore, Frances. *Papago Music.* DC, 1929, illus. .....*$14–$18*

Derby, W.L.A. *The Tall Ships Pass.* Lon, 1937, illus. ..*$75–$110*

Derleth, August. *Night's Yawning Peal.* Arkham House, 1952, 1st ed, presentation copy, dj. ....*$30–$50*

Derleth, August. *Oliver, the Wayward Owl.* Arkham House, 1945, 1st ed, dj. ....$35–$42

Derleth, August. *The House on the Mound.* Duell, Sloan & Pearce, 1958, 1st ed, sgn, dj. ....$60–$80

Derleth, August. *The Narracong Riddle.* NY, 1940, 1st ed, dj. ....$20–$40

Derleth, August. *The Shuttered Room and Other Pieces.* Arkham House, 1959, 1st ed, dj. ....$75–$100

Derleth, August. *Thirty Years of Arkham House.* Sauk City, 1970, 1st ed, dj. ....$50–$85

Derry, Joseph. *Story of the Confederate States.* Rich, 1895, 1st ed, illus. ....$35–$50

Descharnes, Robert. *The World of Salvador Dali.* Atide Books, nd, dj. ....$50–$80

Deutsch, Babette. *Take Them, Stranger.* NY, 1944, 1st ed, sgn. ....$22–$44

Deutsch, Hermann B. *The Huey Long Murder Case.* Garden City, 1963, 1st ed, sgn. ....$20–$25

Dewees, William. *A Compendious System of Midwifery.* Phila, 1847, illus, lea. ....$75–$120

Dewees, William. *A Treatise on the Diseases of Females.* Phila, 1840, illus, 7th ed, calf, steel plates. ....$48–$60

Dewey, John. *Experience and Education.* 1938, 1st ed, sgn. ....$45–$55

Dewitt, David Miller. *The Judicial Murder of Mary E. Surratt.* Balt, 1895, 1st ed. ....$185–$250

Di San Lazzaro, G. *Klee.* NY, 1957, illus, dj. ....$18–$23

Dichter, Harry. *Handbook of American Sheet Music.* Phila, 1947, wrps, 1st American ed. ....$18–$22

Dick, P.K. *The Game-players of Titan.* NY, 1963, 1st ed, paperback. ....$15–$25

Dick, Thomas. *Celestial Scenery or Wonders of the Planetary System Displayed.* NY, 1838, illus. ....$18–$25

Dick, William B. *Dick's Hand Book of Cribbage.* NY, 1885. ....$18–$25

Dickens, Charles. *Barnaby Rudge.* Phil, 1842, illus. ....$85–$110

Dickens, Charles. *Barnaby Rudge.* Lon, 1841, 1st ed, ½ mor.
....$150–$275

Dickens, Charles. *Barnaby Rudge and Hard Times.* Ticknor &
Fields, 1867, illus by S. Eytinge, Jr. ....$50–$85

Dickens, Charles. *Dombey & Son.* NY, 1847, wrps. ...$100–$210

Dickens, Charles. *Little Dorrit.* Lon, 1857, illus by H.K. Browne,
1st ed in book form, engr, ½ calf, mar bds. ....$285–$500

Dickens, Charles. *Martin Chuzzlewit.* Ticknor & Fields, 1867,
illus by S. Eytinge, Jr. ....$50–$85

Dickens, Charles. *Our Mutual Friend.* Lon, 1865, 2 vols, 1st ed
in book form. ....$250–$525

Dickens, Charles. *The Chimes.* 1931, illus by Arthur Rackman,
slipcase. ....$400–$500

Dickens, Charles. *The Life and Adventure of Nicholas Nickelby.*
Chapman & Hall, 1839, 1st ed in book form. ....$200–$385

Dickens, Charles. *The Old Curiosity Shop and Reprinted Pieces.*
Ticknor & Fields, 1867, illus by S. Eytinge, Jr. ....$50–$85

Dickerson, M.C. *The Frog Book: North American Toads and
Frogs Life Histories.* 1906, illus. ....$32–$40

Dickey, James. *Deliverance.* Bos, 1970, 1st ed, 1st prntg, dj.
....$45–$70

Dickey, James. *Sorties.* Doubleday, 1971, 1st ed, dj. .....$22–$30

Dickey, James. *The Zodiac.* NY, Doubleday, 1976, 1st ed, sgn, dj.
....$40–$45

Dickinson, Emily. *Bolts of Melody.* NY, 1945, 1st ed, Todd and
Bingham (eds). ....$25–$40

Dickinson, Emily. *The Letters of Emily Dickinson.* Bos, 1894,
2 vols, 1st ed, M.L. Todd (ed). ....$200–$350

Dickinson, Harris. *An Old Fashioned Senator.* NY, 1925, 1st ed,
dj. ....$18–$22

Didion, Joan. *A Book of Common Prayer.* NY, 1977, 1st ed, dj.
....$15–$25

Didion, Joan. *Democracy.* 1984, 1st ed, dj. ....$22–$30

Didion, Joan. *Play It As It Lays.* NY, 1970, 1st ed, dj...*$18–$25*

Didion, Joan. *Run River.* Obolensky, 1963, 1st ed, dj. ....*$75–$125*

Dietz, August. *Postal Service of the C.S.A.* Rich, 1929, 1st ed, sgn. ....*$200–$350*

Digges, Jeremiah. *Cape Cod Pilot.* Provincetown/NY, WPA, 1937, 2nd prntg, dj. ....*$22–$32*

Dillard, Maud E. *Old Dutch Houses of Brooklyn.* NY, 1945, illus, dj. ....*$10–$15*

Dillon, Richard H. *Hatchet Men.* NY, 1962, illus. ....*$10–$15*

Dillon, Wallace. *Salmon.* Chi, 1962, 1st ed, illus by Bill Barss, dj. ....*$8–$15*

Dimitri, Ivan. *Flight to Everywhere.* NY, 1944, 1st ed, illus, maps, photos. ....*$35–$50*

Dimmick, Ralph W. *Canada Geese of Jackson Hole.* WY, 1968, 1st ed, illus by K. Wiegand, photos. ....*$8–$12*

Dimock, A.W. *Florida Enchantments.* NY, 1915, illus. ..*$30–$40*

Dimsdale, Thomas J. *The Vigilantes of Montana.* Butte, 1949, photos. ....*$18–$30*

Dimsdale, Thomas J. *The Vigilantes of Montana.* Helena, 1915, 4th ed. ....*$55–$85*

Dinesen, Isak. *Out of Africa.* 1938, 1st ed. ....*$85–$145*

Dinesen, Isak. *Seven Gothic Tales.* NY, 1934, 1st ed, dj..*$35–$85*

Dinesen, Isak. *Winter's Tales.* 1942, 1st ed, dj. ....*$12–$20*

Disney. *Stories from Fantasia.* Random House, 1940. ....*$35–$48*

Disney, Walt. *Fantasia Program.* 1940, wrps. ....*$48–$75*

Disney, Walt. *Minnie Mouse and the Antique Chair.* Whitman, 1948, illus. ....*$18–$25*

Ditmars, R. *Reptiles of the World.* 1937, illus, photos....*$25–$35*

Ditmars, R.L. *Reptiles of the World.* NY, 1910, 1st ed, illus. ....*$35–$40*

Ditmars, R.L. *The Reptile Book.* NY, 1915. ....*$27–$35*

Dixon, Franklin. *Flickering Torch Mystery.* 1943, Hardy Boys, dj. ....*$10–$15*

Dixon, Franklin. *Over the Rockies with the Air Mail.* Grosset & Dunlap, nd. ....$5–$10

Dixon, Franklin. *The Mystery at Devil's Paw.* NY, 1959, Hardy Boys, dj. ....$7–$15

Dixon, Franklin. *The Mystery of Cabin Island.* Grosset & Dunlap, nd. ....$5–$10

Dixon, Franklin. *The Mystery of the Flying Express.* NY, 1941, dj. ....$10–$15

Dixon, H. *John Howard and the Prison World of Europe.* 1852. ....$35–$50

Dixon, J. *A Guide to the Practical Study of Diseases of the Eye.* Phila, 1860. ....$38–$45

Dixon, Joseph K. *The Vanishing Race, The Last Great Indian Council. . . .* NY, 1914, illus. ....$85–$125

Dixon, Peter. *Bobby Benson in the Tunnel of Gold.* 1936, 1st ed, wrps, illus. ....$24–$32

Dixon, William Scarth. *Fox-hunting in the 20th Century.* 1925. ....$25–$35

Dobell, C. *Antony van Leeuwenhoek and His Little Animals.* NY, 1958, dj. ....$14–$18

Dobell, Clifford. *Antony van Leeuwenhoek and His Little Animals.* NY/Lon, 1932. ....$65–$100

Dobell, Horace. *On the Nature, Cause, and Treatment of Tuberculosis.* Lon, 1866. ....$20–$25

Dobie, Charles C. *San Francisco's Chinatown.* NY, 1936, illus. ....$14–$22.50

Dobie, J. Frank. *Apache Gold and Yanqui Silver.* Little Brown, 1939, 1st ed, dj. ....$30–$75

Dobie, J. Frank. *The Ben Lilly Legend.* 1st ed, dj. ....$24–$32

Dobie, J. Frank. *The Mustangs.* Bos, 1952, 1st ed. ....$18–$28

Dobie, J. Frank. *The Voice of the Coyote.* Little Brown, 1949, 1st ed, dj. ....$35–$60

Dockstader, F.J. *Indian Art in North America.* Greenwich, 1961. ....$38–$45

Doctorow, E.L. *Billy Bathgate.* Random House, 1989, 1st ed, ltd 300 cc, sgn, slipcase. ....$125–$150

Doctorow, E.L. *Loon Lake.* Random House, 1980, 1st ed, dj. ....$25–$40

Doctorow, E.L. *Ragtime.* NY, 1975, 1st ed, dj. ....$30–$50

Dodge, Col. Richard I. *Our Wild Indians.* Hartford, 1882. ....$50–$100

Dodge, Emma F. *History of Pleasant Hill. . . .* Private prntg, 1938, 1st ed. ....$18–$24

Dodge, Grenville. *The Battle of Atlanta and Other Campaign Addresses, Etc.* Monarch, 1910, 1st ed, illus. ....$45–$80

Dodge, Mary M. *Hans Brinker.* Scribner's, 1926, illus by Edwards, clr plates. ....$22–$30

Dodge, Mary M. *When Life is Young.* Century Co., 1894, 1st ed, illus. ....$28–$35

Dodge, Richard I. *The Black Hills. . . .* Minn, 1965, rprnt, dj. ....$22–$32

Dodge, Richard I. *The Plains of the Great West and Their Inhabitants.* NY, 1877, 1st ed, illus, fldg map. ....$50–$75

Dodge, Theodore Ayrault. *Riders of Many Lands.* Harper & Bros., 1894, 1st ed, illus. ....$40–$55

Dodge, William E. *Influence of the War on Our National Prosperity.* NY, 1865, wrps. ....$28–$45

Dodsley, J. *A Collection of Poems in Six Vols. by Several Hands with Notes.* Lon, 1782, 6 vols. ....$200–$250

Dolan. *Yankee Peddlers of Early America.* NY, 1964, illus, dj. ....$20–$35

Dolbear, A.E. *The Telephone.* 1877, 1st ed, illus. ....$60–$95

Donleavy, J.P. *The Ginger Man.* 1958, 1st ed. ....$60–$75

Donnelly, Ivon A. *Chinese Junks.* Shanghai, 1938, illus, 2nd ed, rbnd, tip-in illus. ....$85–$100

Donnelly, Ivon A. *Chinese Junks.* Shanghai, 1938, illus, 2nd ed. ....$100–$135

Donnelly, Ivon A. *Chinese Junks and Other Native Craft.* Shanghai, 1939, illus, 3rd ed, b/w plates, tip-in clr plates. .....$65–$100

Doran, John. *Habits and Men Touching the Makers of Both.* NY, 1857, 1st ed. ....$22–$35

Dore, G. *Milton's Paradise Lost.* nd, illus by Dore. ....$25–$55

Dore, Gustave. *Gallery of Bible Stories.* nd, illus by Dore. ....$30–$45

Dore, Gustave. *The Adventures of Baron Munchausen.* Lon, nd, illus by Dore. ....$25–$35

Dormon, C. *Wild Flowers of Louisiana.* NY, 1934, wrps, illus, presentation copy, sgn. ....$32–$45

Dorr, Julia C.R. *Bermuda, an Idyl of the Summer Islands.* NY, 1884, 1st ed. ....$25–$35

Dorsey, G.A. *The Ponca Sun Dance.* Field Museum, 1905, illus. ....$25–$75

Dorsey, Sarah A. *Recollections of Henry Watkins Allen . . . Confederate Army.* NY, 1866, 1st ed, lea. ....$45–$55

Dos Passos, John. *42nd Parallel.* Harper, 1930, 1st ed. ..$14–$20

Dos Passos, John. *Adventures of a Young Man.* NY, 1939, 1st ed, dj. ....$45–$55

Dos Passos, John. *Grand Design.* NY, Houghton Mifflin, 1949, 1st ed, dj. ....$35–$50

Dos Passos, John. *One Man's Initiation, 1917.* Lon, 1920, 1st ed. ....$75–$125

Dos Passos, John. *The Big Money.* NY, 1936, 1st ed, dj..$60–$90

Dos Passos, John. *The Prospect before Us.* Bos, 1950, 1st ed, dj. ....$25–$30

Douglas, F.H. *Indian Art of the U.S.* MOMA, 1941, 1st ed, illus. ....$25–$30

Douglas, Norman. *In the Beginning.* NY, 1928, 1st American ed, dj. ....$28–$37

Douglas, William. *Of Men and Mountains.* NY, 1950, 1st ed, illus, sgn. ....$30–$50

Douglas, William O. *Of Men and Mountains.* NY, 1950, 1st ed, illus. ....$18–$25

Douglas-Lithgow, R.A. *Nantucket: A History.* NY, 1914, illus, fldg map. ....$30–$45

Douglass, Frederick. *Life and Times.* 1893. ....$15–$22

Douglass, Frederick. *Life and Times.* Hartford, 1881, illus. ....$28–$35

Douglass, Frederick. *My Bondage and My Freedom.* NY/Auburn, 1855, 1st ed. ....$125–$185

Dow, Edson. *Adventure in the Northwest.* 1st ed, dj. .....$22–$35

Dow, George Francis. *Slave Ships and Slaving.* Salem, 1927, 1st ed. ....$85–$100

Downing, A.J. *The Fruits and Fruit Trees of America.* ... NY, 1870, illus. ....$55–$70

Dowsett, H.M. *Wireless Telephony and Broadcasting.* 1924, 1st ed, illus. ....$75–$100

Doyle, Arthur Conan. *Pheneas Speaks.* NY, 1927. ....$30–$45

Doyle, Arthur Conan. *Sir Nigel.* NY, 1906, 1st American ed. ....$30–$45

Doyle, Arthur Conan. *The Adventures of Gerard.* NY, 1903, 1st ed. ....$18.50–$22

Doyle, Arthur Conan. *The Adventures of Sherlock Holmes.* NY, 1892, 1st U.S. ed. ....$150–$275

Doyle, Arthur Conan. *The Adventures of Sherlock Holmes.* Lon, 1892, 1st ed, illus. ....$900–$1,000

Doyle, Arthur Conan. *The Case for Spirit Photography.* NY, 1923. ....$40–$55

Doyle, Arthur Conan. *The Green Flag.* NY, 1900, 1st American ed. ....$35–$65

Doyle, Arthur Conan. *The Hound of the Baskervilles.* NY, 1902, 1st American ed. ....$75–$100

Doyle, Arthur Conan. *The Hound of the Baskervilles.* NY, 1902, 1st American ed, 3rd state. ....$40–$55

Doyle, Arthur Conan. *The Lost World.* NY, 1912, 1st American ed. ....$40–$75

Doyle, Arthur Conan. *The New Revelation.* NY, 1918, 1st ed. ....$50–$65

Doyle, Arthur Conan. *The War in South Africa.* Lon, 1902, 1st ed, dj. ....$35–$40

Doyle, Arthur Conan. *The White Company.* NY, Cosmopolitan Book Corp., 1922, illus by N. C. Wyeth, dj. ....$50–$60

Doyle, Arthur Conan. *The White Company.* NY, 1891, 1st U.S. ed. ....$95–$125

Doyle, Arthur Conan. *Through the Magic Door.* Lon, 1907, illus. ....$65–$135

Drago, H. *Wild, Woolly, and Wicked.* NY, dj. ....$30–$40

Drake and Caton. *Black Metropolis.* NY, 1945, dj. ....$14–$18

Drake, Benjamin. *Life of Tecumseh and of His Brother the Prophet. . . .* Cinc, 1855. ....$65–$90

Drake, D. *Dr. Daniel Drake's Letters on Slavery.* NY, 1940, 1st ed, ltd 250 cc, dj. ....$50–$65

Drake, Daniel, M.D. *Pioneer Life in Kentucky, 1785–1800.* Schuman, 1948, dj. ....$14–$18

Drake, Ensg. Robert. *The Boy Allies under the Sea, or the Vanishing Submarine.* NY, 1916, illus. ....$25–$45

Drake, Samuel A. *Old Boston Taverns and Tavern Clubs.* Bos, 1917, illus. ....$18–$25

Drane, Maude Johnston. *History of Henry County, Kentucky.* 1948, 1st ed. ....$65–$85

Draper, John William. *Thoughts on the Future Civil Policy of America.* Harper & Bros., 1865, 1st ed. ....$35–$40

Draper, Keith. *Tie a Fly.* New Zealand, 1973, 1st ed, wrps, photos, drawings. ....$7–$12

Dreiser, Theodore. *A Gallery of Women.* NY, 1929, 2 vols, 1st ed, dj. ....$38–$70

Dreiser, Theodore. *Chains.* NY, 1927, 1st ed. ....$11–$25

Dreiser, Theodore. *Dawn.* Liveright, 1931, 1st ed. ....$12–$18

Dreiser, Theodore. *Sister Carrie.* Heritage Press, 1939, illus by Reginald Marsh, slipcase. ....$10–$14

Dreiser, Theodore. *The Bulwark.* NY, 1946, 1st ed, dj. ....$15–$35

Driggs, Howard R. *The Old West Speaks.* NY, 1956. ....$25–$45

Driggs, Howard R. *The Pony Express Goes Through.* NY, 1935. ....$35–$45

Drinker, Frederick E. and James G. Lewis. *Radio—Miracle of the 20th Century.* 1922, 1st ed, illus. ....$15–$20

Driscoll, Joseph. *War Discovers Alaska.* Phila, 1943, 2nd prntg. ....$10–$15

Drummond, Henry. *Natural Law in the Spiritual World.* NY, 1888. ....$8–$12

Du Bois, Theodora. *Murder Strikes an Atomic Unit.* NY, 1946, 1st ed, dj. ....$20–$30

Du Bois, W.E.B. *Darkwater.* Harcourt, 1920, 1st ed. ....$95–$130

Du Bois, W.E.B. *Souls of Black Folk.* Chi, 1924. ....$35–$50

Du Bois, W.E.B. *The World and Africa.* NY, 1947. ....$25–$35

Du Chaillu, Paul. *Land of the Long Night.* NY, 1903, illus. ....$20–$35

Du Chaillu, Paul. *My Apingi Kingdom.* NY, 1871, illus. .$16–$25

Du Chaillu, Paul. *Stories of the Gorilla Country.* NY, 1868, 1st ed. illus. ....$95–$125

Du Maurier, Daphne. *The Scapegoat.* NY, 1957, 1st ed, dj. ....$14–$20

Du Maurier, George. *Trilby.* Harper, 1894, illus. ....$22–$35

Dubourg, George. *The Violin.* Lon, 1852, 4th ed. ....$30–$40

Dubus, Andre. *The Lieutenant.* NY, 1967, 1st ed, dj. ....$40–$65

Duchaussois, P. *Mid Snow and Ice: The Apostles of the Northwest.* Lon, 1923, 1st ed, illus. ....$60–$85

Dufer, S.M. *Over the Dead Line or Tracked by Bloodhounds.* Burlington, VT, 1902. ....$45–$55

Duffy, Herbert S. *William Howard Taft.* NY, 1930, 1st ed. illus. ....$10–$18

Duffy, Warden C. *The San Quentin Story.* 1950, 1st ed. ....$15–$20

Duggan, I.W. and Paul Chapman. *Round the World with Cotton.* DC, GPO, 1941. ....$18–$25

Dulac, Edmund. *Edmund Dulac's Picture Book.* Hodder & Stoughton, 1st ed, dj, illus. ....$125–$150

Dulac, Edmund. *Stories for the Arabian Nights.* Hodder & Stoughton, nd, illus by Dulac. ....$85–$125

Dulac, Edmund. *Stories from Hans Anderson.* Duran, nd, 1st ed, illus by Dulac, clr plates. ....$95–$135

Dulac, Edmund. *The Rubaiyat of Omar Khayham.* Garden City, 1952, illus by Dulac, clr plates, dj. ....$18–$25

Dumas, Lt. Gen. M. *Memoirs of His Own Time Including the Revolution.* Phila, 1839, 2 vols. ....$175–$250

Dunaway, W.F. *Reminiscences of a Rebel.* NY, 1913. .$130–$175

Dunbar, Alice Moore. *Masterpieces of Negro Eloquence.* NY, 1914. ....$140–$180

Dunbar, Paul Laurence. *Candle-lightin' Time.* NY, 1901, 1st ed. ....$125–$150

Dunbar, Paul Laurence. *Lyrics of Love and Laughter.* Dodd Mead, 1903, 1st ed. ....$50–$115

Dunbar, Paul Laurence. *Poems of Cabin and Field.* NY, 1908, illus, photos. ....$70–$95

Dunbar, Paul Laurence. *Poems of Cabin and Field.* NY, 1899, 1st ed, illus. ....$125–$150

Duncan, F. Martin. *Cassell's Natural History.* Cassell, 1922, illus, rprnt, b/w and clr plates. ....$22–$30

Duncan, Isadore. *My Life.* NY, 1927, illus, ltd #105/650 cc. ....$40–$50

Duncan, J. *The National History of Foreign Butterflies.* Edin, 1837, illus, 30 hand-clr plates. ....$30–$50

Duncan, J. *The Naturalist's Library, Introduction to Entomology.* Edin, 1840, illus. ....$57–$70

Dunham, Sam C. *The Men Who Blaze the Trail.* NY, 1913. ....$10–$15

Dunlap, Orrin E. *Marconi: The Man and His Wireless.* 1937, 1st ed, illus. ....$30–$40

Dunlop, William. *History of the American Theatre.* NY, 1832. ....$75–$90

Dunne, Burt. *Play Ball!* NY, 1947, 1st ed, dj, illus. ......$25–$50

Dunne, Peter M. *Early Jesuit Missions in Tarahumara.* Berkeley, CA, 1948, 1st ed, illus, fldg map. ....$40–$75

Dunsany, Lord. *The Charwoman's Shadow.* NY, 1926, 1st U.S. ed, dj. ....$25–$75

Dunsany, Lord. *The Sword of Welleran.* Lon, 1908, illus..$25–$45

Dupont, F. and W. Roepke. *Heterocera Javanica Family Sphingidae, Hawk Moths.* Amsterdam, 1941, wrps, illus. ....$35–$50

Dupont, H.A. *Admiral Samuel Francis Du Pont, United States Navy.* NY, 1926, illus, dj. ....$20–$30

Dupre, Bernard. *World Treasury of Mushrooms.* W. Germany, 1974, 1st ed, illus. ....$16–$20

Durant, John and A. Durant. *Pictorial History of American Ships.* NY, 1953, illus, dj. ....$25–$40

Durant, Will. *The Story of Philosophy.* 1926. ....$10–$14

Durant, Will and Ariel Durant. *A Dual Autobiography.* Simon & Schuster, 1977, 1st ed, illus, photos, dj. ....$10–$15

Durrell, Lawrence. *Collected Poems.* Lon, 1960, 1st ed, dj. ....$30–$35

Durrell, Lawrence. *Monsieur.* NY, 1975, 1st American ed, dj. ....$25–$35

Durrell, Lawrence. *Numquam.* Faber, 1970, 1st ed, dj. ....$20–$45
Durrell, Lawrence. *The Ikons.* Lon, 1966, 1st ed, dj. ....$12–$20

Durrell, Lawrence. *Zero and Asylum in the Snow: Two Excursions into Reality.* 1947, 1st ed. ....$45–$50

Dussauce, H. *A General Treatise on the Manufacture of Vinegar.* Phila, 1871, 1st ed. ....$28–$35

Dustin, Fred. *The Custer Tragedy.* Ann Arbor, 1965, fldg maps in pocket. ....$30–$45

Dutton, Clarence E. *Tertiary History of the Grand Canyon District.* GPO, 1882. ....$22–$35

Dwight, N. *The Lives of the Signers of the Declaration of Independence.* NY, 1851, 1st ed. ....$35–$60

Dyer, Walter A. and Esther S. Fraser. *The Rocking Chair: An American Institution.* NY/Lon, 1928, 1st ed, illus. ....$25–$45

Dyess, Lt. Col. William. *The Dyess Story (The Bataan Death March).* NY, 1944, 1st ed, dj. ....$18–$25

Dyke, A.L. *Dyke's Autmobile and Gasoline Engine Encyclopedia.* Chi, 1924, illus, dj. ....$45–$85

Earhart, Amelia. *Last Flight.* NY, 1937, 1st ed, illus, dj. ...$40–$65

Earhart Amelia. *Last Flight.* NY, 1937, illus, 3rd prntg. .....$15–$22

Earle, Alice Morse. *Customs and Fashions in Old New England.* Scribner's, 1893, sgn. ....$35–$55

Earle, Alice Morse. *Sun Dials and Roses of Yesterday.* NY, 1902, 1st ed, illus. ....$40–$50

Earle, Alice Morse. *Two Centuries of Costume in America.* NY, 1903, 2 vols. ....$55–$85

Earle, Pliny. *Memoirs of Pliny Earle.* Bos, 1898, 1st ed..$45–$80

Eastlake, William. *The Long Naked Descent into Boston.* Viking, 1977, 1st ed, dj. ....$20–$27

Eastman, Charles A. *Indian Boyhood.* NY, 1914, illus, sgn. ....$35–$45

Eastman, Edson. *Guide Book for the Eastern Coast of New England.* Concord, 1871, 1st ed, fldg map. ....$32–$45

Eastman, F. *A History of the State of New York.* NY, 1830, lea. ....$35–$55

Eastman, Mary Elizabeth. *East of the White Hills.* North Conway, NH, 1900, 1st ed, illus, photos. ....$55–$75

Eaton, Allen H. *Handicrafts of the Southern Highlanders.* illus, 2nd prntg, dj. ....$50–$65

Eaton, Elon Howard. *Birds of New York.* Albany, 1909–14, 2 vols, illus by L.A. Fuertes, clr plates. ....$45–$100

Eaton, John H. *The Life of Andrew Jackson.* Phila, 1824, 2nd ed. ....$54–$60

Eaton, John P. and Charles A. Haas. *Titanic.* NY, 1986, illus, dj.
....*$30–$45*

Eaton, Seymour. *The Traveling Bears in Outdoor Sports.* Barse & Hopkins, 1915, illus. ....*$40–$55*

Ebenstein, H. *Pierced Hearts and True Love.* Lon, 1954..*$16–$20*

Eddington, A.S. *Space, Time, and Gravitation.* . . . Camb, 1921, 1st ed. ....*$40–$60*

Edison Institute. *Dedication of Wright Bros. Home.* Dearborn, 1938, illus. ....*$18–$25*

Edison Swan Co. *The Pageant of the Lamp.* 1948, 1st ed, illus.
....*$50–$65*

Edmonds, Walter R. *Drums along the Mohawk.* Bos, 1936, 1st ed. ....*$25–$85*

Edwards, E. and J. Rattray. *Whale Off.* NY, 1932, 1st ed, illus.
....*$27–$40*

Edwards, George Wharton. *Vanished Towers and Chimes of Flanders.* Phila, 1925, illus. ....*$22–$30*

Edwards, John E. *Life of Rev. John Wesley Childs.* . . . Early, 1852, 1st ed. ....*$90–$125*

Edwards, Jonathan. *A History of the Work of Redemption.* NY, 1786. ....*$50–$80*

Edwards, T.J. *Standards, Guidons, and Colours of the Commonwealth Forces.* Lon, 1953. ....*$20–$35*

Edwards, William B. *Civil War Guns.* Harrisburg, 1952, illus, dj.
....*$22–$35*

Edwards, William B. *Story of Colts Revolver.* 1953, 1st ed, dj.
....*$42–$50*

Eickemeyer, Carl. *Among the Pueblo Indians.* NY, 1895.
....*$50–$65*

Eidinoff, Maxwell Leigh and Hyman Ruchlis. *Atomics for the Millions.* NY/Lon, 1947, 1st ed, illus by Maurice Sendak.
....*$100–$120*

Einarsen, Arthur. *Pronghorn Antelope and Its Management,* DC, 1948, 1st ed, illus. ....*$22–$30*

Einstein, Albert. *Relativity: The Special and General Theory.* NY, 1920. ....$55–$75

Einstein, Albert. *Uber Die Spezielle Und Die Allgemeine Relativitatstheorie.* wrps, 4th ed. ....$50–$65

Einstein, Albert and Leopold Infeld. *The New Physics.* Palestine, 1947, 1st Hebrew ed, sgn, dj. ....$85–$125

Eisely, Loren. *The Firmament of Time.* NY. ....$15–$25

Eiseley, Loren. *The Unexpected Universe.* NY, dj. ....$15–$25

Eisenhower, Dwight. *At Ease: Stories I Tell My Friends.* 1967, dj. ....$10–$14

Eisenhower, Dwight. *Peace and Justice.* NY, 1961, dj. .$10–$15

Eisenhower, Dwight. *The White House Years.* 1963, 1st ed, illus, dj. ....$12–$20

Eisenhower, Julie Nixon (ed). *Eye on Nixon.* Hawthorn, 1972, 1st ed, dj. ....$18–$30

Eisenschiml, Otto. *The Story of Shiloh.* Chi, 1946. ....$22–$40

Eldredge, Charles Q. *Illustrated Catalogue of Private Museum . . . Old Mystic, Conn.* CT, 1931, illus, 6th ed. ....$10–$14

Eldridge, Eleanor. *Slave Narrative.* Prov, 1842. ....$125–$150

Eliot, Elizabeth. *Portrait of a Sport: Story of Steeplechasing.* Woodstock, 1957, 1st ed. ....$20–$30

Eliot, George. *The Legend of Jubal and Other Poems.* Bos, 1874, 1st U.S. ed. ....$95–$150

Eliot, T.S. *Old Possum's Book of Practical Cats.* 1939, dj. ....$30–$45

Eliot, T.S. *The Cocktail Party.* Faber, 1950, 1st ed, dj. ..$65–$90

Eliot, T.S. *The Confidential Clerk.* NY, 1954, 1st ed, dj. ....$35–$40

Eliot, T.S. *The Elder Statesman.* NY, 1959, 1st American ed, dj. ....$55–$65

Ellett, Charles Jr. *The Position and Prospects of the Schuylkill Navigation Co.* Phila, 1845, 1st ed. ....$75–$100

Elliot, Maj. George H. *Rep. of Tour of Inspection of European Lighthouse Est. . . . 1873.* GPO, 1874, illus. ....$25–$45

Ellis, Havelock. *The Dance of Life.* Bos/NY, 1923, 6th ed. ....*$20–$25*

Ellis, Havelock. *The World of Dreams.* Bos, 1915. ....*$35–$85*

Ellis, R.A. *Spiderland.* Lon, 1912, illus. ....*$20–$35*

Ellison, Harlan. *Alone Against Tomorrow.* NY, 1971, 1st ed, dj. ....*$35–$100*

Ellison, Harlan. *Approaching Oblivion.* NY, 1974, 1st ed, sgn, dj. ....*$75–$100*

Ellison, Harlan. *Strange Wine.* Harper, 1978, 1st ed, dj..*$45–$65*

Ellison, Ralph. *Invisible Man.* 1952, 1st ed, dj. ....*$350–$650*

Elmer, Robert P. *Target Archery with a History of the Sport in America.* 1946. ....*$15–$20*

Elzas, Barnett. *The Jews of South Carolina.* Phila, 1905, ltd #104/ 175 cc. ....*$55–$65*

Embick, Milton. *Military History of the Third Division, 9th Corp. Army Potomac.* np, 1913, 1st ed, illus. ....*$37–$48*

Emerson, Adaline E. *Ralph Emerson, Jr.: Life and Letters. Edited by his Mother.* Rockford, IL, 1891, 1st ed, illus. ....*$90–$125*

Emerson, R.L., M.D. *Legal Medicine and Toxicology.* NY, 1909. ....*$28–$38*

Emerson, Ralph Waldo. *Essays. . . .* Bos, 1841, 1844, 2 vols, 1st ed. ....*$950–$1,500*

Emmons, Samuel B. *The Vegetable Family Physician. . . .* Bos, 1842. ....*$30–$40*

Endell, Fritz. *Old Tavern Signs: An Excursion in the History of Hospitality.* Houghton Mifflin, 1916, 1st ed, illus, ltd #327/500 cc. ....*$35–$45*

Endicott, William. *Wrecked among Cannibals in the Fijis.* Marine Research Soc., 1923. ....*$50–$95*

Engen, Rodney K. *Kate Greenaway.* Lon/NY, 1976, illus, b/w and clr plates, dj. ....*$10–$18*

Ephron, Nora. *Heartburn.* Knopf, 1983, 1st ed, dj. ....*$20–$28*

Eppes, Mrs. N. *The Negro of the Old South.* Chi, 1925. .*$20–$35*

Epstein, Geo. J., M.D. *Strabismus: A Clinical Handbook.* Phila, 1948, illus. ....$35–$48

Erickson. *Panhandle Cowboy.* Lincoln, dj. ....$16–$20

Esmeralda, Aurora. *Life and Letters of a 49er's Daughter.* SF, 1929. ....$35–$45

Eustis, Celestine. *Cooking in Old Creole Days.* NY, 1903, 1st ed. ....$25–$40

Evans, Augusta Inez. *A Tale of the Alamo.* NY, 1889. .$55–$68

Evans, Frederick William. *Egyptian Sphinx.* Mt. Lebanon, nd, 8 pp, wrps. ....$87–$110

Evans, G.B. *The Best of Nash Buckingham.* NY, 1973, dj. ....$25–$35

Evans, Joan. *A History of Jewelry, 1100–1870.* Boston Book & Art, 1970, 1st ed, dj. ....$32–$45

Evans, John. *Ancient Bronze Implements, Weapons . . . Great Britain and Ireland.* NY, 1881. ....$65–$85

Evans, John. *The Ancient Stone Implements. . . .* NY, 1872, 1st ed. ....$35–$45

Evans, Mary. *How to Make Historic American Costumes.* NY, 1942, illus, dj. ....$22–$35

Evans, R. *Sailor's Log.* 1908. ....$20–$30

Evans, Robley. *An Admiral's Log.* NY, 1910, 1st ed. illus. ....$27–$35

Evashevski, F. and D. Nelson. *Scoring Power with the Winged T Offense.* Dubuque, 1957, 1st ed, dj. ....$18–$22

Everett, Marshall. *The Book of the Fair.* 1904, illus. ....$27–$30

Ewing, Juliana Horatia. *The Story of a Short Life.* Dutton, 1892, illus. ....$15–$25

Eyre, John. *The European Stranger in America.* NY, 1839, 84 pp, 1st ed. ....$55–$100

Faber, Eduard. *Nobel Prize Winners in Chemistry, 1901–1961.* Abelard-Schuman, 1963, rev. ....$25–$35

Fabre, J. *Fabre's Book of Insects.* NY, 1927, clr plates..$15–$18

Fabre, J. Henri. *The Glow-worm and Other Beetles.* NY, 1919, 1st ed. ....*$16–$25*

Fagg, William and J. Pemberton. *Yoruba Sculpture of West Africa.* Knopf, 1982, 1st ed, dj. ....*$35–$40*

Fahie, J.J. *A History of Wireless Telegraphy, 1838–1899.* 1900, 1st ed, illus. ....*$125–$150*

Fahnestock, W.P., M.D. *Artificial Somnambulism, Called Mesmerism, or Animal Magnetism.* Phila, 1869. ....*$85–$125*

Fairbridge, Dorothea. *Historic Farms of South Africa.* Lon, 1931, 1st ed, illus, dj. ....*$125–$150*

Fairbridge, Dorothea. *The Pilgrim's Way in South Africa.* Lon, 1928, 1st ed. ....*$35–$50*

Fairchild, David. *Garden Islands of the Great East.* Scribner's, 1943, 1st ed, illus. ....*$16–$20*

Fairchild, David. *The World Was My Garden.* Scribner's, 1938, 1st ed, illus. ....*$18–$25*

Fairchild, T.B. *The History of the Town of Cuyahoga Falls, Summit County, Ohio.* Cleve, 1876, 1st ed. ....*$65–$75*

Fajans, K. *Radioactivity.* Dutton, 1922, 4th ed. ....*$18–$25*

Fales, E.N. *Learning to Fly in the U.S. Army.* NY, 1917, 1st ed, illus, photos. ....*$16–$20*

Fall, Bernard. *Hell in a Very Small Place.* Phila, 1966, 1st ed, dj. ....*$40–$50*

Fall, Bernard B. *Street without Joy.* Harrisburg, 1961, 1st ed, dj. ....*$425–$500*

Fall, Bernard B. *Vietnam in the Balance.* 1966, wrps. ..*$15–$30*

Farga, Franz. *Violins and Violinists.* NY, 1950, illus. ......*$25–$30*

Faris, John T. *Roaming the Rockies. . . .* Farrar & Rinehart, 1930, illus. ....*$32–$40*

Farish, Hunter D. *The Circuit Rider Dismounts.* Rich, 1938. ....*$14–$18*

Farley, Walter. *Son of the Black Stallion.* 1947, 1st ed, dj. ....*$16–$20*

Farmer, Fannie. *Chafing Dish Possibilities.* Bos, 1898, 1st ed. ....$80–$98

Farmer, Philip Jose. *The Magic Labyrinth.* Berkley, Putnam, 1980, 1st ed, sgn, dj. ....$20–$30

Farnham, Eliza W. *Life in Prairie Land.* NY, 1847. .....$67–$85

Farnol, Jeffrey. *Murder by Nail.* Lon, 1942, 1st ed. ......$35–$45

Farquhar, Roger Brooke. *Historic Montgomery County Old Homes and History.* 1952, sgn. ....$35–$50

Farr, Finis. *Black Champion.* NY, 1964, 1st ed, illus, dj..$35–$45

Farrel, James. *Calico Shoes.* NY, 1934, dj. ....$15–$40

Farrington, Oliver. *Meteorites.* Chi, 1941, wrps. ....$7.50–$12

Farrington, S. Kip. *Atlantic Game Fishing.* 1939. ....$28–$35

Farrington, S. Kip. *Atlantic Game Fishing.* NY, 1937, illus, sgn. ....$145–$185

Fast, Howard. *The Story of Lola Gregg.* NY, Blue Heron, 1956, dj. ....$10–$15

Faubion, Nina Lane. *Some Edible Mushrooms and How to Know Them.* OR, 1938, illus. ....$14–$20

Faulkner, William. *A Fable.* Random House, 1954, 1st ed, dj. ....$45–$60

Faulkner, William. *Absolom.* NY, 1936, 1st ed. ....$75–$250

Faulkner, William. *As I Lay Dying.* NY, Jonathan Cape, 1930, 1st ed, 2nd issue. ....$75–$85

Faulkner, William. *Faulkner's County.* Lon, 1955. ....$30–$60

Faulkner, William. *Intruder in the Dust.* Lon, 1949, 1st British ed, dj. ....$80–$100

Faulkner, William. *Intruder in the Dust.* NY, 1948, 1st ed, dj. ....$100–$250

Faulkner, William. *Light in August.* NY, Smith & Haas, 1932, 1st ed, dj. ....$400–$750

Faulkner, William. *Light in August.* NY, 1932, 1st ed, dj missing. ....$125–$150

Faulkner, William. *Pylon.* Smith, 1935, 1st ed, dj. ....$350–$425

Faulkner, William. *Pylon.* NY, 1967, 1st Modern Library ed, dj. ....*$15–$20*

Faulkner, William. *Pylon.* Signet, 1951, pb. ....*$15–$22*

Faulkner, William. *Requiem for a Nun.* Random House, 1951, 1st ed, dj. ....*$45–$80*

Faulkner, William. *Sartoris.* NY, 1929, 1st ed, dj. .*$1,300–$2,600*

Faulkner, William. *The Faulkner Reader.* NY, 1959. .....*$20–$25*

Faulkner, William. *The Mansion.* NY, Random House, 1959, 1st ed, dj. ....*$60–$100*

Faulkner, William. *The Reivers.* Random House, 1962, 1st ed, dj. ....*$35–$50*

Faulkner, William. *The Town.* Random House, 1957, 1st ed, dj. ....*$65–$125*

Faulkner, William. *The Town.* Chatto & Windus, 1957, 1st English ed. ....*$50–$65*

Faulkner, William. *The Unvanquished.* Signet, 1952, pb. ....*$15–$20*

Faunce, Hilda. *Desert Wife.* Bos, 1934. ....*$20–$25*

Faust, Albert. *The German Element in the United States.* Bos, 1909, 2 vols. ....*$22–$30*

Federal Writers' Project. *New Hampshire.* 1st ed. ....*$20–$40*

Federal Writers' Project. *New Jersey.* 1st ed, map. ......*$35–$40*

Feek, Andrew J. *Every Man His Own Trainer or How to Develop . . . Trotter or Pacer.* NY, 1889, 1st ed. ....*$68–$85*

Fehrenbach, T.R. *This Kind of War.* NY, 1963, 1st ed, illus, dj. ....*$24–$30*

Feiffer, Jules. *Harry, the Rat with Women.* McGraw-Hill, 1963, 1st ed, dj. ....*$20–$25*

Feldman, Leibl. *The Jews of Johannesburg.* 1956, illus, dj. ....*$18–$20*

Fellows, John. *The Mysteries of Freemasonry. . . .* Lon, nd, 1st ed. ....*$25–$32*

Felt, E.P. *Insects Affecting Park and Woodland Trees.* Alb, 1905, illus. ....*$45–$60*

Ferber, Edna. *Giant.* Garden City, 1952, 1st ed, sgn, dj..*$40–$65*

Ferber, Edna. *Giant.* Garden City, 1952, 1st ed, dj. ......*$27–$35*

Ferber, Edna. *Saratoga Trunk.* Garden City, 1941, 1st ed, dj.
....*$12–$20*

Ferguson, Erna. *Our Southwest.* NY, 1946. ....*$20–$30*

Ferlinghetti, Lawrence. *A Trip to Italy and France.* 1979, ltd 250
cc, sgn. ....*$50–$75*

Ferlinghetti, Lawrence. *The Canticle of Jack Kerouac.* Spotlight
Press, 1987, ltd ed, sgn. ....*$25–$40*

Ferlinghetti, Lawrence. *The Mexican Night.* New Directions,
1970, 1st ed, wrps. ....*$20–$25*

Ferlinghetti, Lawrence. *The Secret Meaning of Things.* 1968, dj.
....*$25–$30*

Fermi, Enrico. *Thermodynamics.* Prentice-Hall, 1937, 1st ed.
....*$28–$36*

Fermi, Laura. *Atoms in the Family—My Life with Enrico Fermi.*
1955, 1st ed, illus. ....*$8–$15*

Ferris, Benjamin G. *Utah and the Mormons.* NY, 1854, illus.
....*$60–$75*

Ferris, Timothy. *Spaceshots.* Pantheon, 1984, 1st ed, dj..*$20–$30*

Ferris, W.A. *Life in the Rocky Mountains.* Rosenstock, 1940.
....*$150–$325*

Fessenden, T. *The New American Gardener.* NY, 1828, 1st ed, lea.
....*$65–$90*

Ficklen, John Rose. *History of Reconstruction in Louisiana.* Balt,
1910, 1st ed. ....*$55–$75*

Field, Eugene. *A Little Book of Tribune Verse.* Grosset & Dunlap,
1901, illus. ....*$12–$25*

Field, Eugene. *Conky Stiles.* Cleve, 1925, wrps, ltd 153 cc.
....*$55–$65*

Field, Eugene. *Love-songs of Childhood.* NY, 1894, 1st ed.
....*$25–$35*

Field, Eugene. *The House.* NY, 1896, 1st ed. ....*$35–$65*

Field, Henry M. *History of the Atlantic Telegraph.* NY, 1866, 1st ed, illus. ....$55–$90

Field, Kathleen. *The Yellow Bird.* Oxford Univ. Press, 1930, dj. ....$22–$30

Figuier. *Mammalia, Popularly Described by Typical Species.* Lon, 1870, illus. ....$35–$45

Finck, H. *Chopin and Other Musical Essays.* NY, 1889. .$10–$20

Findley, Palmer. *Priests of Lucina: Story of Obstetrics.* Bos, 1939, 1st ed. ....$22–$35

Finger, Charles J. *Frontier Ballads Heard and Gathered By.* NY, 1927, illus, woodcuts. ....$25–$30

Finkelstein, L. (ed). *The Jews: History, Culture, Religion.* 4 vols, 1st ed. ....$55–$85

Finley, John. *Pilgrim in Palestine.* NY, 1919, illus, cloth and bds, photos. ....$14–$20

Finley, Rev. James B. *Life among the Indians.* Cinc, 1857, 1st ed. ....$55–$65

Firebaugh, W.G. *The Inns of the Middle Ages.* Covici, 1924, illus, ltd #751/ 900 cc. ....$50–$85

Fish, Carl R. *The Civil Service.* Camb, 1920. ....$15–$20

Fishbein, M., et al. *Bibliography of Infantile Paralysis, 1789–1944.* Phila, 1946, 1st ed. ....$50–$65

Fisher, Harrison. *Dream of Fair Women.* NY, 1907, illus. ....$100–$135

Fisher, Harrison. *Harrison Fisher's American Girls in Miniature.* NY, 1912, illus, clr plates. ....$40–$75

Fisher, Harrison. *Hiawatha.* Ind, 1906, 1st ed. ....$50–$95

Fisher, M.F.K. *Here Let Us Feast.* NY, 1946, 1st ed, dj..$18–$25

Fisher, Rev. H.D. *The Gun and the Gospel.* Kansas City, 1902. ....$35–$45

Fisher, Vardis. *Children of God. . . .* NY, 1939, 1st ed, dj. ....$50–$70

Fisk, Wilbur. *Calvinistic Controversy.* NY, 1851. ....$12–$18

Fisk, Wilbur. *Travels in Europe.* NY, 1838, 4th ed, lea..$22–$30

Fiske. *Dutch and Quaker Colonies in America.* Bos, 1899, 2 vols. ....$30–$40

Fiske. *John Fiske's Historical Writings.* Bos, 1902. .... $50–$65

Fiske, J.N. *Dutch and Quaker Colonies in America.* Bos, 1899, 2 vols, maps. ....$24–$32

Fiske, John. *The Beginnings of New England.* Bos, 1898, fldg map. ....$18–$20

Fiske, John. *The Discovery of America.* Bos, 1900, 2 vols, illus. ....$45–$75

Fiske, John. *The Mississippi Valley in the Civil War.* NY, 1900, 1st ed, maps. ....$22–$45

Fiske, Lt. Bradley A. *Electricity in Theory and Practice.* 1890, illus, 8th ed. ....$50–$65

Fitch, Samuel S., A.M., M.D. *A Popular Treatise on the Diseases of the Heart....* NY, 1866, illus. ....$22–$35

Fite, Emerson D. *A Book of Old Maps.* Camb, 1926, 1st ed, folio, maps. ....$150–$195

Fitz, G. *North American Head Hunting.* 1st ed, dj. ....$20–$30

Fitzgerald, F. Scott. *The Basil and Josephine Stories.* NY, 1973, 1st ed. ....$40–$50

Fitzgerald, F. Scott. *The Beautiful and Damned.* Scribner's, 1922, 1st ed. ....$65–$90

Flammarion, Camille. *Astronomy for Amateurs.* NY/Lon, 1921. ....$14–$20

Flammarion, Camille. *The Atmosphere.* NY, 1896, illus. .$28–$45

Flammarion, Camille. *The Atmosphere.* NY, 1873, illus, lithos, woodcuts. ....$75–$90

Flammarion, Camille. *The Unknown.* 1900, 1st ed. ....$18–$25

Fleischer, Nat. *50 Years at Ringside.* NY, 1958, 1st ed, dj. ....$35–$50

Fleming, Alexander (ed). *Penicillin, Its Practical Application.* Lon, Butterworth, 1946, 1st ed. ....$65–$100

Fleming, Ian. *Moonraker.* J. Cape, 1955, 1st ed. ....$60–$75

Fleming, Ian. *Octopussy and the Living Daylights.* J. Cape, 1966, 1st ed. ....$35–$50

Fleming, Ian. *On Her Majesty's Secret Service.* NY, 1963, 1st ed, dj. ....$10–$15

Fleming, Ian. *You Only Live Twice.* NY, 1964, 1st American ed, dj. ....$15–$35

Fleming, John Ambrose. *Electrons, Electric Waves, and Wireless Telephony.* 1923, 1st ed, illus. ....$45–$65

Flexner, J.T. *Mohawk Baronet, Sir William Johnson of New York.* NY, 1959. ....$18–$25

Flint, Timothy. *The Life and Adventures of Daniel Boone.* Cinc, 1868. ....$22–$30

Florain, Lambert. *Alaska, the Yukon, and Ghost Towns of British Columbia.* Seattle, 1971, illus. ....$10–$15

Foerste, Aug. F. *An Introduction to the Geology of Dayton and Vicinity.* OH, 1915, 1st ed, illus. ....$45–$55

Foley, Edwin. *The Book of Decorative Furniture.* NY, 1911, 2 vols, tip-in clr plates. ....$100–$165

Folig, Fred. *Lucy Boston on Women's Rights and Spiritualism.* NY, 1855, 1st ed, illus. ....$37–$65

Follet, Ken. *Lie Down with Lions.* Morrow, 1986, 1st American ed, dj. ....$20–$35

Follet, Ken. *The Gentlemen of 16 July.* Arbor House, 1978, 1st U.S. ed, dj. ....$22–$30

Foner, Philip S. *The Fur and Leather Workers Union.* NJ, 1950. ....$18–$25

Fonteyn, Margo. *Autobiography.* NY, 1976, illus. ....$15–$20

Forbes. *Autobmobile Giants of America.* NY, 1926. ....$12–$15

Forbes, Alexander. *California, a History of Upper and Lower California.* Lon, 1839, 1st ed, illus. ....$925–$1,200

Forbes, Esther. *Paul Revere and the World He Lived In.* Bos, 1942, illus. ....$14–$18

Forbes, Murray. *A Treatise upon Gravel and upon Gout. . . .* Lon, 1793. ....$45–$55

Forbes-Lindsay, C.H. *India Past and Present.* Phila, 1903, 2 vols, illus, fldg map. ....$22–$35

Forbush, Edward Howe. *Birds of Massachusetts and Other States.* Bos, 1925–29, 3 vols, 1st ed. ....$90–$125

Forbush, Edward Howe. *Game Birds, Wild Fowl, and Shore Birds.* 1912, illus. ....$45–$60

Forbush, Edward Howe. *History of Game Birds . . . of Massachusetts.* 1912, illus by Fuertes, plates. ....$45–$50

Forbush, Edward Howe. *Portraits of New England Birds.* MA, 1932, illus by L.A. Fuertes and Alan Brooks. ....$50–$75

Forbush, Edward Howe. *Useful Birds and Their Protection.* Bos, 1905, 1st ed. ....$22–$30

Force, Manning Ferguson. *General Sherman.* NY, 1899, 1st ed. ....$48–$65

Ford, Ford Maddox. *Great Trade Routes.* NY, 1937, 1st ed, dj. ....$75–$125

Ford, Paul. *The Greak K. & A. Train Robbery.* Dodd Mead, 1897. ....$15–$18

Foreman, Grant. *Indian Justice: A Cherokee Murder Trial at Tahlequah in 1840.* Oklahoma City, 1934. ....$75–$85

Forester, C.S. *Captain Horatio Hornblower.* Bos, 1940, illus by N.C. Wyeth, dj. ....$45–$50

Forester, C.S. *Commodore Hornblower.* Curtis Pub. Co., 1945, 1st ed. ....$16–$20

Forester, C.S. *Lord Hornblower.* Little Brown, 1946, 1st ed, dj. ....$22–$35

Forester, C.S. *Randall and the River of Time.* Little Brown, 1950, 1st ed, dj. ....$30–$38

Forester, Frank. *Fishing with Hook and Line.* Hurst & Co., 1858, illus. ....$50–$60

Forester, Frank. *Hints to Horse-keepers.* NY, 1859. ......$48–$75

Formby, John. *The American Civil War. . . .* NY, 1918, 2 vols, illus, maps. ....$30–$45

Forney, Hon. John A. *Life and Military Career of Winfield Scott Hancock. . . .* Phila, 1880, illus. ....$35–$45

Forster, E.M. *Marianne Thornton.* NY, 1956, 1st American ed, dj.
....$20–$30

Forster, Frank J. *Country Houses.* NY, 1931, 1st ed. .$125–$175

Fossett, Frank. *Colorado: Its Gold and Silver Mines.* NY, 1880, illus, 2nd ed, fldg maps. ....$30–$42

Fossett, Frank. *Colorado: Its Gold and Silver Mines.* NY, 1879, illus. ....$45–$65

Foster, R.F. *Dice and Dominoes.* NY, 1897, 1st ed. ....$22–$35

Foster, W. *New England Grouse Shooting.* NY, 1947, illus. ....$35–$47

Foster, William Z. *American Trade Unionism.* NY, 1947, sgn. ....$14–$22

Fowler, H.W. *A Dictionary of Modern English Usage.* Ox, 1926, 1st ed. ....$50–$75

Fowler, Harlan D. *Camels to California.* Stanford Univ. Press, 1950, illus, dj. ....$25–$35

Fowler, L.N. *The Principles of Phrenology and Physiology....* NY, 1842, 1st ed. ....$47–$55

Fowler, O.S. *A Home for All, or the Gravel Wall and Octagon Mode of Building.* NY, 1877, illus. ....$45–$60

Fowles, John. *The French Lieutenant's Woman.* Little Brown, 1969, 1st ed, dj. ....$28–$35

Fox, Charles K. *This Wonderful World of Trout.* Carlisle, PA, 1963, ltd ed, dj. ....$30–$45

Fox, John. *Trail of the Lonesome Pine.* NY, 1908, 1st ed..$12–$18

Fox, John R. *In Happy Valley.* Scribner's, 1917, illus by Yohn. ....$12–$30

Fox, Paula. *The Widow's Children.* Dutton, 1976, 1st ed, dj. ....$15–$20

Fox, T. *Skin Diseases.* NY, 1877, illus. ....$24–$30

Frame, Janet. *Owls Do Cry.* 1960, 1st ed. ....$10–$25

France, Anatole. *The Revolt of the Angels.* NY, 1928, illus by Frank Pape. ....$14–$20

Francetalli. *The Modern Cook.* Phila, 1878, illus. ....$25–$30

Franchere, Gabriel. *Narr. of a Voyage to the NW Coast of Amer, 1811, '12, '13, '14.* NY, 1854, 1st ed in English. ....$250–$350

Francis, Dick. *Longshot.* Putnam, 1990, 1st U.S. ed, dj..$18–$20

Francis, Dick. *Risk.* Harper, 1978. ....$25–$50

Francis, Dick. *The Danger.* Putnam, 1984, 1st U.S. ed, dj. ....$16–$25

Francis, Dick. *The Sport of Queens.* NY, 1st ed. ....$100–$150

Francis, Dick. *Trial Run.* Lon, 1978, dj. ....$15–$20

Francis, H.E. *A Disturbance of Gulls and Other Stories.* NY, 1983, 1st ed, sgn, dj. ....$16–$20

Francis, John W. *Old New York or Reminiscences of the Past Sixty Years.* NY, 1858, 1st ed. ....$30–$50

Frank, Larry. *Indian Silver Jewelry, 1868–1930.* Bos, 1978, 1st ed. ....$45–$75

Frank, Waldo. *Summer Never Ends.* 1941, dj. ....$16–$20

Frankel, H. *Finger Print Expert.* Phila, 1932, 1st ed. ....$15–$20

Franklin, John. *Narrative of a Journey to the Shores of the Polar Sea, 1819–22.* Lon, 1823, 1st ed illus, maps, plates. ...$400–$885

Fraser, C. Lovat. *Pirates.* NY/Lon, 1921–22, illus, woodcuts. ....$25–$40

Fraser, Chelsea. *Heroes of the Air.* NY, 1936, illus, maps. ....$10–$14

Freece, Hans P. *The Letters of an Apostate Mormon to His Son.* NY, private prntg, 1908. ....$65–$85

Freeman. *Studies of Travel, Greece.* NY, 1893, 1st ed. ..$18–$25

Freeman, H. *Brief History of Butte, Montana.* Shepard, 1900, 1st ed. ....$65–$75

Freeman, John R. *On the Safeguarding of Life in Theaters. . . .* NY, 1906, illus. ....$20–$30

Freeman, Joseph. *A Discourse of the Proper Training of Children.* Ludlow, VT, 1862, wrps. ....$15–$25

Fremont, Capt. J.C. *Report of the Exploring Expedition to the Rocky Mountains. . . .* DC, 1845, 2nd ed. ....$200–$300

French, A.P. (ed.). *Einstein: A Centenary Volume.* Camb, Harvard Univ. Press, 1979, illus, 2nd prntg, dj. ....*$12–$20*

French, Joseph Lewis (ed). *The Big Aviation Book for Boys.* Springfield, 1929, 1st ed, dj. ....*$22–$25*

Frere-Cook, Gervis. *The Decorative Arts of the Mariner.* 1966, 1st ed. ....*$32–$40*

Freuchen, Peter. *Ice Floes and Flaming Water—A True Adventure in Melville Bay.* Julian Messner, 1955, 3rd prntg, dj. ...*$8–$12.50*

Freud, Sigmund. *A Note on the Unconscious in Psycho-Analysis.* Lon, 1912, wrps. ....*$25–$30*

Freud, Sigmund. *Interpretation of Dreams.* NY, 1937, dj..*$30–$40*

Freud, Sigmund. *Introductory Lectures on Psycho-Analysis.* Lon, 1929. ....*$50–$80*

Freud, Sigmund. *The Problem of Lay-Analyses.* NY, 1927, 1st American ed, dj. ....*$65–$85*

Friedman, Bruce Jay. *Stern.* NY, 1962, 1st ed, dj. ....*$50–$60*

Frost, John. *American Naval Biography.* Phila, 1844, illus, ¾ mor. ....*$87–$185*

Frost, John. *Pictorial History of Mexico and the Mexican War.* Phila, 1849, maps. ....*$35–$50*

Frost, John. *The Book of Travels in Africa.* NY/Phila, 1848, illus. ....*$20–$25*

Frost, Robert. *A Boy's Will.* NY, 1915, 2nd state. ....*$45–$55*

Frost, Robert. *A Further Range.* NY, 1936, ltd 803 cc, sgn. ....*$150–$275*

Frost, Robert. *A Masque of Mercy.* NY, 1947, 1st ed. ...*$50–$85*

Frost, Robert. *A Masque of Reason.* NY, 1945, 1st ed, dj..*$35–$50*

Frost, Robert. *A Masque of Reason.* NY, 1945, 1st ed. .*$14–$20*

Frost, Robert. *A Witness Tree.* NY, 1942, 1st ed, dj. .....*$45–$60*

Frost, Robert. *In the Clearing.* NY, 1962, 1st ed, dj. ....*$20–$42*

Frost, Robert. *Steeple Bush.* NY, 1947, 1st ed, dj. ....*$25–$55*

Frost, Robert. *The Complete Poems of Robert Frost.* 2 vols, slip-case, sgn. ....*$350–$385*

Frost, Stanley. *The Challenge of the Klan.* Ind, 1924, 1st ed.
....*$25–$40*

Frothingham, Richard. *Life and Times of Joseph Warren.* Bos,
1865. ....*$12–$20*

Fry, Christopher. *The Dark is Light Enough.* NY, 1954, 1st Amer-
ican ed, dj. ....*$12–$25*

Fry, J. Reese. *A Life of Gen. Zachary Taylor.* Phila, 1848, illus.
....*$37–$45*

Fryer, Jane E. *Mary Frances Sewing Book.* illus, patterns present.
....*$55–$65*

Fryer, Jane E. *The Mary Frances Cook Book.* 1912. ....*$35–$65*

Fryer, Mary Ann. *John Fryer of the Bounty.* Lon, Golden Cock-
erel Press, 1939, illus by Averil MacKenzie-Grieve, ltd #226/ 300
cc, sgn, colophon. ....*$325–$375*

Fuchs, Sir Vivian and Sir Edmund Hillary. *The Crossing of Ant-
arctica.* Box, 1958, illus, 1st American ed, dj. ....*$14–$20*

Fuentes, Carlos. *Myself with Others.* Farrar, 1988, 1st U.S. ed, dj.
....*$15–$20*

Fuentes, Carlos. *The Old Gringo.* NY, 1985, 1st ed, 2nd prntg, dj.
....*$20–$30*

Fuller and Steuart. *Firearms of the Confederacy.* Huntington,
WV, 1944. ....*$95–$135*

Fuller, Andrew S. *The Small Fruit Culturist.* NY, Orange Judd
Co., 1867, 1st ed, illus. ....*$12–$18*

Fuller, Frederick L. *My Half Century as an Inventor.* np, 1938,
illus. ....*$24–$45*

Fuller, J.F.C. *The Generalship of Ulysses S. Grant.* NY, 1929.
....*$37–$45*

Fuller, R. Buckminster. *Nine Chains to the Moon.* Phila, 1938, 1st
ed. ....*$20–$50*

Fuller, R. Buckminster. *Synergetics.* NY, 1957, 1st ed, sgn, dj.
....*$85–$110*

Fulton, Frances I. Sims. *To and through Nebraska.* Lincoln, 1884,
1st ed. ....*$65–$100*

Fulton, J. *Palestine: The Holy Land.* 1900. ....$25–$35

Fulton, James A. *Peach Culture.* NY, 1905. ....$25–$50

Furlong, Charles W. *Let 'er Buck.* NY, 1921, 1st ed, sgn..$55–$65

Furneaux, W. *British Butterflies and Moths.* Lon, 1911, plates. ....$45–$55

Fuzzlebug, Fritz. *Prison Life during the Rebellion....* Singers Glen, VA, 1869, 48 pp, wrps. ....$60–$70

Gade, John A. *Book Plates—Old and New.* NY, 1898, illus. ....$25–$30

Gage, W.L. *Palestine: Historical and Descriptive.* Bos, 1883, illus. ....$55–$95

Gaines, P.W. *Political Works of Concealed Authorship, 1789–1809.* New Haven, 1959. ....$25–$35

Galbraith, Winifred. *In China Now.* NY, 1941, dj. ....$15–$22

Gallico, P. *Mrs. 'arris Goes to Paris.* NY, 1958, 1st ed, dj. ....$20–$40

Gallico, Paul. *The Poseidon Adventure.* NY, 1969, 1st ed, dj. ....$12–$18

Galsworthy, John. *Memories.* NY, 1914, illus. ....$30–$40

Galsworthy, John. *Swan Song.* Lon, 1928, ltd #157/525 cc, sgn. ....$50–$60

Galsworthy, John. *The Dark Flower.* Lon, 1913, 1st ed, sgn. ....$45–$65

Galsworthy, John. *The Eldest Son.* Scribner's, 1912, 1st ed. ....$22–$30

Gambrall, Rev. T. *Early Maryland: Civil, Social, and Ecclesiastical.* 1893, 1st ed. ....$16–$22

Gammons, Rev. John G. *The Third Massachusetts Regiment Volunteer ... 1861–1863.* Prov, 1906, 1st ed, illus. ....$75–$100

Ganpat. *The Voice of Dashin.* Lon, 1926, 1st ed. ....$40–$50

Gapen, D. *River Fishing.* 1978, dj. ....$16–$20

Gardiner, John. *Longevity, The Means of Prolonging Life after Middle Age.* Lon, 1874. ....$25–$30

Gardner, Erle Stanley. *Hovering Over Baja.* NY, 1961, 1st ed. ....*$22–$30*

Gardner, John. *October Light.* Knopf, 1976, 1st ed, dj. ..*$8–$15*

Gardner, John. *The Sunlight Dialogues.* Cape, 1973, 1st English ed, dj. ....*$37–$45*

Garland, H. *The Life of John Randolph of Roanoke.* NY, 1851, 2 vols. ....*$30–$40*

Garland, Hamlin. *A Son of the Middle Border.* NY, 1917, 1st ed. ....*$10–$35*

Garland, Hamlin. *Trail-makers of the Middle Border.* Macmillan, 1st ed, dj. ....*$25–$35*

Garnett, David. *First "Hippy" Revolution.* Cerrillos, NM, 1970, 1st ed, wrps, sgn. ....*$35–$40*

Garrard, Lewis H. *Wah-To-Yah and the Taos Trail.* SF, Grabhorn Press, 1936, illus, ltd 550 cc. ....*$125–$140*

Garside, Alston H. *Cotton Goes to Market.* NY, 1934. .*$18–$25*

Garwood, Darrell. *Artist in Iowa: A Life of Grant Wood.* NY, W.W. Norton, 1944, 1st ed, illus, photos, dj. ....*$25–$30*

Gask, Norman. *Old Silver Spoons of England.* Lon, 1926, illus, rbnd, ¼ lea. ....*$75–$125*

Gaster, M. *Hebrew Illuminated Bibles of the 9th and 10th Centuries.* Lon, 1901, folio, plates. ....*$85–$125*

Gatty, Mrs. A. *The Book of Sun Dials.* Lon, 1872, 1st ed, illus, plates. ....*$68–$75*

Gay, John. *The Beggar's Opera.* Lon, 1922, illus, ltd 1,000 cc, dj. ....*$45–$65*

Gee, E.P. *The Wild Life of India.* NY, 1964, 1st ed, photos, dj. ....*$25–$45*

Gee, Ernest R. *Early American Sporting Books, 1734–1844.* NY, Derrydale Press, 1928, illus, sgn. ....*$50–$66*

Gee, Hugh and Sally Gee. *Belinda and the Magic Journey.* NY, Chanticleer Press, 1948, dj. ....*$25–$35*

Geer, J. *Beyond the Lines: Or a Yankee Prisoner Loose in Dixie.* Phila, 1864, illus. ....*$40–$50*

Geer, J. *Beyond the Lines: Or a Yankee Prisoner Loose in Dixie.* Phila, 1863, 1st ed, illus. ....*$55–$65*

Geer, Walter. *Campaigns of the Civil War.* 1926, 1st ed..*$75–$110*

Geiberger, Al. *Tempo Golfs Master Key.* Norwalk, 1980, 1st ed, dj. ....*$18–$25*

Geike, Cunningham. *The Holy Land and the Bible.* NY, 1888, 2 vols. ....*$20–$30*

Geikie, James. *Mountains: Their Origin, Growth, and Decay.* Van Nostrand, 1914. ....*$20–$30*

Genet, Jean. *Miracle of the Rose.* NY, 1966, 1st American ed, dj. ....*$20–$25*

Genet, Jean. *Our Lady of the Flowers.* NY, 1963, 1st American ed, dj. ....*$40–$50*

Genthe, Arnold. *Old Chinatown.* NY, 1908, 2nd ed. ...*$80–$100*

George, Todd M. *Just Memories, and Twelve Years with Cole Younger.* np, 1959. ....*$18–$25*

Gerlach, Rex. *Fly Fishing the Lakes.* NY, 1972, 1st ed, dj. ....*$18–$25*

Germaine, Ina M. *Handbook of Drapery Patterns.* NY, 1945, illus, 3rd prntg. ....*$25–$40*

Gernsbach, Hugo. *Radio for All.* 1922, 1st ed, illus. .....*$30–$40*

Gernsbach, Hugo. *Ralph 124C41+ A Romance of the Year 2660.* 1925, 1st ed. ....*$175–$245*

Gerstaecker, Frederick. *Wild Sports of the Far West.* NY, nd. ....*$45–$60*

Gerstaecker, Friedrich. *Narrative of a Journey Round the World. . . .* NY. 1854, 3 vols. ....*$65–$75*

Gharpurey, K.G. *The Snakes of India and Pakistan.* Bombay, 1954. ....*$18–$35*

Gibbs, C.W. *Paper Negatives.* NY, 1934, 1st ed, illus. ..*$18–$25*

Gibrain, Kahlil. *The Prophet.* 1966, illus by author, 10th prntg. ....*$24–$30*

Gibson, Charles Dana. *Sketches in Egypt.* Doubleday/McClure, 1899, illus by Gibson, b/w drawings, large paper. ....*$35–$55*

Gibson, W.H. *Camp Life in the Woods and the Tricks of Trapping and Trap Making.* NY, 1881. ....$16–$25

Gibson, W.H. *Our Edible Toadstools and Mushrooms.* NY, 1895, illus. ....$85–$125

Gibson, Walter. *Houdini's Fabulous Magic.* NY, 1961, illus, dj. ....$20–$30

Gilbert, A.C. *The Man Who Lives in Paradise.* NY, 1954, 1st ed, dj. ....$32–$45

Gilchrest, Beth Bradford. *The Life of Mary Lyon.* Bos, 1910. ....$5–$10

Giles, Rosean A. *Shasta County California.* CA, 1949, 1st ed, illus, map, ltd 1,000 cc. ....$30–$50

Gillespie, W. Bro. Nelson. *History of Apollo Lodge No.13 ... Troy, N.Y.* NY, 1886, illus, plates. ....$30–$40

Gillette, Mrs. F. L. *White House Cook Book.* Chi, 1889..$65–$85

Gilley. *Art of Bird Carving.* 1976, sgn, dj. ....$25–$30

Gimonds and McEnnis. *The Story of Manual Labor.* Chi, 1887, illus. ....$18–$25

Ginsberg, Allen. *Bixby Canyon Ocean Path Word Breeze.* Botham, 1972, sgn, ltd 100 cc. ....$100–$125

Ginsberg, Allen. *Iron Horse.* NY, 1972, 1st ed, sgn. ......$35–$50

Ginsberg, Allen. *Planet News 1961–1967.* CA, 1968, 1st U.S. ed. ....$25–$35

Ginzburg, R. *An Unhurried View of Erotica.* NY, 1958, slipcase. ....$15–$20

Glackens, Ira. *William Glackens and the Ashcan Group.* NY, 1957, illus. ....$20–$25

Gladstone, J.H. *Michael Faraday.* Lon, 1874, 2nd ed, repairs. ....$22–$35

Glasgow, Ellen. *They Stoop to Folly.* Garden City, 1929, 1st ed, dj. ....$45–$60

Glasser, Otto. *Dr. Wilhelm C. Rontgen.* 1945, 1st ed, dj..$25–$50

Glazier, Capt. Willard. *Down the Great River.* Phila, 1893. ....$25–$35

Glazier, Capt. Willard. *Headwaters of the Mississippi.* NY, 1893.
....*$30–$45*

Glenister, A.G. *Birds of the Malay Peninsula.* Oxford Univ. Press, 1951, illus, dj. ....*$25–$50*

Glover, T. *An Account of Virginia and Their Manner of Planting Tobacco. . . .* Ox, 1904, ltd 250 cc, lea, bds. ....*$65–$95*

Glueck, Nelson. *River Jordan.* Phila, 1946, illus, dj. ....*$7–$14*

Godbey, J.E. and A.H. Godbey. *Light in Darkness.* St. Louis, 1891. ....*$14–$20*

Goddard, Henry Herbert. *The Kallikak Family.* NY, 1916.
....*$18–$25*

Godwin, G.N. *A Guide to the Maltese Islands.* Malta, 1880, fldg map. ....*$32–$45*

Godwin, Gail. *Glass People.* NY, 1972, 1st ed, dj. ....*$35–$45*

Goebbels, Joseph. *Kampf um Berlin.* Munchen, 1938, illus.
....*$24–$30*

Goerg, Alfred J. *Pacific and Northwest Hunting.* NY, 1952, 1st ed, dj. ....*$15–$22*

Gold, Herbert. *Fathers.* NY, 1966, 1st ed, dj. ....*$18–$28*

Gold, Herbert. *Love and Like.* NY, 1960, 1st ed, sgn, presentation copy, dj. ....*$40–$65*

Gold, Herbert. *The Optimist.* Atlantic/Little Brown, 1959, 1st ed, dj. ....*$20–$25*

Goldberg, Alfred. *A History of the United States Air Force.* NJ, 1957, 1st ed, illus, photos. ....*$18–$25*

Goldberg, R. *Rube Goldberg's Guide to Europe.* NY, 1954, 1st ed, presentation copy, sgn. ....*$30–$45*

Goldenberg, Samuel. *Lace: Its Origin and History.* NY, 1904, 1st ed, illus, presentation copy. ....*$50–$85*

Golding, William. *Lord of the Flies.* NY, 1955, 1st American ed.
....*$100–$350*

Golding, William. *Rites of Passage.* NY, 1980, 1st ed, dj..*$20–$25*

Golding, William. *The Pyramid.* Faber, 1967, 1st ed, dj..*$40–$45*

Golding, William. *The Pyramid.* Harcourt, 1967, 1st U.S. ed, dj.
....*$28–$35*

Goldman, Emma. *The Place of the Individual in Society.* Chi, Free Society Forum, nd, wrps. ....*$35–$45*

Goldman, Emma. *The Social Significance of the Modern Drama.* Bos, 1914. ....*$30–$67*

Goldschmidt, S.G. *Stable Wise.* 1929. ....*$18–$25*

Goldsmith, Oliver. *The Vicar of Wakefield.* Phila, 1929, illus by Arthur Rackham, clr plates. ....*$150–$225*

Goldwater, Barry. *Arizona.* 1978, 1st ed, dj. ....*$28–$35*

Goldwater, Barry. *Delightful Journey down the Green and Colorado Rivers.* Tempe, 1970, illus. ....*$20–$30*

Goldwater, Barry. *The Face of Arizona.* np, 1964, 1st ed, ltd #769/ 1,000 cc, sgn. ....*$125–$180*

Gommez, R. *Cake Decoration: Flower and Classic Piping.* Lon, 1899. ....*$65–$90*

Goodall. *How to Train Your Own Gun Dog.* 1983. ....*$11–$14*

Goodison, N. *English Barometers, 1680–1860. . . .* Potter, 1968, 1st ed, illus, plates, dj. ....*$60–$75*

Goodman, Paul. *Compulsory Mis-Education.* NY, 1964, dj.
....*$15–$20*

Goodman, Paul. *Hawkweed.* Random House, 1967, 1st ed, dj.
....*$16–$20*

Goodman, Paul. *Speaking and Language: Defense of Poetry.* 1971, dj. ....*$10–$18*

Goodman, Paul. *The Break Up of Our Camp.* NY, 1949, dj.
....*$25–$35*

Goodrich, L. *Winslow Homer.* NY, 1944. ....*$35–$47*

Goodrich, Samuel Griswold. *History of the Indians of North and South America.* NY, 1844, 1st ed, illus. ....*$45–$60*

Goodrich, Ward L. *The Modern Clock.* Chi, 1905, 1st ed, illus.
....*$40–$55*

Goodrich-Freer, A. *Things Seen in Palestine.* NY, 1913..*$45–$65*

Goodwin, C.C. *The Comstock Club.* SLC, 1891, 1st ed. .*$50–$75*

Goodwin, Grace Duffield. *Anti-Suffrage: Ten Good Reasons.* NY, 1913. ....$20–$25

Goodwyn, Frank. *Lone-star Land.* NY, 1955. ....$14–$20

Goody, J. *Death, Property, and the Ancestors.* Stanford, 1962, illus. ....$25–$35

Goodyear, W.A. *The Coal Mines of the Western Coast of the United States.* SF, 1877, 1st ed. ....$75–$100

Goor, A. and M. Nurock. *The Fruits of the Holy Land.* Jerusalem, 1968, dj. ....$25–$30

Gorbachev, Mikhail. *Perestroika Is the Concern of All Soviet Peoples.* Moscow, 1989, wrps, 1st English ed. ....$35–$40

Gordimer, Nadine. *A Sport of Nature.* NY, 1987, 1st ed, dj. ....$20–$25

Gordimer, Nadine. *Burger's Daughter.* Viking, 1979, 1st U.S. ed, dj. ....$28–$35

Gordimer, Nadine. *July's People.* Viking, 1981, 1st ed, dj. ....$25–$33

Gordimer, Nadine. *My Son's Story.* Farrar, 1990, 1st U.S. ed, dj. ....$18–$25

Gordon, A.C. and Page Thomas Nelson. *Befo' de War—Echoes in Negro Dialect.* NY, 1888. ....$38–$50

Gordon, Armistead Churchill. *In the Picturesque Shenandoah Valley.* Rich, 1930, 1st ed. ....$30–$45

Gordon, Elizabeth. *Bird Children.* Volland, 1912, illus by M.T. Ross. ....$50–$85

Gordon, Elizabeth. *Flower Children.* Volland, 1910, illus by M.T. Ross, bds. ....$30–$50

Gordon, Elizabeth. *Really-so Stories.* Joliet, 1924, 1st ed, illus by Rae. ....$18–$28

Gordon, John B. *Reminiscences of The Civil War.* NY, 1904. ....$40–$80

Gordon, T. *A Gazetteer of the State of Pennsylvania.* Phila, 1832, 1st ed, lea. ....$55–$65

Gordon, T. *The History of Pennsylvania.* Phila, 1829, 1st ed. ....$95–$125

Gordon, T.F. *Gazetteer of the State of New York.* Phila, 1836.
....*$65–$85*

Goren, Charles. *The Sports Illustrated Book of Bridge.* NY, 1961,
illus, dj, slipcase. ....*$50–$70*

Gorey, Edward. *Amphigorey, Too.* Putnam, 1975, 1st ed, dj.
....*$25–$35*

Gorey, Edward. *The Blue Aspic.* NY, 1968, 1st ed, dj. ...*$35–$52*

Gorey, Edward. *The Unstrung Harp.* Duell, 1953, 1st ed, dj.
....*$150–$300*

Gorey, Edward. *The Utter Zoo Alphabet.* 1st ed. dj. .....*$20–$27*

Gorey, Edward. *Water Flowers.* NY, 1982, 1st ed, dj, sgn.
....*$50–$70*

Gorky, Maxim. *Orloff and His Wife.* NY, 1901, 1st English ed.
....*$30–$40*

Gorrie, P. Douglas. *Black River and Northern New York Confer-
ence Memorial—2nd Ser.* Watertown, 1881. ....*$35–$55*

Gould, Charles E., Jr. *The Toad at Harrow.* Lon, 1981, ltd 500
cc. ....*$25–$30*

Gould, E. *The Housing of the Working People.* DC, GPO, 1895,
illus. ....*$24–$35*

Gould, J. *A Century of Birds from the Himalaya Mountains.* Lon,
1832, 1st ed, illus, large folio, 80 hand-clr plates. ..*$7,800–$10,000*

Gould, J. *Birds of Australia.* Lon, 1967, plates. ....*$25–$30*

Gould, J. *The Birds of Great Britain.* Lon, 1873, 5 vols, illus,
large folio, 367 clr plates. ....*$20,000–$58,000*

Gould, Marcus. *Report of the Trial of Friends.* Phila, 1829, ¼
mor. ....*$95–$150*

Gould, Mary E. *Early American Wooden Ware and Other Kitchen
Utensils.* Springfield, MA, 1942, illus. ....*$22–$32*

Gould, R.T. *The Case for the Sea Serpent.* Lon, 1930, illus.
....*$55–$95*

Gould, R.T. *The Loch Ness Monster.* Lon, 1934, illus. ..*$25–$40*

Grafton, Sue. *F is for Fugitive.* NY, 1989, dj. ....*$45–$60*

Graham, Col. W.A. *The Custer Myth.* Harrisburg, 1953, illus.
....*$50–$75*

Graham, D.M. *The Life of Clement Phinney.* NH, Free Will Baptist, 1851. ....*$40–$45*

Graham, F. Lanier. *Hector Guimard.* NY, MOMA, 1970, illus.
....*$8–$14*

Graham, Stephen. *Through Russian Central Asia.* Lon, 1916, illus, fldg map, photos. ....*$20–$30*

Grahame, Kenneth. *Dream Day.* Lon, 1902, illus by Maxfield Parrish. ....*$85–$150*

Grahame, Kenneth. *The Wind in the Willows.* Scribner's, 1908, 1st ed. ....*$65–$75*

Grainge, William. *Daemonologia: Discourse on Witchcraft.* Harrogate, 1882. ....*$24–$30*

Granados, J. *The Birth of Israel.* Knopf, 1948, 1st ed...*$13–$18*

Grand, Gordon. *The Silver Horn.* NY, 1932, illus by J. Alden Twachtman, ltd 950 cc. ....*$75–$130*

Grand Rapids & Indiana Railroad. *Michigan in Summer.* 1898, 22 pp, wrps, illus, brochure, fldg maps. ....*$30–$48*

Granger, Stewart. *Sparks Fly Upward.* NY, 1981, 1st ed, dj.
....*$22–$30*

Grant, Blanche C. (ed). *Kit Carson's Own Story of His Life.* Taos, 1926, softbound. ....*$75–$125*

Grant, Douglas. *The Fortunate Slave: An Illustration of African Slavery. . . .* Lon, 1968, 1st ed, dj. ....*$33–$45*

Grant, E. *The Peasantry of Palestine.* Bos, 1907. ....*$20–$25*

Grant, George F. *Montana Trout Flies.* np, 1971, 1st ed, wrps, unpaged. ....*$20–$35*

Grant, George Monro (ed). *Picturesque Canada: The Country As It Was and Is.* Tor, 1882, 1st ed, mor, engr. ....*$125–$200*

Grant, Madison. *The Passing of the Great Race.* NY, 1926, sgn, presentation copy. ....*$18–$27*

Grant, Ulysses S. *Personal Memoirs of U.S. Grant.* NY, 1885, 2 vols, 1st ed. ....*$50–$85*

Grant, Ulysses S. *Report of Lt.-General U.S. Grant . . . 1864–65.* DC, 1865, 44 pp, wrps. ....$75–$90

Grass, Gunter. *Cat and Mouse.* NY, 1963, 1st English ed, dj. ....$25–$30

Grass, Gunter. *Local Anaesthetic.* 1969, 1st ed, dj. ....*$16–$20*

Grass, Gunter. *The Tin Drum.* Pantheon, 1962, 1st U.S. ed, dj. ....$70–$150

Grau, Shirley Ann. *The Condor Passes.* Knopf, 1971, 1st ed, dj. ....$25–$30

Grau, Shirley Ann. *The Hard Blue Sky.* Knopf, 1958, 1st ed, dj. ....$30–$40

Grau, Shirley Ann. *The House on Coliseum Street.* NY, 1964, 1st ed, dj. ....$25–$35

Grau, Shirley Ann. *The Keepers of the House.* NY, 1964, 1st ed, sgn, dj. ....$55–$65

Graves, Jackson A. *My Seventy Years in California, 1857–1927.* Los Angeles, Times-Mirror, 1927. ....$60–$85

Graves, Robert J. *Clinical Lectures on the Practice of Medicine.* Lon, 1884, 2 vols. ....$20–$35

Gray, Alonzo and C.B. Adams. *Elements of Geology.* Harper, 1853, lea. ....$15–$25

Gray, Asa. *Gray's Botanical Text-book (6th Ed).* American Book Co., 1879, vol 1. ....$60–$125

Gray, Asa. *Introduction to Structural and Systematic Botany.* NY, 1860, 5th ed. ....$25–$32

Gray, Henry. *Anatomy, Descriptive and Surgical.* Phila, 1862, 2nd American ed, lea. ....$95–$120

Gray, W., et al. *The New Fun with Dick and Jane.* Scott, 1951. ....$28–$35

Gray, W., et al. *The New Fun with Dick and Jane.* Scott, 1946–47. ....$30–$45

Gray, W., et al. *The New Fun with Dick and Jane.* Scott, 1940. ....$38–$50

Gray, W.H. *A History of Oregon, 1792–1849. . . .* Portland, 1870, 1st ed. ....$175–$225

Grayson, William J. *The Hireling and the Slave Chicora and Other Poems.* Charleston, 1856, 1st ed. ....$45–$65

Greeley, Horace. *Political Text Book for 1860.* NY, 1860..$35–$65

Greeley, Horace. *The American Conflict.* Hartford, 1865, 2 vols. ....$40–$50

Greely, Adolphus W. *Handbook of Alaska.* 1909, map. .$17–$25

Greely, Adolphus W. *Three Years of Arctic Service.* NY, 1886, 2 vols, 1st ed, illus, pocket maps. ....$120–$300

Green. *History of English People.* Lon, 1895, 8 vols. ....$50–$75

Green, Arthur R. *Sundials, Incised Dials, or Mass Clocks.* NY/ Tor, 1926, 1st ed, illus. ....$30–$45

Green, Calvin and Seth Y. Wells. *A Brief Exposition of . . . the Shakers.* NY, 1851. ....$115–$150

Green, Edwin L. *The Indians of South Carolina.* Columbia, SC, 1904, 1st ed. ....$45–$75

Green, Jerry. *Year of the Tiger.* 1969, 1st ed, dj. ....$15–$20

Green, Lydia Marshall. *Perennials in a Bishop's Garden.* Phila, 1953, sgn, dj. ....$20–$30

Green, S. *Crime: It's Nature, Causes, Treatment, and Prevention.* 1889, 1st ed. ....$22–$29

Greene, Graham. *Our Man in Havana.* NY, 1958. ....$25–$35

Greene, Graham. *Our Man in Havana.* Lon, 1958, dj. .$50–$60

Greene, Graham. *The Comedians.* NY, 1966, 1st ed, dj. .$15–$26

Greene, Graham. *The End of the Affair.* NY, 1951, 1st American ed, dj. ....$45–$65

Greene, Graham. *The Human Factor.* Simon, 1978, 1st U.S. ed, dj. ....$25–$30

Greene, Graham. *The Man Within.* NY, 1947, dj. ....$25–$35

Greene, Graham. *The Shipwrecked.* NY, 1953, dj. ....$35–$45

Greene, Graham. *Travels with My Aunt.* 1970, 1st ed, dj..$8–$15

Greene, W.T. *Favourite Foreign Birds for Cages and Aviaries.* Lon, 1891, illus, engr. ....$25–$38

Greene, Welcome Arnold. *The Providence Plantations.* Prov, 1886, 1st ed, illus, folio. ....$45–$55

Greenwalt, Crawford H. *Hummingbirds.* 1960, illus, dj.
....*$145–$175*

Greenway, James A. Jr. *Extinct and Vanishing Birds of the World.* NY, 1958, illus. ....*$28–$35*

Gregg, Josiah. *Commerce on the Prairies.* dj. ....*$18–$20*

Gregory, Dick. *Dick Gregory's Political Primer.* NY, 1968, dj.
....*$15–$20*

Gremillion, Nelson. *Company G, 1st Regiment, Louisiana Cavalry, CSA.* np, private prntg, 1986, 1st ed. ....*$28–$37*

Grenfell, Wilfred. *40 Years for Labrador.* NY, 1932, presentation copy, sgn, dj. ....*$44–$50*

Grenfell, Wilfred. *A Labrador Doctor.* NY, 1919, illus, original sketch on flyleaf by author. ....*$50–$65*

Grenfell, Wilfred. *Adrift on an Ice Pan.* Bos, 1909, illus, 5th ed.
....*$18–$25*

Grenfell, Wilfred. *Down North on Labrador.* Chi, 1911, 1st ed, illus. ....*$16–$20*

Grenfell, Wilfred. *The Romance of Labrador.* NY/Lon, 1934, illus. ....*$22–$30*

Grey, Zane. *Arizona Ames.* Grosset & Dunlap, 1932, rprnt, dj.
....*$7–$9*

Grey, Zane. *Forlorn River.* Grosset & Dunlap, 1927, rprnt, dj.
....*$8–$12*

Grey, Zane. *Riders of the Purple Sage.* Grosset & Dunlap, 1940, rprnt, dj. ....*$10–$14*

Grey, Zane. *Roping Lions in the Grand Canyon.* NY, nd. .*$15–$20*

Grey, Zane. *Tales of Fishes.* 1919, 2nd prntg. ....*$40–$47*

Grey, Zane. *Tales of Fishing Virgin Seas.* Harper, 1925, 1st ed.
....*$70–$95*

Grey, Zane. *Tales of Fresh-water Fishing.* NY/Lon, 1928, 1st ed.
....*$95–$125*

Grey, Zane. *Tales of Lonely Trails.* NY, Harper, 1922, 1st ed, illus.
....*$55–$115*

Grey, Zane. *Tales of Southern Rivers.* Grosset & Dunlap, rprnt, dj. ....*$30–$100*

Grey, Zane. *Tales of the Angler's Eldorado.* NY, Grosset & Dunlap, 1926, illus, photos, dj. ....*$45–$75*

Grey, Zane. *Tappan's Burro.* Harper, 1923, 1st ed. ....*$35–$50*

Grey, Zane. *The Desert of Wheat.* Grosset & Dunlap, 1919, rprnt, dj. ....*$7–$10*

Grey, Zane. *The Hash Knife Outfit.* Grosset & Dunlap, 1933, rprnt, dj. ....*$8–$13*

Grey, Zane. *The Last of the Plainsmen.* NY, 1908, 1st ed, illus by Zane Grey, dj. ....*$200–$300*

Grey, Zane. *The Man of the Forest.* Grosset & Dunlap, 1920, rprnt, dj. ....*$8–$12*

Grey, Zane. *The Mysterious Rider.* NY, 1921, 1st ed. ....*$35–$45*

Grey, Zane. *The Red Headed Outfield.* NY, 1915, dj. ....*$14–$18*

Grey, Zane. *The Shepherd of Guadaloupe.* Grosset & Dunlap, 1930, rprnt, dj. ....*$10–$15*

Grey, Zane. *The Thundering Herd.* Grosset & Dunlap, 1925, rprnt, dj. ....*$10–$14*

Grey, Zane. *Wanderer of the Wasteland.* Grosset & Dunlap, 1923, rprnt, dj. ....*$10–$14*

Gridley, A.D. *History of the Town of Kirkland.* NY, 1874, sgn. ....*$45–$55*

Griffen, Jeff. *The Hunting Dogs of America.* NY, 1964. .*$14–$18*

Griffen, J.H. *Church and the Black Man.* 1969, illus. ....*$20–$25*

Griffiths, Capt. *The Modern Fencer.* Lon, illus, 6th ed..*$18–$25*

Grimm. *Snow-White and the Seven Dwarfs.* Chi, Rand McNally, 1938, illus. ....*$10–$22*

Grimm Bros. *Little Brother and Little Sister, and Other Tales.* NY, 1917, illus by Arthur Rackham. ....*$30–$40*

Grimm, Wilhelm. *Dear Mili.* 1988, 1st ed, illus by Maurice Sendak, dj. ....*$20–$35*

Grimshaw, Beatrice. *Isles of Adventure.* Lon, 1930, 1st ed, illus. ....$20–$35

Grinnel, J., H.C. Bryant, and T.I. Storer. *The Game Birds of California.* Berkeley, 1918, illus, dj. ....$175–$350

Grinnel, G. *American Duck Shooting.* NY, 1901. ....$45–$65

Grinnel, George Bird. *Blackfoot Lodge Tales.* NY, 1913..$30–$45

Grinnel, George Bird. *Blackfoot Lodge Tales.* NY, 1892, 1st ed. ....$50–$85

Grinnel, George Bird. *The Fighting Cheyennes.* NY, 1915, maps. ....$100–$125

Grinnel, George Bird. *The Indians of Today.* NY, 1915, 3rd prntg, plates. ....$45–$75

Griswold, Freeman C. *Canadian Excursion, Summer of 1885.* MA, 1885, wrps. ....$15–$25

Groot, Roy A. (ed). *The Hive and the Honey Bee.* Dadant, 1949. ....$25–$35

Gross, Chaim. *The Technique of Wood Sculpture.* NY, 1965, illus, photos, dj. ....$9–$13

Gross, H.I. *Antique and Classic Cameras.* NY, 1965, 1st ed, illus, dj. ....$35–$50

Grover, Eulalie Osgood. *The Overall Boys.* 1st ed, illus by Bertha L. Corbett. ....$45–$50

Grover, Eulalie Osgood. *The Sunbonnet Babies Book.* Rand McNally, 1928, illus by Bertha L. Corbett. ....$20–$30

Grover, Eulalie Osgood. *The Sunbonnet Babies Book.* NY, 1902. ....$30–$40

Gruelle, Johnny. *Raggedy Andy Stories.* Donohue, 1920, illus by Gruelle, dj. ....$20–$30

Gruelle, Johnny. *Raggedy Ann and Andy and the Camel with the Wrinkled Knees.* Bobbs-Merrill, 1951. ....$8–$10

Gruelle, Johnny. *Raggedy Ann Stories.* Volland, 1918, 1st ed, illus by Gruelle. ....$25–$45

Gruelle, Johnny. *Raggedy Ann's Alphabet Book.* Donohue, 1925, dj. ....$30–$40

Guggisberg, A.W. *The Game Animals of Africa.* Nairobi, 1959, illus. ....*$5–$12*

Gunnison, J.W. *The Mormons.* Phila, 1852, 1st ed. ...*$150–$200*

Gunther, Erna. *Indian Life on the Northwest Coast of North America. . . .* Univ. of Chicago Press, 1972, illus, dj. ......*$15–$20*

Gunther, R.T. *Historic Instruments for the Advancement of Science.* Humphrey Milford, 1925, glassine wrapper. ....*$25–$35*

Guptill, A. *Norman Rockwell Illustrator.* NY, 1946, 1st ed, dj. ....*$30–$45*

Gussow, H.T. and W.S. Odell. *Mushrooms and Toadstools.* Ottawa, 1927, 1st ed, illus. ....*$27–$38*

Guthrie, A.B. *The Big Sky.* Sloane, 1947, 1st ed, dj. ......*$45–$50*

Guthrie, A.B. *The Way West.* NY, 1949. ....*$25–$35*

Hagedorn, Hermann. *Boy's Life of Theodore Roosevelt.* Harper, 1918. ....*$24–$32*

Hagedorn, Hermann. *Roosevelt in the Badlands.* Bos/NY, 1921, illus, dj. ....*$40–$60*

Haggard, H. Rider. *Allan's Wife and Other Tales.* Lon, 1915, illus, rprnt. ....*$15–$20*

Haggard, H. Rider. *Ayesha.* NY, 1905. ....*$45–$65*

Haggard, H. Rider. *Cleopatra.* Lon, 1893. ....*$75–$95*

Haggard, H. Rider. *Dr. Thorne.* Lon, 1898, 1st ed. .....*$85–$100*

Haggard, H. Rider. *Finished.* NY, Longmans Green, 1917, 1st U.S. ed. ....*$35–$45*

Haggard, H. Rider. *Maiwa's Revenge.* Lon, 1888, 1st ed. ....*$50–$115*

Haggard, H. Rider. *Red Eve.* Grosset & Dunlap, rprnt. .*$20–$30*

Haggard, H. Rider. *Regeneration.* Lon, Longmans Green, 1910, 1st ed, presentation copy. ....*$225–$350*

Haggard, H. Rider. *The Ancient Allan.* NY, Longmans Green, 1920, 1st American ed. ....*$25–$35*

Haggard, H. Rider. *When the World Shook.* Longmans Green, 1919, 1st ed. ....*$30–$37*

Haggard, Lilias Rider. *I Walked by Night.* 1936, 1st ed..*$38–$47*

Hahn, W.L. *Some Habits and Sensory Adaptations of Cave Inhabiting Bats.* DC, 1908, wrps. ....$14–$20

Haig-Brown, Roderick. *The Western Angler.* Morrow, 1947. ....$25–$35

Haig-Brown, Roderick. *The Western Angler.* Derrydale Press, 1939, 2 vols, ltd ed, map. ....$375–$450

Haines, Elijah M. *The American Indian (Uh-Nish-In-Na-Ba).* Chi, 1888. ....$90–$100

Haines, Flora E. *A Keramic Study.* Bangor, ME, 1895. .$18–$25

Haines, Francis. *The Nez Percees.* Univ. of Oklahoma, 1955, 1st ed. ....$50–$75

Hajek, Karl. *Weidemanshiel!* Czechoslovakia, 1954, illus, ribbon bookmark, photos, dj. ....$14–$22

Hakes, H. *Landmarks of Steuben County, NY.* Syracuse, 1896. ....$95–$130

Haldane, J.S. *Respiration.* New Haven, 1922. ....$28–$35

Haldeman, Joe. *All My Sins Remembered.* St. Martin, 1977, 1st American ed, dj. ....$18–$24

Hale, Edwin M. *A Systematic Treatise on Abortion.* Chi, 1866, illus, clr plates. ....$65–$95

Haley, Alex. *Roots.* Doubleday, 1976, 1st ed, dj. ....$50–$60

Hall, Ben. *Best Remaining Seats.* NY, 1961, 1st ed, dj...$25–$30

Hall, Charles W. *Adrift in the Ice-fields.* Bos, 1877, illus..$28–$55

Hall, Donald. *A Roof of Tiger Lilies: Poems.* Lon, 1964, 1st ed, sgn, dj. ....$30–$40

Hall, Dr. W.W. *Sleep.* NY, 1865, 5th ed. ....$35–$55

Hall, Dr. W.W. *Soldier Health.* NY, 1861, wrps. ....$30–$65

Hall, Fred S. *Sympathetic Strikes and Sympathetic Lockouts.* NY, 1898, softbound. ....$25–$35

Hall, Hiland. *History of Vermont.* Alb, 1868, 1st ed, inscr. ....$100–$125

Hall, James Norman. *My Island Home.* Bos, 1952, 1st ed, dj. ....$16–$22

Hall, Radclyffe. *The Well of Loneliness.* NY, 1928, 1st ed, ltd 500 cc, boxed. ....$45–$50

Halliday, Andrew. *Observations on Emphysema.* ... Lon, 1807, bds. ....$150–$200

Hallock, Charles. *Camp Life in Florida: A Handbook for Sportsmen and Settlers.* NY, 1876. ....$25–$35

Hallowell, A. Irving. *The Role of Conjuring in Saulteaux Society.* Univ. of Pennsylvania Press, 1942, 1st ed, waxine dj. .....$25–$35

Hallows, R.W. *Atoms and Atomic Energy.* 1946, 1st ed. ..$14–$20

Halsey, F.W. *The Pioneers of Unadilla Village.* Unadilla, NY, 1902, ltd 650 cc. ....$45–$55

Halsey, Margaret. *Color Blind: A White Woman Looks at the Negro.* NY, 1946. ....$20–$30

Halstead, W.C. *Brain and Intelligence: A Quantitative Study of Frontal Lobes.* Chi, 1947, 1st ed, dj. ....$100–$125

Haluck, Paul. *Harness Making.* Phila, 1904. ....$28–$35

Hamerton, Philip, G. *Harry Blount: Passages in a Boy's Life on Land and Sea.* Bos, 1875, 1st American ed. ....$27–$45

Hamilton, William T. *My Sixty Years on the Plains.* ... NY, 1905, 1st ed, illus by C.M. Russell. ....$150–$175

Hammett, Dashiell. *The Dain Curse.* NY, Grosset & Dunlap, nd, rprnt, dj. ....$16–$22

Hammett, Dashiell. *The Glass Key.* NY, 1931, 1st ed, 4th prntg. ....$75–$150

Hammett, Dashiell. *The Maltese Falcon.* NY, Pocket Books, 1944, paperback. ....$25–$70

Hammett, Dashiell. *The Maltese Falcon.* NY/Lon, 1930. ....$500–$2,000

Hammett, Dashiell. *The Thin Man.* NY, 1934, 1st ed, 5th prntg. ....$75–$150

Hanaford, Mrs. P.A. *The Young Captain: A Memorial of Capt. Richard C. Berby.* ... Bos, 1865. ....$25–$35

Hanaford, Phebe A. *Daughters of America.* 1882, illus. ..$15–$20

Hancock. *Life at West Point.* 1902, 1st ed. ....$22–$30

Hankins, Arthur P. *Canyon Gold.* NY, 1925, illus. ....$24–$35

Hannum. *Spin a Silver Dollar.* NY, 1945, 2nd prntg. ....$10–$15

Hansard, George Agar. *The Book of Archery.* Lon, 1840, illus by F.P. Stephanoff, rbnd. ....$75–$125

Hansberry, Lorraine. *Les Blancs: Collected Last Plays Of.* Random House, 1972. ....$24–$37

Hansen. *Mingling of Canadian and American Peoples.* New Haven, 1940. ....$30–$40

Hansen, Ron. *Desperadoes.* NY, 1979, dj. ....$14–$20

Hardee, W. *Rifle and Light Infantry Tactics.* NY, 1862, wrps. ....$38–$45

Harding, A. *Wolf and Coyote Trapping.* St. Louis, 1909, 1st ed, illus. ....$18–$25

Harding, A.R. *Deadfalls and Snares.* Columbus, 1907. ..$14–$20

Harding, A.R. *Fox Trapping.* Columbus, 1906, illus. .....$15–$30

Harding, A.R. *Fur Farming.* OH, Harding Pub., 1916, 2nd ed. ....$14–$20

Harding, A.R. *Ginseng and Other Medicinal Plants.* Columbus, illus, photos, rev ed. ....$18–$40

Harding, A.R. *Mink Trapping.* Columbus, 1934. ....$10–$15

Harding, A.R. *Mink Trapping.* Columbus, 1906, illus. ...$20–$28

Hardy, Ronald. *The Iron Snake, the Story of the Uganda Railway.* NY, 1965. ....$22–$28

Hardy, Thomas. *A Group of Noble Dames.* NY, 1891, 1st U.S. ed. ....$50–$65

Hardy, Thomas. *Human Shows, Far Fantasies, Songs and Trifles.* Lon, 1925, 1st ed. ....$20–$30

Hardy, Thomas. *Tess of the D'Urbervilles.* Lon, 1926, ltd 325 cc, sgn. ....$800–$1,000

Hardy, Thomas. *The Well-Beloved.* 1897. ....$25–$60

Harlan, James R. and Everett B. Speaker. *Iowa Fish and Fishing.* IA, 1951, 1st ed, illus by Maynard Reece, dj. ....$12–$20

Harlow, Alvin F. *Old Wires and New Waves.* 1936, 1st ed, illus. ....$65–$85

Harrell, Isaac S. *Loyalism in Virginia.* Durham, 1926. ..*$18–$24*

Harris, Frank. *My Life and Loves.* Grove, 1963, 5 vols in 1, 1st ed, dj. ....*$25–$30*

Harris, Frank. *The Women of Shakespeare.* 1912. ....*$50–$60*

Harris, H.G. *Handbook of Watch Repair.* NY, 1966, 3d prntg. ....*$8–$15*

Harris, Joel Chandler. *A Little Union Scout.* NY, 1904, 1st ed, illus. ..../...*$25–$45*

Harris, Joel Chandler. *Aaron in the Wildwood.* Bos, 1898, 1st ed. ....*$40–$55*

Harris, Joel Chandler. *Free Joe and Other Georgian Sketches.* NY, 1887, 1st ed. ....*$20–$65*

Harris, Joel Chandler. *Gabriel Tolliver.* NY, 1902, 1st ed. ....*$75–$300*

Harris, Joel Chandler. *Nights with Uncle Remus: Myths and Legends. . . .* Bos, 1883, 1st ed. ....*$30–$55*

Harris, Joel Chandler. *On the Plantation.* NY, 1892, illus. ....*$35–$50*

Harris, Joel Chandler. *On the Wings of Occasion.* NY, 1900. ....*$18–$30*

Harris, Joel Chandler. *Told by Uncle Remus.* 1905, rprnt. ....*$10–$20*

Harris, Joel Chandler. *Uncle Remus.* NY, 1911, illus by A.B. Frost. ....*$30–$45*

Harris, Joel Chandler. *Uncle Remus and His Friends.* Bos, 1892, 1st ed. ....*$35–$55*

Harris, Joel Chandler. *Uncle Remus: His Songs and His Sayings.* NY, Appleton, 1881, 1st ed. ....*$300–$650*

Harris, Joel Chandler. *Wally Wanderoon and His Story Telling Machine.* NY, 1903, 1st ed, illus. ....*$50–$60*

Harris, K. *Outback in Australia.* 1929, 4th ed, photos, maps, sgn. ....*$14–$18*

Harris, Stanley. *Playing the Game.* NY, 1925, illus. ....*$22–$28*

Harris, T.W. *Treatise on Insects Injurious to Vegetation.* Bos, 1862, illus, plates. ....$125–$175

Harris, Thomas. *Silence of the Lambs.* NY, 1988, 1st ed, dj. ....$45–$65

Harris, Thomas L. *A Lyric of the Golden Age.* NY, 1856, 1st ed. ....$115–$175

Harris, Walter. *Salmon Fishing in Alaska.* S. Brunswick, 1967, 1st ed, illus. ....$22–$30

Harrison, Michael. *The History of the Hat.* Lon, 1960, illus, dj. ....$14–$20

Harrold, Ernest. *Life in New York. . . .* NY, 1903. ....$35–$50

Hart, George. *The Violin and Its Music.* Lon, 1881, illus..$30–$40

Harte, Bret. *Clarence.* Bos, 1895, 1st American ed. ......$20–$40

Harte, Bret. *East and West Poems.* Bos, 1871, 1st ed. ..$30–$37

Harte, Bret. *In the Hollow of the Hills.* Bos, 1895. ....$28–$35

Harte, Bret. *Tales of Trail and Town.* 1898. ....$20–$35

Harte, Bret. *The Luck of Roaring Camp.* SF, Grabhorn Press, 1948, ltd 300 cc, 40 clr engr. ....$14–$50

Hartshorne, A. *Old English Glasses.* Lon, 1897, folio, plates. ....$110–$150

Hartwell, Dickson. *Dogs against Darkness: The Story of the Seeing Eye.* NY, 1942, illus. ....$12–$18

Hartwig, G. *The Polar and Tropical Worlds. . . .* Springfield, 1874, illus, maps. ....$35–$40

Harvey, E. Newton. *A History of Luminescence.* 1957, 1st ed. ....$35–$50

Harvey, Rev. M. *Newfoundland in 1897.* Lon, 1897, illus. ....$25–$40

Haskell, Frank Aretas. *The Battle of Gettysburg.* WI, 1908, 1st ed, illus. ....$30–$50

Haskins, S. *Cowboy Kate and Other Stories.* NY, 1965, 1st ed, illus, dj. ....$27–$40

Hathaway, B. *The League of the Iroquois.* Chi, 1882. ...$35–$40

Haupt, Herman. *German Theory of Bridge Construction.* NY, 1856. ....*$45–$60*

Havighurst, Walter. *Long Ships Passing: Story of Great Lakes.* NY, 1942. ....*$20–$25*

Havighurst, Walter. *Vein of Iron.* Cleve, 1958, 1st ed, illus, dj. ....*$15–$22*

Haweis, Rev. H.R. *Old Violins.* Lon, 1898, illus. ....*$40–$50*

Hawker, P. *Instructions to Young Sportsmen . . . Guns and Shooting.* 1858. ....*$45–$50*

Hawkes, Clarence. *Master Frisky.* NY, 1902. ....*$5–$10*

Hawley, Walter A. *Oriental Rugs, Antique and Modern.* NY, 1937, clr plates, slipcase. ....*$125–$150*

Hawthorne, Nathaniel. *A Wonder Book.* NY, nd, illus by Arthur Rackham. ....*$95–$140*

Hawthorne, Nathaniel. *A Wonder Book and Tanglewood Tales.* NY, 1910, illus by Maxfield Parrish. ....*$60–$75*

Hawthorne, Nathaniel. *A Wonder Book for Girls and Boys.* Bos, 1902, 1st ed, illus by Walter Crane, 18 clr plates. ....*$95–$135*

Hawthorne, Nathaniel. *Doctor Grimshawe's Secret.* Osgood, 1883, 1st ed. ....*$85–$160*

Hawthorne, Nathaniel. *Our Old Home.* Ticknor & Fields, 1863, 1st ed, 1st state. ....*$95–$125*

Hawthorne, Nathaniel. *The House of the Seven Gables.* Bos, 1851, 1st ed, 3rd prntg, ltd 2,051 cc. ....*$115–$125*

Hawthorne, Nathaniel. *The Marble Faun.* Bos, 1860, 2 vols, 1st American ed. ....*$160–$200*

Hawthorne, Nathaniel. *The Scarlet Letter.* Bos, 1850, 2nd ed. ....*$200–$450*

Hawthorne, Nathaniel. *The Scarlet Letter.* Bos, 1850, 1st ed. ....*$850–$1,000*

Hayden, A. *Spode and His Successors.* Lon, 1925. ....*$60–$75*

Hayden, A.S. *Early History of the Disciples in the Western Reserve, Ohio. . . .* Cinc, 1876, 1st ed. ....*$50–$125*

Haydn, Ruff. *Pine Mountain Americans.* NY, 1947. ......*$25–$30*

Hayes, I. *The Open Polar Sea.* NY, 1874. ....$25–$30

Hayes, Isaac. *An Arctic Boat Journey.* Bos, 1860, 1st ed..$25–$45

Hayes, Isaac. *Cast Away in the Cold.* Bos, 1885, illus...$25–$32

Haynes, Warden G. *Pictures from Prison Life and Suggestions on Discipline.* 1869. ....$50–$65

Haynes, William B. *Goose and Duck Shooting.* TX, 1961, dj. ....$25–$35

Hayward, Charles B. *Practical Aeronautics.* 1917, 1st ed, illus. ....$40–$65

Head, Maj. Sir Francis. *The Life and Adventures of Bruce, the African Traveller.* NY, 1842, ¼ lea, mar bds. ....$28–$45

Head, Mrs. *The Lace and Embroidery Collector.* Lon, 1922. ....$24–$30

Headland, Isaac Taylor. *Court Life in China.* NY, 1909, illus, 2nd ed, photos. ....$22–$35

Headley, J.T. *The Achievements of Stanley and Other African Explorers.* Phila, 1878, illus, fldg map. ....$14–$20

Headley, P.C. *Fighting Phil.* Bos, 1889, illus. ....$35–$45

Heaney, Seamus. *Door into the Dark.* 1969, 1st ed, dj. .$95–$125

Heaney, Seamus. *Selected Poems, 1966–1987.* Farrar, 1990, ltd 200 cc, sgn, dj. ....$75–$90

Hearn, Lafcadio. *Chita: A Memory of Last Island.* NY/Lon, 1917. ....$50–$85

Hearn, Lafcadio. *Dokoro: Hints and Echoes of Japanese Life.* Bos, 1896, 1st ed. ....$18–$25

Hearn, Lafcadio. *Editorials.* Bos/NY, 1926, 1st ed. ....$23–$30

Hearn, Lafcadio. *Essays in European and Oriental Literature.* NY, 1923, 1st ed. ....$10–$20

Hearn, Lafcadio. *Japan.* NY, 1904, 1st ed, dj. ....$95–$325

Hearn, Lafcadio. *Kwaidan.* Tokyo, 1932, illus, sgn, silk case. ....$150–$200

Hearn, Lafcadio. *Out of the East.* Bos, 1895, 1st ed. .$110–$125

Hearn, Lafcadio. *The Romance of the Milky Way.* Bos, 1905, 1st ed. ....$20–$25

Heathcote, J.M. and C.G. Tebbutt. *Skating with T.M. Witham's Figure-skating.* . . . 1909, illus. ....$60–$85

Hebert, Frank. *40 Years Prospecting and Mining in the Black Hills of So. Dakota.* Rapid City, 1921, 1st ed, sgn. ....$30–$37

Heckewelder, John. *A Narr. of United Brethren among Delaware and Mohegan Indians.* Cleve, 1907, large paper copy. .$140–$180

Hedges, Isaac A. *Sugar Canes and Their Products, Culture, and Manufacture.* St. Louis, 1881, illus. ....$18–$25

Hedrick, U.P. *The Pears of New York.* Alb, 1921. ....$30–$40

Heilner, Van Campen. *A Book of Duck Shooting.* Knopf, 1947, illus by Lynn Bogue Hunt, dj. ....$20–$27

Heinlein, Robert. *Assignment in Eternity.* Fantasy Press, 1953, 1st ed, dj. ....$100–$135

Heinlein, Robert. *Farmer in the Sky.* Scribner's, 1950, 1st ed, dj. ....$120–$150

Heinlein, Robert. *Rocket Ship Galileo.* NY, 1957, illus by Voter, Junior Literary Guild. ....$10–$20

Heinlein, Robert. *Space Cadet.* NY, 1948, 1st ed, sgn, dj. ....$625–$850

Heinlein, Robert. *Stranger in a Strange Land.* NY, Putnam, 1961, 1st ed, dj. ....$500–$1,200

Heinlein, Robert A. *Cat Who Walks through Walls.* Ny, 1985, 1st ed, dj. ....$19–$30

Heinlein, Robert A. *Orphans of the Sky.* NY, 1964, 1st American ed, dj. ....$225–$300

Heinlein, Robert A. *The Number of the Beast.* Lon, 1980, 1st ed, dj. ....$30–$35

Heisenberg, Werner. *Physical Principles of the Quantum Theory.* Chi, 1930. ....$18–$26

Heller, Joseph. *Catch-22.* NY, 1961, 2nd prntg, sgn, dj..$50–$65

Heller, Joseph. *God Knows.* NY, 1984, 1st ed, sgn, dj. .$35–$40

Heller, Joseph. *Good as Gold.* Simon, 1979, 1st ed, sgn, dj. ....$35–$45

Heller, Joseph. *Something Happened.* Knopf, 1974, 1st ed, dj. ....$22–$30

Hellman, Lillian. *Pentimento.* Bos, 1973, 1st ed, dj. .....$10–$15

Hellman, Lillian. *The Children's Hour.* NY, 1934, 1st ed, dj. ....$250–$300

Hellman, Lillian. *The Little Foxes.* NY, 1939, 1st ed, dj..$30–$45

Helper, Hinton Rowan. *The Impending Crisis of the South.* NY, 1857. ....$24–$32

Hemingway, Ernest. *A Farewell to Arms.* Scribner's, 1929, 1st ed, dj. ....$800–$1,200

Hemingway, Ernest. *A Moveable Feast.* Jonathan Cape, 1964, 1st English ed, dj. ....$50–$75

Hemingway, Ernest. *A Moveable Feast.* Scribner's, 1964, 1st ed, dj. ....$35–$45

Hemingway, Ernest. *For Whom the Bell Tolls.* 1940, 1st ed, dj. ....$95–$250

Hemingway, Ernest. *Green Hills of Africa.* Scribner's, 1935, 1st ed, dj missing. ....$50–$90

Hemingway, Ernest. *Green Hills of Africa.* Scribner's, 1935, 1st ed, dj. ....$400–$475

Hemingway, Ernest. *Men without Women.* Scribner's, 1927, 1st ed, dj. ....$125–$150

Hemingway, Ernest. *The Old Man and the Sea.* Jonathan Cape, 1952, 1st English ed, dj. ....$75–$150

Hemingway, Ernest. *The Old Man and the Sea.* NY, Scribner's, 1952, 1st ed, dj. ....$200–$450

Hemingway, Ernest. *Winner Take Nothing.* NY, 1933, 1st ed, dj. ....$600–$900

Hemingway, Gregory. *Papa: A Personal Memoir.* Bos, 1976, dj. ....$25–$30

Hendericks. *Albert Bierstadt: Painter of the American West.* Abrams, 1973, 1st ed, dj. ....$50–$75

Henderson, Mrs. Mary F. *Practical Cooking and Dinner Giving.* NY, 1881, rprnt. ....$28–$35

Henderson, Peter. *Gardening for Profit.* NY, 1883. ....$14–$18

Henderson, W.A. *Modern Domestic Cookery and Useful Receipt Book.* Bos, 1844. ....$135–$170

Hendrick, B. *The Jews in America.* 1923, 1st ed. ....$12–$15

Hendrick, U.P. *The Cherries of New York.* Alb, 1915. .$85–$110

Henry, Capt. W.S. *Campaign Sketches of the War with Mexico.* NY, 1847, 1st ed, illus. ....$190–$250

Henry, O. *Heart of the West.* McClure, 1907, 1st ed. ....$35–$60

Henry, O. *Let Me Feel Your Pulse.* NY, 1910, 1st ed. ...$15–$30

Henry, O. *Options.* NY, 1909, 1st ed. ....$40–$45

Henry, O. *Strictly Business.* NY, 1910, 1st ed. ....$20–$45

Henry, Robert Mitchell. *The Evolution of Sinn Fein.* Dublin, 1920, 1st ed, sgn by Sean Cullen. ....$35–$95

Henry, Robert Selph. *The Story of Reconstruction.* NY, 1938, 1st ed. ....$18–$22

Henslow, T. Geoffrey. *Ye Sundial Booke.* Lon, 1914, illus, engr. ....$65–$90

Henty, G. *Out with Garibaldi.* Lon, 1901. ....$50–$70

Henty, G.A. *A Knight of the White Cross.* NY, 1895, 1st ed, illus. ....$12–$15

Henty, G.A. *Both Sides of the Border.* NY, 1898, 1st ed, illus. ....$40–$50

Henty, G.A. *By England's Aid.* Rahway, NJ, nd. ....$15–$20

Henty, G.A. *By Pike and Dyke.* NY, 1897, 1st ed. ....$25–$30

Henty, G.A. *In the Irish Brigade.* Scribner's, 1900, 1st ed. ....$30–$35

Henty, G.A. *The Young Franc-Tireurs.* NY, nd, illus. .....$12–$15

Henty, G.A. *With Buller in Natal.* Lon, nd, 1st English ed. ....$35–$55

Henty, G.A. *With Cochrane the Dauntless.* NY, 1896. ...$20–$30

Herbert, Frank. *Charterhouse Dune.* NY, 1985, 1st ed, sgn, dj. ....$35–$50

Herbert, Frank. *Dune.* NY, 1984, 1st ed, sgn, dj. ....$50–$75

Herbert, Frank. *God Emperor of Dune.* NY, 1981, 1st ed, sgn, dj.
....*$50–$75*

Herbert, Frank. *Heretics of Dune.* NY, 1984, 1st ed, sgn, dj.
....*$50–$75*

Herbert, George B. *The Popular History of The Civil War in America.* NY, 1884, 1st ed, illus. ....*$10–$15*

Herbert, H.W. *Frank Forester's Fish and Fishing in the U.S.* NY, 1850, 1st ed. ....*$35–$50*

Herbert, J.A. *Illuminated Manuscripts.* NY/Lon, 1911, illus.
....*$50–$75*

Herbert, T.E. *Telegraphy.* 1916, illus, 3rd ed. ....*$22–$35*

Herford, Oliver. *An Alphabet of Celebrities.* Bos, 1899, 1st ed, illus. ....*$28–$35*

Herford, Oliver. *The Rubaiyat of a Persian Kitten.* NY, 1904.
....*$12–$20*

Hergesheimer, Joseph. *Sheridan; A Military Narrative.* Bos/NY, 1931, 1st ed, illus. ....*$25–$40*

Hermann, Robert. *Tobacco and Americans.* NY, 1960, dj.
....*$30–$45*

Herrick, Francis Hobart. *The American Eagle: A Study in Natural and Civil History.* NY, 1934. ....*$30–$40*

Hersey, John. *Hiroshima.* NY, Knopf, 1946, 1st ed, dj. .*$25–$45*

Herter, George. *Professional Fly-tying and Tackle Making.* 1953.
....*$20–$30*

Hertz, Louis. *Handbook of Old American Toys.* Wetherfield, 1947, 1st ed. ....*$27–$33*

Hesse, Hermann. *Demian.* NY, 1965, intro by T. Mann. .*$30–$35*

Hesse, Hermann. *Demian.* NY, 1948, dj. ....*$15–$20*

Hethmon, R. *Strasberg at Actors Studio.* NY, 1965, 1st ed.
....*$40–$55*

Hewitt, Abram S. *On the Statistics and Geography of the Production of Iron.* NY, 1856, wrps. ....*$45–$70*

Hewlett, John. *Harlem Story.* NY, 1948, 1st ed, dj. ....*$20–$25*

Heydecker, Joe J. and J. Leeb. *The Nuremberg Trial: A History of Nazi Germany.* . . . Cleve, 1962, 1st cd. ....$25–$30

Heyerdahl, Thor. *Fatu-Hiva, Back to Nature.* Garden City, 1975, 1st American ed, dj. ....$20–$30

Hibben, Frank C. *Hunting in Africa.* NY, 1962, 1st ed, photos, dj. ....$22–$35

Hibbert and Buist. *The American Flower Garden Dictionary.* Phila, 1832. ....$60–$100

Hicks, Albert. *The Life, Trial, and Execution of the Pirate and Murderer.* NY, 1860, 1st ed, illus. ....$50–$75

Hielscher, Kurt. *Picturesque Spain.* NY/Berlin, 1925, folio. ....$30–$45

Higgins, Colin. *Harold and Maude.* NY, 1971, 1st ed, dj..$20–$25

Hildreth, Richard. *Despotism in America.* . . . Bos, 1854. ....$32–$47

Hildreth, Samuel C. and James R. Crowell. *The Spell of the Turf.* NY, 1926, 1st ed, illus. ....$18–$24

Hill, B.L. *An Epitome of the Homoeopathic Healing Arts.* Detroit, 1869. ....$37–$45

Hill, Grace Livingston. *Through These Fires.* Phila, 1943, 1st ed, dj. ....$35–$47

Hill, L. *Meteorological and Chronological Register, 1806 to 1869.* Plymouth, MA, 1869, 1st ed. ....$20–$30

Hill, Ralph Nading. *Sidewheeler Saga.* Rinehart, 1953, 1st ed, illus, dj. ....$22–$35

Hill, Robin. *Australian Birds.* NY, 1967, 1st ed, illus, clr plates, dj. ....$25–$35

Hill, W. Henrey, et al. *Antonio Stradivari, His Life and Work (1644–1737).* Lon, Macmillan, 1909, illus. ....$75–$150

Hillary, William. *Observations on the Changes of the Air* . . . *Yellow Fever.* Lon, 1766, 2nd ed, bds. ....$125–$235

Hillerman, Tony. *A Thief of Time.* NY, 1988, 1st ed, dj..$35–$40

Hillerman, Tony. *Talking God.* Harper, 1989, 1st ed, dj..$18–$25

Hillerman, Tony. *Words, Weather, and Wolfmen.* NM, 1989, 1st ed, ltd 400 cc, sgn, dj. ....*$100–$150*

Hindle, Brooke. *The Pursuit of Science in Revolutionary America, 1735–1789.* 1956, dj. ....*$28–$38*

Hinton, H.E. and A.M.S. Dunn. *Mongooses, Their Natural History and Behaviour.* Edin, 1967, illus. ....*$5–$10*

Hinton, S.E. *That Was Then, This Is Now.* NY, 1971, 1st ed, dj. ....*$60–$80*

Hinton, S.E. *The Outsiders.* NY, 1967, 1st ed, dj. ......*$100–$250*

Hipkins, A.J. *Musical Instruments.* . . . Lon, 1945, illus by William Gibb. ....*$65–$75*

Hitchcock, Edward. *Final Report of the Geology of Massachusetts.* Amherst, 1841, rbnd. ....*$90–$125*

Hitchcock, Edward, et al. *Report on the Geology of Vermont.* . . . Claremont, NH, 1861, 2 vols, illus, fldg maps. ....*$60–$100*

Hitler, Adolf. *Mein Kampf.* 1939. ....*$16–$20*

Hitler, Adolf. *Mein Kampf.* Munchen, 1938. ....*$35–$42*

Hitler, Adolf. *Mein Kampf.* Munchen, 1933, dj, text in German. ....*$35–$50*

Hively, W. (ed). *Nine Classic California Photographers.* Berkeley, 1980, illus. ....*$22–$30*

Hobbs, William H. *Exploring about the North Pole of the Winds.* NY, 1930, 1st ed, photos. ....*$16–$20*

Hobley, C.W. *Bantu Beliefs and Magic.* Lon, 1922, illus. ....*$75–$125*

Hochbaum, H. Albert. *Travels and Traditions of Waterfowl.* MN, 1955, 1st ed, illus, dj. ....*$18–$30*

Hochwalt, A.F. *Bird Dogs.* Cinc, 1922, 1st ed, illus. .....*$18–$25*

Hodge, Frederick. *Handbook of American Indians, North of Mexico.* 1911, 2 vols, 3rd prntg. ....*$65–$110*

Hodge, Frederick. *Handbook of American Indians, North of Mexico.* DC, GPO, 1907–1910, 2 vols, 1st ed, illus, map. .*$125–$200*

Hodge, Hirim. *Arizona.* . . . NY, 1877, 1st ed, sgn. ....*$175–$225*

Hodge, O.J. *Reminiscences, Vol. II.* Brooks, 1910. ....*$10–$18*

Hodgkin, A.E. *The Archers Craft.* NY, Barnes, nd, illus, dj. ....*$30–$45*

Hoegh, Leo A. and Howard Doyle. *Timberwolf Tracks.* DC, 1946, 1st ed, illus, photos, maps. ....*$45–$60*

Hoffman, Abbie. *Square Dancing in the Ice Age.* NY, 1982, dj. ....*$25–$30*

Hoffman, Abbie. *Steal This Book.* NY, 1971, 1st ed, sgn. ....*$50–$100*

Hoffman, Abbie. *Woodstock Nation.* 1st ed, wrps. ....*$15–$20*

Hoffman, Daniel. *Striking the Stones: Poems.* NY, 1968, 1st ed, sgn, dj. ....*$25–$30*

Hoffman, Heinrich. *Struwwelpeter.* Lon/NY, nd, illus. ...*$35–$50*

Hoffman, Prof. *Drawing-room Amusements and Evening Party Entertainments.* Lon, 1883, illus. ....*$75–$145*

Hoffman, Ralph. *Birds of the Pacific States.* Bos/NY, 1927, illus, b/w and clr plates, dj. ....*$14–$20*

Hohman, Elmo P. *The American Whaleman.* NY, 1928, illus, rprnt. ....*$15–$25*

Holbrook, Florence. *Hiawatha Alphabet.* Chi, 1910, 1st ed, illus by H.D. Pohl. ....*$35–$50*

Holbrook, S. *Old Post Road.* 1st ed. ....*$20–$30*

Holbrook, Stewart. *The Columbia.* NY, 1956, 1st ed, sgn, dj. ....*$30–$50*

Holbrook, Stewart H. *The Story of American Railroads.* NY, 1947, 1st ed, illus, dj. ....*$20–$25*

Holder, C. *The Ivory King: A Popular Hist. of the Elephant and Its Allies.* 1886, 1st ed, illus. ....*$75–$95*

Holder, Charles Frederick. *Big Game at Sea.* NY, 1908, presentation copy, sgn. ....*$37–$45*

Holland, Mrs. Mary. *Economical Cook and Frugal House-wife....* Lon, 1853, 16th ed. ....*$125–$155*

Holland, R. *Historic Airships.* 1928. ....*$18–$25*

Holland, Ray P. *My Dog Lemon.* 1945, dj. ....*$25–$30*

Holland, Ray P. *My Gun Dogs.* Bos, 1929, 1st ed, illus..*$30–$65*

Holland, W.J. *The Butterfly Book.* NY, 1922, clr plates..*$25–$35*

Holland, W.J. *The Butterfly Book.* NY, 1901, clr plates..*$45–$70*

Holland, W.J. *The Moth Book.* 1913. ....*$15–$18*

Holley, Marietta. *Samantha on the Race Problem.* Bos, 1892, illus. ....*$45–$75*

Holliday, Carl. *A History of Southern Literature.* NY, 1906. ....*$30–$68*

Holling, H.C. *The Book of Cowboys.* NY, 1936, 1st ed, dj. ....*$14–$25*

Hollis, H. *Bass and Tackle Tactics.* Barnes, 1942, 2nd ed..*$12–$15*

Hollister, Mary Brewster. *River Children.* NY, 1935, illus by Kurt Wiese, sgn. ....*$8–$14*

Hollister, U.S. *The Navajo and His Blanket.* 1974, rprnt..*$20–$25*

Hollon, W. Eugene. *The Lost Pathfinder.* Univ. of Oklahoma Press, 1949, dj. ....*$25–$35*

Holme, C.G. *Children's Toys of Yesterday.* Lon, 1932, illus, dj. ....*$37–$45*

Holmes, Oliver Wendell. *A Mortal Antipathy.* Bos, 1885, 1st ed. ....*$35–$45*

Holmes, Oliver Wendell. *The Guardian Angel.* Bos, 1867, 1st ed. ....*$15–$45*

Holt, Bessie Belle. *Rugs, Oriental and Occidental.* Chi, 1901, illus, plates. ....*$60–$75*

Holt, P.G. *Fifty Dollars a Week with Car and Camera.* Bos, 1926, illus, dj. ....*$14–$20*

Holt, Rosa Belle. *Oriental and Occidental Rugs, Ancient and Modern.* Garden City, 1937, illus. ....*$75–$90*

Holzworth, John M. *The Wild Grizzlies of Alaska.* NY, 1930, 1st ed, illus, dj. ....*$37–$60*

Homans, James E. *Self-Propelled Vehicles.* NY, 1910, 7th ed. ....*$35–$65*

Honey, W.B. *Dresden China.* Lon, 1934. ....*$35–$50*

Honig, Donald. *Baseball When the Grass Was Real.* 1975, 1st ed, dj. ....*$15–$20*

Hood, Grant. *Modern Methods in Horology.* IL, 1944, illus. ....*$32–$45*

Hood, Jennings and Charles J. Young. *American Orders and Societies and Their Decorations.* Phila, 1917, illus, clr plates. ....*$30–$45*

Hood, Thomas. *The Epping Hunt.* NY, Derrydale Press, 1930, ltd #229, 490 cc, bds. ....*$50–$75*

Hook, Sidney. *Reason, Social Myths, and Democracy.* NY, 1940, 1st ed, dj. ....*$25–$35*

Hooker, William F. *The Prairie Schooner.* Chi, 1918, 1st ed, illus. ....*$60–$100*

Hooper, Bert and Jas. M. Flagg. *Virgins in Cellophane.* NY, 1932, 1st ed, illus. ....*$22–$30*

Hooper, Lucy. *The Lady's Book of Flowers and Poetry.* Phila, 1863, illus, clr plates. ....*$40–$95*

Hoover, Herbert. *A Boyhood in Iowa.* NY, 1931, ltd, sgn. ....*$125–$150*

Hope, Bob. *They Got Me Covered.* Hollywood, 1941, 1st ed wrps. ....*$25–$38*

Hope, Laura Lee. *Bobbsey Twins at Indian Hollow.* Grossett & Dunlap, 1940. ....*$2–$4*

Hopkins, Ernest J. *Our Lawless Police.* NY, 1931, 1st ed. ....*$25–$45*

Hopkins, Gen. Frederick W. *Eulogy at Norwich, Vt., Feb. 22, 1848 ... Truman R. Ransom. ...* Hanover, 1848, 1st ed, wrps. ....*$45–$75*

Hopkins, Samuel. *The Life and Character of Miss Susanna Anthony.* Portland, 1810, calf. ....*$15–$22*

Hopkinson, E. *Records of Birds Bred in Captivity.* Lon, 1926. ....*$45–$60*

Hopkinson, F. *An Account of the Impeachment of the Late Francis Hopkinson. ...* Phila, 1794, 1st ed. ....*$65–$90*

Hoppe, Willie. *30 Years of Billiards.* NY, 1925, 1st ed, illus. ....*$30–$40*

Horan, Jack. *Burnt Leather.* MT, 1937, wrps. ....*$30–$40*

Horgan, Paul. *Josiah Gregg and His Vision of the Early West.* NY, 1979, 1st ed, dj. ....$20–$28

Horgan, Paul. *Peter Hurd.* Fort Worth, 1965, 1st ed, sgn, dj. ....$25–$38

Horn, Stanley F. *Invisible Empire: The Story of the Ku Klux Klan.* Bos, 1939, 1st ed, illus, dj. ....$45–$60

Horn, Stanley Fitzgerald. *The Decisive Battle of Nashville.* Baton Rouge, 1956, 1st ed, presentation copy, dj. ....$25–$35

Hornaday, W.T. *Thirty Years War for Wildlife.* Stamford, 1931, 1st ed. ....$25–$30

Horne, George. *Pheasant Keeping for Amateurs.* Lon, illus. ....$55–$95

Horton, William E. *About Stage Folk.* Free Press, 1902..$18–$25

Horwood, A.R. *The Outdoor Botanist.* Lon, 1920, illus, photos. ....$20–$25

Hough, Horatio Gates. *Diving . . . Attempt to Describe Method of Supplying Diver with Air.* Hartford, 1813, 1st ed. ....$50–$170

Houghton, P. *Football and How to Watch It.* Bos, 1922. .$14–$20

House, Edward J. *A Hunter's Camp-fires.* 1909. ....$35–$55

House, Homer D. *Wildflowers of New York.* Univ. of New York, 1923, 2 vols, illus. ....$50–$85

House, Homer D. *Wildflowers of New York.* Alb, 1918, 2 vols, illus, folio, plates. ....$75–$100

Houseman, A.E. *A Shropshire Lad and Last Poems.* Alcuin Press, 1929, 2 vols, ltd, 325 cc, slipcase. ....$175–$225

Houston, John W. *Address on the Hist. of the Boundaries of the St. of Delaware.* Wilmington, DE, 1879, 1st ed, wrps. ...$35–$50

Hovey and Call. *The Mammoth Cave of Kentucky.* Louisville, 1899, illus. ....$18–$23

Hovgaard, William. *The Voyages of the Norsemen to America.* NY, 1914. ....$25–$35

Howard, F.E. *English Church Woodwork.* Lon, 1917, illus. ....$40–$57

Howard, Oliver O. *Nez Perce Joseph: An Account of.* . . . Bos, 1881, illus, plates, fldg maps. ....*$125–$150*

Howard, Robert. *A Treatise on Salt.* . . . Lon, 1850, 2nd ed. ....*$45–$55*

Howard, Robert E. *Conan the Barbarian.* NY, Gnome Press, 1954, 1st ed, dj. ....*$75–$95*

Howard, Robert E. *King Conan.* Gnome Press, 1953, 1st ed, dj. ....*$75–$100*

Howard, Robert E. *The Coming of Conan.* Gnome Press, 1953, 1st ed, dj. ....*$75–$100*

Howbert, Irving. *Memories of a Lifetime in the Pike's Peak Region.* NY, 1925. ....*$28–$35*

Howe, James Virgil. *The Modern Gunsmith.* NY, 1934, 2 vols, sgn. ....*$25–$35*

Howe, Julia Ward. *Reminiscences, 1819–1899.* Houghton Mifflin, 1899, 1st ed, illus. ....*$20–$28*

Howe, William H. *The Butterflies of North America.* Garden City, 1975, 1st ed, illus, clr plates, dj. ....*$25–$55*

Howell, A.H. *Florida Bird Life.* NY, 1932. ....*$50–$95*

Howells, W.D. *A Boy's Town.* Harper, 1890, 1st ed, illus..*$14–$18*

Howison, Robert R. *A History of Virginia, from Its Discovery* . . . *Present Time.* Phila/Rich, 1846/1848, 2 vols. ....*$125–$200*

Hrdlicka, Ales. *Alaska Diary, 1926–1931.* PA, 1943, illus. ....*$18–$25*

Hubbard, B.V. *Socialism, Feminism, and Suffragism.* Chi, 1914, 1st ed, dedication copy, sgn. ....*$67–$75*

Hubbard, Charles D. *Camping in the New England Mountains.* ME, 1952, illus. ....*$25–$35*

Hubbard, Elbert. *Joaquin Miller.* East Aurora, NY, 1903, 1st ed, illus, suede. ....*$25–$35*

Hubbard, Elbert. *Little Journeys to the Homes of Famous Women.* 1911. ....*$12–$15*

Hubbard, Harlan. *Shantyboat.* NY, 1954, dj. ....*$18–$25*

Hubbard, L. Ron. *Dianetics.* 1951, dj. ....*$45–$75*

Hubbard, L. Ron. *Dianetics.* NY, 1950, 1st ed, dj. ...*$100–$225*

Hubbard, L. Ron. *Lives You Wished to Lead But Never Dared.* . . . Clearwater, 1978, 1st ed. ....*$45–$75*

Hubbard, L. Ron. *Typewriter in the Sky/Fear.* Gnome Press, 1951, 1st ed. ....*$45–$100*

Hubbard, W. *A Narrative of the Troubles with the Indians in New England.* . . . Bos, 1677, illus, map. ....*$22,000–$45,000*

Hudson, Robert. *Two Princes of Science: Edison and Marconi.* 1907, 1st ed, illus. ....*$25–$45*

Hudson, W.H. *Birds of LaPlata.* Lon/NY, 1920, 2 vols, illus. ....*$50–$75*

Hudson, W.H. *Dead Man's Plack and an Old Thorn.* Lon, 1920, 1st ed. ....*$40–$45*

Hudson, W.H. *Far Away and Long Ago.* Limited Edition Club, 1943, illus, ltd 1,500 cc. ....*$75–$125*

Hudson, W.H. *The Purple Land.* Lon, 1929, illus. ....*$65–$125*

Huey, Pennock. *A True Hist. of Charge of 8th Pa. Cavalry at Chancelorsville.* Phila, 1885, 2nd ed. ....*$95–$115*

Hughes, Elizabeth and Marion Lester. *The Big Book of Buttons.* ME, 1991, illus, rprnt. ....*$95–$125*

Hughes, Langston. *Black Misery.* NY, 1969, 1st ed, illus, dj. ....*$35–$50*

Hughes, Langston. *The Big Sea.* 1940, 1st ed. ....*$37–$45*

Hughes, Langston and Roy De Carava. *The Sweet Flypaper of Life.* NY, 1955, wrps, illus, 1st prntg. ....*$35–$75*

Hughes, T. *Tom Brown's School Days.* NY, 1911, illus. ..*$14–$20*

Hughes, Therle. *English Domestic Needlework.* Lon, nd, illus, dj. ....*$14–$20*

Hulbert, Archer. *Forty-Niners: Chronicle of California Trail.* Bos, 1931. ....*$25–$35*

Hulten, Pontus. *The Surrealists Look at Art.* Venice, CA, 1990. ....*$20–$25*

Hulton, Ann. *Letters of a Loyalist Lady.* . . . Camb, 1927, 1st ed, illus, ltd 750 cc. ....*$30–$50*

Humbard, A.E. *My Life Story.* Cleve, 1945. ....$12–$22

Humphrey, Maude. *Treasury of Stories, Jingles, and Rhymes.* Stokes, 1894, illus by Humphrey, clr plates. ....$135–$160

Humphries, Sydney. *Oriental Carpets, Runners, and Rugs.* Lon, 1910. ....$150–$250

Hunt, Blanche Seale. *Little Brown Koko.* 1940, 1st ed. .$22–$35

Hunt, Blanche Seale. *Little Brown Koko Has Fun.* Chi, 1945, 1st ed. ....$25–$35

Hunt, Blanche Seale. *Stories of Little Brown Koko.* Chi/NY, 1940, 1st ed, illus, dj. ....$35–$45

Hunt, Frazier. *I Fought with Custer.* NY, 1945, 1st ed, dj. ....$22–$30

Hunt, Maj. Elvid. *History of Fort Leavenworth, 1827–1927.* Ft. Leavenworth, KS, 1926, illus, sgn. ....$25–$40

Hunter, George L. *Tapestries, Their Origin, History, and Renaissance.* NY, 1912, 1st ed, illus. ....$26–$35

Hunter, J.A. *Hunter.* NY, 1952, illus, dj. ....$15–$25

Hunter, J.A. *Hunters Tracks.* 1st ed, dj. ....$20–$25

Hunter, M. *Utah, Story of Her People.* Salt Lake, 1946..$16–$20

Huntington, D. *Our Big Game.* NY, 1904, 1st ed. ....$22–$28

Hurlimann, M. *Die Schweiz.* Zurich, 1938, illus, folio...$18–$25

Hurok, S.S. *Hurok Presents.* 1953, dj, sgn. ....$14–$20

Huse, Caleb. *The Supplies for the Confederate Army....* Bos, 1904, 1st ed, wrps. ....$80–$100

Hutchins, Samuel. *A Theory of the Universe.* NY, 1868. .$60–$75

Hutchinson, Francis. *An Historical Essay concerning Witchcraft.* Lon, 1718, 1st ed, ¾ calf. ....$325–$375

Hutchinson, H.G. *The Badminton Library Golf.* Lon, 1898, illus. ....$75–$85

Hutchinson, William T. *Cyrus Hall McCormick, Harvest, 1856–1884.* NY, 1935, 1st ed, illus. ....$12–$20

Hutton, F.W. and J. Drummond. *The Animals of New Zealand.* Aukland, 1923. ....$35–$45

Huxley, Aldous. *Antic Hay.* NY, 1923, 1st U.S. ed. ....$18–$25

Huxley, Aldous. *Brave New World.* Lon, 1932, 1st ed, dj.
....$225–$300

Huxley, Aldous. *Brave New World Revisited.* NY, 1932, 1st ed, dj.
....$60–$80

Huxley, Elspeth. *On the Edge of the Rift: Memories of Kenya.*
1962, 1st ed, dj. ....$10–$25

Huxley, Elspeth. *Scott of the Antarctic.* NY, 1978, illus, 1st American ed, dj. ....$13–$18

Huxley, Elspeth. *Their Shining Eldorado.* 1967, 1st ed, dj.
....$12–$16

Huxley, Julian. *African View.* NY, 1931, 1st ed, dj. ....$22–$30

Huxley, Thomas. *A Manual of the Anatomy of Invertebrate Animals.* Appleton, 1888. ....$30–$50

Huxley, Thomas. *Evidence as to Man's Place in Nature.* NY, 1878, 1st American ed. ....$40–$75

Huxley, Thomas. *On the Origin of the Species.* NY, 1863, 1st ed.
....$32–$45

Huxley, Thomas H. *American Address with a Lecture on the Study of Biology.* NY, 1877, 1st ed, illus. ....$25–$30

Huxley, Thomas H. *Lay Sermons, Addresses, and Reviews.* Appleton, 1871. ....$18–$25

Huxley, Thomas H. *Science and the Hebrew Tradition Essays.* NY, 1899. ....$22–$30

Hyde, John. *Wonderland, or the Pacific Northwest and Alaska.* St. Paul, 1888, softbound. ....$25–$45

Hyde, Walter Woodburn. *Ancient Greek Mariners.* NY, 1947, 1st ed, dj. ....$25–$35

Hylander, Clarence J. *Feathers and Flight.* NY, 1959, 1st ed, illus, dj. ....$12–$18

Ibsen, Henrik. *The Doll's House.* NY, 1889. ....$20–$35

Ickes, Anna Wilmarth. *Mesa Land: The History and Romance of the American Southwest.* Bos, 1933. ....$25–$35

Ingersoll, Ernest (ed). *Alaskan Bird Life.* NY, 1914, illus.
....$25–$35

Ingham, George Thomas. *Digging Gold among the Rockies.* Phila, 1888. ....$28–$35

Ingham, George Thomas. *Digging Gold among the Rockies.* Phila, 1880, 1st ed. ....$125–$165

Ingham, J. Washington. *A Short History of Asylum, Pennsylvania.* Towanda, PA, 1916, wrps, illus. ....$33–$42

Ingraham, I. (ed). *Sunny South or Southerner at Home.* 1860, 1st ed. ....$42–$50

Inman, Col. *A Pioneer from Kentucky.* Topeka, 1898, 1st ed. ....$28–$40

Inman, Col. Henry. *The Old Santa Fe Trail, The Story of a Great Highway.* Topeka, 1916, illus. ....$25–$35

Inman, Col. Henry and Col. William Cody. *The Great Salt Lake Trail.* NY, 1898, 1st ed. ....$75–$100

Inn, Henry. *Chinese Houses and Gardens.* Honolulu, 1940, illus, ltd 2,000 cc, sgn. ....$50–$85

Ionesco, Eugene. *The Hermit.* NY, 1973, 1st ed, dj. ......$25–$35

Ionesco, Eugene. *The Killer and Other Plays.* Grove, 1960, 1st U.S. ed. ....$18–$28

Irons, Neville John. *Last Emperor.* Lon, 1983, illus, dj..$12–$20

Irving, John. *Cider House Rules.* Franklin Library, 1985, lea, aeg, sgn. ....$55–$75

Irving, John. *Cider House Rules.* Morrow, 1985, 1st ed, sgn, dj. ....$60–$85

Irving, John. *Hotel New Hampshire.* 1981, 1st ed, dj. ...$35–$85

Irving, John. *The World according to Garp.* NY, 1978, 1st ed, dj. ....$60–$75

Irving, John Treat. *Indian Sketches Taken during an Expedition to the Pawnee....* Lon, 1835, 2 vols, 1st English ed, ½ mor. ....$150–$235

Irving, Washington. *A History of New York by Diedrich Knickerbocker.* Lon, 1825. ....$45–$50

Irving, Washington. *Adventures of Capt. Bonneville, or Scenes beyond the Rocky Mts.* Paris, 1837. ....$175–$200

Irving, Washington. *Astoria, or Anecdotes of an Enterprise Beyond Rocky Mountains.* Phila, 1836, 2 vols, 1st American ed. ....*$350–$500*

Irving, Washington. *Life of George Washington.* 1856, 5 vols. ....*$90–$100*

Irving, Washington. *Life of George Washington.* nd, 4 vols in 2. ....*$20–$30*

Irving, Washington. *Old Christmas.* 1908, 1st ed, illus by Cecil Alden, clr plates. ....*$37–$45*

Irving, Washington. *The Legend of Sleepy Hollow.* Bobbs-Merrill, 1906, illus by Arthur Keller. ....*$40–$75*

Isham, Charles. *The Fishery Question.* Putnam, 1887, 1st ed, map. ....*$18–$25*

Isham, Frederic S. *Under the Rose.* Bobbs-Merrill, 1903, illus by Howard Chandler Christy. ....*$18–$25*

Isherwood, Christopher. *My Guru and His Disciple.* 1980, 1st ed, sgn, dj. ....*$30–$75*

Isherwood, Christopher. *The Condor and the Cows.* Lon, 1949, illus, photos, dj. ....*$18–$25*

Jackson, C. *Foreign Bodies in the Air and Food Passages.* MA, 1924. ....*$40–$48*

Jackson, Daniel. *Religious Experience . . . of Rev. Daniel Jackson. . . .* Cinc, 1859, 1st ed, illus. ....*$60–$75*

Jackson, Frederick G. *A Thousand Days in the Arctic.* NY, 1899, 1st ed, illus, fldg maps. ....*$85–$140*

Jackson, Helen Hunt (H.H.). *Ramona.* 1900, village scene on cover. ....*$18–$30*

Jackson, Helen Hunt (H.H.). *Ramona.* 1889, thistles on cover. ....*$45–$75*

Jackson, Helen Hunt (H.H.). *Ramona.* Roberts Bros., 1884, 1st ed. ....*$350–$500*

Jackson, Joseph H. *Anybody's Gold: The Story of California's Mining Towns.* NY, 1941, illus. ....*$15–$22*

Jackson, S. *Report on Introduction of Domestic Reindeer in Alaska.* GPO, 1909, illus, map. ....*$55–$75*

Jackson, Sheldon. *Alaska and the Missions on the North Pacific Coast.* NY, 1880, engr. ....$25–$40

Jackson, Shirley. *Hangsaman.* NY, 1951, 1st ed, dj. ....$55–$65

Jackson, Shirley. *Life among the Savages.* NY, 1953, 1st ed, dj. ....$45–$55

Jackson, Shirley. *The Sundial.* NY, 1958, 1st ed, dj. ...$75–$145

Jacobs, Michael. *The Rebel Invasion of Maryland, Penn., and Battle of Gettysburg.* Gettysburg, 1909, wrps. ....$18–$25

Jacobson, H.P. *Fungus Diseases.* Springfield, 1932, 1st ed, illus. ....$14–$18

Jakes, John. *And So to Bed.* Monarch, 1962, 1st ed, wrps. ....$10–$15

Jalovec, Karel. *Italian Violin Makers.* Lon, 1964, illus...$40–$90

Jamal, H. *From the Dead Level—Malcolm X and Me.* 1st ed. ....$12–$18

James, Edgar. *The Allen Outlaws and Their Career of Crime....* Balt, 1912, 1st ed, wrps, illus. ....$45–$55

James, George W. *Through Ramona's Country.* Bos, 1909, 1st ed. ....$55–$65

James, George Wharton. *California, Romantic and Beautiful.* Bos, 1914, 1st ed, illus. ....$40–$55

James, Henry. *A Landscape Painter.* NY, Scott & Seltzer, 1919. ....$20–$30

James, Henry. *English Hours.* Bos, 1905, 1st ed, illus by Pennell. ....$75–$100

James, Henry. *Hawthorne.* Lon, Macmillan, 1870. ....$35–$45

James, Henry. *The Finer Grain.* NY, 1910, 1st ed. ....$30–$40

James, Henry. *The Other House.* NY, 1896, 1st American ed. ....$125–$150

James, Jesse Jr. *James My Father.* Cleve, 1906, wrps. ...$75–$85

James, Marques. *The Life of Andrew Jackson.* Ind, 1938..$20–$25

James, P.D. *Skull beneath the Skin.* 1982, Lester/Orpen Denys. ....$12–$22

James, Will. *Lone Cowboy: My Life Story.* NY, 1930, 1st ed, illus by author. ....*$25–$40*

James, Will. *Smoky the Cow Horse.* Scribner's, 1958, clr plates. ....*$15–$25*

James William. *Pragmatism.* NY, 1908, 3rd ed. ....*$12–$20*

Jane, Fred T. *The Imperial Russian Navy.* Lon, 1899, illus. ....*$125–$200*

Janis, H and S. Janis. *Picasso the Recent Years, 1939–1946.* NY, 1946, 1st ed, dj. ....*$18–$23*

Janney, Samuel. *Peace Principles Exemplified in the Early History of Penn.* Phila, 1876. ....*$30–$48*

Jansen, Murk. *Feebleness of Growth and Congenital Dwarfism. . . .* Lon, 1921, 1st ed. ....*$50–$60*

Janvier, T.A. *The Aztec Treasure-house.* NY, 1890. ....*$45–$85*

Jaques, Florence Page. *Francis Lee Jaques: Artist of the Wilderness World.* Garden City, 1973, 1st ed, illus, boxed. ....*$25–$40*

Jaquet and Chapuis. *The Swiss Watch. . . .* Switzerland, 1953. dj. ....*$95–$120*

Jarvis, C.S. *Yesterday and Today in Sinai.* Edin/Lon, 1938, illus, fldg map. ....*$5–$10*

Jay, William. *A View of the Action of the Federal Govt. in Behalf of Slavery.* NY, 1839, 1st ed. ....*$65–$85*

Jay, William. *Inquiry into Character and Tendency of American Anti-Slavery Soc.* 1838, 6th ed. ....*$30–$40*

Jebb, E. and R. Jebb. *Belloc the Man.* 1957. ....*$10–$12*

Jeffers, Leroy. *Call of the Mountains.* 1922, 1st ed. ......*$22–$30*

Jeffers, Rob. *Be Angry at the Sun.* NY, 1941, 1st ed, dj..*$27–$35*

Jefferson, Joseph. *"Rip Van Winkle": The Autobiography of Joseph Jefferson.* Lon, 1949, 1st ed, illus. ....*$13–$22*

Jehl, Francis. *Menlo Park Reminiscences.* 1936, 1st ed, illus, softcover. ....*$35–$45*

Jekyll, Gertrude. *Home and Garden.* Lon, 1900, illus. .*$31–$50*

Jekyll, Gertrude. *Wood and Garden. . . .* Lon, 1899, 1st ed, illus. ....*$75–$85*

Jellicoe, Viscount. *The Crisis of the Naval War.* NY/Lon, 1920, illus, plates, pocket charts. ....$40–$65

Jenkins, Dan. *Best 18 Golf Holes in America.* NY, 1966, 1st ed, dj. ....$22–$32

Jenkins, Rolland. *The Mediterranean Cruise Handbook for Travellers.* NY, 1928, illus, clr plates, maps. ....$30–$45

Jennings. *Book of Trout Flies.* 1970, 4th ed, dj. ....$22–$28

Jennings, Robert. *The Horse and His Diseases.* Phila, 1860, 1st ed, illus. ....$18–$22

Jensen, Ronald J. *The Alaska Purchase and Russian-American Relations.* Seattle, 1975. ....$14–$20

Jillson, Willard R. *The Coal Industry in Kentucky: An Historical Sketch.* Frankfort, 1922, 1st ed, illus. ....$35–$50

Job, H.K. *Propagation of Wild Birds.* Garden City, 1915, illus. ....$22–$30

Johnson. *The National Flag.* NY, illus, dj. ....$16–$20

Johnson, Capt. Charles. *The Lives and Actions of the Most Noted Highwaymen. . . .* Lon, 1839, 3rd ed. ....$100–$175

Johnson, Clifton. *The Picturesque Hudson.* NY, 1909, 1st ed, illus. ....$16–$20

Johnson, Clifton. *What to See in America.* NY, 1919, dj..$20–$28

Johnson, Edward, M.D. *The Domestic Pratice of Hydropathy.* NY, 1856, illus. ....$30–$40

Johnson, Harold. *Who's Who in the American League.* 1935. ....$27–$35

Johnson, Helen. *Woman and The Republic.* 1897, 1st ed. .$37–$50

Johnson, Howard F. *Researches into the Effects of Cold Water upon the Healthy Body.* Lon, 1850. ....$15–$20

Johnson, J.H. *Great Western Gun Works.* 1873, cat. ....$95–$150

Johnson, James Weldon (ed). *The Book of American Negro Spirituals.* NY, 1925. ....$15–$22

Johnson, Martin. *Safari.* NY, 1928, illus. ....$12–$22.50

Johnson, Merle. *American First Editions.* NY, 1936, 3rd ed. ....$25–$30

Johnson, Merle. *American First Editions.* 1932, ltd 1,000 cc.
....*$40–$45*

Johnson, Osa. *I Married Adventure.* Phila, 1940, illus. ...*$10–$20*

Johnson, W. Fletcher. *Life of Sitting Bull and History of the Indian War of 1890–91.* Edgewood Publishing Co., 1891, 1st ed, illus. ....*$40–$50*

Johnson, Walter R. *A Report to the Navy Dept. of the U.S. on American Coals....* GPO, 1844, 1st ed. ....*$60–$75*

Johnston, F.B. and T.T. Waterman. *The Early Architecture of North Carolina.* Univ. of North Carolina, 1947, 2nd prntg, folio, plates. ....*$150–$200*

Johnston, Harry V. *My Home on the Range.* Webb, 1942.
....*$22–$30*

Johnston, Henry P. *The Storming of Stony Point.* NY, 1900, 1st ed, illus, maps, plates. ....*$18–$25*

Johnston, Mary. *The Witch.* Houghton Mifflin, 1914, dj..*$30–$40*

Johnston, Mary. *To Have and to Hold.* Houghton Mifflin, 1900, illus by Howard Pyle. ....*$30–$40*

Johnstone, Annie Fellows. *Ole Mammy's Torment.* Bos, 1897.
....*$25–$45*

Johnstone, J. *An Account of the Discovery of the Power of Mineral Acid....* Lon, 1802. ....*$30–$40*

Jolly, W.P. *Marconi.* 1972, 1st ed, illus. ....*$22–$30*

Jones and Brown. *Swinging into Golf.* NY, 1937, 6th prntg.
....*$18–$22*

Jones, Addrienne. *Wild Voyageur: The Story of a Canada Goose.* Bos, 1966, 1st ed, dj, sgn. ....*$12–$17*

Jones, Bobby. *Golf is My Game.* NY, 1960, 1st ed, dj. .*$22–$30*

Jones, Howard. *Key for the Identification of Nests and Eggs of Common Birds.* OH, 1927, wrps. ....*$25–$30*

Jones, James. *From Here to Eternity.* NY, Scribner's, 1951, 1st ed, dj. ....*$110–$175*

Jones, James. *From Here to Eternity.* NY, 1951, dj. ......*$50–$85*

Jones, James. *Some Came Running.* NY, 1957, 1st ed, dj..*$28–$35*

Jones, Laurence Clifton. *Piney Woods and Its Story.* Revell, 1922, 1st ed, illus. ....$32–$45

Jones, LeRoi (aka Imamu Amiri Baraka). *Dutchman and the Slave.* Morrow, 1964, 1st ed, paperback. ....$15–$20

Jones, LeRoi (aka Imamu Amiri Baraka). *Home: Social Essays.* Morrow, 1966, 1st ed, dj. ....$30–$50

Jones, LeRoi (aka Imamu Amiri Baraka). *Raise: Essays since 1965.* Random House, 1971, 1st ed, dj. ....$25–$35

Jones, Louise Seymour. *The Human Side of Bookplates.* Ward Ritchie Press, 1951, illus. ....$22–$35

Jones, N.E. *The Squirrel Hunters of Ohio. . . .* Cinc, 1898, 1st ed, illus. ....$70–$85

Jones, P. *Annals and Recollections of Oneida County.* Rome, NY, 1851. ....$60–$80

Jones, Robert Edmond. *Drawings for the Theatre.* NY, 1925. ....$60–$80

Jones, Thomas. *The Experience of Thomas Jones . . . a Slave for Forty-three Years.* Bos, 1850, wrps, 2nd ed. ....$175–$450

Jones, Virgil Carrington. *Ranger Mosby.* Chapel Hill, 1944, 1st ed. ....$40–$85

Jong, Erica. *Parachutes and Kisses.* New American Library, 1984, 1st ed, dj. ....$20–$25

Jong, Erica. *Witches.* NY, 1981, 1st ed, illus by Jos. Smith, dj. ....$20–$30

Jordan, Weymouth T. *Hugh Davis and His Alabama Plantation.* Univ. of Alabama Press, 1948, 1st ed, dj. ....$30–$40

Josephson, Matthew. *Sidney Hillman: Statesman of American Labor.* NY, 1952, dj. ....$14–$20

Josephus, Ben Gorion. *The Wonderful and Most Deplorable Hist. of Latter Times of Jews.* Bellow Falls, VT, 1819, calf over bds. ....$45–$75

Josiah Allen's Wife. *Samantha at the Centennial.* Hartford, 1880, illus. ....$12–$18

Joyce, James. *Finnegan's Wake.* Lon, 1939, 1st trade ed, dj. ....$125–$450

Joyce, James. *Ulysses.* NY, Random House, 1st Authorized American ed. ....$135–$175

Joyce, James. *Ulysses.* Paris, 1932, 2 vols, wrps, 1st Odyssey Press ed. ....$150–$200

Jubb, Samuel. *History of the Shoddy-trade.* Lon, 1860, 1st ed, wrps. ....$37–$45

Jung, Carl. *Studies in Word-association.* NY, 1919. 1st American ed. ....$65–$90

Jung, Carl G. *Contributions to Analytical Psychology.* Harcourt, 1928, 1st English ed. ....$20–$30

Kael, Pauline. *The Citizen Kane Book.* Bos, 1971, 1st ed, illus, dj. ....$28–$35

Kafka, Franz. *The Trial.* Lon, 1937, 1st English ed. .....$30–$50

Kahn, E.J. *The Voice.* NY, 1947. ....$50–$75

Kahn, Edgar. *Cable Car Days in San Francisco.* Stanford, 1946, sgn presentation copy, 9th prntg. ....$20–$25

Kamm, Minnie W. *200 Pattern Glass Pitchers.* MI, 1941. .$8–$12

Kane, Elisha Kent. *Arctic Explorations: . . . in Search of Sir John Franklin.* Phila/Lon, 1856, 2 vols, illus. ....$95–$175

Kantor, MacKinlay. *Again the Bugle.* NY, 1958, 1st ed, illus, sgn. ....$35–$45

Kantor, MacKinlay. *The Children Sing.* Garden City, 1973, 1st ed, sgn, dj. ....$25–$35

Karloff, Boris (ed). *And the Darkness Falls.* Cleve, 1946, 1st ed. ....$17–$25

Katayev, Valentin. *A White Sail Gleams.* Moscow, 1954, illus. ....$22–$35

Katz, Doris. *Lady Was a Terrorist.* NY, 1953, dj. ....$10–$20

Kay, S. *Travels and Researches in Caffaria.* NY, 1834, fldg map. ....$30–$45

Keene, Carolyn. *The Spider Sapphire Mystery.* Grossett & Dunlap, 1968, dj. ....$3–$5

Keillor, Garrison. *Lake Wobegone Days.* Viking, 1985, 1st ed, dj. ....$30–$50

Keithahn, Edward. *Monuments in Cedar.* 1963, dj. ....$20–$30

Keithahn, Edward. *Monuments in Cedar.* Ketchikan, 1945, 1st ed, illus. ....$40–$95

Kelemen, P. *Medieval American Art.* NY, 1943, 2 vols, 1st ed. ....$30–$50

Keller, A.J. *A Theatre of Machines.* Lon, 1964, illus, folio, dj. ....$20–$30

Keller, Helen. *Optimism.* NY, 1903, 1st ed. ....$25–$35

Keller, Helen. *Our Duties to the Blind.* Bos, 1904, 1st ed. ....$25–$40

Keller, Helen. *The Story of My Life.* NY, 1904, 1st ed, illus. ....$37–$50

Kelley, Robert (ed). *The Sportsman's Anthology.* NY, 1944. ....$10–$15

Kelly, Col. Francis J. *U.S. Army Special Forces, 1961–1971.* DC, 1973, illus, maps. ....$9–$13

Kelly, Emmet. *Clown.* NY, 1954, 1st ed, ARC, dj. ....$35–$55

Kelly, Fanny. *Narrative of My Captivity among the Sioux Indians.* Hartford, 1871, 1st ed, illus. ....$125–$275

Kelly, Fred. *The Wright Brothers.* NY, 1943, 1st ed, dj..$18–$24

Kelly, H. *Some American Medical Botanists.* NY, 1914, illus, dj. ....$25–$35

Kelly, Walt. *Pogo.* 1951, wrps. ....$5–$10

Kelly, Walt. *Pogo a la Sundae.* NY, 1961, 1st ed, wrps..$18–$25

Kelly, Walt. *Positively Pogo.* NY, 1957, 1st ed, wrps. ...$18–$25

Kelly, Walt. *Song of the Pogo.* Simon & Schuster, 1956, 1st ed, illus by Kelly. ....$35–$60

Kelly, Walt. *The Incomplete Pogo.* NY, 1954, 1st ed, wrps. ....$18–$25

Kelly, Walt. *The Pogo Peek-a-Book.* NY, 1955, 1st ed, wrps, illus. ....$27–$30

Kelly, Walt. *The Pogo Sunday Book.* NY, 1956, 1st ed, wrps. ....$20–$25

Kelly, Walt. *Uncle Pogo So-So Stories.* NY, 1953, 1st ed, wrps.
....*$18–$25*

Kelsey, Albert. *The Architectural Annual.* Phila, 1900, illus.
....*$28–$35*

Kelsey, D.M. *Deeds of Daring by Both Blue and Gray.* Phila/St. Louis, 1884. ....*$47–$60*

Kelso, Isaac. *The Stars and Bars; or The Reign of Terror in Missouri.* Bos, 1863, 1st ed. ....*$40–$60*

Kemelman, Harry. *Sunday the Rabbi Stayed Home.* NY, 1969, 1st ed, dj. ....*$25–$30*

Kendall, J.B. *A Treatise on the Horse and His Diseases.* VT, 1891. ....*$25–$40*

Kennedy, Edward. *Our Day and Generation.* 1979, sgn, dj.
....*$30–$40*

Kennedy, John. *The History of Steam Navigation.* Liverpool, 1903, illus. ....*$90–$110*

Kennedy, John F. *Profiles in Courage.* NY, 1955, 1st ed, dj.
....*$65–$100*

Kennedy, Joseph P. *I'm for Roosevelt.* NY, 1936. ....*$95–$125*

Kennedy, Robert. *To Seek a Newer World.* 1967, 1st ed, dj.
....*$14–$25*

Kennedy, Sen. John F. *The Strategy of Peace.* NY, 1960, 1st ed.
....*$35–$40*

Kent, Rockwell. *A Northern Christmas.* NY, 1941, dj. ..*$35–$40*

Kent, Rockwell. *Candide.* Random House, 1928, ltd ed, sgn.
....*$125–$150*

Kent, Rockwell. *How I Make a Woodcut.* Pasadena, 1934, 1st ed, dj. ....*$18–$25*

Kent, Rockwell. *N by E.* Brewer & Warren, 1930, 1st ed, illus by Rockwell Kent, dj. ....*$25–$35*

Kent, Rockwell. *Rockwell Kent's Greenland Book.* Harcourt, 1935, 1st ed, dj. ....*$35–$50*

Kent, Rockwell. *Rockwell Kentiana.* NY, 1933, 1st ed, dj.
....*$35–$50*

Kent, Rockwell. *Salamina.* NY, 1935, 1st ed, dj. ....*$35–$40*

Kerouac, Jack. *Lonesome Traveler.* NY, 1960, 1st ed, dj..*$30–$60*

Kerouac, Jack. *On the Road.* Viking, 1957, 1st ed, dj. .*$325–$700*

Kerouac, Jack. *Pull My Daisy.* Grove Press, 1959, 1st ed, dj. ....*$80–$85*

Kerouac, Jack. *Satori in Paris.* NY, 1966, 1st ed, dj. ...*$35–$75*

Kerouac, Jack. *The Dharma Bums.* NY, 1958, 1st ed, dj. ....*$125–$200*

Kerouac, Jack. *Tristessa.* NY, 1960, 1st ed, wrps. ....*$40–$60*

Kerouac, Jack. *Visions of Cody.* McGraw-Hill, 1972, 1st ed, dj. ....*$65–$85*

Kerouac, John (Jack). *The Town and the City.* NY, 1950, 1st ed, dj. ....*$175–$450*

Kersh, Gerald. *The Battle of the Singing Men.* Lon, 1944, 1st ed, dj. ....*$12.50–$20*

Kersh, Gerald. *The Horrible Dummy and Other Stories.* Lon, 1944, 2nd ed, dj. ....*$35–$45*

Kertesz, A. *Americana, Mayflower Books.* 1979, stiff wrps. ....*$16–$22*

Kesey, Ken. *Kesey's Garage Sale.* NY, Viking, 1973, 1st ed, sgn, dj. ....*$125–$150*

Kesey, Ken. *Kesey's Garage Sale.* NY, Viking, 1973, 1st ed, dj. ....*$50–$100*

Kesey, Ken. *One Flew Over the Cuckoo's Nest.* Viking, 1962, 1st ed, dj. ....*$150–$400*

Kesey, Ken. *Sometimes a Great Notion.* 1964, 1st ed, dj. ....*$150–$200*

Key, Alexander. *The Red Eagle.* NY, 1930, illus. ....*$20–$35*

Keynes, J.M. *The Economic Consequences of the Peace.* NY, 1920, 1st ed. ....*$20–$25*

Keynes, Milo. *Essays on John Maynard Keynes.* Camb, 1976, illus, rprnt, dj. ....*$10–$15*

Khayyam, Omar. *The Rubaiyat.* Lon, nd, illus by Doris Palmer, folio, tip-in plates. ....*$50–$85*

Khayyam, Omar. *The Rubaiyat.* Houghton Mifflin, 1894, illus by Elihu Vedder. ....$45–$75

Kidder, Daniel P. *Mormonism and the Mormons.* NY, 1844. ....$65–$75

Kieran, John. *The American Sporting Scene.* NY, 1941, illus, clr and b/w, dj. ....$10–$15

Kiernan, Dr. P.F. *Hints on Horse-shoeing.* np, nd, illus..$37–$40

Kincaid, Jamaica. *A Small Place.* NY, 1988, 1st ed, dj..$25–$35

King, Clarence. *Mountaineering in the Sierra Nevada.* Lon, 1903. ....$24–$30

King, Constance Eileen. *The Collector's History of Dolls.* NY, 1981, 1st ed, dj. ....$18–$20

King, Coretta Scott. *My Life with Martin Luther King, Jr.* NY, 1969, 1st ed, dj. sgn. ....$50–$75

King, F.H. *Farmers of Forty Centuries.* WI, 1911, illus, photos. ....$20–$30

King, Martin Luther Jr. *Where Do We Go from Here: Chaos or Community?* NY, 1967, 1st ed, dj. ....$75–$125

King, Stephen. *Cujo.* 1981, 1st ed, dj. ....$10–$20

King, Stephen. *The Dark Half.* Hodder & Stoughton, 1989, 1st English ed, dj. ....$25–$45

King, Stephen. *The Dark Tower: The Gunslinger.* West Kingston, 1982, 1st ed, dj. ....$300–$600

King, Stephen. *The Dark Tower II: The Drawing of the 3.* Grant Pub., 1987, 1st ed. ....$60–$125

King, Stephen. *The Shining.* Doubleday, 1977, 1st ed, dj. ....$75–$225

King, Stephen. *The Tommyknockers.* 1987, 1st ed, dj. ...$15–$20

Kingsford, Anna Bonus. *The Ideal in Diet.* Lon, 1898. .$24–$35

Kingsley, Charles. *Westward Ho!* NY, 1936, illus by N.C. Wyeth. ....$40–$45

Kinnell, Galway. *The Essential Whitman.* Ecco Press, 1987, 1st ed, dj. ....$20–$28

Kinnell, Galway. *What a Kingdom It Was.* Bos, 1960, 3rd prntg, sgn, dj. ....*$60–$75*

Kinney, Bruce. *Frontier Missionary Problems, Their Character and Solution.* NY, 1918. ....*$18–$25*

Kip, William I. *The Early Jesuit Missions in North America.* NY, 1846, 2 vols in 1. ....*$140–$200*

Kipling, R. *Barrack Room Ballads.* 1899, 1st ed, illus...*$20–$30*

Kipling, Rudyard. *Collected Dog Stories.* Lon, 1939, illus. ....*$10–$15*

Kipling, Rudyard. *Dipsey Chanty.* 1898, illus. ....*$50–$75*

Kipling, Rudyard. *Kim.* NY, 1901, 1st American ed. ....*$45–$70*

Kipling, Rudyard. *Kim.* Lon, 1901, 1st ed. ....*$65–$75*

Kipling, Rudyard. *Puck of Pooks Hill.* illus by Arthur Rackham. ....*$50–$75*

Kipling, Rudyard. *Sea Warfare.* Lon, 1916. ....*$30–$35*

Kipling, Rudyard. *Stalky & Company.* NY, 1899, 1st U.S. ed, dj. ....*$22–$45*

Kipling, Rudyard. *The Drums of Fore and Aft.* 1898, 1st ed. ....*$18–$30*

Kipling, Rudyard. *The Second Jungle Book.* Lon, 1895, 1st ed. ....*$75–$100*

Kipling, Rudyard. *The Works of Rudyard Kipling.* Doubleday/McClure, 1898, 14 vols, ¾ lea, bds, teg. ....*$150–$175*

Kirby, Georgiana B. *Years of Experience: An Autobiographical Narrative.* NY, 1887, 1st ed. ....*$120–$200*

Kirk, Russell. *Lord of the Dark Hollow.* NY, 1979, 1st ed, dj. ....*$20–$30*

Kitto, John. *Palestine: Physical Geography, Natural History....* Lon, 1841, illus, ¾ calf. ....*$45–$75*

Kittredge, George. *Witchcraft in Old New England.* Harvard, 1929. ....*$45–$62*

Kittredge, Henry. *Shipmasters of Cape Cod.* 1935, 1st ed, dj. ....*$15–$20*

Kittredge, Henry C. *Cape Cod.* Bos, 1930, sgn. ....*$18–$25*

Kitzmiller, Helen H. *One Hundred Years of Western Reserve.* OH, 1926, photos. ....$10–$15

Klein, Frederic Shriver (ed). *Just South of Gettysburg, Carroll County, Md., in the Civil War.* MD, 1963, 1st ed, sgn, dj. .$42–$50

Klingberg, Frank. *An Appraisal of the Negro in Colonial S.C.* DC, 1941, 1st ed. ....$35–$45

Knapp, Samuel L. *A Memoir of the Life of Daniel Webster.* Bos, 1831, 1st ed. ....$30–$45

Knight, Lucian. *Stone Mountain.* Atlanta, 1923. ....$14–$18

Knight, Mrs. Helen C. *Hannah More. . . .* NY, American Tract Society, 1862, rev ed. ....$42–$55

Knohl, D. *Siege in Hills of Hebron.* 1958. ....$14–$21

Knowles, James D. *Memoir of Mrs. Ann H. Judson.* Bos, 1829, fldg map, calf. ....$45–$60

Knox, Dudley W. *The Naval Genius of George Washington.* Bos, 1932, 1st ed, ltd 550 cc. ....$65–$85

Knox, Thomas W. *Adventures of Two Youths in a Journey to Egypt and Holy Land.* NY, 1883, illus. ....$20–$30

Knox, Thomas W. *Boy Travellers in Central Europe.* NY, 1893, illus. ....$20–$30

Knox, Thomas W. *Boy Travellers in the Russian Empire.* NY, 1887, illus. ....$30–$45

Knox, Thomas W. *The Underground World.* Hartford, 1882, illus. ....$65–$110

Koch, R. *Louis Tiffany Rebel in Glass.* NY, 1966, dj. ....$18–$25

Koehn, A. *Art of Japanese Flower Arrangement.* Japan, 1933. ....$22–$30

Koestler, Arthur. *Thieves in the Night.* Macmillan, 1946, 1st American ed, dj. ....$18–$25

Kolpacoff, V. *Prisoners of Quai Dong.* 1967, wrps. ....$18–$20

Koontz, Dean R. *Coldfire.* Putnam, 1991, ltd 750 cc, dj, slipcase. ....$175–$225

Koontz, Dean R. *Dark of the Woods/Soft Come the Dragons.* NY, 1970, 1st ed, paperback. ....$10–$45

Kopp, Marie. *Birth Control in Practice.* NY, 1934, 1st ed, dj. ....$40–$50

Korn, Bertram Wallace. *American Jewry and the Civil War.* Phila, 1951, 1st ed, illus. ....$35–$45

Kornbluth, C.M. *A Mile beyond the Moon.* NY, 1958, 1st ed, dj. ....$30–$40

Kornbluth, Jesse. *Pre-Pop Warhol.* NY, 1988, 1st ed. ...$58–$70

Kouwenhoven, John. *The Columbia Historical Portrait of New York.* NY, 1953, dj. ....$40–$60

Kowalski, Isaac. *A Secret Press in Nazi Europe.* NY, 1969, dj. ....$20–$30

Krauss, Ruth. *A Hole Is To Dig.* Harper & Row, illus by Maurice Sendak, dj. ....$20–$22

Krider, John. *Forty Years Notes of a Field Ornithologist.* Phila, 1879. ....$30–$50

Krieger, L.C. *The Mushroom Handbook.* NY, 1936, illus, clr and b/w, dj. ....$14–$23

Krige, E.J. *The Social System of the Zulus.* Lon, 1957, illus, 3rd ed. ....$35–$45

Krug, J.A. *The Columbia River.* DC, 1947, illus, folio, pocket maps. ....$35–$50

Kunstler, William M. *Deep in My Heart.* NY, 1966, 1st ed, sgn, dj. ....$22–$30

Kunz, George Frederick. *The Curious Lore of Precious Stones.* Phila, 1913, illus. ....$125–$150

Kuran, Aptullah. *The Mosque in Early Ottoman Architecture.* Chi, 1968, illus. ....$35–$50

Kurtz and Erlich. *The Art of the Toy Soldier.* NY, 1987, illus, folio. ....$40–$60

Kurtz, Wilbur. *Atlanta and the Old South.* Atlanta, 1969. ....$8–$12

Kyne, Peter B. *Never the Twain Shall Meet.* Cosmopolitan, 1923, 1st ed. ....$14–$18

L'Amour, Louis. *Over on the Dry Side.* NY, 1975, 1st ed, dj. ....$50–$75

L'Amour, Louis. *Rivers West.* NY, 1975, 1st ed, dj. ......$50–$75

L'Engle, Madeleine. *A Wrinkle in Time.* NY, 1987, 1st ed, dj. ....$65–$75

L'Engle, Madeleine. *Ladder of Angels.* Seabury, 1979, 1st ed, illus, dj. ....$18–$25

La Fontaine, Jean de. *Fables.* Whitman Pub., 1934, illus. ....$14–$20

La Monte, Francesca. *North American Game Fishes.* NY, 1945, 1st ed, illus, limp lea, clr plates. ....$14–$18

Lacroix, Paul. *The Arts in the Middle Ages.* NY, 1875, illus. ....$22–$30

Lafarge, John. *The Higher Life in Art.* NY, 1908, 1st ed..$45–$50

LaFarge, Oliver. *As Long as the Grass Will Grow.* Alliance Book Corp., 1940, illus, sgn. ....$35–$55

LaFarge, Oliver. *Laughing Boy.* Houghton Mifflin, 1929, 1st ed, dj. ....$25–$175

LaFayette, Gen. *Memoirs of Embracing Details of Public and Private Life.* Hartford, 1825, 1st ed, lea. ....$50–$65

Lafflin, John. *British Campaign Medals.* NY, 1964. ....$12–$20

Lahee, Henry C. *Famous Violinists of To-day and Yesterday.* Bos, 1906, illus. ....$25–$35

Laing, Alexander. *Clipper Ship Men.* NY, 1944, 1st ed, dj. ....$14–$20

Laing, Alexander. *Dr. Scarlett.* NY, 1936, 1st ed, dj. .$14–$17.50

Lair, John. *Songs Lincoln Loved.* NY, 1954, illus. ....$18–$22

Lake, Simon. *The Submarine in War and Peace.* Phila, 1918, 1st ed, illus, photos, presentation copy, sgn. ....$50–$75

Lamb, Charles. *Grass of Parnassus.* Lon, 1888, 1st ed. .$16–$22

Lamb, Charles and Mary. *Tales from Shakespeare.* Lon/NY, 1909, illus by Arthur Rackham. ....$50–$75

Lamb, Frank W. *Indian Baskets of North America.* Riverside, CA, 1972, illus, dj. ....$45–$75

Lamb, M. *The Homes of America.* NY, 1879, illus. ....$50–$65

Lamb, Mrs. Martha. *History of the City of New York: Its Origin, Rise, and Progress.* NY, Barnes, 1877, 2 vols, illus, maps, plates. ....*$35–$45*

Lamb, Wallace E. *The Lake Champlain and Lake George Valleys.* NY, 1940, 3 vols, illus, maps. ....*$100–$165*

Lamon and Slocum. *The Mating and Breeding of Poultry.* NY, 1920, illus. ....*$40–$60*

Lancaster, Bruce. *No Bugles Tonight.* Bos, Little Brown, 1948, 1st ed, dj. ....*$18–$25*

Land, Barbara. *The New Explorers.* NY, 1981, illus. ......*$5–$10*

Landis, C.S. *Twenty-two Caliber Varmint Rifles.* Small Arms Tech, 1957, 1st ed, dj. ....*$25–$35*

Lane, Mark. *Rush to Judgement.* NY, 1968, 1st ed, dj. .*$15–$25*

Lane, Rev. *12 Years in a Reformatory.* Self-published, 1934. ....*$14–$22*

Lang, Andrew. *The Disentanglers.* NY, 1902, 1st U.S. ed. ....*$35–$45*

Lang, Andrew. *The True Story Book.* Lon, 1893, 1st ed, illus by H.J. Ford. ....*$40–$60*

Lang, H.O. *History of the Willamette Valley.* Portland, 1885, rbnd. ....*$125–$200*

Langdon, Amelie. *Just for Two: Recipes Designed for Two Persons.* Minn, 1907. ....*$15–$22*

Langdon, W.C. *The American Telephone Historical Collection.* 1924, 1st ed, softcover. ....*$10–$15*

Langley, S. *Experiments in Aerodynamics.* DC, 1891, 1st ed. ....*$150–$200*

Laqueur, Walter. *A History of Zionism.* NY, 1971, 1st ed, dj. ....*$18–$25*

Lardner, Rev. Dionysius. *The Cabinet Cyclopaedia.* Phila, 1832, illus. ....*$50–$65*

Lardner, Ring. *Gullible's Travels, Etc.* Ind, 1917, 1st ed, dj. ....*$30–$35*

Lardner, Ring. *My Four Weeks in France.* Ind, 1918, 1st ed, dj. ....*$60–$72*

Lardner, Ring. *Round Up.* Lon, 1935, 1st English ed, dj..*$15–$30*

Lardner, Ring. *The Big Town.* NY, 1925, 1st ed. ....*$28–$40*

Lardner, Ring. *The Story of a Wonder Man.* NY, 1927, 1st ed. ....*$28–$40*

Lardner, Ring. *You Know Me Al.* NY, 1925. ....*$30–$37*

Larned, Linda H. *The New Hostess To-day.* NY, 1917. .*$14–$21*

Lartigue, Jacques-Henri. *Les Femmes Aux Cigarettes.* NY, 1980, illus, 1st American ed, dj. ....*$35–$45*

Lathrop, Elise. *Early American Inns and Taverns.* NY, 1936. ....*$18–$22*

Lathrop, Elise. *Historic Houses of Early America.* NY, 1927, illus. ....*$12–$25*

Lathrop, Elise. *Historic Houses of Early America.* NY, 1927, 1st ed, illus, dj. ....*$65–$88*

Latil, Pierre De. *Thinking by Machine.* 1957, 1st ed illus, dj. ....*$22–$30*

Latimer, Elizabeth. *Familiar Talks on Some of Shakespeare's Comedies.* Bos, 1886, 1st ed. ....*$18–$25*

Lattimore, Owen. *Inner Asian Frontiers of China.* NY, 1940, illus. ....*$18–$25*

Laurie, J. and R.S. Gutteridge. *The Homeopathic Domestic Medicine.* . . . Lon, 1888. ....*$35–$45*

Laut, Agnes C. *Pathfinders of the West.* NY, 1927, dj. ......*$25–$40*

Laut, Agnes C. *Pathfinders of the West.* NY, 1904, 1st ed. ....*$40–$50*

Laut, Agnes C. *Story of the Trapper.* Tor, 1902, 1st ed..*$25–$35*

Laut, Agnes C. *The Blazed Trail of the Old Frontier.* NY, 1926, 1st ed, illus by Chas. M. Russell, fldg maps. ....*$125–$175*

Laut, Agnes C. *The Conquest of Our Western Empire.* NY, 1927, 1st ed. ....*$25–$35*

Laut, Agnes C. *The Conquest of the Great Northwest.* . . . NY, 1908, 2 vols, 1st ed, illus. ....*$30–$65*

Laut, Agnes C. *The Fur Trade of America.* NY, 1921, 1st ed. ....*$30–$50*

Laut, Agnes C. *Vikings of the Pacific.* Macmillan, 1905, 1st ed. ....$25–$30

Lawrence, A. *A Present for M. Lincoln.* Macon, 1961, 1st ed, illus, dj. ....$22–$30

Lawrence, D.H. *Amores.* NY, 1916, 1st American ed. ...$60–$75

Lawrence, D.H. *David.* Knopf, 1926, dj. ....$65–$75

Lawrence, D.H. *Lady Chatterley's Lover.* Knopf, 1932, 1st American ed. ....$75–$125

Lawrence, D.H. *Lady Chatterley's Lover.* Florence, Italy, private prntg, 1928, 1st ed, ltd 1,000 cc, sgn, dj. ....$250–$3,000

Lawrence, D.H. *Pornography and Obscenity.* Faber & Faber, 1929, 1st English ed. ....$50–$65

Lawrence, D.H. *We Need One Another.* NY, Equinox, 1933, 1st ed, illus by J.P. Heins, dj. ....$50–$70

Lawrence, D.H. *Women in Love.* NY, 1922, 1st ed, 2nd prntg. ....$50–$65

Lawrence, Josephine. *The Berry Patch.* Cupples & Leon, 1925, illus by Thelma Gooch. ....$12–$20

Lawrence, T.E. *Revolt in the Desert.* NY, 1927, 1st U.S. ed, dj. ....$50–$250

Lawrence, T.E. *Seven Pillars of Wisdom.* Doubleday/Duran, 1935, 1st ed, dj. ....$50–$75

Lawson, Cecil C.P. *Naval Ballads and Sea Songs.* Lon, 1933, illus. ....$25–$35

Lawson, Charles. *Lawson's Switcher Guide on the Game of Checkers.* Worcester, MA, 1899, 1st ed. ....$22–$35

Lawson, John. *The History of North Carolina.* Raleigh, 1860, 1st ed. ....$115–$150

Lawson, Robert. *Rabbit Hill.* NY, 1944, 1st ed, dj. ....$35–$65

Lawson, Robert. *Rabbit Hill.* NY, 1944, 3rd prntg, dj. ...$18–$20

Lawson, Robert. *Rabbit Hill.* NY, 1944, illus by Lawson, 2nd prntg. ....$25–$35

Layard, Austen H. *Discoveries in the Ruins of Nineveh and Babylon.* NY, 1853, 1st ed, illus, maps, lithos. ....$115–$150

Layard, Austen H. *Nineveh and Its Remains.* . . . NY, 1849, mor, aeg. ....$80–$95

Lazarus, Emma. *Songs of a Semite.* NY, 1882, 1st ed. .$65–$90

Lazenby, Marion B. *History of Methodism in Alabama and West Florida.* Birmingham, 1960. ....$25–$45

Le Carre, John. *A Small Town in Germany.* Coward, 1968, 1st U.S. ed, dj. ....$25–$35

Le Carre, John. *Call for the Dead.* 1962, 1st American ed, dj. ....$40–$50

Le Carre, John. *The Little Drummer Girl.* Lon, Hodder & Stoughton, 1983, 1st U.K. ed, dj. ....$45–$60

Le Carre, John. *The Looking Glass War.* NY, 1965. .....$28–$35

Le Carre, John. *The Looking Glass War.* Lon, 1965, 1st English ed, dj. ....$40–$85

Le Carre, John. *The Russia House.* Knopf, 1989, 1st American ed, dj. ....$75–$110

Le Carre, John. *The Secret Pilgrim.* Lon, Hodder & Stoughton, 1991, 1st U.K. ed, sgn, dj. ....$85–$100

Le Carre, John. *Tinker, Tailor, Soldier, Spy.* NY, 1974, dj. ....$20–$25

Le Gallienne, Richard. *Pieces of Eight.* . . . NY, 1918, 1st ed, dj. ....$20–$35

Le Gallienne, Richard. *The Romance of Perfume.* NY/Paris, 1928, 1st ed, illus by George Barbier, clr plates, Richard Hudnut brochure in rear pocket. ....$125–$185

Le Moine, J.M. *Picturesque Quebec.* Montreal, 1882, softcover. ....$24–$30

Lea, Elizabeth E. *Domestic Cookery, Useful Receipts, Etc.* Balt, 1853, 5th ed. ....$50–$85

Lea, Isaac. *Descriptions of the Soft Parts . . . of Unionidae of the U.S.* Phila, 1863, 1st ed, wrps, illus, folio. ....$75–$100

Lea, Tom. *Bullfight Manual for Spectators.* El Paso, 1957. ....$14–$20

Lea, Tom. *The King Ranch.* Little Brown, 1957, 2 vols, 1st ed. ....$40–$65

Lea, Tom. *The King Ranch.* Bos, 1957, 2 vols, sgn, slipcase. ....*$125–$200*

Lea, Tom. *The Wonderful Country.* Bos, 1952, 1st ed, dj..*$25–$35*

Leacock, Stephen. *My Discovery of England.* NY, 1922. .*$10–$14*

Leadbeater, C.W. *Some Glimpses of Occultism.* Lon, 1903. ....*$14–$20*

Leaf, Earl. *Isles of Rhythm.* NY, 1948, 1st ed, illus, dj. .*$14–$20*

Leaf, Munro. *Wee Gillis.* NY, 1938, 1st ed, illus by Robert Lawson. ....*$35–$55*

Leakey, Dr. L.S.B. *White African.* 1966, dj. ....*$10–$15*

Leary, Timothy. *High Priest.* NY, 1968, 1st ed. ....*$25–$35*

Lederer, William and Eugene Burdick. *The Ugly American.* 1958, 1st ed, dj. ....*$25–$35*

Lee, Art. *Fishing Dry Flies for Trout on Rivers and Streams.* NY, 1982, 1st ed, dj. ....*$30–$50*

Lee, Gypsy Rose. *Gypsy.* NY, 1957, 1st ed. ....*$14–$18*

Lee, Harper. *To Kill a Mockingbird.* Lon, 1960, 1st British ed. ....*$100–$250*

Lee, Harper. *To Kill a Mockingbird.* Phila, 1960, 1st ed, dj. ....*$900–$1,250*

Lee, Laurie. *I Can't Stay Long.* 1976, 1st ed, dj. ....*$10–$15*

Lee, Robert. *Clinical Midwifery.* Phila, 1849, 1st American ed. ....*$125–$150*

Lee-Elliot, Theyre. *Paintings of the Ballet.* Lon, 1947, illus. ....*$18–$25*

Leeson, F. *Identification of Snakes of the Gold Coast.* Lon, 1950, illus. ....*$65–$100*

Leffingwell. *The Art of Wing Shooting.* Chi/NY, 1894. ..*$38–$45*

Leffingwell, William Bruce (ed). *Shooting on Upland, Marsh, and Stream.* Chi/NY, 1890. ....*$75–$125*

Leger, Jacques Nicolas. *Haiti, Her History and Her Detractors.* NY/Wash, 1907, 1st ed. ....*$95–$150*

Lehner, Joseph C. *Worlds Fair Menu and Recipe Book.* SF, 1915. ....*$37–$50*

Leiber, Fritz. *A Specter is Haunting Texas.* NY, 1969, 1st ed, dj.
....*$45–$60*

Leiber, Fritz. *Gather Darkness.* NY, Grosset & Dunlap, 1950, dj.
....*$14–$22*

Leiber, Fritz. *Heroes and Horrors.* Chappel Hill, 1978, 1st ed, illus by Tim Kirk, dj. ....*$14–$17.50*

Leighton, A. *Early American Gardens.* 1970, 2nd ed, dj..*$14–$20*

Leighton, Clare. *Four Hedges.* NY, 1935, illus by Leighton, sgn.
....*$28–$35*

Leisenring, James E. and Vernon S. Hidy. *The Art of Tying the Wet Fly and Fishing the Flymph.* NY, 1972, dj. ....*$25–$35*

Leiser, Eric. *The Complete Book of Fly Tying.* NY, 1977, 1st ed, dj. ....*$14–$18*

Leland, E.H. *Farm Homes.* NY, 1881, illus. ....*$30–$67*

Lennon, John. *A Spaniard in the Works.* Lon, 1965. ...*$85–$125*

Lennon, John. *A Spaniard in the Works.* NY, 1965, 1st American ed. ....*$60–$80*

Lenski, Lois. *High-rise Secret.* Lippincott, 1966, illus by Lensky, 4th prntg. ....*$10–$15*

Lenski, Lois. *Strawberry Girl.* Lippincott, 1945, 1st ed, illus by Lenski. ....*$25–$35*

Lenski, Lois. *The Little Fire Engine.* 1946, 1st ed. ....*$16–$20*

Lenski, Lois. *The Little Train.* 1940, 11th prntg. ....*$10–$15*

Lentz, Harold. *The Pop-up Pinnochio.* NY, 1932. ....*$95–$125*

Leslie, Frank. *Famous Leaders and Battle Scenes of the Civil War.* NY, 1896, 1st ed, folio. ....*$135–$160*

Leslie, Miss. *75 Receipts for Pastry, Cakes, and Sweetmeats.* Bos, nd. ....*$145–$185*

Leslie, Miss. *Directions for Cookery.* Phila, 1863, 59th ed.
....*$18–$25*

Leslie, Miss. *Miss Leslie's New Recipes for Cooking.* Phila, 1854.
....*$120–$150*

Lessing, Doris. *African Stories.* NY, 1965, 1st ed, dj. ....*$25–$35*

Lessing, Doris. *The Habit of Loving.* Crowell, 1957, 1st U.S. ed, dj. ....*$30–$40*

Lessing, Doris. *The Sirian Experiments.* Lon, 1st ed, dj..*$30–$60*

Leutz, Charles R. *Modern Radio Reception.* 1924, 1st ed, illus. ....*$40–$55*

Levi, Wendell M. *The Pigeon.* Sumter, SC, 1963, illus, sgn. ....*$50–$65*

Levine, Philip. *A Walk with Tom Jefferson.* NY, 1988, 1st ed, sgn, dj. ....*$55–$72*

Lewis, Alfred Henry. *Wolfville.* Stokes, NY, 1897, 1st ed, illus by Frederick Remington. ....*$60–$90*

Lewis, Franklin. *The Cleveland Indians.* 1949, 2nd imp, dj. ....*$15–$22*

Lewis, G. Griffin. *The Practical Book of Oriental Rugs.* Phila/Lon, 1920, illus, 5th ed. ....*$65–$100*

Lewis, Oscar. *Sagebrush Casinos.* NY, 1953, dj. ....*$15–$20*

Lewis, Sinclair. *Arrowsmith.* Tor, 2d prntg. ....*$18–$25*

Lewis, Sinclair. *Babbitt.* NY, 1922, 1st ed, dj. ....*$75–$90*

Lewis, Sinclair. *Dodsworth.* NY, 1929, 1st ed. ....*$20–$35*

Lewis, Sinclair. *Elmer Gantry.* NY, 1927, 1st ed, dj. .....*$25–$35*

Lewis, Sinclair. *Free Air.* Harcourt, 1938, 1st ed, dj.......*$30–$45*

Lewis, Sinclair. *The Prodigal Parents.* Doubleday, 1938, 1st ed, dj. ....*$45–$60*

Lewis, Willie Newbury. *Between Sun and Sod.* TX, 1939, 1st ed, dj. ....*$45–$60*

Lichten, Frances. *Folk Art of Rural Pennsylvania.* Scribner's, 1946, 1st ed. ....*$18–$25*

Lincoln, Mrs. *Boston Cook Book.* Bos, 1894. ....*$45–$60*

Lincoln, Mrs. *Boston Cook Book.* Bos, 1884. ....*$150–$350*

Lincoln, Mrs. *Boston School Kitchen Textbook.* Bos, 1887. ....*$27–$45*

Lincoln, Mrs. D.A. *Boston Cook Book.* Bos, 1886. ....*$50–$75*

Lindbergh, Anne Morrow. *Dearly Beloved.* Harcourt, 1962, sgn, dj. ....*$25–$30*

Lindbergh, Anne Morrow. *Gift from the Sea.* 1955, 1st ed, illus by George W. Thompson, slipcase. ....*$25–$35*

Lindbergh, Anne Morrow. *Listen! The Wind.* Harcourt, 1938, 1st ed, dj. ....*$18–$22*

Lindbergh, Charles A. *The Spirit of St. Louis.* Scribner's, 1953. ....*$10–$20*

Lindbergh, Charles A. *We.* NY, 1927, 1st ed, dj. ....*$35–$65*

Lindley and Widney. *California of the South.* NY, 1888, 1st ed, illus. ....*$32–$45*

Lindsay, David Moore. *A Voyage to the Arctic in the Whaler "Aurora."* Bos, 1911, 1st ed, illus. ....*$60–$75*

Lindsay, Merrill. *100 Great Guns: An Illustrated History of Firearms.* NY, 1967, 1st ed, dj. ....*$28–$35*

Lionni, Leo. *Fish is Fish.* 1970. ....*$12–$15*

Lipman, Jean. *American Primitive Painting.* Lon, 1942. .*$60–$75*

Lipman, Jean. *The Collector in America.* NY, 1971. ......*$16–$20*

Lipton, Lawrence. *The Holy Barbarians.* NY, 1959, 1st ed, dj. ....*$45–$65*

Littlejohn, F.J. *Legends of Michigan and the Old Northwest.* MI, 1875. ....*$40–$60*

Livingstone, David. *Missionary Travels and Researches in South Africa.* NY, 1858, illus, maps. ....*$120–$150*

Lloyd, Freeman. *All Spaniels.* NY, nd, illus. ....*$15–$25*

Lobel, Anita. *Potatoes, Potatoes.* Harper & Row, 1967, sgn, dj. ....*$20–$35*

Lobel, Arnold. *On Market Street.* Greenwillow, 1981, 1st ed, illus by Anita Lobel, sgn, dj. ....*$15–$25*

Lockhart, J.G. *Mysteries of the Sea.* Lon, 1924, illus. ..*$16–$20*

Lockwood, Thomas D. *Electricity, Magnetism, and Electric Telegraphy.* 1883, 1st ed, illus. ....*$45–$65*

Lodge, Edmund. *Lodges Portraits.* Bos, 1902, 12 vols, ltd 1,000 cc, lea. ....*$500–$750*

Lodge, Henry Cabot. *The Senate and the League of Nations.* NY, 1925, dj. ....*$15–$22*

Lodge, Sir Oliver. *Atoms and Rays.* 1924, 1st ed. ....*$32–$40*

Lodge, Sir Oliver. *Past Years: An Autobiography.* 1932, 1st ed, illus. ....*$30–$40*

Loeb, Leo. *The Biological Basis of Individuality.* Springfield, 1945. ....*$25–$40*

Lofting, Hugh. *Doctor Dolittle in the Moon.* Stokes, 1928, 1st ed, illus. ....*$45–$55*

Lofting, Hugh. *Dr. Dolittle and the Secret Lake.* Lippincott, 1948, 1st ed. ....*$30–$40*

Lofting, Hugh. *Dr. Doolittle's Circus.* Stokes, 1924, 1st ed, illus. ....*$25–$30*

Logan, H. and L.C. Cosper. *Orchids Are Easy to Grow.* Englewood Cliffs, 1949, dj. ....*$25–$35*

Logan, Olive. *Apropos of Women and Theatres.* NY, 1870. ....*$27–$35*

Logue, Roscoe. *Tumbleweeds and Barb Wire Fences.* Amarillo, 1936, 1st ed, illus. ....*$30–$45*

Logue, Roscoe. *Under Texas and Border Skies.* Amarillo, 1935, wrps, 2nd prntg. ....*$45–$65*

Lomax, A. *Mister Jelly Roll.* NY, 1950, dj. ....*$20–$60*

Lomax, John. *Adventures of a Ballad Hunter.* NY, 1947, 1st ed, dj. ....*$30–$50*

Lomax, John. *American Ballads and Folk Songs.* NY, 1934, 1st ed. ....*$30–$45*

London, Charmian K. *The Log of the Snark.* NY, 1916, illus. ....*$45–$50*

London, H.R. *Portraits of Jews by Gilbert Stuart and Other Early Amer. Artists.* Rutland, VT, 1969, 1st ed, dj. ....*$25–$35*

London, Jack. *Best Short Stories of Jack London.* Garden City, 1945, dj. ....*$18–$30*

London, Jack. *Burning Daylight.* Macmillan, 1910, 1st ed. ....*$100–$125*

London, Jack. *Daughter of Snows.* NY, 1902, 2nd ed. ..*$22–$35*

London, Jack. *Jerry of the Islands.* Macmillan, 1917, 1st ed. ....$85–$100

London, Jack. *Love of Life.* 1st ed. ....$100–$115

London, Jack. *Scarlet Plague.* Macmillan, 1915, 1st ed. ....$125–$200

London, Jack. *Smoke Bellew.* Century, 1912, 1st ed. .....$75–$90

London, Jack. *The Cruise of the Snark.* NY, 1911, illus. ....$125–$200

London, Jack. *The Game.* Macmillan, 1905, 1st ed. ....$85–$125

London, Jack. *The Little Lady of the Big House.* Macmillan, 1916, 1st ed, illus. ....$65–$85

London, Jack. *The Turtles of Tasman.* Macmillan, 1916, 1st ed. . ...$225–$300

London, Jack. *White Fang.* NY, 1906, 1st ed, illus, clr plates. ....$75–$110

Long, E. *History of Pathology.* Balt, 1928, 1st ed. ....$25–$35

Long, Huey. *My First Days in the White House.* Telegraph Press, 1935, 1st ed. ....$45–$50

Long, Mason. *The Life of Mason Long, the Converted Gambler.* Ind, 1887. ....$28–$35

Longfellow, Henry Wadsworth. *Evangaline.* Ind, 1905, illus by Howard Chandler Christy. ....$50–$75

Longfellow, Henry Wadsworth. *Tales of a Wayside Inn.* Bos, 1863, 1st ed. ....$70–$145

Longfellow, Henry Wadsworth. *The Courtship of Miles Standish.* Ind, 1903, illus by Howard Chandler Christy, 1st thus, clr and b/w illus. ....$50–$85

Longfellow, Henry Wadsworth. *The Hanging of the Crane.* Bos, 1875, 1st ed, lea. ....$90–$110

Longstreet, Augustus Baldwin. *Georgia Scenes . . . by a Native Georgian.* NY, 1840, illus, 2nd ed. ....$75–$125

Longstreet, Helen D. *Lee and Longstreet at High Tide: Gettysburg. . . .* Gainesville, GA, 1905, illus, 2nd ed. ....$50–$75

Longworth, Mike. *Martin Guitars: A History.* Colonial Press. ....*$18–$25*

Lonn, Ella. *Reconstruction in Louisiana after 1868.* NY/Lon, 1918, 1st ed, maps. ....*$87–$125*

Lonn, Ella. *Salt as a Factor in the Confederacy.* NY, 1933, 1st ed. ....*$85–$125*

Loomis, Noel M. *Wells Fargo.* NY, 1st ed, dj. ....*$35–$50*

Loos, Anita. *Gentlemen Prefer Blondes.* NY, 1925, 1st ed, dj. ....*$65–$95*

Lorentz, H.A. *The Theory of Electrons ... Light and Radiant Heat.* Leipzig, 1969, 2nd ed, Nobel Prize–winning author. ....*$35–$55*

Lossing, Benjamin J. *Pictorial History of the Civil War in the United States.* . . . Phila, 1866, 3 vols, ½ lea. ....*$65–$85*

Lossing, Benson J. *History of the Civil War, 1861–1865.* NY, 1895, illus. ....*$65–$90*

Lossing, Benson J. *The Pictorial Field Book of the American Revolution.* Freeport, NY, 1969, 2 vols, rprnt. ....*$35–$55*

Lossing, J.G. *Bio. Sketches of Signers of Declaration of American Independence.* 1848. ....*$27–$40*

Love, Robertus. *Rise and Fall of Jesse James.* NY, 1939..*$22–$33*

Lovecraft, H.P. *Dagon.* Arkham House, 1965, 1st ed, dj..*$50–$75*

Lovecraft, H.P. *Dunwich Horror and Others.* Arkham House, 1963, 1st ed, dj. ....*$65–$75*

Lovecraft, H.P. *Something about Cats.* Arkham House, 1949, 1st ed, dj. ....*$100–$125*

Lovecraft, H.P. *Three Tales of Horror.* Arkham House, 1967, 1st ed, dj. ....*$100–$150*

Lovecraft, H.P. and August Derleth. *The Watchers Out of Time.* Arkham House, 1974, 1st ed, dj. ....*$30–$45*

Lovell, Mrs. F.S. and L.C. Lovell. *History of the Town of Rockingham, VT.* Bellows Falls, 1958, illus. ....*$22–$37*

Loving, Brady Antoine. *Thornton Kelly Tyson: Pioneer Home Missionary.* . . . Kansas City, 1915, 1st ed, illus. ....*$45–$75*

Lowell, James Russell. *Conversations on Some of the Old Poets.* Bos, 1862, 3rd ed. ....$18–$40

Lowell, James Russell. *Under the Willows.* Bos, 1869, 1st ed. ....$40–$50

Lowell, Robert. *Lord Weary's Castle.* NY, 1946, 1st ed. ....$125–$175

Lowell, Robert. *The Dolphin.* NY, 1973, 1st ed, dj. ......$18–$25

Lowell, Robert. *The Mills of the Kavanaughs.* NY, 1951, 1st ed. ....$100–$125

Lowther, Minnie Kendall. *Blennerhassett Island in Romance and Tragedy.* 1939, presentation copy. ....$20–$25

Lubbock, Basil. *The Log of the "Cutty Sark."* Chas. Lauriat, 1924, 1st ed, illus, dj. ....$22–$30

Lubbock, Basil. *The Opium Clippers.* Glasgow, 1946–1948, illus, 2nd ed. ....$35–$50

Lubbock, Sir John. *Ants, Bees, and Wasps.* NY, 1890. .$37–$40

Ludlow, Fitz Hugh. *Heart of the Continent: A Record of Travel across the Plains. . . .* NY, 1870. ....$100–$150

Ludlum, Robert. *Osterman Weekend.* NY, 1972, 1st ed, dj. ....$30–$40

Ludlum, Robert. *The Bourne Identity.* NY, Marek, 1980, 1st ed, dj. ....$15–$40

Ludlum, Robert. *The Bourne Supremacy.* NY, 1986, 1st ed, dj. ....$10–$15

Ludlum, Robert. *The Matarese Circle.* 1979, 1st ed. ......$7–$16

Ludy, Llewellyn. *Locomotive Boilers and Engines.* Amer. School of Corres., 1913. ....$30–$50

Lummis, Charles F. *The King of the Broncos and Other Stories of New Mexico.* NY, 1897. ....$30–$40

Lunt, Dudley Cammett. *Thousand Acre Marsh.* NY, 1959, 1st ed, dj. ....$15–$22

Lutz, Frank. *Fieldbook of Insects.* NY, 1921, illus, clr plates. ....$18–$25

Lyell, Charles. *Elements of Geology.* Troutman & Hayes, 1852, 2nd American ed, clr litho, rbkd. ....$35–$50

Lynch, Jeremiah. *Egyptian Sketches.* Lon, 1890, illus. ..$40–$75

Lynch, V.E. *Thrilling Adventures . . . Rio Grande to the Wilds of Maine.* Private prntg, 1928, sgn. ....$30–$45

Lynch, W.F. *Narrative of the U.S. Expedition to the River Jordan and Dead Sea.* Phila, 1849, illus. ....$75–$150

Lyon, W.E. (ed). *In My Opinion: Being a Book of Dissertations on Horses.*... NY, 1929, illus. ....$18–$22

Lytle, Horace. *Breaking a Bird Dog.* NY, 1924, illus. ...$14–$20

Lytle, Horace. *Breaking a Bird Dog: A Treatise on Training.* Fenno Pub., 1923, 1st ed, illus. ....$18–$25

Lytle, Horace. *How to Train Your Bird Dog.* Dayton, 1940, 1st ed, illus. ....$15–$20

M'Clintock, Capt. *Narrative of the Discovery of the Fate of Sir John Franklin.*... Bos, 1860, illus, maps. ....$30–$45

MacDiarmid, Hugh. *Selected Poems.* Lon, 1934, wrps. .$30–$45

MacDonald, Alexander. *Design for Angling: The Dry Fly on Western Trout Streams.* Bos, 1947. ....$65–$100

MacDonald, Betty. *Mrs. Piggle Wiggle.* 1947, 1st ed, sgn. ....$20–$45

Macdonald, John D. *Cinnamon Skin.* NY, 1982, 1st ed, dj. ....$10–$20

MacDougall, Arthur Jr. *The Trout Fisherman's Bedside Book.* NY, 1963, 1st ed, dj. ....$30–$35

MacFall, Haldane. *Aubrey Beardsley: The Man and His Work.* Lon, 1928, illus by Beardsley. ....$75–$100

Machen, Arthur. *Dog and Duck.* NY, 1924, 1st ed. ..... $10–$25

Machen, Arthur. *Far Off Things.* NY, 1923, 2nd U.S. ed..$15–$20

Machen, Arthur. *The Great God Pan and the Inmost Light.* Lon, 1894, 1st ed. ....$60–$250

Machen, Arthur. *The Shining Pyramid.* Covici, 1923, 1st ed, ltd 875 cc. ....$55–$65

Mack, Connie. *My 66 Years in the Big Leagues.* Phila, 1950, 1st ed. ....$18–$25

Mackay, David N. *Clan Warfare in the Scottish Highlands.* Paisley, 1922, illus. ....$16–$25

MacKay, Douglas. *The Honourable Company—A History of the Hudson's Bay Company.* Ind, 1936, 1st ed, dj. ....$30–$42

MacKaye. *Tall Tales of Kentucky Mountains.* NY, 1926..$18–$20

Mackenzie, R. Shelton. *Bits of Blarney.* 1854, 1st U.S. ed. ....$40–$55

Mackey, William F. Jr. *American Bird Decoys.* Bonanza, 1965, dj. ....$12–$18

Maclean, Norman. *A River Runs through It and Other Stories.* Chi, 1976, illus by R. Williams, woodcuts, dj. ....$12–$15

Macleish, Archibald. *Conquistador.* Bos, 1932, 1st ed, map, dj. ....$69–$90

MacLeish, Archibald. *Herakles.* Bos, 1967, 1st ed, dj...$20–$25

MacManus, Seaumas. *The Red Poocher.* 1903, 1st U.S. ed. ....$25–$35

Macmillan, Donald B. *Four Years in the White North.* Bos, 1925, illus. ....$35–$60

MacNiece, Louis. *Holes in the Sky.* NY, 1949, 1st ed. ...$30–$35

Maeterlinck, Maurice. *Life of the White Ant.* 1939, illus by Victor Wolfgang von Hagen, sgn by von Hagen. ....$20–$25

Maeterlinck, Maurice. *The Blue Bird.* NY, 1913, illus by F.C. Robinson. ....$125–$145

Maeterlinck, Maurice. *The Children's Life of the Bee.* Dodd Meade, 1920, illus. ....$18–$25

Maeterlinck, Maurice. *The Intelligence of the Flowers.* 1907. ....$65–$85

Mahan, A.T. *Sea Power in Its Relation to the War of 1812.* Lon, 1905, 2 vols, dj. ....$78–$95

Mahan, A.T. *Types of Naval Officers.* Lon, 1902, illus, plates. ....$55–$74

Mahan, Captain A.T. *The Influence of Sea Power upon History.* Lon, illus, 1st English ed. ....$115–$150

Mahan, D.H. *A Treatise on Field Fortification.* NY, 1861, 3rd rev ed. ....$22–$30

Mahan, D.H. *An Elementary Course of Civil Engineering.* . . . NY, 1838, 2nd ed, fldg plates. ....$125–$200

Mailer, Norman. *Advertisements for Myself.* NY, Putnam, 1959, 1st ed, dj. ....$35–$45

Mailer, Norman. *Advertisements for Myself.* NY, Putnam, 1959, 1st ed, sgn, dj. ....$75–$85

Mailer, Norman. *An American Dream.* Dial, 1965, 1st ed, dj. ....$28–$35

Mailer, Norman. *Marilyn: A Biography.* NY, 1973, 1st ed, dj. ....$35–$125

Mailer, Norman. *The Last Night: A Story of Armageddon.* NY, 1984, ltd 250 cc, sgn. ....$85–$125

Mailer, Norman. *The Naked and the Dead.* NY, Rinehart, 1948, 1st ed, dj. ....$95–$200

Mailer, Norman. *The Prisoner of Sex.* NY, 1971, dj. ....$20–$30

Malamud, Bernard. *A New Life.* Farrar, 1961, 1st ed, dj. ....$35–$45

Malamud, Bernard. *Pictures of Fidelman.* Farrar, 1969, 1st ed, dj. ....$32–$40

Malamud, Bernard. *The Magic Barrel.* Farrar Straus, 1958, 1st ed, dj. ....$75–$100

Malamud, Bernard. *The Tenants.* Farrar, 1971, 1st ed, dj. ....$28–$35

Malcolm, Ross. *Machine Age in the Hills.* NY, 1933, 1st ed, illus, photos. ....$16–$20

Mallory, Arthur. *The Fiery Serpent.* NY, 1929, 1st ed. ....$14–$17.50

Malraux, Andre. *Man's Hope.* NY, 1938, 1st American ed, dj. ....$25–$35

Maltin, Leonard. *Of Mice and Magic.* NY, 1980, 1st ed, dj. ....$28–$35

Manchester, William. *Shadow of the Monsoon.* NY, 1956, 1st ed, dj. ....*$18–$30*

Manley, William Lew. *Death Valley in '49.* San Jose, 1894. ....*$115–$125*

Mann, A. *History of the Forty-fifth Regiment (Mass.).* 1908. ....*$65–$85*

Mann, F.W. *The Bullet's Flight from Powder to Target.* Huntington, WV, 1942, illus, photos, 2nd ed. ....*$50–$95*

Mann, H. *Historical Annals of Dedham, MA, to 1847.* Dedham, MA, 1847. ....*$65–$85*

Mann, Horace. *Speech of Hon. Horace Mann of Mass. on Slavery and the Slave Trade.* Phila, 1849, 48 pp, unbound. ....*$60–$85*

Mann, Kathleen. *Peasant Costume in Europe.* Lon, 1931, illus by Mann, clr plates. ....*$25–$35*

Mann, Mrs. Horace. *Christianity in the Kitchen. . . .* Bos, 1861. ....*$50–$72*

Mann, Thomas. *Joseph and His Brothers.* NY, 1938, 6th prntg of American ed, sgn. ....*$125–$150*

Mann, Thomas. *Joseph the Provider.* NY, Knopf, 1944, 1st U.S. ed, dj. ....*$45–$50*

Mann, Thomas. *The Holy Sinner.* NY, Knopf, 1951, 1st ed, dj. ....*$22–$28*

Manning, Bernard L. *The Hymns of Wesley and Watts.* Lon, 1948. ....*$10–$12*

Mansfield, Katherine. *Poems.* NY, Knopf, 1924, 1st ed. .*$35–$45*

Manson, F.L. *Wright to 1910: The First Golden Age.* Reinhold, 1958, dj. ....*$120–$150*

Manwaring, Christopher. *Essays, Historical, Moral, Political, and Agricultural.* New London, CT, 1829, 1st ed, bds. .*$85–$125*

Mao Tse-Tung. *On New Democracy.* Peking, 1960, 2nd ed. ....*$8–$12*

Marcus, G. *The Maiden Voyage.* NY, 1969, 1st ed, dj. ..*$30–$60*

Marcus, J. *The Rise and Destiny of the German Jew.* 1934, 1st ed. ....*$16–$20*

Margulies, Leo. *Flying Wildcats.* NY, 1943, dj. ....*$12–$18*

Marquand, John P. *Stopover: Tokyo.* Bos, 1957, 1st ed, dj. ....*$27–$35*

Marquis, Don. *Danny's Own Story.* Garden City, 1912, 1st ed. ....*$55–$65*

Marquis, Don. *Revolt of the Oyster.* NY, 1922, dj. ....*$30–$45*

Marriott, Alice. *Maria, The Potter of San Idelfonso.* Univ. of Oklahoma Press, 1976, illus. ....*$22–$32*

Marriott, Alice. *The Ten Grandmothers.* Univ. of Oklahoma Press, 1948, 3rd prntg, dj. ....*$18–$25*

Marryat, Capt. Frederick. *The Settlers in Canada.* Lon, 1844, 2 vols, 1st ed, mor, mar bds. ....*$100–$150*

Marsh, Othniel Charles. *Dinocerata: A Monograph of an Extinct Order of Gigantic Mammals.* DC, GPO, 1886, illus, plates. ....*$125–$175*

Marshall, A.M. *The Frog.* Lon, 1912. ....*$15–$25*

Marshall, J. *A History of the Colonies Planted by the English.* Phila, 1824. ....*$40–$55*

Marshall, John. *Life of George Washington. . . .* Phila, 1836, 2 vols. ....*$50–$90*

Marshall, Logan. *The Sinking of the Titanic and Great Sea Disasters.* Myers, 1912, illus, photos, rbnd. ....*$20–$45*

Marshall and Evans. *A Day in Natchez.* MS, 1946. ......*$10–$15*

Martin, Sadie E. *The Life and Professional Career of Emma Abbott.* Minn, 1891, illus, photos. ....*$25–$35*

Martin and Martin. *Harness, Sadlery, Horse Clothing.* NY/Phila, 1890s, cat. ....*$45–$60*

Martindale, T. *With Gun and Guide.* Phila, 1910. ....*$18–$25*

Martineau, Harriet. *Retrospect of Western Travel.* NY, 1838, 2 vols, 1st ed. ....*$25–$45*

Marx, Groucho. *Memoirs of a Lousy Lover.* NY, 1963, 1st ed. ....*$20–$25*

Marx, H. *Harpo Speaks.* NY, 1961. ....*$10–$15*

Masefield, John. *A Letter from Pontus and Other Verse.* Lon, 1936, 1st ed, dj. ....$25–$30

Masefield, John. *Reynard the Fox.* NY, 1919, 1st ed. .....$20–$40

Mason, Bernard S. *Roping.* NY, 1940, 4th prntg, dj. .....$12–$15

Mason, Bobbie Ann. *In Country.* 1985, 1st ed, dj. ....$16–$20

Mason, Charles F. *Medical Electricity.* 1887, 1st ed. .....$30–$45

Mason, Michael H. *Where the River Runs Dry.* Lon, 1934, illus, dj. ....$20–$30

Mason, Otis Tufton. *Aboriginal American Harpoons.* DC, 1900, illus. ....$18–$65

Massengill, Samuel Evans. *A Sketch of Medicine and Pharmacy.* Bristol, 1942. ....$20–$35

Masters, Edgar Lee. *The Great Valley.* NY, 1916, 1st ed..$45–$60

Masters, Edgar Lee. *The New Spoon River.* NY, 1924, ltd 360 cc, sgn. ....$65–$87

Matheson, R. *Handbook of the Mosquitoes of North America.* Ithaca, 1944. ....$25–$35

Mathews. *The Writing Table of the 20th Century.* NY, 1900, illus. ....$35–$40

Mathews, John Joseph. *Wah'Kon-Tah: The Osage and the White Man's Road.* Univ. of Oklahoma, 1932, 1st ed, illus, fldg map. ....$14–$20

Mathewson, Christy. *Pitcher Pollock.* NY, 1914, 1st ed, illus by Chas. Relyea. ....$30–$40

Mathewson, Christy. *Pitching in a Pinch.* NY, 1912, illus, Boy Scout Ed. ....$12–$20

Matthews, B. *Tales of Fantasy and Fact.* NY, 1896, 1st ed. ....$60–$75

Matthews, Brander. *A Book about the Theater.* NY, 1916, 1st ed, illus, sgn. ....$15–$20

Maude, Mrs. Raymond. *The Life of Jenny Lind.* Lon, 1926, illus. ....$25–$35

Maugham, W.S. *Cakes and Ale.* Garden City, 1930, dj. .$25–$45

Maugham, W. Somerset. *Summing Up.* Doubleday, 1938, 1st ed, dj. ....*$12–$18*

Maugham, W. Somerset. *The Bread-winner.* Doubleday, 1931, 1st ed, dj. ....*$18–$22*

Maugham, W. Somerset. *Then and Now.* 1946, 1st U.S. ed, dj. ....*$10–$20*

Mauldin, Bill. *This Damn Tree Leaks: A Collection of War Cartoons.* Stars & Stripes, 1945, 1st ed. ....*$10–$30*

Mauldin, Bill. *Up Front.* NY, 1945, 1st ed. ....*$9–$12*

Maurice, Sir Frederick. *Statesmen and Soldiers of The Civil War.* Bos, 1926, 1st ed. ....*$45–$110*

Mauriceau, Dr. A.M. *The Married Woman's Private Medical Companion.* NY, 1852. ....*$150–$275*

Maury, M.F. *The Physical Geography of the Sea.* NY, 1856, illus, fldg plates, 6th ed. ....*$65–$80*

Maxim, Sir Hiram. *Artificial and Natural Flight.* NY, 1908, 1st ed, illus. ....*$50–$100*

Maxwell, Aymer. *Pheasants and Covert Shooting.* 1913, illus, clr plates. ....*$60–$85*

Maxwell, Robt. S. and Robert Baker. *Sawdust Empire: The Texas Lumber Industry, 1830–1940.* Texas A & M Univ., 1983, 1st ed, dj. ....*$20–$30*

May, J.B. *The Hawks of North America.* NY, 1935. ....*$60–$90*

May, Sophie. *Dotty Dimple's Flyaway.* Bos, 1897, illus..*$10–$14*

Mayer, Brantz. *Mexico, As it Was and As it Is.* Phila, 1848, 3rd ed. ....*$32–$45*

Mayo, Katherine. *Isles of Fear.* 1935, 1st ed. ....*$18–$22*

Mayo, Katherine. *Mother India.* 1927, photos. ....*$14–$18*

McCarthy, Cormac. *Blood Meridian. . . .* Random House, 1985, 1st ed, dj. ....*$40–$85*

McCarthy, John J. *The Science of Fighting Fire.* NY, 1943, 1st ed, illus. ....*$45–$55*

McCarthy, Mary. *Memories of a Catholic Girlhood.* 1957, 1st ed, sgn, dj. ....*$20–$35*

McCarthy, Mary. *The Group.* NY, 1963, 1st ed, dj. ......$25–$30

McCarthy, Mary. *Vietnam.* NY, 1967, wrps. ....$18–$25

McClellan, Elisabeth. *History of American Costume.* NY, 1937. ....$30–$45

McClellan, George B. *Rept. on the Organization and Campaigns ... Army of the Potomac.* NY, 1864, 1st ed, illus, maps. ....$35–$60

McClintock, John S. *Pioneer Days in the Black Hills.* Deadwood, 1939, 1st ed. ....$100–$145

McClure, J.B. *Edison and His Inventions.* 1879, 1st ed, illus. ....$65–$100

McCormick, A. *The Tinker Gypsies of Caloway.* Dumfries, 1906, illus, sgn. ....$25–$38

McCracken, H. *Alaska Bear Trails.* NY, 1931, 1st ed. ..$40–$50

McCracken, H. *The Charles M. Russell Book.* Garden City, 1957, 1st ed, dj. ....$45–$60

McCracken, Harold. *George Catlin and the Old Frontier.* NY, 1959, 1st ed, illus, buckram, dj. ....$35–$70

McCracken, Harold. *George Catlin and the Old Frontier.* NY, 1959, 1st ed, illus, sgn, dj. ....$60–$85

McCracken, Harold. *God's Frozen Children.* NY, 1930, 1st ed, illus, dj. ....$15–$20

McCracken, Harold. *The Flaming Bear.* Phila/NY, 1951, 1st ed, presentation copy, sgn. ....$55–$75

McCracken, Harold. *The Frank Tenny Johnson Book.* NY, 1974, 1st ed, folio, dj. ....$48–$65

McCracken, Harold. *The Great White Buffalo.* NY, 1946, 1st ed, illus, dj. ....$10–$18

McCullagh, Rev. Joseph H. *The Sunday-school Man of the South. . . .* Phila, 1889, 1st ed, illus. ....$55–$75

McCullers, Carson. *The Member of the Wedding.* Bos, Houghton Mifflin, 1946, 1st ed, dj. ....$50–$125

McCullough, Colleen. *A Creed for the Third Millennium.* Harper, 1985, 1st ed, sgn, dj. ....$35–$45

McCullough, Colleen. *Tim.* Angus & Robertson, 1975, 1st English ed, dj. ....*$35–$50*

McCutcheon, G.B. *Graustark.* Grosset & Dunlap, 1901, illus. ....*$10–$15*

McDaniel, Ruel. *Vinegarroon: The Saga of Judge Roy Bean.* .... TN, 1936, illus. ....*$16–$22*

McDuddie, Franklin. *History of the Town of Rochester, NH.* Manchester, 1892, 2 vols, 1st ed, illus. ....*$50–$65*

McDuff, James M. *U.S. Army Officer's Collar Insignia, 1902–1976, Vol. 1.* ....*$8–$12*

McElroy, John. *The Struggle for Missouri.* DC, 1909, 1st ed, illus. ....*$28–$45*

McEwan, Ian. *In Between the Sheets.* Lon, 1978, 1st ed, dj. ....*$175–$250*

McFee, William. *Pilgrims of Adversity.* Doubleday/Doran, 1928, 1st ed, dj. ....*$45–$50*

McGowan, Archibald. *The Prisoners of War: A Reminiscence of the Rebellion.* NY, 1901, 1st ed. ....*$75–$125*

McGroarty. *California: Its History and Romance.* Los Angeles, 1911, illus. ....*$14–$20*

McGuire, J. *Diary of a Southern Refugee during the War.* NY, 1867, 1st ed. ....*$60–$75*

McKay, Claude. *Banjo.* NY, 1929, 1st ed, dj. ....*$110–$300*

McKee, Edwin. *Ancient Landscapes of the Grand Canyon Region.* 1931, 1st ed, illus. ....*$15–$25*

McKenney, Thomas L. and Jason Hall. *The Indian Tribes of North America.* Edin, 1933, 3 vols, dj. ....*$500–$625*

McKinney, E. and W. *Aunt Caroline's Dixie-land Recipes.* Chi, 1922. ....*$15–$20*

McLeod, Robert R. *In the Acadian Land.* Bos, 1899, 1st ed, illus. ....*$20–$30*

McMasters, William H. *Revolt: An American Novel.* Bos, 1919, 1st ed. ....*$25–$35*

McMillan, George. *The Old Breed.* DC, 1949, 1st ed. ..*$30–$50*

McMullen, Joseph V. *Islamic Carpets.* NY, 1965. .....*$150–$200*

McMullen, Thomas. *Handbook of Wines.* NY, 1852, 1st ed. ....*$28–$40*

McMurtry, Larry. *Anything for Billy.* Simon & Schuster, 1988, 1st ed, dj. ....*$30–$50*

McNamara, Brooks. *The American Playhouse in the 18th Century.* Harvard Univ. Press, 1969, 1st ed, dj. ....*$20–$25*

McNemar, Richard. *A Concise Answer . . . Who, or What Are the Shakers.* Stockbridge, 1826, 1st ed. ....*$200–$250*

McPhee, J. *The Control of Nature.* Farrar Strauss, 1989, 1st ed, dj. ....*$20–$35*

McPhee, John. *A Roomful of Hovings.* NY, 1968, dj. ....*$60–$85*

McPhee, John. *Coming into the Country.* Lon, 1978, 1st ed, dj. ....*$30–$45*

McQuade, James. *The Cruise of the Montauk to Bermuda, the West Indies, and Florida.* NY, Thos. R. Knox, 1885, 1st ed, illus. ....*$62–$75*

McRae, D.G.W. *The Arts and Crafts of Canada.* Tor, 1944, illus, dj. ....*$25–$35*

McTaggart, M. *Stable and Saddle.* NY, 1930, illus. ....*$20–$25*

McTaggart, M.F. *Mount and Man.* Lon, 1925, illus by Lionel Edwards. ....*$16–$20*

Mead, Margaret. *Male and Female.* NY, 1st ed, dj. ......*$45–$65*

Mead, Margaret. *Twentieth Century Faith, Hope, and Survival.* NY, 1972, 1st ed, dj. ....*$28–$45*

Meade, Robert D. *Judah P. Benjamin, Confederate Statesman.* NY, 1943, illus, 4th prntg, presentation copy, dj. ....*$20–$35*

Meadowcroft, William H. *The Boy's Life of Edison.* 1949, illus, 3rd ed, dj. ....*$10–$20*

Meany, Tom. *Babe Ruth.* 1947, 1st ed. ....*$20–$25*

Meany, Tom. *The Boston Red Sox.* 1956, 1st ed, dj. .....*$22–$30*

Medbery, J.K. *Men and Mysteries of Wall Street.* Bos, 1870, 1st ed. ....*$24–$30*

Medical Society of Va. *Confederate Medicine, 1861–1865.* np, 1961, wrps. ....$54–$75

Meeker, Ezra. *The Ox Team, or the Old Oregon Trail, 1852–1906.* Omaha, 1906, 1st ed. ....$45–$75

Mehling. *Scandalous Scamps.* NY, 1959. ....$12–$15

Meignan, Victor. *From Paris to Peking Over Siberian Snows.* Lon, 1889, illus, 2nd ed. ....$125–$245

Meigs, Charles D. *A Complete Treatise on Midwifery.* Phila, 1852, illus, 4th American ed, calf, steel plates. ....$60–$75

Meigs, Charles D. *Woman: Her Diseases and Remedies.* Phila, 1851. ....$25–$50

Meigs, Cornelia. *Railroad West.* Little Brown, 1944. .....$18–$20

Meisel, Martin. *Shaw and the Nineteenth Century Theatre.* Princeton Univ. Press, 1963, dj. ....$12–$20

Mellen, Kathleen D. *In a Hawaiian Valley.* NY, 1947, 1st ed, illus. ....$25–$45

Menaboni, A. and S. Menaboni. *Menaboni's Birds.* 1st ed, dj. ....$20–$30

Mencken, H.L. *A Book of Burlesques.* Lon, 1923, 1st English ed. ....$24–$32

Mencken, H.L. *Happy Days.* NY, 1940, 1st ed, dj. ....$25–$35

Mencken, H.L. *Minority Report—Notebooks.* NY, 1956, 1st ed, dj. ....$30–$40

Mencken, H.L. *The Philosophy of Friedrich Nietzsche.* Bos, 1913, 3rd ed. ....$35–$50

Mencken, H.L. *Treatise on Right and Wrong.* NY, 1934, 1st ed, dj. ....$30–$50

Menninger, Karl A. *Man against Himself.* NY, 1938, sgn. ....$65–$95

Menocal, A.G. *Report of the U.S. Nicaragua Surveying Party, 1885.* 1886, 1st ed, illus, folio, fldg maps, drawings. ...$75–$250

Meredith, D.L. *Search at Loch Ness. . . .* NY, 1977, illus..$12–$20

Meredith, George. *Poems.* Lon, 1892, 1st ed. ....$35–$45

Merryweather, James C. *Fire Protection of Mansions.* Lon, 1899, 3rd ed. ....$60–$110

Mertins, Louis and Esther. *The Intervals of Robert Frost.* Berkeley, 1947. ....$50–$65

Merton, H.W. *Descriptive Mentality from the Head, Face, and Hand.* Phila, 1899, 1st ed, illus. ....$65–$75

Merton, Thomas. *Exile Ends in Glory: The Life of a Trappistine.* Milw, 1948, 2nd prntg, dj. ....$16–$20

Merton, Thomas. *The Sign of Jonas.* NY, 1953, 1st ed, dj. ....$20–$40

Merton, Thomas. *The Waters of Siloe.* Harcourt, 1949, 1st ed, dj. ....$50–$75

Merwin, Samuel. *Silk.* Bos, 1923, 1st ed, illus by N.C. Wyeth. ....$20–$30

Meyersberg, Dorothy. *Seventh Avenue.* 1941, 1st ed, sgn, dj. ....$14–$22

Michener, C.K. *Heirs of the Incas.* NY, 1924, 1st ed, illus, dj. ....$16–$20

Michener, James. *Alaska.* NY, 1988, 1st ed, dj. ....$10–$18

Michener, James. *Chesapaeake.* NY, 1978, 1st ed, dj. ...$18–$25

Michener, James. *Journey.* NY, 1989, 1st American ed, dj. ....$10–$15

Michener, James. *Kent State.* NY, 1971, 1st ed, dj. ....$20–$50

Michener, James. *Poland.* Random House, 1983, 1st ed, dj. ....$13–$18

Michener, James. *Texas.* 1985, 1st ed. ....$14–$18

Michener, James. *The Bridge at Andau.* NY, 1957, dj. .$30–$40

Michener, James A. *Hawaii.* NY, 1959, 1st ed, dj. ....$17–$24

Michener, James A. *The People and the Land.* 1981, 1st ed, dj. ....$16–$20

Michener, James A. *The Voice of Asia.* NY, 1951, 1st ed, dj. ....$22–$45

Middlecoff, Cary. *The Golf Swing.* Englewood Cliffs, NJ, 1974, illus. ....$18–$20

Milburn, William H. *Ten Years of Preacher Life.* NY, 1859.
....$12–$15

Milham, Willis I. *Time and Timekeepers.* NY, 1941, illus..$22–$40

Mill, John Stuart. *Autobiography.* NY, 1874, 1st American ed.
....$60–$85

Millay, Edna St. Vincent. *A Few Figs from Thistles.* NY, 1922.
....$15–$20

Millay, Edna St. Vincent. *Fatal Interview.* Harper, 1931, 1st ed, dj. ....$25–$35

Millay, Edna St. Vincent. *Mine the Harvest.* NY, 1954, 1st ed, dj.
....$27–$35

Millay, Edna St. Vincent. *The Princess Marries the Page.* Harper & Bros., 1932, 4th prntg, dj. ....$22–$35

Millburn, William Henry. *The Rifle, Axe, and Saddlebags and Other Lectures.* NY, 1857. ....$35–$75

Miller. *The World in the Air: Story of Flying in Pictures.* NY, 1930, 2 vols. ....$75–$95

Miller, Arthur. *A View from the Bridge.* NY, Viking, 1955, 1st ed, dj. ....$38–$50

Miller, Arthur. *Death of a Salesman.* NY, 1949, 1st ed, dj.
....$75–$125

Miller, Arthur. *Focus.* Reynal & Hitchcock, 1945, 1st ed, dj.
....$38–$50

Miller, Arthur. *Incident at Vichy.* NY, 1965, 1st ed, dj...$10–$20

Miller, C.C. *Fifty Years among the Bees.* Medina, 1915, 1st ed, illus. ....$10–$15

Miller, Elizabeth S. *In the Kitchen.* Bos, 1875. ....$25–$35

Miller, F. *Thomas A. Edison.* Phila, 1931, 1st ed. ....$22–$30

Miller, F.T. *History of World War II.* Phila, 1945, illus, photos.
....$20–$25

Miller, Francis Trevelyan (ed). *The Photographic History of the Civil War.* NY, 1912, 10 vols, illus by Brady, lea and cloth.
....$350–$400

Miller, Henry. *Opus Pistorum.* NY, 1983. ....$18–$20

Miller, Henry. *Tropic of Cancer.* NY, 1940. ....$22–$30

Miller, Henry. *Tropic of Capricorn.* Calder, 1964, 1st English ed, dj. ....$20–$30

Miller, Henry. *Tropic of Capricorn.* NY, Grove, 1961, 1st U.S. ed, dj. ....$45–$75

Miller, Lieut.-Col. *Fifty Years of Sport.* NY, nd. ....$16–$20

Miller, Max. *Land Where Time Stands Still.* NY, 1943, dj. ....$20–$35

Miller, O.B. *Little Pictures of Japan.* 1925. ....$25–$35

Miller, O.B. *My Book House.* Chi, 1937, 12 vols. ....$75–$95

Miller, O.B. *My Book House: The Latchkey.* Chi, 1921. .$18–$25

Miller, O.B. *My Book House: The Treasure Chest.* Chi, 1920, illus. ....$18–$25

Miller, O.B. *Tales Told in Holland.* 1926. ....$25–$35

Miller, Olive Beaupre. *Nursery Friends from France.* 1927, illus. ....$20–$35

Miller, W. *Structure of the Lung.* Bos, 1893, sgn. ....$25–$32

Miller, W. *The American Hunting Dog.* 1926. ....$20–$30

Millet, Rev. Joshua. *A History of the Baptists in Maine.* Portland, 1845. ....$37–$50

Milligan, D.E. *Fist Puppetry.* Barnes, 1938. ....$14–$20

Milligan, Harold Vincent. *Stephen Collins Foster: A Biography....* NY, 1920, illus. ....$35–$45

Mills, G. *The People of the Saints.* Taylor Museum, 1965, illus, photos. ....$12–$15

Milne, A. *By Way of Introduction.* NY, 1929, 1st American ed, ltd 166 cc, sgn, slipcase. ....$200–$300

Milne, A.A. *Four Days' Wonder.* Lon, 1933, 1st ed, dj. .$35–$45

Milne, A.A. *Michael and Mary.* Lon, 1930. ....$25–$30

Milne, A.A. *Now We Are Six.* Lon, 1927, 1st ed, illus by Shepard, teg. ....$150–$275

Milne, A.A. *Toad of Toad Hall.* Lon, 1929, 1st ed, dj. .....$65–$115

Minarik. *No Fighting, No Biting!* 1958, 1st ed, illus by Maurice Sendak. ....$8–$15

Minarik, Else. *Little Bear's Friend.* 1960, illus by Maurice Sendak, dj. ....$14–$18

Minarik, Else Holmelund. *Little Bear.* Harper & Row, illus by Maurice Sendak. ....$15–$18

Minkoff, George R. *Bibliography of the Black Sun Press.* Great Neck, 1970. ....$50–$95

Mintorn, John and Horatio Mintorn. *The Handbook for Modelling Wax Flowers.* Lon, 1849, 3rd ed. ....$22–$37

Mishima, Yukio. *The Sailor Who Fell from Grace with the Sea.* Knopf, 1965, 1st American ed, dj. ....$85–$125

Miss Leslie. *Directions for Cookery.* Phila, 1839, 7th ed..$75–$100

Mitchell, Margaret. *Gone with the Wind.* NY, 1936, 1st ed, 1st issue, dj, "Published May 1936" appears on copyright page. ....$1,000–$2,500

Mitchell, R.C. *Old San Francisco.* 1933, 4 vols, 1st ed, boxed. ....$45–$75

Mitchell, S.A. *Mitchell's New Atlas of the United States.* Phila, 1874, illus, hand-clr maps. ....$115–$135

Mitchell, W. *Trail Life in the Canadian Rockies.* NY, 1924, 1st ed, illus cvr. ....$18–$22

Mitchell, William. *Winged Defense.* NY/Lon, 1925, 1st ed, illus. ....$30–$50

Mitchener, C.H. (ed). *Historic Events in the Tuscarawas and Muskingham Valleys.* Dayton, 1876. ....$40–$65

Mivart, St. George. *On Genesis of Species.* NY, 1871, illus, 1st American ed. ....$26–$35

Mogannam, Mrs. Matiel E.T. *The Arab Woman.* Lon, 1936, 1st ed. ....$32–$44

Mollo, John. *Military Fashion.* NY, 1972. ....$20–$30

Monroe, James. *Message from the President.* DC, 1821, 1st ed, wrps, sewn. ....$75–$95

Monroe, Marilyn. *My Story.* NY, 1974, 1st ed, dj. ....$30–$35

Monroe, Marilyn. *My Story.* NY, 1974, dj. ....*$15–$20*

Montgomery, Frances. *Billy Whiskers Tourist.* Saalfield, 1929, illus. ....*$20–$35*

Montgomery, J.M. *Golden Road.* 1913, 1st ed. ....*$25–$35*

Montgomery, L.M. *Anne of Avonlea.* L.C. Page. ....*$25–$35*

Montgomery, L.M. *Anne of Green Gables.* illus. ....*$8–$25*

Montgomery, L.M. *Anne of the Island.* A.L. Burt, dj. ...*$25–$35*

Montgomery, L.M. *Anne's House of Dreams.* A.L. Burt, dj. ....*$25–$37*

Montgomery, L.M. *Chronicles of Avonlea.* NY, 1912, dj. ....*$12–$18*

Montgomery, L.M. *Jane of Lantern Hill.* Grosset & Dunlap, 1937, dj. ....*$25–$35*

Montgomery, L.M. *Rainbow Valley.* NY, 1919, dj, rprnt. ....*$30–$40*

Moore, Brian. *Judith Hearne.* Lon, 1955, 1st ed, sgn, dj. ....*$300–$650*

Moore, C. *History of Ancient and Honorable Frat. of Free and Accepted Masons.* Lon, 1902, ½ lea. ....*$30–$40*

Moore, Charles. *Lincoln's Gettysburg Address and Second Inaugural.* Bos, 1927, illus, paper-covered bds. ....*$18-$24*

Moore, Clement C. *The Night before Christmas.* Chi, 1908, illus by J.R. Neill. ....*$40–$50*

Moore, Frank. *Rebel Rhymes and Rhapsodies.* NY, 1864, 1st ed, calf spine, bds. ....*$55–$100*

Moore, Frank. *Women of the War.* Scranton, 1866, 1st ed, steel engr. ....*$25–$35*

Moore, George Henry. *Notes on the History of Slavery in Massachusetts.* NY, 1866, 1st ed. ....*$150–$175*

Moore, H.N. *Life and Services of Gen. Anthony Wayne.* Phila, 1845, illus. ....*$45–$50*

Moore, John Hamilton. *The Seaman's Complete Daily Assistant and New Mariner's Compass.* Lon, 1796, 5th ed, sailcloth over calf. ....*$190–$235*

Moore, Joseph. *Penicillin in Syphilis.* Chas. Thomas, 1946, 1st ed, dj. ....$22–$25

Moore, Marianne. *Complete Poems.* Viking, 1981, 1st ed, dj. ....$10–$35

Moore, William. *Wall Street Mysteries Revealed Secrets Exposed.* NY, 1921, 1st ed. ....$18–$28

Moore-Wilson, Minnie. *The Seminoles of Florida.* NY, Moffat, Yard, 1910, 1st ed, illus. ....$20–$25

Morgan, Alfred P. *The Boy Electrician.* 1914, 1st ed, illus. ....$25–$35

Morgan, Alma L. *The Elk Walker.* NY, 1976, 1st ed, dj, sgn. ....$25–$30

Morgan, E. and H. Morgan. *Stamp Act Crisis.* Chapel Hill, 1953, dj. ....$16–$20

Morgan, James M. *Recollections of a Rebel Reefer.* Bos, 1917, 1st ed, illus. ....$40–$100

Morgan, Lewis H. *Ancient Society . . . Savagery through Barbarism to Civilization.* Chi, 1877. ....$20–$25

Morgan, Lewis H. *House and House-life of the American Aborigines.* DC, GPO, 1881, illus, litho and photo plates. ......$95–$125

Morison, S.E. *The Founding of Harvard College.* Camb, 1935, 1st ed. ....$30–$45

Morley, Christopher. *Seacoast of Bohemia.* 1929, 1st ed. ....$15–$20

Morley, Christopher. *The Old Mandarin.* NY, 1947, 1st ed. ....$22–$30

Morley, Christopher. *Where the Blue Begins.* NY, 1922, 1st ed, illus by Rackham, dj. ....$30–$75

Morley, S.G. *The Ancient Maya.* Stanford Univ. Press, 1947, illus, dj. ....$18–$22

Morris, Barbara. *Victorian Embroidery.* NY, 1962, illus, dj. ....$40–$50

Morris, Clara. *Life on the Stage.* NY, McClure, 1902. ..$14–$20

Morris, Earl H. *The Temple of the Warriors.* NY, 1931, illus. ....$15–$20

Morris, Frank and E.A. Eames. *Our Wild Orchids.* NY, 1929, 1st ed, illus, dj. ....*$28–$35*

Morris, Gouveneur. *Diary and Letters....* NY, 1888, 2 vols, 1st ed, illus. ....*$45–$75*

Morris, J. *Memoirs of South Farms in Litchfield.* NY, 1933, 1st ed. ....*$24–$30*

Morris, Robert *Freemasonry in the Holy Land.* LaGrange, KY, 1880. ....*$50–$125*

Morris, Wright. *Ceremony in Lone Tree.* NY, 1960, 1st ed, dj. ....*$45–$70*

Morrison, Toni. *Tar Baby.* 1981, 1st ed, dj. ....*$30–$60*

Morrison, Toni. *The Bluest Eye.* Lon, 1979, 1st ed, dj. ..*$65–$75*

Morse, A.H. *Radio: Beam and Broadcast.* 1925, 1st ed, illus. ....*$70–$90*

Morse, Edward Lind. *Samuel F.B. Morse: His Letters and Journals.* 1914, 2 vols, 1st ed, illus. ....*$65–$115*

Morse, J. *Geography Made Easy.* Utica, NY, 1819. ....*$30–$50*

Morse, J. and E. Parish. *A Compendious History of New England.* Charlestown, 1820. ....*$20–$30*

Morse, Jedidiah. *American Universal Geography.* Bos, 1800, 7th ed. ....*$65–$90*

Morse, Jedidiah. *Annals of the American Revolution....* Hartford, 1824, illus. ....*$85–$100*

Morse, Samuel (ed). *Confessions of a French Catholic Priest.* NY, 1873. ....*$14–$20*

Morse, Samuel F.B. *Examination of the Telegraphic Apparatus, Vol. 4.* GPO, 1869. ....*$30–$40*

Moton, Robert Russa. *What the Negro Thinks.* Garden City, 1929, 1st ed, sgn. ....*$60–$95*

Moton, Robert Russa. *What the Negro Thinks.* Garden City, 1929. ....*$25–$35*

Mott, Frank Luther. *Golden Multitudes.* NY, 1947, 1st ed, dj. ....*$16–$25*

Muir, John. *My First Summer in the Sierra.* Bos, 1911, 1st ed. ....*$95–$125*

Muir, John. *Our National Parks.* Bos, 1902, 2nd prntg. .*$37–$45*

Muir, John (ed). *Picturesque California.* . . . NY, 1894, illus, folio. ....*$140–$180*

Muir, John. *The Mountains of California.* NY, 1922, illus. ....*$22–$40*

Muir, John. *Travels in Alaska.* Bos, 1916, illus. ....*$28–$35*

Mulfurd, Clarence. *Hopalong Cassidy's Coloring Book.* NY, 1951, wrps. ....*$15–$20*

Mullins, Michael A. *The Fremont Rifles: A Hist. of 37th Ill. Vet. Vol. Infantry.* NC, 1990, illus, sgn, dj. ....*$35–$50*

Mulock, Dinah Maria. *The Woman's Kingdom.* NY, 1869, 1st ed, illus. ....*$33–$40*

Mulock-Craik, Dinah M. *Adventures of a Brownie.* Chi, 1923, illus by Milo Winter. ....*$35–$40*

Mumford, John Kimberly. *Oriental Rugs.* NY, 1923, illus, 4th ed. ....*$35–$50*

Mumford, John Kimberly. *Oriental Rugs.* NY, 1902. ...*$50–$75*

Mumford, Lewis. *The City in History.* Harcourt, 1961, 1st ed. ....*$18–$25*

Munro, Alice. *Who Do You Think You Are?* Macmillan of Canada, 1978, 1st ed, dj. ....*$35–$45*

Munro, H.R. ("Saki"). *When William Came.* NY, 1926, dj. ....*$15–$20*

Munsey, Cecil. *The Illustrated Guide to the Collectibles of Coca-Cola.* NY, 1972. ....*$8–$10*

Munson, John W. *Reminiscences of a Mosby Guerilla.* NY, 1906, 1st ed, illus. ....*$75–$100*

Murdoch, Iris. *The Unicorn.* Lon, 1963, 1st ed, dj. ....*$35–$45*

Murphy, Robert Cushman. *Oceanic Birds of So. America.* NY, 1936, 2 vols, illus, boxed. ....*$80–$125*

Murray, Arthur. *Arthur Murray's Dance Secrets.* NY, 1946, illus by Olga Ley. ....*$18–$25*

Murray, W.H. *Lake Champlain and Its Shores.* Bos, De Wolfe, 1890, 1st ed. ....$20–$28

Murray, W.H.H. *Daylight Land.* 1888, illus. ....$28–$37

Murray, W.H.H. *How John Norton the Trapper Kept His Christmas.* Private prntg, 1885. ....$25–$30

Murrey, Thomas J. *Luncheon.* NY, 1888. ....$20–$30

Murrow, Edward R. *In Search of Light ... Broadcasts of E.R. Murrow, 1938–1961.* 1967, 1st ed, illus, dj. ....$10–$15

Mursell, James L. *Music in American Schools.* NY, 1943, illus. ....$10–$12

Musgrove, J. *Waterfowl in Iowa.* 1943, 1st ed. ....$18–$25

Myers, Frank. *Soldiering in Dakota among the Indians.* SD, 1936. ....$20–$35

Myers, Gustavus. *History of the Great American Fortunes.* NY, Modern Library, 1936, dj. ....$12–$18

Nabokov, V. *Lectures on Russian Literature.* 1981, 1st ed. ....$25–$30

Nabokov, Vladimir. *Invitation to a Beheading.* Putnam, 1959, 1st U.S. ed, dj. ....$45–$75

Nabokov, Vladimir. *Lolita.* Paris, 1955, 2 vols, 1st ed, wrps, 1st issue. ....$275–$400

Nabokov, Vladimir. *Look at the Harlequins!* McGraw-Hill, 1974, 1st ed, dj. ....$25–$30

Nabokov, Vladimir. *Nabokov's Quartet.* NY, 1966, 1st ed. ....$35–$55

Nabokov, Vladimir. *Notes on Prosody.* NY, 1964, dj. ....$50–$75

Nabokov, Vladimir. *Pale Fire.* Putnam, 1962, 1st U.S. ed, dj. ....$95–$125

Nabokov, Vladimir. *The Enchanter.* 1986, 1st ed, dj. ......$5–$10

Nagel, Charles. *Boy's Civil War Story.* St. Louis, 1934, 1st ed, presentation copy, sgn. ....$20–$30

Nansen, F. *Farthest North.* NY, 1897, 2 vols, 1st American ed. ....$125–$175

Nansen, Fridt Jof. *The First Crossing of Greenland.* Lon, 1892, illus, fldg map. ....$45–$65

Nash, E.B. *Leaders in Homeopathic Therapeutics.* Phila, 1901, 2nd ed. ....$35–$40

Nash, Ogden. *The Moon Is Shining Bright as Day.* Lippincott, 1953, 1st ed. ....$25–$35

Nash, Wallis. *Two Years in Oregon.* Appleton, 1882, 2nd ed. ....$60–$75

Nasmyth, James and James Carpenter. *The Moon: Considered as a Planet, a World, and a Satellite.* Lon, 1885, illus, 3rd ed. ....$75–$150

Nassau, R.H. *Fetishism in West Africa.* NY, 1904, illus..$60–$80

Nathan, George Jean. *Art of the Night.* NY, 1928, 1st ed, ltd #192/200 cc, sgn. ....$45–$75

Nation, Carry A. *The Use and Need of the Life of Carry A. Nation....* Topeka, 1905, wrps, illus. ....$85–$125

Naylor, P.I.H. *Astrology—An Historical Examination.* Lon, 1967, dj. ....$7–$14

Neal, E. *Diet for the Sick and Convalescent.* Phila, 1861, 1st ed. ....$28–$45

Near, I.W. *A History of Steuben County, NY, and Its People.* Chi, 1911, 2 vols. ....$100–$135

Nearing, Scott. *Maple Sugar Book.* 2nd ed, dj. ....$18–$25

Nearing, Scott. *The Conscience of a Radical.* ME, 1965, 1st ed, dj. ....$22–$30

Neate, W.R. *Mountaineering and Its Literature.* Seattle, 1980, dj. ....$14–$18

Neely, Flora. *Hand-book for the Kitchen and Housekeeper's Guide.* NY, 1910. ....$20–$30

Neff, Jackob. *The Army and Navy of America from the French and Indian Wars....* Phila, 1845, fldg plates. ....$52–$60

Neil, Marion Harris. *Favorite Recipes Cook Book.* NY, 1917, illus. ....$14–$20

Neill, Edward. *The History of Minnesota....* Phila, 1858, 1st ed, fldg map. ....$50–$95

Neill, Miss E. *The Every-day Cook-book and Encyclopedia of Practical Recipes.* NY, 1888. ....$25–$35

Nelson, E.W. *Report upon the Natural History of Collections ... Alaska.* DC, 1887, illus. ....$85–$125

Nelson, Truman. *The Old Man: John Brown at Harper's Ferry.* NY, 1973, 1st ed, dj. ....$14–$18

Nemes, Sylvester. *The Soft-hackled Fly Addict.* Chi, 1981, 1st ed, dj. ....$25–$35

Nesbit, W. *Oh Skin-Nay!* Volland, 1913. ....$25–$35

Nevill, Ralph. *Sporting Days and Sporting Ways.* NY, 1910. ....$15–$20

Nevins, Allan. *Ordeal of the Union.* NY, 1971, 8 vols, 1st ed. ....$130–$175

Nevins, Allan. *Sail On.* NY, 1946, illus. ....$10–$15

Nevins, W.S. *Witchcraft in Salem Village.* Salem/Bos, 1892, illus. ....$60–$85

New, Egan. *Battersea Enamels.* Lon/Bos, 1926, illus. ....$50–$95

Newcomb, H. *Young Ladies Guide.* Bos, 1840, 2nd ed. ..$22–$25

Newcomb, W. *Story of Nudism.* NY, 1934, 1st ed, illus, dj. ....$25–$40

Newcombe, Rexford. *Old Kentucky Architecture.* NY, 1940, 1st ed, plates. ....$35–$45

Newell, Peter. *The Hole Book.* NY, 1908, 1st ed, illus..$70–$125

Newhall, B. *Latent Image: The Discovery of Photography.* Garden City, 1967, illus, dj. ....$22–$30

Newhall, Walter S. *A Memoir.* Phila, 1864, 1st ed, regimental. ....$60–$75

Newhouse, S. *The Trapper's Guide: A Manual. . . .* NY, 1869, illus, 3rd ed. ....$35–$47

Newton, Helmut. *White Women.* 1976, 1st ed, presentation copy, dj. ....$75–$150

Newton, Issac. *Opticks.* Lon, 1931, rpnt, 4th ed of 1730, ed. ....$18–$25

Newton, Robert R. *The Moon's Acceleration and Its Physical Origins.* MD, 1979, 2 vols. ....*$27–$35*

Nibley, Preston. *Brigham Young.* 1936, 1st ed, dj. ....*$16–$20*

Nichol, J.P. *The Phenomena and Order of the Solar System.* NY, 1843, illus. ....*$30–$50*

Nichols, J.T. *The Freshwater Fishes of China.* NY, 1943, illus. ....*$95–$150*

Nichols, Mary E. *366 Dinners by "M.E.N."* NY, 1892. .*$20–$25*

Nichols, Roy, William C. Bagley, and Charles A. Beard. *America Yesterday.* NY, 1938, illus. ....*$12–$20*

Nichols, Rudge and Caroline N. Poole. *Peter Powers Pioneer: First Settler in Hollis, New Hampshire.* Concord, 1930, 1st ed, illus, ltd #3/550 cc, woodcuts, presentation copy, sgn. ....*$30–$50*

Nicolls, William Jasper. *The Story of American Coals.* Phila, 1897. ....*$10–$25*

Nightingale, Florence. *Notes on Nursing....* NY, 1860, 1st ed. ....*$95–$150*

Nimoy, Leonard. *I Am Not Spock.* Millbrae, 1975, 1st ed, softbound, photos. ....*$30–$40*

Nin, Anais. *Children of the Albatross.* Dutton, 1947, 1st U.S. ed, dj. ....*50–$95*

Nin, Anais. *Ladders to Fire.* Dutton, 1946, 1st ed, dj...*$50–$110*

Nin, Anais. *Spy in the House of Love.* NY, 1954. ....*$50–$60*

Nin, Anais. *The Four Chambered Heart.* 1950, 1st ed, dj. ....*$75–$175*

Nixon, Oliver. *Whitman's Ride through Savage Lands.* np, 1905. ....*$20–$25*

Nixon, Richard. *No More Vietnams.* sgn. ....*$45–$75*

Nixon, Richard. *The Memoirs of Richard Nixon.* NY, Grosset & Dunlap, 1978, 1st ed, boxed, sgn. ....*$145–$175*

Nobel, Alfred. *Les Explosifs Modernes.* Paris, 1876, 1st ed. ....*$200–$230*

Nordhoff and Hall. *Pitcairn's Island.* 1934, 2nd ed. ......*$12–$15*

Norman, Dorothy. *Alfred Stieglitz: An American Seer.* NY, 1973, 1st ed, illus, dj. ....$20–$35

Norris, Frank. *McTeague: A Story of San Francisco.* NY, 1899, 1st ed. ....$100–$245

Norris, Frank. *The Pit.* NY, 1903, 1st ed. ....$50–$80

Northend, Mary Harrod. *Historic Doorways of Old Salem.* Bos, 1926, 1st ed, illus, photos. ....$22–$25

Northrop, Solomon. *Narr. of a Citizen of N.Y. Kidnapped . . . in 1841, Rescued in 1853.* Derby & Miller, 1853. ....$75–$100

Northrup, H.D. *Chinese Horrors and Persecutions of Christians. . . .* Phila, 1900, 1st ed, illus, engr, photos. ....$135–$225

Northup, Henry D. *Marvelous Wonders of the Whole World.* Phila, 1891. ....$22–$30

Norton, A. Tiffany. *History of Sullivan's Campaign against Iroquois.* Lima, NY, 1879, fldg map. ....$65–$70

Norton, Andre. *Cats Eye.* Harcourt, 1961, 1st ed, dj. ....$30–$45

Norton, Andre. *Night of Masks.* Harcourt, 1964, 1st ed, dj. ....$65–$85

Norton, Andre. *Ordeal in Otherwhere.* World, 1964, 1st ed, dj. ....$20–$85

Norton, Caroline T. *The Rocky Mountain Cook Book.* Denver, 1903. ....$30–$40

Norton, Roy. *The Garden of Fate.* NY, 1910, 1st ed, illus by J.C. Coll. ....$25–$35

Nossiter, Harold. *Southward Ho! . . .* 1938, 1st ed, fldg map, dj. ....$27–$45

Noyes, A.J. *In the Land of Chinook, or the Story of Blaine County.* Helena, MT, 1917, 1st ed, illus. ....$75–$145

Noyes, Alfred. *Watchers of the Sky.* NY, 1922, 1st ed. ..$16–$20

Noyes, Katherine M. *Jesse Macy: An Autobiography.* Springfield, IL, 1933, 1st ed, illus. ....$50–$75

Nutt, Frederick. *The Complete Confectioner. . . .* Lon, 1809, illus, plates, calf. ....$150–$225

Nuttall, T. *Manual of Ornithology.* Bos, 1834. ....$45–$75

Nutting, Wallace. *England Beautiful.* NY, 1928, illus. ...*$15–$22*

Nutting, Wallace. *Furniture of the Pilgrim Century, 1620–1720.* Bos, 1921, 1st ed, illus. ....*$50–$60*

Nutting, Wallace. *Ireland Beautiful.* NY, 1925, 1st ed....*$14–$22*

Nutting, Wallace. *Maine Beautiful.* ....*$15–$20*

Nutting, Wallace. *Massachusetts Beautiful.* 1923, dj. .....*$18–$25*

Nutting, Wallace. *New Hampshire Beautiful.* 1923, 1st ed. ....*$25–$45*

Nutting, Wallace. *Pennsylvania Beautiful.* 1935, illus.....*$12–$20*

Nutting, Wallace. *Pennsylvania Beautiful.* 1924, 1st ed, illus. ....*$18–$25*

Nutting, Wallace. *The Clock Book.* Old America, 1924, 1st ed. ....*$55–$67*

Nutting, Wallace. *Vermont Beautiful.* 1st ed. ....*$20–$22*

O'Brien. *Best Short Stories of 1923.* NY, 1924. ....*$20–$30*

O'Brien, F. *Mystic Isles of the South Seas.* NY, 1921, 1st ed, illus, photos, map. ....*$10–$20*

O'Brien, F. *White Shadows in the South Seas.* NY, 1924, illus. ....*$10–$20*

O'Casey, Sean. *Cock-a-doodle Dandy.* 1949, 1st ed, dj..*$16–$20*

O'Cathasaigh, P. *The Story of the Irish Citizen Army.* Dublin, 1919, 1st ed, wrps. ....*$150–$225*

O'Conner, Jack. *The Art of Hunting Big Game in North America.* 1967, 1st ed, dj. ....*$18–$27*

O'Connor, Flannery. *Mysteries and Manners.* NY, 1969, 1st ed, dj. ....*$45–$60*

O'Connor, Flannery. *Wise Blood.* NY, 1952, 1st ed, dj. ....*$350–$725*

O'Connor, J. *Art of Big Game Hunting in North America.* 1967. ....*$13–$20*

O'Connor, J. *The Big Game Animals of North America.* NY, 1961, folio, dj. ....*$45–$60*

O'Connor, Jack. *Jack O'Connor's Big Game Hunts.* NY, 1963, illus. ....*$60–$75*

O'Connor, Jack. *The Art of Hunting Big Game in North America.* NY, 1967, 1st ed, illus, dj. ....*$35–$50*

O'Connor, Jack. *The Big Game Rifle.* NY, 1952, 1st ed, dj. ....*$60–$100*

O'Connor, R. *Sheridan the Inevitable.* Ind, 1953, 1st ed, dj. ....*$20–$35*

O'Donnell, Elliot. *The Menace of Spiritualism.* NY, 1920, 1st ed, dj. ....*$15–$20*

O'Faolain, Sean. *Come Back to Erin.* Viking, 1940, 1st U.S. ed, dj. ....*$45–$50*

O'Faolain, Sean. *The Life Story of Eamon De Valera.* Dublin, 1933, 1st ed. ....*$60–$75*

O'Hara, John. *A Family Party.* NY, 1956, dj. ....*$15–$20*

O'Hara, John. *A Rage to Live.* Cresset, 1950, 1st English ed, dj. ....*$25–$40*

O'Hara, John. *And Other Stories.* 1968, 1st ed, dj. ....*$8–$18*

O'Hara, John. *From the Terrrace.* NY, Random House, 1958, 1st ed, dj. ....*$30–$40*

O'Hara, John. *Ten North Frederick.* Random House, 1955, 1st ed, dj. ....*$28–$35*

O'Hara, John. *The Farmers Hotel.* Random House, 1951, 1st ed, dj. ....*$30–$40*

O'Hara, John. *Waiting for Winter.* NY, 1966, 1st ed, dj..*$30–$45*

O'Keefe, Georgia. *Georgia O'Keefe.* NY, 1976, 1st ed, folio, dj. ....*$75–$100*

O'Neal, Bill. *Encyclopedia of Western Gun-fighters.* 1979, 1st ed, dj. ....*$30–$65*

O'Neil, George. *Tomorrow House, or the Tiny Angel.* Dutton, 1930, illus by Rose O'Neil. ....*$15–$25*

O'Neill, Eugene. *Ah, Wilderness!* NY, Random House, 1933, 1st ed, dj. ....*$40–$75*

O'Neill, Eugene. *Lazarus Laughed.* NY, 1927, 1st ed, dj. ....*$75–$125*

O'Neill, Eugene. *Mourning Becomes Electra.* Boni, 1925, 1st ed, dj. ....*$45–$75*

O'Neill, Eugene. *Strange Interlude.* 1928, 1st ed, dj. .....*$25–$45*

O'Neill, Eugene. *The Iceman Cometh.* NY, 1982, illus by Leonard Baskin, ltd 2,000 cc, sgn by Baskin, slipcase. ....*$65–$95*

O'Rourke, Kathleen. *Shades and Echoes of Old Killarney.* 1936, 1st ed. ....*$10–$15*

Oates, Joyce Carol. *Angel of Light.* Dutton, 1981, 1st ed, dj. ....*$20–$25*

Oates, Joyce Carol. *On Boxing.* NY, 1987, illus, sgn, dj..*$45–$55*

Oates, Joyce Carol. *The Assignation.* 1988, 1st ed, dj. ..*$10–$14*

Oates, Joyce Carol. *Triumph of the Spider Monkey.* ltd 350 cc, presentation copy, sgn. ....*$75–$85*

Oates, Joyce Carol. *With Shuddering Fall.* 1964, 1st ed, dj. ....*$18–$30*

Oberdorfer, Don. *The Story of a Battle and Its Historic Aftermath.* NY, 1971. ....*$22–$30*

Odets, Clifford. *Golden Boy.* NY, 1937, 1st ed, sgn. .*$135–$150*

Odum, Howard. *Rainbow Round My Shoulder: The Blue Trail of Black Ulysses.* Bobbs-Merrill, 1928, 1st ed, dj. ....*$37–$65*

Odum, Howard W. *The Negro and His Songs.* Chapel Hill, 1925. ....*$45–$75*

Oemler, Marie Conway. *The Holy Lover.* NY, 1927. ....*$8–$15*

Ogg, Frederick Austin. *The Opening of the Mississippi.* NY, 1904, 1st ed, illus, maps. ....*$37–$50*

Okada, Barbara. *Netsuke: The Small Sculptures of Japan.* NY, 1980, illus, clr and b/w. ....*$14–$26*

Okaura, Kakuzo. *The Book of Tea.* NY, 1912. ....*$20–$45*

Olbermann, Keith. *The Major League Coaches, 1921–1973.* nd. ....*$15–$20*

Oliver, W.R.B. *New Zealand Birds.* Wellington, 1955, 2nd ed, clr plates. ....*$67–$75*

Oliver, W.R.B. *The Moas of New Zealand and Australia.* Wellington, 1949. ....*$50–$65*

Olmstead, A.T. *History of Palestine and Syria to the Macedonian Conquest.* NY/Lon, 1931, 1st ed, illus, fldg map. ....$25–$40

Oppenheimer, J. Robert. *Science and the Common Understanding.* NY, 1954, 1st ed. ....$25–$30

Optic, Oliver. *Careless Kate.* Bos, 1865, illus. ....$8–$12

Optic, Oliver. *On Time, or The Young Captain of the Ucayga Steamer.* Lee & Shepard, 1869. ....$13–$18

Optic, Oliver. *Through by Daylight, or The Young Engineer of the Lake Shore RR.* Lee & Shepard, 1870. ....$10–$15

Orcutt, Samuel. *The Indians of the Housatonic and Naugatuck Valleys.* Hartford, 1882, illus. ....$90–$135

Ordway, Samuel H. Jr. *A Conservation Handbook.* NY, 1949. ....$18–$25

Ormond, Clyde. *Bear!* Harrisburg, 1961, illus. ....$14–$20

Ormond, Clyde. *Hunting Our Biggest Game.* Harrisburg, 1956, illus, dj. ....$20–$25

Ormsbee, T.H. *Early American Furniture Makers.* NY, 1935. ....$28–$35

Orwell, George. *Animal Farm.* NY, Harcourt, 1946, 1st U.S. ed, dj. ....$65–$110

Orwell, George. *Animal Farm.* Lon, 1945, 1st ed. ....$75–$125

Orwell, George. *Nineteen Eighty Four.* NY, 1949, 1st American ed, red dj. ....$125–$250

Osborn, Gardner. *The Streets of Old New York.* Harper & Bros., 1939. ....$10–$15

Osborne, Russell. *Journal of a Trapper.* Boise, 1921. ...$37–$50

Osgood, C. *Ingalik Material Culture.* New Haven, 1940, illus. ....$60–$80

Osler, Sir William. *Aequanimitas.* Phila, 1932, 3rd ed. ..$17–$20

Osler, W. *Lectures on the Diagnosis of Abdominal Tumors.* Lon, 1900. ....$20–$25

Osler, William. *An Alabama Student and Other Biographical Essays.* Lon, 1926, illus, 2nd imp. ....$40–$55

Osler, William. *Principles and Practice of Medicine.* NY, 1892.
....*$540–$900*

Osler, William. *Science and Immortality: Ingersoll Lecture.* Bos, 1904, 1st ed. ....*$45–$60*

Osler, William. *The Old Humanities and the New Science.* Bos, 1920, dj. ....*$95–$125*

Osler, William D. *The Student Life and Other Essays.* Lon.
....*$18–$22*

Osofsky, Gilbert (ed). *Puttin' on Ole Massa: The Slave Narr. of Bibb, Brown, and Northup.* NY, 1969, 1st ed. ....*$30–$35*

Oswald, John Clyde. *Printing in the Americas.* NY/Lon, 1937, 1st ed, illus, dj. ....*$45–$85*

Otis, James. *Toby Tyler or Ten Weeks with the Circus.* Phila, 1937. ....*$12–$15*

Oudemans, A.C. *The Great Sea-serpent.* Lon, 1892, illus.
....*$55–$150*

Owen, Catherine. *Choice Cookery.* NY, 1889. ....*$30–$45*

Owen, Catherine. *Culture and Cooking.* NY, 1881. ....*$30–$45*

Owen, Charles H. *The Justice of the Mexican War.* NY, 1908.
....*$18–$25*

Owen, Russell. *The Antarctic Ocean.* NY, Whittlesey House, 1941, 1st ed. ....*$18–$25*

Owen, Sir R. *Memoir on the Gorilla.* Lon, 1865. ......*$500–$750*

Owens, John A. *Sword and Pen: Ventures and Adventures of Willard Glazier.* Phila, 1883, illus. ....*$20–$25*

Ozick, Cynthia. *The Cannibal Galaxy.* 1983, 1st ed, dj. ..*$5–$12*

Ozick, Cynthia. *The Pagan Rabbi and Other Stories.* Knopf, 1971, 1st ed, dj. ....*$15–$25*

Paddock, Mrs. A.G. *The Fate of Madame La Tour: A Tale of Great Salt Lake.* NY, 1861, 1st ed. ....*$37–$45*

Page, V. *Ford V-8 Cars and Trucks.* NY, 1940. ....*$30–$35*

Page, Victor W. *The Model T Ford Car.* NY, 1917. ......*$45–$65*

Paige, Satchel. *Maybe I'll Pitch Forever.* NY, 1962, 1st ed.
....*$35–$50*

Paine, A.B. *Mark Twain, A Biography.* NY, 1912, 3 vols, 1st ed, illus. ....*$50–$95*

Paine, A.B. *The Great White Way.* NY, 1901, 1st ed. ....*$35–$45*

Paine, Thomas. *The Rights of Man.* Lon, 1791, 6th ed. ....*$200–$225*

Paley, Grace. *Later the Same Day.* NY, 1985, 1st ed, dj..*$15–$25*

Paley, Grace. *The Little Disturbances of Man.* Garden City, 1959, 1st ed, dj, sgn. ....*$95–$140*

Palmborg, Rilla. *The Private Life of Greta Garbo.* NY, 1931. ....*$40–$75*

Palmer, C.H. *The Salmon Rivers of Newfoundland.* Bos, 1928, illus, fldg map. ....*$75–$95*

Panchard, M. Edouard. *Meats, Poultry, and Game: How to Buy, Cook and Carve. . . .* NY, 1919. ....*$15–$20*

Pannell, Walter. *Civil War on the Range.* Los Angeles, 1943, 1st ed. ....*$22–$30*

Pansy. *Cunning Workmen.* Lothrop & Co., nd. ....*$28–$35*

Paret, J. Parmly. *Methods and Players of Modern Lawn Tennis.* 1915, illus. ....*$30–$50*

Parker, Dorothy. *After Such Pleasures.* NY, 1933, ltd #189/250 cc, slipcase, sgn. ....*$100–$125*

Parker, Dorothy. *Death and Taxes.* NY, 1931. ....*$15–$25*

Parker, Dorothy. *Sunset Gun.* NY, 1928, 1st ed. ....*$40–$60*

Parker, Thomas V. *The Cherokee Indians . . . Their Relations with the U.S. Govt.* NY, 1097, 1st ed, illus. ....*$65–$75*

Parkman, Francis. *The Old Regime in Canada.* Bos, 1874, 1st ed, map. ....*$20–$35*

Parkman, Francis. *The Oregon Trail.* 1946, illus by T.H. Benton. ....*$20–$30*

Parkman, Francis. *The Oregon Trail.* Bos, 1925, illus by N.C. Wyeth and F. Remington, ltd #907/975 cc. ....*$100–$145*

Parkman, Francis. *The Oregon Trail.* Bos, Little Brown, 1892, 1st ed, illus by F. Remington. ....*$125–$550*

Parloa, Maria. *Choice Receipts.* Dorchester, 1895, softbound.
....*$15–$25*

Parloa, Maria. *Miss Parloa's New Cook Book.* Bos, 1881, 1st ed.
....*$45–$55*

Parrish, Maxfield. *Knave of Hearts.* NY, 1925, 1st ed, hardbound.
....*$950–$1,250*

Parrish, Randall. *Beth Norvell.* McClurg, 1907. ....*$25–$18*

Parsons, Cochrane. *The Story of Newfoundland.* Tor, 1949, illus.
....*$10–$15*

Parsons, F. *The Story of New Zealand.* Phila, 1904, 1st ed.
....*$14–$18*

Parsons, Francis. *A Time of Preservation.* Bos, 1935, illus, photos.
....*$20–$25*

Parsons, Mary. *Wild Flowers of California.* Wm. Doxey, 1897,
1st ed. ....*$14–$20*

Partington, James. *A Text-book of Thermodynamics.* Lon, 1913,
1st ed. ....*$15–$25*

Parton, J. *Life of Andrew Jackson.* NY, 1861, 3 vols. ...*$45–$75*

Pasley. *Al Capone: The Biography of a Self-made Man.* NY, 1930,
1st ed. ....*$30–$40*

Pasternak, Boris. *An Essay in Autobiography.* Collins, 1959, 1st
English ed, dj. ....*$30–$35*

Pasternak, Boris. *Doctor Zhivago.* Pantheon, 1959, 1st American
ed. ....*$45–$60*

Pasteur, M. Louis. *Inoculation against Hydrophobia.* NY, 1886.
....*$30–$45*

Patchen, Kenneth. *Hurrah for Anything.* 1957, 1st ed, wrps.
....*$37–$45*

Paton, Alan. *Cry, The Beloved Country.* NY, 1948, sgn.
....*$125–$150*

Paton, Alan. *Oh, But Your Land is Beautiful.* NY, 1982, sgn, dj.
....*$30–$35*

Paton, Alan. *Too Late the Phalarope.* Scribner's, 1953, 1st U.S.
ed, dj. ....*$37–$45*

Paton, Alan. *Too Late the Phalarope.* Capetown, 1953, 1st ed, dj. ....*$65–$100*

Patrick, Rembert Wallace. *Jefferson Davis and His Cabinet.* Baton Rouge, 1944, 1st ed. ....*$35–$50*

Patterson, A. *Notes on Pet Monkeys.* Lon, 1888. ....*$60–$85*

Patterson, Haywood and Earle Conrad. *Scottsboro Boy.* Garden City, 1950, 1st ed, dj. ....*$35–$65*

Patterson, J.H. *The Man-eaters of Tsavo.* Lon, 1908, illus. ....*$10–$16*

Patterson, J.H. *With the Zionists in Gallipoli.* NY, 1916, 1st ed. ....*$22–$35*

Patterson, R.M. *Buffalo Head.* NY, 1961.........................*$20–$27*

Patterson, Robert. *A Narrative of the Campaign in the Valley of the Shenandoah.* Phila, 1865, map, sgn. ....*$112–$120*

Pauling, Linus. *No More War!* NY, 1958, sgn. ....*$40–$60*

Pauling, Linus and E. Bright Wilson. *Introduction to Quantum Mechanics.* NY/Lon, 1935, dj. ....*$30–$40*

Pauling, Linus and Roger Hayward. *The Architecture of Molecules.* SF/Lon, 1964, 1st ed, illus, dj. ....*$14–$20*

Pavlov, Ivan Petrovich. *Lectures on Conditioned Reflexes. . . .* NY, 1928, illus, 1st English ed. ....*$125–$150*

Payne, W. Floyd. *Hunting in the High Mountains.* El Paso, nd, presentation copy, photos. ....*$25–$35*

Peabody, F. *Education for Life: The Story of Hampton Institute.* 1918, 1st ed. ....*$27–$38*

Peach, Arthur W. *The Country Rod and Gun Book.* VT, 1938, 1st ed, illus, sgn, dj. ....*$10–$15*

Pearson, Edmund. *Dime Novels.* Little Brown, 1929, 1st ed, illus. ....*$20–$35*

Pearson, Emily. *Gutenberg and the Art of Printing.* Bos, 1871, illus. ....*$25–$35*

Peary, Robert E. *The North Pole.* Stokes, 1910, 1st ed, illus. ....*$100–$130*

Peattie, Roderick. *Black Hills.* NY, 1952. ....*$20–$25*

Peck, J.M. *A New Guide for Emigrants to the West.* Bos, 1836, 2nd ed. ....$150–$225

Peckham, G.W. and E.G. *On the Instincts and Habits of the Solitary Wasps.* Madison, WI, 1898. ....$30–$45

Peel, Edgar and Pat Southern. *The Trials of the Lancashire Witches. . . .* Taplinger, 1969, dj. ....$12–$17

Peery, Paul D. *Chimes and Electric Carillons.* NY, 1948, illus. ....$15–$20

Peil, Margaret. *The Ghanaian Factory Worker: Industrial Man in Africa.* Lon, 1972, 1st ed, dj. ....$20–$30

Peixotto, Ernest. *Our Hispanic Southwest.* NY, 1916. ...$18–$25

Pendergast, A. *Cigar Store Figures.* Chi, 1953, 1st ed, illus. ....$35–$40

Pendray, G. Edward. *The Coming Age of Rocket Power.* NY/Lon, Harper & Bros., 1945, 1st ed, illus. ....$35–$60

Pennell, Elizabeth Robins. *French Cathedrals.* NY, 1909, illus by Joseph Pennell, teg, plans and diagrams. ....$25–$45

Penzer, N.M. *The Book of the Wine Label.* Lon, 1947, 1st ed, illus. ....$38–$45

Pepper, Adeline. *Glass Gaffers of New Jersey. . . .* NY, 1971, illus. ....$20–$28

Percy, J. *Metallurgy: Iron and Steel.* Lon, 1864, 1st ed..$25–$35

Percy, Walker. *Lancelot.* NY, Farrar, 1977, 1st ed, dj.....$25–$50

Percy, Walker. *Love in the Ruins.* 1971, dj. ....$28–$35

Percy, Walker. *The Last Gentleman.* Farrar, 1966, 1st ed, dj. ....$60–$125

Percy, Walker. *The Second Coming.* NY, 1980, 1st ed, dj..$8–$15

Percy, William Alexander. *Lanterns on the Levee.* NY, 1941, 1st ed, sgn, dj. ....$50–$75

Perelman, S.J. *Chicken Inspector No. 23.* 1966, 1st ed, dj. ....$15–$20

Perkins, D.A.W. *History of O'Brien County, Iowa.* Sioux Falls, 1897, illus. ....$45–$65

Perkins, Jacob B. *JB's Final Bulletin.* 1937, ltd #8/300 cc, presentation copy. ....$25–$30

Perkins, James. *Annals of the West.* Cinc, 1846, 1st ed, maps. ....$58–$70

Perkins, Lucy Fitch. *The Indian Twins.* Houghton Mifflin, 1930, illus. ....$18–$30

Perkins, Lucy Fitch. *The Italian Twins.* Houghton Mifflin, 1920, illus. ....$22–$40

Perkins, Lucy Fitch. *The Japanese Twins.* Houghton Mifflin, 1912, illus. ....$14–$25

Perkins, P.D. and Ione Perkins. *Bibliography of Lafcadio Hearne.* NY, 1968. ....$45–$60

Perrault, Charles. *Cinderella.* Scribner's, 1954, 1st ed, illus by Marcia Brown, sgn by Brown. ....$75–$85

Perry, John. *Spinning Tops.* Lon, 1890, illus. ....$25–$37

Perry, R. *The Jeannette.* Chi, 1883. ....$25–$35

Peters, F.J. *Currier & Ives Railroad, Indian and Pioneer Prints.* NY, 1930, folio, dj. ....$35–$45

Peters, Madison C. *Justice to the Jew.* NY, 1899. ....$18–$25

Petersham, Maud and Miska. *The Silver Mace.* NY, 1956, 1st ed, dj. ....$18–$27

Peterson, Roger Tory. *A Field Guide to Birds.* . . . Bos, 1947, illus, 2nd ed, sgn. ....$35–$45

Peto, Florence. *Historic Quilts.* NY, 1939, 1st ed, illus, dj. ....$55–$125

Pettigrew, Thomas F. *A Profile of the Negro American.* Van Nostrand, 1964, dj. ....$12–$18

Pettingill, Eleanor Rice. *Penguin Summer.* NY, 1960, 1st ed, illus, dj. ....$16–$20

Pfeiffer, Ida. *The Last Travels of Ida Pfeiffer.* Harper & Bros, 1861, 1st U.S. ed. ....$65–$75

Phillips, John. *China Trade Porcelain.* Harvard Univ. Press, 1956, 1st ed, illus, clr and b/w. ....$75–$185

Phillips, Paul Chrisler. *The Fur Trade.* OK, 1961, 2 vols, 1st ed, illus, slipcase. ....*$50–$100*

Phillips, Ulrich B. *American Negro Slavery.* Appleton, 1928. ....*$20–$35*

Phillips, W.S. *Indian Tales for Little Folks.* NY, Platt & Munk, 1928, illus by Phillips, clr plates. ....*$35–$50*

Piaget, H.E. *The Watch.* 1860, illus. ....*$100–$200*

Picard, Mary Ann. *Official Star Trek Cooking Manual.* NY, 1978, 1st ed, paperback, sgn. ....*$12.50–$18*

Picasso, Pablo. *Desire: A Play.* NY, 1948, 1st ed, dj. ....*$25–$35*

Pidgin, Charles Felton. *Blennerhassett: A Romance Founded upon Events of American Hist.* 1901, illus. ....*$10–$15*

Pierce, Gerald S. *Texas under Arms . . . Rep. of Texas, 1836–1846.* Austin, 1969, dj. ....*$27–$35*

Pike, Nicholas. *A New and Complete System of Arithmetick.* Bos, 1808, 3rd ed, calf. ....*$22–$45*

Pike, Warburton. *The Barren Ground of Northern Canada.* Lon, 1892, 1st ed, fldg maps. ....*$85–$125*

Pike, Zebulon M. *Exploratory Travels through the Western Territories.* Denver, 1889. ....*$100–$125*

Pilat, Oliver and Jo Ranson. *Sodom by the Sea: An Affectionate History of Coney Island.* Garden City, 1941, illus. ....*$25–$35*

Pilling, James Constantine. *Bibliography of the Eskimo Language.* GPO, 1887, wrps. ....*$55–$75*

Pinkerton, Allan. *Claude Melmotte, as a Detective and Other Stories.* Chi, 1875, 1st ed. ....*$50–$65*

Pinto, Edward H. *Treen or Small Woodware throughout the Ages.* Lon, 1949, 1st ed, illus, dj. ....*$32–$40*

Piper, Watty (ed). *My Picture Story Book.* NY, 1941, dj. ....*$14–$18*

Piquion, Rene. *Manuel de Negritude.* Haiti, nd. ....*$18–$20*

Pitchford R. and Combs, F. *The Projectionist's Handbook.* 1933, 1st ed, illus. ....*$30–$40*

Planck, Max. *Das Weltbild der Neuen Physik.* Leipzig, 1947. ....*$15–$20*

Playtner, R.H. *An Analysis of the Lever Escapement.* Chi, 1895, 1st ed, illus. ....*$30–$45*

Plowden, E. *The History of Ireland.* Lon, 1812, 2 vols, 2nd ed, ¼ lea. ....*$50–$75*

Plummer, Peter W. *Carpenters' and Builders' Guide.* NY, 1891, 4 plates. ....*$18–$25*

Pocock, Roger. *Following the Frontier.* NY, 1903. ....*$85–$115*

Poe, Edgar Allan. *Tales of Mystery and Imagination.* NY, Tudor Pub., 1935, illus by Harry Clarke. ....*$40–$75*

Poe, Edgar Allan. *The Works of Edgar A. Poe.* NY, 1902, 10 vols, Library Ed. ....*$100–$135*

Point, Fr. Nicolas. *Wilderness Kingdom: . . . Indian Life in the Rocky Mtns., 1840–1847.* NY, 1967. ....*$25–$35*

Pollard, Edward A. *Southern History of the Great Civil War.* Tor, 1863. ....*$75–$100*

Pollard, Edward A. *The First Year of the War.* Rich, 1862, 1st ed, Confederate imprint. ....*$225–$250*

Pollard, Edward A. *The Lost Cause: A New Southern Hist. of War of the Confederates.* NY, 1866. ....*$25–$35*

Pollard, Edward A. *The Lost Cause Regained.* NY, 1868, 1st ed. ....*$25–$30*

Pollard, Eliza. *Florence Nightingale: The Wounded Soldier's Friend.* Lon, nd. ....*$20–$25*

Pollock, Thomas C. *The Philadelphia Theater in the 18th Century.* 1933. ....*$24–$30*

Poolman, K. *Zeppelins against London.* NY, 1961, 1st ed, illus, dj. ....*$22–$30*

Poore, Ben Perley. *Life and Public Services of Ambrose E. Burnside.* Prov, 1882, illus, engr, maps. ....*$25–$35*

Popp, A. *The Autobiography of a Working Woman.* Lon, 1912, 1st English ed. ....*$50–$78*

Porter, Gene Stratton. *Birds of the Bible.* Cinc, 1909, 1st ed. ....*$150–$200*

Porter, Gene Stratton. *Laddie.* Doubleday, 1st ed. ....*$15–$18*

Porter, Gene Stratton. *Michael O'Halloran.* Doubleday, 1915, 1st ed. ....$32–$40

Porter, Gene Stratton. *Moths of the Limberlost.* NY, 1926. ....$125–$140

Porter, Gene Stratton. *Music of the Wild.* Cinc, 1910, 1st ed. ....$120–$170

Porter, Gene Stratton. *The Firebird.* Garden City, 1922, 1st ed, illus by Gordon Grant. ....$22–$35

Porter, Gene Stratton. *The Magic Garden.* NY, 1927, 1st ed. ....$35–$48

Porter, Gene Stratton. *The Song of the Cardinal.* Bobbs Merrill, 1903, illus, buckram. ....$80–$90

Porter, Gene Stratton. *The White Flag.* NY, 1923, 1st ed. ....$22–$35

Porter, Gene Stratton. *What I Have Done with Birds.* Ind, 1907, 1st ed. ....$165–$220

Porter, Katherine. *My Chinese Marriage.* NY, 1921. ....$50–$65

Porter, Katherine Ann. *A Christmas Story.* NY, 1958, 1st ed. ....$30–$40

Porter, Katherine Ann. *Ship of Fools.* Bos, 1962, 1st ed, dj. ....$20–$30

Porter, Katherine Anne. *The Leaning Tower.* Harcourt, 1944, 1st ed, dj. ....$45–$55

Porter, Kenneth W. *The Jacksons and the Lees: . . . Massachusetts Merchants, 1765–1844.* Camb, 1937, 2 vols, 1st ed, illus, dj. ....$65–$100

Posse, Baron Nils. *The Special Kinesiology of Educational Gymnastics.* Bos, 1894, 1st ed, pocket chart. ....$22–$35

Post, C.C. *Driven from Sea to Sea.* Phila, 1888, illus.....$62–$75

Potok, Chaim. *The Promise.* NY, 1969, 1st ed, dj. ....$20–$25

Potter. *Art of Hanging.* NY, 1965, dj. ....$16–$20

Potter, Beatrix. *Tale of Jemima Puddle Duck.* F. Warne, 1936, dj. ....$15–$20

Potter, Beatrix. *The Pie and the Patty Man.* NY, 1905. .$45–$60

Potter, Beatrix. *The Story of Peter Rabbit and Other Stories.* Whitman, 1928. ....*$14–$18*

Potter, Beatrix. *The Tale of Benjamin Bunny.* Lon, 1904, 1st ed. ....*$375–$495*

Potter, Beatrix. *The Tale of Mr. Toad.* 1939, illus, dj. ....*$20–$35*

Potter, Beatrix. *Wag-by-Wall.* Horn Book, 1944, 1st ed, illus, dj. ....*$45–$65*

Pound, Arthur. *Lake Ontario.* Bobbs Merrill, 1945, illus, dj. ....*$10–$15*

Pound, Ezra. *70 Cantos.* Lon, 1950, 1st English ed, ltd, 1,622 cc, dj. ....*$90–$120*

Pound, Ezra. *Kulchur.* NY, 1952, 2nd American ed. ......*$15–$25*

Pound, Ezra. *Personae: The Collected Poems.* NY, 1926, 1st ed. ....*$75–$100*

Pound, Ezra. *The Classic Anthology Defined by Confucius.* Harvard Univ. Press, 1954, 1st ed, dj. ....*$50–$125*

Powell, Agnes Baden. *Handbook for Girl Scouts.* 1917, 1st ed. ....*$30–$45*

Powell, E. Alexander. *By Camel and Car to the Peacock Throne.* NY/Lon, 1923, illus, fldg map. ....*$10–$15*

Powell, E. Alexander. *Where the Strange Trails Go Down.* Scribner's, 1921, 1st ed, illus, dj. ....*$18–$25*

Powell, J.W. *14th Annual Report of the Bureau of Ethnology.* DC, GPO, 1896, illus, maps. ....*$65–$95*

Powell, John Wesley. *Down the Colorado.* Promontory Press, 1969, illus, dj. ....*$16–$20*

Powys, John Cowper. *Morwyn, or The Vengeance of God.* NY, 1976, rprnt. ....*$30–$40*

Poyas, Mrs. Elizabeth A. *Carolina in Olden Time.* Charleston, 1855, 1st ed. ....*$50–$75*

Prager, Hans G. *Through Artic Hurricanes.* Lon, nd. ....*$16–$22*

Prescott, W. *History of the Conquest of Peru.* Phila, 1874, 2 vols. ....*$14–$18*

Prescott, W. *History of the Conquest of Peru.* NY, 1847, 2 vols, 1st American ed. ....*$100–$145*

Prescott, W.H. *Conquest of Mexico.* NY, 1848, 3 vols, 1st ed. ....*$85–$110*

Prescott, William H. *History of the Conquest of Peru.* 1865, 2 vols. ....*$35–$45*

Preston, T. *Historical Sketches of the Holston Valley.* TN, 1926, map. ....*$20–$28*

Price, Henry C. *How to Make Pictures, Easy Lessons.* . . . NY, 1882, 1st ed, illus. ....*$28–$35*

Price, Mary and Vincent. *Treasury of Great Recipes.* NY, 1965, lea. ....*$50–$70*

Price, Vincent and Mary. *A Treasury of Great Recipes.* 1965. ....*$14–$20*

Prideaux, Humphrey. *The Old and New Testament . . . Hist. of Jews and Neighbouring Nations.* Balt, 1833, illus, fldg maps, calf. ....*$50–$65*

Priest, Josiah. *American Antiquities and Discoveries in the West.* Alb, 1833, illus, fldg map, calf. ....*$90–$135*

Priestley, J. *Discourses Relating to the Evidences of Revealed Religion.* Phila, 1796, 1st ed, lea. ....*$95–$120*

Priestley, J.B. *Angel Pavement.* Lon, 1930, ltd #842/1,025 cc, sgn. ....*$40–$50*

Priestley, J.B. and Gerald Bullett. *I'll Tell You Everything.* NY, 1933, 1st ed. ....*$14–$20*

Prieur, J.C. *Boyer's Royal Dictionary.* Dublin, 1796, full lea, 17th ed. ....*$55–$85*

Prime, William C. *Boat Life in Egypt and Nubia.* NY, Harper, 1865, illus, 2nd ed. ....*$22–$20*

Prince Philip. *Seabirds in Southern Waters.* 1962. ....*$25–$35*

Pritchard, J. Laurence. *Sir George Cayley.* NY, 1962, 1st ed, illus, 1st American ed. ....*$40–$55*

Proctor, Mary. *The Young Folks Book of the Heavens.* Bos, 1929, illus. ....*$12–$20*

Proctor, R. *Chance and Luck.* Lon, 1887. ....*$50–$90*

Prosch, Charles. *Reminiscences of Washington Territory.* . . . Seattle, 1904, sgn. ....*$95–$125*

Pullen, John J. *20th Maine: A Volunteer Regiment in the Civil War.* Lippincott, 1957, 2nd imp, dj. ....*$28–$40*

Purdy, James. *Children Is All.* Secker & Warburg, 1963, 1st English ed, dj. ....*$30–$35*

Purdy, James. *Jeremy's Version.* Garden City, 1970, 1st ed, dj. ....*$20–$25*

Purtell, Joseph. *The Tiffany Touch.* NY, 1st ed, illus, dj..*$22–$35*

Pusey, William Allen. *The Wilderness Road to Kentucky.* NY, 1921, dj. ....*$58–$75*

Putnam, George. *A Prisoner of War in Virginia.* NY, 1912, 1st ed. ....*$35–$45*

Putnam, George R. *Lighthouses and Lightships of the United States.* 1933, illus. ....*$30–$45*

Puzo, Mario. *The Runaway Summer of Davie Shaw.* 1976, 1st British ed. ....*$15–$20*

Pyle, Howard. *Men of Iron.* Harper, 1892, 1st ed, illus..*$55–$75*

Pynchon, Thomas. *The Crying of Lot 49.* Phila, 1966, 1st ed, dj. ....*$150–$275*

Pynchon, Thomas. *V.* Lippincott, 1963, 1st ed, dj. .....*$375–$650*

Pyne, Henry R. *The History of the First New Jersey Cavalry.* Trenton, 1871, 1st ed. ....*$125–$175*

Quaife, Milo M. *Checagou: From Indian Wigwam to Modern City, 1673–1835.* Chi, 1933, 1st ed, dj. ....*$20–$35*

Quarles, Benjamin. *The Negro in the American Revolution.* Chapel Hill, 1976, 8th prntg, dj. ....*$14–$17*

Quarles, E.A. *American Pheasant Breeding and Shooting.* Am. Protective Game Assn., 1916, illus. ....*$27–$37*

Queen, Ellery. *Devil to Pay.* NY, 1938, 1st ed, dj. ....*$30–$55*

Queen, Ellery. *Double, Double.* Little Brown, 1950, 1st ed, dj. ....*$45–$70*

Queen, Ellery. *Ellery Queen's Double Dozen.* NY, 1964, 1st ed, dj. ....*$32–$40*

Queen, Ellery (ed). *To the Queen's Taste.* Bos, 1946, 1st ed, dj. ....*$25–$40*

Queeny, Edgar. *Prairie Wings.* 1946, 1st ed, dj. ....*$125–$150*

Queeny, Edgar M. *Cheechako: The Story of an Alaskan Bear Hunt.* NY, 1941, photos. ....*$40–$160*

Quick, Herbert and Edward. *Mississippi Steamboatin'.* 1st ed. ....*$30–$40*

Quiller-Couch. *Adventures in Criticism.* NY, 1896. ....*$10–$15*

Quiller-Couch (ed). *The Oxford Book of English Verse, 1250–1900.* Ox, 1926. ....*$25–$85*

Quiller-Couch. *The Twelve Dancing Princesses.* NY, nd, illus, tip-in plates, dj. ....*$90–$200*

Quiller-Couch, A.T. *The Sleeping Beauty and Other Fairy Tales.* Lon, nd, illus by Edmund Dulac. ....*$125–$175*

Quinn, P.T. *Pear Culture for Profit.* NY, 1900. ....*$12–$15*

Quinton, Capt. *The Strange Adventures of Captain Quinton.* NY, The Christian Herald, 1912. ....*$14–$18*

Quints, Dionne. *Growing Up.* 1935. ....*$35–$55*

Radford. *Stores and Flat Buildings.* Chi/NY, 1909. ....*$58–$75*

Radin, Paul. *The Story of the American Indian.* 1934. ..*$15–$20*

Radley, J.A. *Photography in Crime Detection.* Lon, 1948, illus. ....*$28–$40*

Radziwill, Princess. *My Recollections.* NY, 1904, illus...*$25–$35*

Raht, C.G. *The Romance of Davis Mountains and Big Bend Country.* El Paso, 1919, 1st ed, illus, fldg map, plates. ....*$55–$100*

Ralph, Julian. *On Canada's Frontier.* Harper & Bros., 1892, 1st ed, illus by Remington. ....*$75–$95*

Ramsay, D. *The History of the American Revolution.* Trenton, 1811, 2 vols, 2nd ed, lea. ....*$95–$125*

Ramsdell, Charles W. *Laws and Joint Resolution of Last Session of Confed. Congress.* Durham, 1941. ....*$45–$70*

Rand, Ayn. *Atlas Shrugged.* Random House, 1957, 1st ed, dj. ....*$100–$250*

Rand, Ayn. *The Fountainhead.* Ind, 1943, 1st ed, dj. ..*$125–$200*

Rand, Ayn. *The Fountainhead.* Ind, 1943. ....*$16–$20*

Rand, Ayn. *We the Living.* NY, 1936, 1st ed, dj. ....*$65–$75*

Randall, Henry. *Youatt on the Structure and Diseases of the Horse.* NY, Judd, 1865. ....*$24–$32*

Randolph, Mary. *The Virginia Housewife, or Methodical Cook.* DC, 1830. ....*$200–$500*

Ransom, John L. *Andersonville Diary.* NY, private prntg, 1881, 1st ed. ....*$95–$125*

Raper, Charles. *North Carolina: A Study in English Colonial Government.* NY, 1904, 1st ed. ....*$30–$35*

Rarey, John Solomon. *The Modern Art of Taming Wild Horses.* Columbus, 1856, 1st ed, wrps. ....*$900–$1,500*

Raskin, Saul. *Hagadah for Passover.* NY, 1941, illus, dj..*$20–$25*

Raum, Green B. *The Existing Conflict between Republican Gov. and South. Oligarchy* Cleve, 1884, 1st ed. ....*$48–$65*

Rawlings. *Coins and How to Know Them.* NY, nd, illus. .*$22–$28*

Rawlings, M.K. *Cross Creek Cookery.* NY, 1942, 1st ed, dj. ....*$25–$65*

Rawlings, Marjorie Kinnan. *The Sojourner.* NY, 1953, 1st ed, dj. ....*$30–$40*

Ray, P. *Rep. of the Internat. Polar Expedition to Point Barrow, Alaska.* GPO, 1885, 1st ed. ....*$60–$85*

Rayner, B.L. *Sketches of Life, Writings, and Opinions of Thomas Jefferson. . . .* NY, 1832. ....*$35–$50*

Reagan, R. *Speaking My Mind.* sgn. ....*$98–$125*

Rebold, E. *General History of Free-masonry in Europe.* Cinc, 1868. ....*$35–$50*

Redding, M. Wolcott. *Antiquities of the Orient Unveiled.* 1873, illus. ....*$45–$50*

Redding, M. Wolcott. *Ruins and Relics of the Holy City.* NY, 1872, cloth. ....*$14–$20*

Redford, R.H. *Western Cavaliers . . . Methodist Episcopal Church, Ky, 1832–1844.* Nashville, 1876. ....*$27–$35*

Redpath, James. *John Brown.* Bos, 1860. ....*$20–$40*

Reed, Ishmael. *Flight to Canada.* NY, Random House, 1976, 1st ed, review copy, dj. ....$22–$30

Reed, Ishmael. *Flight to Canada.* NY, Random House, 1976, 1st ed, sgn, dj. ....$65–$85

Reed, Ishmael. *Mumbo Jumbo.* Garden City, 1972, 1st ed, dj. ....$35–$55

Reed, John. *An Apology for the Rite of Infant Baptism . . . Modes of Baptism.* Prov, 1815, calf. ....$25–$30

Reed, John A. *History of the 101st Regiment Pennsylvania Volunteer Infantry.* Chi, 1910. ....$40–$50

Reed, Myrtle. *Master of Vineyard.* NY, 1910. ....$20–$25

Reese, A.M. *The Alligator and Its Allies.* NY, 1915, illus..$55–$75

Reeves, J.E. *A Hand-book of Medical Microscopy.* Phila, 1894, 1st ed, illus. ....$37–$45

Reeves, James J. *History of the 24th Regiment New Jersey Volunteers.* Camden, NJ, 1889, 45 pp, 1st ed, wrps. ....$110–$135

Reichard, Gladys. *Spider Woman: A Story of Navajo Weavers and Chanters.* 1934, 1st ed. ....$25–$48

Reichenbach, W. *Six Guns and Bulls Eyes.* Sam Worth, 1936, 1st ed, dj. ....$40–$50

Reid, Mayne Capt. *The White Chief: A Legend of North Mexico.* NY, 1875. ....$22–$30

Reid, Mrs. Hugo. *Woman: Her Education and Influence.* NY, 1847. ....$30–$45

Reinhardt, Col. G.C. and Lt. Col. W.R. Kintner. *Atomic Weapons in Land Combat.* Harrisburg, 1953, 1st ed, illus. ......$20–$30

Reitman, B.L. *Second Oldest Profession.* NY, 1931. ......$18–$20

Remarque, Erich. *All Quiet on the Western Front.* 1929, 1st American ed, dj. ....$40–$75

Remarque, Erich Maria. *Heaven Has No Favorites.* NY, 1961, 1st American ed, advance copy, dj. ....$30–$35

Remington, Frederic. *Crooked Trails.* NY, Harper & Bros., 1898, illus by Remington. ....$200–$275

Remington, Frederic. *Pony Tracks.* NY, 1895, 1st ed, illus by Remington. ....*$200–$500*

Remington, Frederic. *The Way of an Indian.* NY, 1906, 1st ed, illus by Remington. ....*$350–$475*

Replinger, John G. *The Jewelry Repairer's Handbook.* Peoria, IL, 1914. ....*$18–$25*

Reti, Ladislao (ed). *The Unknown Leonardo.* NY, 1974, illus, folio, dj. ....*$25–$45*

Rexroth, Kenneth. *Saucy Limericks and Christmas Cheer.* Santa Barbara, 1980, 1st ed, ltd #111/ 299 cc. ....*$35–$40*

Reynolds. *Dutchess County Doorways, 1730–1830.* NY, 1931. ....*$18–$25*

Reynolds, B. *Magic, Divination, and Witchcraft among Barotse of N. Rhodesia.* Lon/Berkeley, 1963, illus. ....*$30–$40*

Reynolds, E.W. *The True Story of the Barons of the South....* Bos, 1862. ....*$28–$35*

Reznikoff, Nathan and Charles. *Early History of a Sewing-machine Operator.* Charles Reznikoff, Pub., 1936, 1st ed. ....*$50–$100*

Rheims, Maurice. *The Flowering of Art Nouveau.* NY, nd, dj. ....*$85–$115*

Rice, Anne. *Cry to Heaven.* NY, 1982, 1st ed, dj. ....*$30–$45*

Rice, Anne. *The Queen of the Damned.* Knopf, 1988, sgn, dj. ....*$45–$60*

Rice, Anne. *The Vampire Lestat.* 1985, dj. ....*$100–$150*

Rice, Louise. *Dainty Dishes from Foreign Lands.* Chi, 1911. ....*$15–$22*

Rice, William Gorham. *Carillons of Belgium and Holland.* NY, 1914, illus. ....*$22–$35*

Rich, Louise D. *We Took to the Woods.* Phila, 1942, 1st ed, illus. ....*$6–$12*

Rich, Prof. George. *Artistic Horse Shoeing.* NY, 1890. .*$35–$45*

Richards, H.S. *All about Horse Brasses.* 1944, wrps. ....*$20–$24*

Richards, Laura. *Captain January.* Bos, 1893, illus by Frank Merrill. ....*$35–$45*

Richards, Laura E. *The Golden Windows.* Little Brown, 1903, illus by Arthur Becher. ....*$30–$40*

Richards, Laura E. *The Silver Crown.* Little Brown, 1906, illus by Jessie Wilcox Smith. ....*$20–$40*

Richards, Laura E. *When I Was Your Age.* Bos, 1849, 1st ed. ....*$20–$30*

Richards, Laura Elizabeth Howe. *The Hurdy-gurdy.* Bos, 1902, illus. ....*$65–$85*

Richardson, Albert. *The Secret Service.* Hartford, 1865, 1st ed. ....*$18–$45*

Richardson, Albert D. *The Secret Service, the Field, the Dungeon, and the Escape.* Hartford, 1865, 1st ed, illus. ......*$65–$145*

Richardson, D.N. *Girdle Round the Earth.* Chi, 1894. ..*$14–$25*

Richardson, Frank. *From Sunrise to Sunset: Reminiscence.* Bristol, TN, 1910, 1st ed, illus. ....*$90–$125*

Richardson, Frank. *The Secret Kingdom.* Lon, 1911, 3rd prntg. ....*$50–$75*

Richardson, N. *The Boy Scout Movement Applied by the Church.* NY, 1915. ....*$14–$20*

Richardson, Sir John. *Arctic Searching Expedition for Sir John Franklin.* NY, 1852. ....*$60–$80*

Richmond, Mary. *A Day in the Life of a Spoiled Child.* New Haven, Babcock, nd. ....*$32–$45*

Richter, Conrad. *A Simple Honorable Man.* NY, 1962, 1st ed, sgn, dj. ....*$48–$55*

Richter, Conrad. *The Sea of Grass.* Knopf, 1937, dj. ...*$20–$35*

Rickard, T.A. *The Copper Mines of Lake Superior.* NY, 1905, 1st ed. ....*$33–$45*

Rickenbacker, Edward. *Seven Came Through.* NY, 1943, 1st ed, dj. ....*$5–$25*

Rickett, H. *Wildflowers of the U.S.: The Southeastern States.* 1966, 2 vols, slipcase. ....*$85–$120*

Rickmers. *Skiing for Beginners and Mountaineers.* 1910..*$30–$50*

Rideing, William H. *Overland Express (1837–1875).* Ashland, 1970, ltd #441/650 cc. ....*$35–$45*

Ridgeway, Robert. *A Manual of North American Birds.* Phila, 1887, 1st ed, illus. ....*$65–$78*

Ridgway, Matthew B. *The Korean War.* Garden City, 1967, dj. ....*$14–$18*

Riesen, Rene. *Jungle Mission.* NY, 1957. ....*$25–$40*

Riesenberg, F. *Cape Horn.* NY, 1939. ....*$22–$30*

Riggs and Carvie. *Modern Guns and Smokeless Powder.* Lon, 1892. ....*$48–$60*

Riggs, Stephen Return. *Dakota Grammar, Texts and Ethnography.* DC, GPO, 1893. ....*$60–$95*

Rights, Douglas LeTell. *The American Indian in North Carolina.* NC, 1947, 1st ed. ....*$50–$65*

Riis, J. *How the Other Half Lives.* Scribner's, 1890, 1st ed. ....*$85–$125*

Riis, Jacob. *The Battle with the Slum.* NY, 1902. ....*$25–$45*

Riker, James. *Revised History of Harlem.* NY, 1904, fldg map. ....*$60–$95*

Riley, J.W. *Home Again with Me.* Bobbs-Merrill, 1908, 1st ed, illus by Christy, dj. ....*$18–$24*

Riley, James W. *Riley Child Rhymes.* Bobbs-Merrill, 1905, illus by Vawter. ....*$14–$25*

Riley, James Whitcomb. *The Old Swimmin' Hole and 'leven More Poems. . . .* Ind, 1891, 1st ed, 3rd state. ....*$50–$75*

Rinehart, Mary Roberts. *Tenting Tonight.* Bos/NY, 1918, illus. ....*$45–$60*

Rinehart, Mary Roberts. *The Door.* Farrar & Rinehart, 1930, 1st ed. ....*$20–$40*

Rinehart, Mary Roberts. *The Out Trail.* Doran, 1923. ..*$22–$28*

Rinehart, Mary Roberts. *Through Glacier Park.* Bos, 1916, 1st ed, illus, sgn. ....*$32–$40*

Rinehart, Mary Roberts. *When a Man Marries.* Tor, 1909, illus by Harrison Fisher-Bunker, 1st Canadian ed. ....*$50–$75*

Ripley, Mary Churchill. *Chinese Rug Book.* NY, 1927, illus. ....*$14–$25*

Ripley, Ozark. *Quail and the Quail Dog.* Hunter Trader Trapper, 1929, 1st ed. ....*$10–$18*

Ritchie, George Thomas. *A List of Lincolniana in the Library of Congress.* GPO, 1903. ....*$35–$50*

Ritchie, Leitch. *Ireland Picturesque and Romantic.* Lon, 1837, 1st ed, illus, engr, aeg. ....*$85–$125*

Robb, Alfred A. *A Theory of Time and Space.* Camb, 1914. ....*$25–$35*

Robbins, R.A. *The 91st Infantry Division in WWII.* DC, 1947, 1st ed, illus, maps, photos. ....*$50–$60*

Roberts, Allen E. *House Undivided: The Story of Freemasonry and The Civil War.* NY, 1964, dj. ....*$18–$25*

Roberts, H.H. *Basketry of the San Carlos Apache.* AMNH, 1929, illus. ....*$35–$45*

Roberts, John S. *Life and Explorations of David Livingstone.* Bos, 1874, illus. ....*$22–$28*

Roberts, Kenneth. *Boon Island.* Garden City, 1956, dj. .*$20–$25*

Roberts, Kenneth. *It Must Be Your Tonsils.* NY, 1936, sgn. ....*$45–$55*

Roberts, Kenneth *Lydia Bailey.* Garden City, 1947, 1st ed, dj. ....*$20–$30*

Roberts, Kenneth. *Northwest Passage.* NY, 1937, 1st ed, dj, inscr. ....*$60–$150*

Roberts, Kenneth. *Trending into Maine.* Bos, 1938, 1st ed, illus by N.C. Wyeth. ....*$45–$75*

Roberts, Octavia. *Lincoln in Illinois.* Bos/Houston, 1918, 1st ed, illus, ltd 1,000 cc. ....*$50–$75*

Roberts, Warren E. *Viewpoints on Folklife.* Ann Arbor, 1988, 1st ed, illus, dj. ....*$18–$22*

Robeson, Eslanda Goode (Mrs. Paul Robeson). *African Journey.* NY, 1945, 1st ed, dj. ....*$45–$65*

Robeson, Kenneth. *Quest of the Spider: A Doc Savage Novel.* NY, 1935. ....$95–$130

Robie, Virginia. *Historic Styles in Furniture.* Chi, 1905, 1st ed, illus. ....$35–$40

Robinson, Bert. *The Basket Weavers of Arizona.* Albuquerque, 1954, dj. ....$50–$75

Robinson, Charles. *The Kansas Conflict.* NY, 1892, 1st ed. ....$95–$150

Robinson, E.A. *Avon's Harvest.* NY, 1921, dj. ....$15–$20

Robinson, Edward Arlington. *Cavender's House.* 1929, dj. ....$30–$35

Robinson, Ethel Fay. *Houses in America.* NY, 1936, illus by Thos. P. Robinson. ....$25–$40

Robinson, G. *Travels in Palestine and Syria.* Paris, 1837, 2 vols, illus, half calf, maps, plates. ....$150–$200

Robinson, Leigh. *The South before and at the Battle of the Wilderness.* Rich, 1878, wrps. ....$75–$100

Robinson, Rowland E. *Danvis Folks and a Hero of Ticonderoga.* Rutland, 1934, illus. ....$14–$20

Robinson, Rowland E. *Sam Lovel's Camps.* NY, 1893. .$20–$35

Robinson, Rowland E. *Uncle Lishas's Outing.* Bos/NY, 1897, 1st ed. ....$25–$35

Robinson, S. *Kansas: Interior and Exterior Life.* Bos, 1856. ....$35–$45

Robinson, Will. *The Story of Arizona.* Phoenix, 1919. ...$30–$65

Robison, Capt. S.S. *Robison's Manual of Radio Telegraphy and Telephony, 1919.* 1919, illus, 5th ed. ....$30–$40

Robles, Philip K. *U.S. Military Medals and Ribbons.* Tuttle, 1973, 3d prntg. ....$25–$35

Rockne, Knute. *Coaching.* NY, 1931. ....$28–$35

Rockwell, Norman. *My Adventures as an Illustrator.* NY, 1960, 1st ed, slipcase, dj. ....$40–$45

Rockwell, W.H. *Dissecting Manual Based on Cunningham's Anatomy.* Wood, 1905. ....$12–$20

Rockwood, Roy. *Through the Air to the North Pole.* . . . NY, 1906, 1st ed, illus. ....*$32–$45*

Rodale, J.J. and Mabel Mulock. *The Said Book.* Allentown, PA, 1947, dj. ....*$20–$28*

Roe, Clifford G. *The Great War of White Slavery.* . . . 1911. ....*$20–$35*

Roemer, Ferdinand. *Texas with Particular Reference to German Immigration.* San Antonio, 1935, 1st ed, dj. ....*$100–$150*

Rogers, Dale Evans. *Angel Unaware.* Revell, 1953, dj. .*$15–$22*

Rogers, J.E. *The Shell Book.* NY, 1908, illus. ....*$25–$50*

Rohmer, Sax. *Bat Wing.* Caxton House, rprnt, dj. ....*$20–$25*

Rohmer, Sax. *Dope.* NY, 1919, 2nd prntg. ....*$22–$28*

Rohmer, Sax. *Hanover House.* NY, rprnt, dj. ....*$15–$20*

Rohmer, Sax. *Island of Fu Manchu.* Crime Club, Garden City, 1941, 1st ed, dj. ....*$100–$450*

Rohmer, Sax. *Mask of Fu Manchu.* A.L. Burt, nd. ....*$20–$40*

Rohmer, Sax. *Moon of Madness.* Garden City, 1928. ....*$20–$40*

Rohmer, Sax. *President Fu Manchu.* Crime Club, Garden City, 1936. ....*$35–$40*

Rohmer, Sax. *President Fu Manchu.* Garden City, 1936, 1st ed, dj. ....*$250–$350*

Rohmer, Sax. *The Bat Flies Low.* NY, 1935. ....*$20–$35*

Rohmer, Sax. *The Book of Fu Manchu.* NY, 1929. ....*$25–$35*

Rohmer, Sax. *The Green Eyes of Bast.* NY, 1920, 1st ed..*$45–$75*

Rohmer, Sax. *White Velvet.* Garden City, 1937, dj. ....*$25–$35*

Rolle, Andrew F. *The Lost Cause: The Confederate Exodus to Mexico.* Univ. of Oklahoma Press, 1965, 1st ed. ....*$28–$35*

Rolvaag. *Giants in the Earth.* NY, 1927. ....*$10–$15*

Ronald, Mary. *Luncheons.* NY, 1902. ....*$10–$15*

Ronalds, Alfred. *Fly-fisher's Entomology.* Lon, 1883, illus, 9th ed, plates. ....*$125–$180*

Roosevelt, Franklin D. *The Happy Warrior, Alfred E. Smith.* Bos, 1928, 1st ed. ....*$35–$50*

Roosevelt, Kermit. *The Long Trail.* NY, 1921, sgn. ....*$18–$24*

Roosevelt, Mrs. James. *My Boy Franklin.* NY, 1933, dj. .*$14–$18*

Roosevelt, Theodore. *Hunting Trips of a Ranchman.* Lon, 1886, 1st ed, illus. ....*$175–$200*

Roosevelt, Theodore. *African Game Trails.* NY, 1910, 1st ed, illus. ....*$45–$95*

Roosevelt, Theodore. *Outdoor Pastimes of an American Hunter.* Scribner's, 1905, 1st ed. ....*$50–$95*

Roosevelt, Theodore. *Ranch Life and the Hunting Trail.* NY, 1904, illus by Frederick Remington. ....*$75–$250*

Roosevelt, Theodore. *Rank and File.* NY, 1928, 1st ed. *$30–$50*

Roosevelt, Theodore. *Roosevelt in the Kansas City Star: War-time Editorials. . . .* Bos, 1921, 1st ed, illus, ltd 375 cc. ....*$45–$75*

Roosevelt, Theodore. *The Winning of the West.* NY, 1900, 4 vols. ....*$70–$225*

Roosevelt, Theodore. *Through the Brazilian Wilderness.* NY, 1914, 1st ed. ....*$67–$75*

Roosevelt, Theodore and Kermit. *East of the Sun and West of the Moon.* NY/Lon, 1926, 1st ed, illus, photos by Kermit. ...*$22–$35*

Root, George. *Tramp! Tramp! Tramp!* Troy, 1890. ....*$22–$32*

Root, S. *Primary Bible Questions for Young Children.* Atlanta, 1864, 3rd ed. ....*$125–$150*

Rorer, Sarah Tyson. *Mrs. Roger's Cakes, Icing, and Fillings.* Phila, 1905. ....*$15–$25*

Rose, W. *The Reptiles and Amphibians of Southern Africa.* Cape Town, 1950, 1st ed, illus. ....*$25–$35*

Rosendahl, Carl Otto and Frederic Butters. *Trees and Shrubs of Minnesota.* 1928. ....*$15–$25*

Rosendahl, Commander C.E. *What about the Airship.* NY, 1938, 1st ed, dj. ....*$65–$80*

Ross, Alexander. *Adventures of First Settlers on the Oregon or Columbia River.* NY, 1969, rprnt, dj. ....*$22–$30*

Ross, Alexander. *Adventures of First Settlers on the Oregon or Columbia River.* Lakeside Press, 1928. ....*$40–$45*

Rotch, A. Lawrence. *The Conquest of the Air.* NY, 1909, 1st ed, illus. ....*$15–$25*

Roth, Philip. *Portnoy's Complaint.* Random House, 1969, 1st ed, dj. ....*$65–$85*

Roth, Philip. *The Breast.* Lon, 1973, 1st ed, dj. ....*$15–$20*

Roth, Philip. *The Great American Novel.* NY, 1973, 1st ed, dj. ....*$25–$40*

Roth, Philip. *The Professor of Desire.* NY, 1977, 1st ed, sgn, dj. ....*$55–$65*

Roth, Philip. *When She Was Good.* Random House, 1967, 1st ed, dj. ....*$35–$50*

Rowan, Richard. *Trees.* 1973, illus, 12 litho prints. ....*$15–$20*

Royko, Mike. *I May Be Wrong, But I Doubt It.* Chi, 1968, 1st ed. ....*$24–$37*

Ruark, R. *The Old Man's Boy Grows Older.* 1961, 1st ed, dj. ....*$35–$45*

Ruark, Robert C. *Horn of the Hunter.* 1953, 1st ed, dj..*$70–$125*

Ruark, Robert C. *Horn of the Hunter.* NY, 1953, 1st ed. ....*$50–$85*

Ruark, Robert C. *Something of Value.* Garden City, 1955, 1st ed, illus by Daniel Schwartz. ....*$40–$55*

Ruark, Robert C. *The Honey Badger.* NY, 1965, 1st ed, dj. ....*$30–$50*

Ruark, Robert C. *The Old Man and the Boy.* NY, 1957, 1st ed, illus by Walter Dower. ....*$45–$100*

Ruark, Robert C. *Uhuru.* Lon, 1962, 1st British ed, dj..*$50–$65*

Ruark, Robert C. *Use Enough Gun.* NY, 1966, 1st ed, illus by Ruark, dj. ....*$35–$75*

Ruark, Robert C. *Use Enough Gun.* NY, 1966. ....*$22–$30*

Rubin, Jerry. *We Are Everywhere.* 1971, 1st ed, dj. ......*$20–$25*

Rubin, Ruth (ed). *A Treasury of Jewish Folksongs.* NY, 1950, illus by T. Herzl Rome. ....*$18–$25*

Rudkin, M. *The Margaret Rudkin Pepperidge Farm Cookbook.* Atheneum, 1963, 1st ed. ....*$12–$15*

Rugg, H.W. *History of Freemasonry in Rhode Island.* Prov, 1895. ....*$30–$45*

Ruhen, Olaf. *Land of Dahori.* Lippincott, 1957, 1st ed, dj. ....*$18–$25*

Rundle, Maria Eliza. *A New System of Domestic Cookery....* Lon, 1849, illus, enlarged. ....*$40–$50*

Rundle, Maria Eliza. *A New System of Domestic Cookery....* Lon, 1807, illus. ....*$75–$125*

Rush, Benjamin. *An Account of the Bilious Remiting Yellow Fever....* Phila, Thomas Dobson, 1794, 2nd ed, lea, rbkd. ....*$150–$275*

Rush, Benjamin. *Letters of the American Philosophical Society.* 1951, 2 vols, 1st ed, djs. ....*$45–$65*

Rush, Benjamin. *Medical Inquiries and Observations, Vol 1.* Phila, 1809, 3rd ed. ....*$100–$275*

Rush, Richard. *Memoranda of a Residence at the Court of London.* Phila, 1833, 1st ed. ....*$50–$75*

Rushdie, Salman. *Midnights Children.* NY, Knopf, 1981, 1st ed, dj. ....*$145–$225*

Rushdie, Salman. *Satanic Verses.* NY, 1989, 1st American ed, dj. ....*$45–$60*

Rushdie, Salman. *Shame.* Lon, 1983, 1st ed, sgn, dj. .*$125–$375*

Ruskin, John. *Letters and Advice to Young Girls and Young Ladies.* NY, 1879. ....*$35–$45*

Russell, Bertrand. *The ABC of Relativity.* NY/Lon, 1925, 1st ed. ....*$75–$100*

Russell, Charles M. *Good Medicine.* Garden City, 1930, illus. ....*$50–$75*

Russell, Keith. *The Duck-huntingest Gentlmen: Coll. of Waterfowling Stories.* 1977, ltd, slipcase, sgn. ....*$85–$125*

Russell, Prof. William. *Scientific Horse Shoeing.* 1901, illus, 6th ed. ....*$30–$45*

Russell, William Howard. *My Diary North and South.* NY, 1954, rprnt, dj. ....*$18–$25*

Rutherford, Livingston. *John Peter Zenger: His Press, His Trial . . . Bibliog. of Imprints.* NY, 1904, 1st ed, illus, ltd 325 cc. ....*$150–$250*

Rutledge, Archibald. *An American Hunter.* NY, 1937, illus by Lynne Bogue Hunt, 2nd prntg. ....*$18–$45*

Rutledge, Archibald. *Brimming Chalice.* NY, 1936, 1st ed, sgn, dj. ....*$95–$150*

Rutledge, Archibald. *Etiquette among the Beasts.* np, 1981. ....*$18–$22*

Rutledge, Archibald. *Hunters Choice.* NY, 1946, 1st ed, dj. ....*$35–$50*

Rutledge, Archibald. *Plantation Game Trails.* 1921, 1st ed, dj. ....*$60–$85*

Rutledge, Archibald H. *Home by the River.* Ind, 1941, plates, sgn, dj. ....*$25–$35*

Sabin, Edwin L. *Building the Pacific Railway.* Lippincott, 1919. ....*$25–$37*

Sabin, Joseph. *A Dictionary of Books Relating to America. . . .* Amsterdam, 1961, 15 vols, rprnt. ....*$950–$1,250*

Sachs, B. and L. Hausman. *Nervous and Mental Disorders from Birth through Adolescence.* NY, 1926, 1st ed, illus. ....*$50–$85*

Sachs, Ernest, M.D. *50 Years of Neurosurgery.* Vantage, 1958, 1st ed, sgn. ....*$22–$30*

Sacks, Benjamin. *Carson Mansion and Ingomar Theatre.* Fresno, 1979, 1st ed, illus, dj. ....*$25–$35*

Sackville-West, Vita. *Devil at Westease.* NY, 1947, 1st ed, dj. ....*$20–$25*

Sackville-West, Vita. *Grand Canyon.* 1942, 1st ed, dj. ..*$15–$20*

Sadler, William S. *Race Decadence.* Chi, 1922, 1st ed, dj. ....*$27–$35*

Sadoul, Jacques. *Alchemists and Gold.* Putnam, 1972, dj..*$12–$20*

Safford. *America's Quilts and Coverlets.* 1972. ....*$14–$18*

Sagan, Carl. *Broca's Brain: Reflections on the Romance of Science.* Random House, 1979, 1st ed, dj. ....*$12–$20*

Sagan, Francoise. *Those without Shadows.* Dutton, 1957, 1st U.S. ed, dj. ....$16–$25

Salinger, J.D. *Franny and Zooey.* Bos, 1961, 1st ed, dj. ..$45–$65

Salinger, J.D. *Nine Stories.* Bos, 1953, 1st ed, dj. ......$250–$425

Salinger, J.D. *Raise High the Roof Beam, Carpenters.* Little Brown, 1963, 1st ed, 2nd state. ....$50–$75

Salinger, J.D. *Raise High the Roof Beam, Carpenters.* 1963, 1st ed, 3rd issue, dj. ....$20–$30

Salinger, J.D. *The Catcher in the Rye.* Bos, 1951, 1st ed, dj. ....$200–$850

Salinger, J.D. *The Kitbook for Soldiers, Sailors, and Marines.* 1943, 1st ed. ....$50–$85

Salk and Salk. *World Population and Human Values.* NY, 1981, sgn, dj. ....$55–$70

Salomon, H. *Victory at Sea.* 1959, illus. ....$14–$25

Salten, Felix. *Bambi: A Life in the Woods.* Simon & Schuster, 1928, ltd 1,000 cc. ....$50–$60

Salten, Felix. *Bambi's Children.* Bobbs-Merrill, 1939, 1st ed, dj. ....$30–$40

Sanborn, F.B. (ed). *The Life and Letters of John Brown, Liberator of Kansas. . . .* Bos, 1891, 1st ed. ....$45–$55

Sanborn, Helen. *Winter in Central America and Mexico.* Bos, 1887, 1st ed. ....$32–$45

Sanborn, Kate. *A Truthful Woman in Southern California.* NY, 1893, 1st ed. ....$30–$40

Sanborn, Kate. *Old Time Wallpapers.* NY, 1905, 1st ed. ....$200–$300

Sanborn, Kate. *Old Time Wallpapers.* CT, 1905, illus, ltd 975 cc, sgn and dated. ....$120–$200

Sanchez, Thomas. *Mile Zero.* Knopf, 1989, 1st ed, dj. ..$18–$35

Sandburg, C. *Abraham Lincoln: The War Years.* NY, 1939, 4 vols, 1st ed. ....$45–$80

Sandburg, Carl. *Abraham Lincoln: War Years/Prairie Years.* NY, nd, 6 vols, boxed. ....$60–$85

Sandburg, Carl. *Always the Young Strangers.* NY, 1953, 1st ed, sgn, dj. ....*$30–$50*

Sandburg, Carl. *Chicago Poems.* Holt, 1916, dj. ....*$20–$25*

Sandburg, Carl. *Good Morning America.* Harcourt, 1928, 1st ed, dj. ....*$45–$55*

Sandburg, Carl. *Potato Face.* Harcourt, 1930, 1st ed, dj...*$50–$75*

Sandburg, Carl. *Remembrance Rock.* NY, 1948, 1st ed, presentation to August Derleth, sgn, dj. ....*$150–$275*

Sandburg, Carl. *Remembrance Rock.* NY, 1948, 1st ed, dj. ....*$20–$30*

Sandburg, Carl. *Rootabaga Pigeons.* NY, 1923, 1st ed, illus. ....*$75–$110*

Sandburg, Carl. *The American Songbag.* NY, 1927. ......*$25–$75*

Sanderson, G.P. *Thirteen Years among the Wild Beasts of India.* Lon, 1893. ....*$18–$25*

Sanderson, Ivan. *Book of Great Jungles.* Messner, 1965, 1st ed. ....*$18–$25*

Sandoz, Mari. *Old Jules.* 1935. ....*$5–$10*

Sandoz, Mari. *Son of the Gamblin' Man.* 1st ed, dj. .....*$35–$40*

Sandoz, Mari. *The Cattlemen.* NY, 1958, dj. ....*$27–$35*

Sandoz, Mari. *The Horse Catcher.* 1957, sgn, dj. ....*$25–$30*

Sandoz, Maurice. *The Maze.* NY, 1945, 1st ed, illus by Salvador Dali. ....*$40–$75*

Sanford, William R. *Jewelry: Queen of Crafts.* NY, 1970, illus, dj. ....*$14–$20*

Sanger, Margaret. *Woman and the New Race.* NY, 1920, 1st ed. ....*$75–$90*

Sanger, William W. *The History of Prostitution.* NY, 1859, 1st ed. ....*$35–$40*

Sangree, Allen. *The Jinx: Stories of the Diamond.* NY, 1911, illus. ....*$60–$90*

Sansom, Joseph. *Travels in Lower Canada. . . .* Lon, 1820, ¼ calf. ....*$85–$125*

Santayana, George. *Sonnets and Other Verses.* Camb/Chi, 1894, 1st ed, ltd 450 cc. .... *$75–$100*

Santee, Ross. *The Bar X Gold Course.* Flagstaff, 1971, illus, dj. ....*$10–$14*

Santillana, Giorgio de. *The Crime of Galileo.* Chi, 1955, dj. ....*$10–$18*

Sarafian, Kevork. *A History of Education in Armenia.* Laverne, CA, 1930, maps. ....*$25–$45*

Sarg, Tony. *Tony Sarg's Book of Animals.* Greenberg Pub., 1925, 1st ed. ....*$30–$40*

Sargent, C. *Manual of the Trees of North America.* 1905, 1st ed. ....*$15–$18*

Saroyan, William. *Get Away Old Man.* NY, 1944, 1st ed, dj. ....*$25–$30*

Saroyan, William. *Rock Wagram.* NY, 1951, 1st ed, dj. .*$20–$30*

Saroyan, William. *The Laughing Matter.* Doubleday, 1953, 1st ed, dj. ....*$30–$55*

Saroyan, William. *The Time of Your Life.* Harcourt, 1939, 1st ed. ....*$20–$30*

Sarton, May. *Anger.* NY, 1982, sgn, dj. ....*$25–$40*

Sarton, May. *December Moon.* Ewert, 1988, ltd 36 cc, sgn. ....*$40–$50*

Sarton, May. *Faithful are the Wounds.* Rinehart, 1955, 1st ed, dj. ....*$8–$15*

Sarton, May. *Miss Pickthorn and Mr. Hare.* NY, 1st ed, sgn, dj. ....*$45–$50*

Sarton, May. *The Poet and the Donkey.* NY, 1969, 1st ed, dj. ....*$25–$30*

Sartre, Jean-Paul. *Existentialism.* Philosophical Library, 1947, 1st U.S. ed, dj. ....*$45–$55*

Sartre, Jean-Paul. *Nausea.* CT, 1949, 1st U.S. ed, dj. ..*$40–$55*

Sartre, Jean-Paul. *The Devil and the Good Lord.* Knopf, 1960, 1st U.S. ed, dj. ....*$27–$35*

Sartre, Jean-Paul. *The Wall and Other Stories.* New Directions, 1948, ltd, slipcase. ....*$50–$60*

Sassoon, Siegfried. *Memoirs of an Infantry Officer.* NY, 1931, illus by Barnett Freedman, 1st U.S. ed, dj. ....*$25–$35*

Sassoon, Siegfried. *Nativity.* Lon, nd, 1st ed, dj. ....*$25–$35*

Satterlee, L. *American Gun Makers.* NY, 1940, 1st ed. ..*$35–$40*

Saundby, R. *Lectures on Bright's Disease.* Bristol/Lon, 1889. ....*$22–$25*

Saunders, Ann. *Narrative of the Shipwreck and Sufferings* .... Prov, 1827, 1st ed, wrps. ....*$75–$150*

Saunders, Charles Francis. *The Indians of the Terraced Houses.* NY, 1912. ....*$30–$45*

Saunders, Louise. *The Knave of Hearts.* Racine, WI, 1925, illus by Maxfield Parrish, folio, spiral bound. ....*$500–$750*

Sayler, O. *Inside the Moscow Art Theatre.* NY, 1925, illus. ....*$20–$30*

Sayre, W.W. *Four against Everest.* 1964, dj. ....*$28–$40*

Schaad, Cornelium G. *Ping-Pong.* Bos, 1930. ....*$18–$22*

Schackleton, E.H. *South: The Story of Shackleton's Last Expedition, 1914–1917.* Lon, 1919, 1st ed. ....*$100–$140*

Schackleton, E.H. *The Heart of the Antarctic.* Phila, 1909, 2 vols, 1st American ed. ....*$200–$375*

Schaff, Morris. *The Sunset of the Confederacy.* Bos, 1912, maps. ....*$25–$37*

Schaldach, William J. *Coverts and Casts.* NY, 1943, 1st ed, illus. ....*$35–$45*

Schaldach, William J. *Fish by Schaldach.* Phila, 1937, ltd 1,500 cc. ....*$80–$150*

Schaldach, William J. *Upland Gunning.* VT, 1946, illus by Schaldach, presentation copy, dj. ....*$100–$175*

Schaller, G. *The Deer and the Tiger.* 1967, 1st ed. ....*$14–$20*

Schell, William G. *Is the Negro a Beast.* Moundsville, 1901, 1st ed. ....*$40–$45*

Schenck, David. *North Carolina, 1780–81.* Raleigh, 1889, 1st ed. ....*$75–$100*

Schley, W.S. *Report of Greely Relief Exped. of 1884.* DC, 1887, 1st ed. ....*$85–$110*

Schmidt, C.W. *Footprints of Five Generations.* New Ulm, 1930, 1st ed, photos, dj. ....*$20–$30*

Schmitt, Martin and Dee Brown. *The Settlers' West.* NY, 1955, 1st ed, illus, dj. ....*$24–$30*

Schoenberger, J. *From Great Lakes to Pacific.* 1934, 1st ed. ....*$50–$65*

Schoolcraft, Henry. *The American Indians, Their History.* Rochester, 1851. ....*$115–$145*

Schoonmaker, W.J. *The World of the Grizzly Bear.* Phila/NY, 1968, illus. ....*$30–$40*

Schoonover, T. *Life of General J. Sutter.* 1895, 1st ed....*$60–$75*

Schreiner, Olive. *Woman and Labor.* NY, 1911, 5th ed. .*$10–$12*

Schulberg, Budd. *Love, Action, Laughter.* Random House, 1989, 1st ed, dj. ....*$15–$20*

Schulberg, Budd. *Sanctuary V.* World, 1969, 1st ed, dj..*$20–$25*

Schultz, A.H. *The Life of Primates.* NY, 1969, illus. .....*$35–$45*

Schultz, J.W. *My Life as an Indian.* NY, 1907. ....*$40–$75*

Schulz, Charles M. *Good Grief, More Peanuts.* NY, 1956, wrps. ....*$30–$40*

Schulz, Charles M. *Snoopy and the Red Baron.* NY, 1966, 1st ed, dj. ....*$28–$38*

Schwatka, Frederick. *A Summer in Alaska.* St. Louis, 1894, illus. ....*$30–$35*

Schwatka, Frederick. *A Summer in Alaska.* St. Louis, 1893, illus. ....*$45–$75*

Schweinfurth, Charles. *Orchids of Peru.* Chi, 1958, 2 vols. ....*$50–$60*

Schweizer, Charles H. *Billiard Hints.* LaCrosse, WI, 1906. ....*$20–$28*

Schwiebert, E. *History of the U.S. Air Force Ballistic Missiles.* NY, 1965, 1st ed, dj. ....$25–$30

Scott, Anna. *Glimpses of Life in Africa.* CA, 1867. ....$14–$18

Scott, Emmett. *Scott's Official History of the American Negro in the World War.* 1919, illus. ....$20–$25

Scott, James Brown. *De Grasse at Yorktown.* Balt, Johns Hopkins, 1931, 1st ed. ....$35–$50

Scott, Kenneth. *Counterfeiting in Colonial America.* NY, 1957, 1st ed, illus, dj. ....$14–$18

Scott, Sir Walter. *The Lady of the Lake.* NY, 1869, Riverside Classic ed. ....$20–$45

Scott, W.W. *History of Orange County, Virginia.* Rich, 1907, 1st ed. ....$85–$90

Scott, Winfield. *General Scott and His Staff. . . .* Phila, 1849, illus. ....$37–$45

Seaman, Elizabeth Cochrane. *The Story of Nellie Bly.* 1951, 1st ed, illus, photos. ....$18–$25

Seeger, Alan. *Poems.* 1916, 1st ed. ....$30–$45

Seeger, Ruth Crawford. *American Folk Songs for Children. . . .* NY, 1948, illus by Barbara Cooney. ....$14–$18

Seeley, Eva B. and Martha Lane. *Chinook and His Family: True Dog Stories.* Bos, 1930, illus. ....$15–$20

Seitz, Don. *Famous American Duels.* NY, 1929, 1st ed, illus. ....$10–$12

Sendak, Maurice. *Outside Over There.* NY, 1981, illus by Sendak, dj. ....$25–$40

Sendak, Maurice. *Posters.* Harmony, NY, 1986, 1st ed, dj. ....$28–$35

Sergeant, F.L. *Wright's Usonian House.* 1978, dj. ....$47–$60

Service, Robert W. *Ballads of a Cheechako.* NY, 1909. $6–$12

Service, Robert. *Rhymes of a Rolling Stone.* Tor, 1912, 1st ed. ....$60–$100

Service, Robert W. *Rhymes of a Red Cross Man.* NY, 1909. ....$6–$10

Sessler, Jacob John. *Saints and Tomahawks.* 1940, 1st ed, sgn, dj. ....$27–$35

Seton, Ernest Thompson. *Gospel of the Red Man.* 1st ed, dj. ....$40–$55

Seton, Ernest Thompson. *Lives of the Hunted.* NY, 1901, 1st ed. ....$22–$45

Seton, Ernest Thompson. *Lives of the Hunted.* Scribner's, 1923, illus by Seton. ....$18–$24

Seton, Ernest Thompson. *Monarch, The Big Bear of Tallac.* NY, 1904, 1st ed, illus, 1st imp. ....$25–$50

Seton, Ernest Thompson. *Rolf in the Woods.* NY, 1922, illus. ....$25–$35

Seton, Ernest Thompson. *Rolf in the Woods.* Doubleday, 1911, illus. ....$30–$45

Seton, Ernest Thompson. *The Arctic Prairies.* NY, 1917, illus, rprnt, photos, maps, drawings. ....$40–$55

Seton, Ernest Thompson. *The Biography of a Grizzly.* NY, 1900, illus by Seton, presentation copy, sgn. ....$42–$55

Seton, Ernest Thompson. *The Birchbark Roll of Woodcraft.* NY, 1931, illus, softcover. ....$20–$27

Seton, Ernest Thompson. *The Book of Woodcraft.* Garden City, 1921, illus. ....$30–$35

Seton, Ernest Thompson. *Two Little Savages.* NY, 1903, 1st ed, illus by Seton. ....$40–$55

Seton, Ernest Thompson. *Wild Animals I Have Known.* NY, 1898, 1st ed, illus. ....$40–$50

Seton, Grace. *A Woman Tenderfoot.* Lon, 1900, illus. ....$18–$22

Seton, Grace Thompson. *Yes, Lady Saheb.* NY/Lon, 1925, 1st ed, illus, photos. ....$15–$25

Seton, Julia M. *The Pulse of the Pueblo.* NM, 1939, presentation copy, sgn. ....$25–$30

Seuss, Dr. *More Boners.* NY, 1931. ....$15–$40

Seuss, Dr. *Thidwick: The Big Hearted Moose.* NY, 1948, 1st ed. ....$33–$40

Seward, A.C. *A Summer in Greenland.* Camb, 1922, 1st ed, illus, maps. ....*$24–$30*

Sewel, William. *The History . . . of the People Called Quakers.* Phila, 1823, 2 vols, lea. ....*$40–$65*

Sewell, Anna. *Black Beauty: His Grooms and Companions.* Bos, 1890, 1st thus. American Humane Ed. Soc. ....*$150–$295*

Sextus, Carl. *Hypnotism.* Chi, 1893, 1st ed, illus. ....*$30–$45*

Seymour, C. *Intimate Papers of Colonel House.* 2 vols, 1st ed. ....*$40–$60*

Seymour, George. *Furbearers of California.* Sacramento, 1950, 1st ed, illus, 1st prntg. ....*$14–$10*

Shackleton, Ernest. *South!* NY, 1920, 1st ed. ....*$125–$175*

Shackleton, Ernest. *The Heart of the Antarctic.* Phila, 1914, illus, fldg map, clr plates. ....*$50–$75*

Shackleton, Ernest H. (ed). *Aurora Australis.* New Zealand, 1988, illus, rprnt, dj. ....*$25–$30*

Shackleton, Ernest H. *The Heart of the Antarctic.* Phila, 1909, 2 vols, illus, 1st American ed, pocket maps. ....*$375–$500*

Shahn, Ben. *Hagadah.* Bos, 1965, small folio. ....*$55–$65*

Shakespeare. *Passionate Pilgrim.* Clarendon, 1905, facs of 1st ed, vellum. ....*$115–$150*

Shakespeare, William. *A Winter's Tale.* Lon, 1856, 105 pp. ....*$85–$125*

Shakespeare, William. *Complete Works.* NY, 1856, 3 vols, illus. ....*$185–$225*

Shakespeare, William. *Midsummer Nights Dream.* Lon/NY, 1908, 1st ed, illus by Arthur Rackham, clr plates. ....*$275–$325*

Shakespeare, William. *Romeo and Juliet.* NY, 1936, illus, dj. ....*$50–$75*

Shakespeare, William. *Shakespeare's Comedy As You Like It.* Lon/NY, nd, 1st ed, illus by Hugh Thomson, 39 tip-in clr plates. ....*$195–$250*

Shakespeare, William. *Shakespeare's Comedy of the Tempest.* Lon, 1915, illus by Edmund Dulac. ....*$250–$300*

Shakespeare, William. *The Comedies, Histories and Tragedies of Wm. Shakespeare.* 1939, 37 vols, illus, Limited Edition Club, 8 slipcases. ....$850–$950

Shakespeare, William. *The Dramatic Works.* Bos, Hilliard Gray, 1839, 8 vols. ....$75–$100

Shakespeare, William. *The Works.* Lon/NY, 1892, 12 vols, boxed. ....$50–$75

Shakespeare, William. *The Works of Shakespeare.* NY, Defau, 1903, 12 vols, ltd 1,000 cc, mor, mar bds. ....$275–$350

Shakespeare, William. *Works.* Phila, Porter, nd, 8 vols, limp lea. ....$90–$125

Shakespeare, William. *Works of Shakespeare.* Lon, 1904, 10 vols, Deluxe ed, ltd #197/500 cc. ....$120–$135

Shaler, Nathaniel S. *The Individual: A Study of Life and Death.* Appleton, 1901. ....$14–$20

Shankland, Frank. *Friends of the Forest.* Saalfield, 1932. ....$18–$25

Shankle, George. *American Nicknames.* NY, 1937, dj. ..$20–$27

Shapiro, Karl. *Essay on Rime.* Reynal & Hitchcock, 1945, 1st ed, dj. ....$40–$45

Shapiro, Karl. *White-haired Lover.* NY, 1968, 1st ed, sgn, dj. ....$30–$45

Sharp, H. *Modern Sporting Gunnery Manual. . . .* Lon, 1906, small folio. ....$30–$40

Sharpless and Philips. *Astronomy for Schools and General Readers.* Phila, 1892, illus, 4th ed. ....$7–$14

Shaw, Edward. *Shaw's Civil Architecture.* Bos, 1852. ...$40–$50

Shaw, Edward Richard. *The Pot of Gold: A Story of Fire Island Beach.* Chi/NY, 1888. ....$85–$125

Shaw, George Bernard. *An Intelligent Woman's Guide to Socialism and Capitalism.* NY, 1928, 1st American ed. ....$25–$35

Shaw, George Bernard. *The Adventures of a Black Girl in Her Search of God.* Dodd Mead, 1933, illus, 1st American ed, dj. ....$30–$40

Shaw, Irwin. *Mixed Company.* Random House, 1950, 1st ed, dj.
....*$40–$50*

Shaw, Irwin. *The Troubled Air.* NY, 1951, 1st ed, dj. ....*$35–$40*

Shaw, Irwin. *The Young Lions.* NY, 1st ed, dj. ....*$35–$45*

Shaw, Thomas George. *The Wine Trade and Its History.* Lon, nd.
....*$37–$75*

Sheckley, Robert. *Dramocles.* NY, 1983. ....*$22–$25*

Sheckley, Robert. *Is That What People Do?* NY, 1984, sgn, dj.
....*$15–$20*

Sheehan, Neil. *A Bright Shining Lie.* NY, 1988, 1st ed, dj.
....*$30–$50*

Sheldon, Charles. *The Wilderness of the Upper Yukon.* NY, 1913,
illus, maps. ....*$50–$75*

Sheldon, Sidney. *Master of the Game.* NY, 1982, 9th prntg, sgn.
....*$10–$15*

Shelley, H. *Inns and Taverns of Old London.* Bos, 1909, 1st ed,
illus. ....*$27–$35*

Shepherd, Sam. *Operation Sidewinder.* NY, 1970. ....*$35–$40*

Sheridan, P.H. *Personal Memoirs. . . .* NY, 1888, 2 vols.
....*$60–$85*

Sherman, Gen. *Memoirs. . . .* 1891, 2 vols, 4th ed. ....*$40–$70*

Sherman, H. *Strike Him Out!* NY, 1931. ....*$10–$15*

Sherman, John. *Recollections.* 1895, 2 vols, 1st ed. ......*$45–$65*

Sherman, S.M. *History of the 133rd Regiment, O.V.I.* Columbus,
1896, 1st ed. ....*$95–$125*

Sherman, William Tecumseh. *Home Letters of General Sherman.*
NY, 1909, 1st ed. ....*$40–$50*

Sherrod, Robert. *TARAWA: The Story of a Battle.* NY, 1954, 4th
prntg, dj. ....*$10–$14*

Sherwen, Grayson N. *The Romance of St. Sacrement.* VT, 1912,
illus. ....*$9–$15*

Sherwood, Robert Emmet. *The Queen's Husband.* NY, 1928, 1st
ed. ....*$40–$45*

Shiel, M.P. *Children of the Wind.* NY, 1923, 1st U.S. ed..*$30–$40*

Shillaber, Lydia. *A New Daily Food* . . . *St. Paul's Church, Morrisania, N.Y.* 1885. ....$35–$45

Shine, Ian and Sylvia Wrobel. *Thomas Hunt Morgan: Pioneer of Genetics.* Univ. of Kentucky Press, 1976. ....$18–$25

Shiras, G. *Hunting Wildlife with Gun and Camera.* Nat'l. Geographic, 1936, 2 vols, illus. ....$16–$25

Shirer, William. *Berlin Diary.* NY, 1941, 1st ed, dj. ......$16–$22

Shirer, William. *Berlin Diary.* NY, 1941, 1st ed. ....$10–$15

Shirts, Augustus F. *History of* . . . *Hamilton County, Indiana (1818 to Civil War).* 1901, 1st ed, illus. ....$65–$100

Shlee, Susan. *The Edge of an Unfamiliar World: A History of Oceanography.* Dutton, 1973, dj. ....$14–$25

Short, Wayne. *The Cheechakoes.* NY, 1964, 1st ed, illus, dj. ....$10–$14

Shriner, C.H. *Birds of New Jersey.* 1896. ....$25–$45

Shuckard, W.E. *British Bees.* Lon, nd. ....$18–$25

Shuckers, J.W. *The Life and Public Services of Samuel Portland Chase.* NY, 1874, 1st ed. ....$28–$35

Shurtleff, Nathaniel. *A Topographical and Historical Description of Boston.* Bos, 1871. ....$45–$75

Shute, Miss T.S. *The American Housewife Cook Book.* Phila, 1878. ....$30–$40

Shute, Nevil. *On the Beach.* NY, 1957, 1st ed, dj. ....$30–$40

Sickels, Daniel. *The General Akiman Rezon* . . . *Freemason's Guide.* NY, 1870, illus. ....$30–$40

Sidney, M. *Five Little Peppers Grown Up.* Bos, 1892, 1st ed. ....$20–$30

Siebert, Wilbur H. *A Quaker Section of the Underground Railroad in Northern Ohio.* OH, 1930, rprnt. ....$18–$30

Siebert, Wilbur H. *Vermont's Anti-Slavery and Underground Railroad Record.* . . . Columbus, OH, 1937, 1st ed, illus, map, plates. ....$50–$75

Siedentopf, A.R. *Last Stronghold of Big Game.* NY, 1946, 1st ed, illus, maps. ....$22–$25

Sieg, Harvey. *The ABC of Wall Street.* NY, 1939. ....$14–$20

Siegbahn, M. *Spectroscopy of X-rays.* Lon, 1925, 1st English ed. ....$40–$50

Sikorsky, Igor I. *The Story of the Winged-S with New Material on ... Helicopter.* NY, 1942, illus, photos, inscr, dj. ....$40–$45

Silverstein, Shel. *Different Dances.* 1978, 1st ed, dj. ....$55–$100

Simkins, Francis Butler and James Welch Patton. *The Women of the Confederacy.* Rich/NY, 1936, 1st ed, dj. ....$90–$125

Simmonds, Thomas. *Wood Carving with Suggestions in Chip Carving.* Lon. ....$20–$30

Simmons, Amelia. *American Cookery.* NY, 1958, ltd, 800 cc, boxed. ....$35–$50

Simmons, L.W. (ed). *Sun Chief: The Autobiography of a Hopi Indian.* New Haven, 1942, illus. ....$30–$40

Simms, Florence. *Etoffe du Pays: Lower St. Lawrence Sketches.* Tor, 1913. ....$20–$25

Simms, W. Gilmore. *The Lily and The Totem.* NY, 1850. ..$35–$45

Simon, R. *Lectures on the Treatment of the Common Diseases of the Skin.* Birmingham, 1888. ....$10–$12

Simonds, Frederic Wm. *Geography of Texas.* Bos, 1905, illus, maps. ....$14–$20

Sinclair, Upton. *A World to Win.* NY, 1946, 1st ed, dj...$15–$20

Sinclair, Upton. *Presidential Mission.* NY, 1947, 1st ed, dj. ....$14–$20

Sinclair, Upton. *The Flivver King: A Story of Ford-America.* Published by author, 1937, 1st ed, dj. ....$45–$50

Singer, Isaac Bashevis. *Old Love.* NY, 1979, 1st ed, dj..$15–$30

Singer, Isaac Bashevis. *Short Friday.* NY, 1964, 1st ed. ..$35–$40

Singer, Isaac Bashevis. *The Estate.* NY, 1969, 1st ed, dj..$25–$35

Singleton, Esther. *The Shakespeare Garden.* NY, 1931. ..$20–$25

Sinnett, A.P. *The Occult World.* Bos, 1882, 1st ed. ....$45–$85

Siringo, Charles. *Riata and Spurs.* Bos, 1931. ....$25–$35

Siringo, Charles. *Riata and Spurs.* Bos, 1927, 1st ed. ..$95–$150

Siringo, Charles. *Lone Star Cowboy.* Sante Fe, 1919, 1st ed.
....$85–$100

Siringo, Charles A. *A Cowboy Detective.* Chi, 1912, 1st ed, photos. ....$200–$250

Sitwell, Sacheverell. *Great Palaces of Europe.* NY, illus..$14–$25

Sizer, Nelson. *Forty Years in Phrenology.* NY, 1882. .....$18–$27

Skinner, Charles M. *Myths and Legends of Our Own Land.* Phila/Lon, 1896, 2 vols, 1st ed, illus. ....$25–$35

Skinner, Maude and Otis Skinner. *One Man in His Time....* Phila, 1938...$18–$25

Skinner, Otis. *Footlights and Spotlights.* Bobbs-Merrill, 1924, ltd #27/ 500 cc, sgn. ....$35–$45

Skinner, William. *The Belle Skinner Collection of Old Musical Instruments.* Holyoke, MA, 1933, illus, softcover. ....$35–$44

Slim, Field Marshal the Viscount. *Defeat into Victory.* NY, 1965, illus, 4th prntg, maps, dj. ....$18–$23

Sloane, Eric. *A Reverence for Wood.* Funk, Inc., 1965, 1st ed, dj.
....$20–$30

Sloane, T. O'Connor. *Rubber Handstamps.* NY, 1891, illus.
....$18–$25

Slocum, Joshua. *The Voyage of the Liberdade.* Bos, 1894, illus.
....$125–$255

Smalley. *A Brief History of the Republican Party....* NY, 1888.
....$24–$32

Smith, A. *Dental Microscopy.* Lon/Phila, 1895, plates. ..$35–$45

Smith, Adam. *An Inquiry into the Nature and Causes of the Wealth of Nations.* Lon, 1799, 3 vols, lea, bds. ....$150–$210

Smith, Amanda. *An Autobiography....* Chi, 1893, 1st ed.
....$45–$175

Smith, Betty. *Joy in the Morning.* NY, 1963, 1st ed, sgn, dj.
....$25–$40

Smith, Clark Ashton. *Other Dimensions.* Sauk City, Arkham House, 1970, 1st ed, dj. ....$30–$85

Smith, Clark Ashton. *Tales of Science and Sorcery.* Arkham House, 1964, 1st ed, dj. ....$75–$125

Smith, Daniel. *Company K, First Alabama Regiment....* Prattville, AL, 1885. ....$900–$1,000

Smith, Erroll A. *The American Checker Player's Handbook.* Chi, 1931, 1st ed. ....$10–$15

Smith, F.L. *Wright: A Study in Architectural Content.* 1979, dj. ....$50–$75

Smith, George. *Assyrian Discoveries.* Scribner's, 1875, illus. ....$47–$65

Smith, Gustavus Woodson. *The Battle of Seven Pines.* NY, 1891, 1st ed, wrps. ....$175–$200

Smith, H. *Stina: Story of a Cook.* 1942. ....$12–$14

Smith, H. Allen. *Low Man on the Totem Pole.* NY, 1941, 1st ed, sgn. ....$16–$20

Smith, James Power. *General Lee at Gettysburg.* VA, nd, 1st ed. ....$50–$75

Smith, Jerome V.C. *Natural History of the Fishes of Mass....* *Essay on Angling.* Bos, 1833. ....$150–$175

Smith, Joseph. *The Book of Mormon.* 1891. ....$65–$75

Smith, Joseph. *The Book of Mormon.* Liverpool, 1841, 1st English ed. ....$1,500–$2,500

Smith, Martin Cruz. *Gorky Park.* Random House, 1981, 1st ed, dj. ....$20–$30

Smith, Mrs. *The Female Economist ... for the Use of Families.* Lon, 1810, ½ calf. ....$45–$65

Smith, Nicol. *Burma Road.* Ind/NY, 1940, illus. ....$14–$18

Smith, Sara R. *Manchurian Crisis, 1931–1932.* NY, 1948, dj. ....$14–$18

Smith, Thorne. *Lazy Bear Lane.* NY, 1931, 1st ed. ....$36–$60

Smucker, S. *Life and Times of T. Jefferson.* Phila, 1857..$40–$45

Smucker, Samuel. *Life of Fremont.* NY, 1856, 1st ed, illus. ....$32–$40

Smucker, Samuel S. (ed). *Arctic Exploration and Discoveries.* NY, 1857, 1st ed, ½ lea. ....$48–$60

Smyth, Henry D. *Atomic Energy for Military Purposes.* Princeton Univ. Press, 1945, 1st ed, dj. ....$90–$95

Smyth, Henry Dewolf. *Atomic Energy for Military Purposes.* 1945, illus, 2nd ed, softcover. ....$35–$55

Smythies, Bertram E. *Birds of Burma.* Edin, 1953, illus, 2nd ed, dj. ....$40–$70

Snively and Furbee. *Satan's Ferryman.* np, 1968, illus, dj. ....$16–$20

Snow, Edward Rowe. *Pirates and Buccaneers of the Atlantic Coast.* Bos, 1944, 1st ed, dj. ....$25–$35

Snow, Edward Rowe. *Unsolved Mysteries of Sea and Shore.* NY, 1963, illus, dj. ....$15–$22

Snowden, R. *The History of North and South America.* Phila, 1813, 2 vols in one, lea, maps. ....$75–$100

Snyder, Gary. *Earth House Hold.* 1969, 1st ed, sgn, dj..$60–$85

Snyder, Gary. *Regarding Wave.* Lon, 1970, 1st ed, dj. ..$35–$45

Snyder, Gary. *The Old Ways.* City Lights, 1977, 1st ed..$20–$25

Solomon. *Why Smash Atoms?* Camb, 1940, 1st ed. ....$30–$60

Solzhenitsyn, Alexander. *Cancer Ward.* Bodley Head, 1968, 1st English ed, dj. ....$35–$40

Solzhenitsyn, Alexander. *Gulag Archipelago.* NY, 1973, 1st ed, dj. ....$25–$30

Solzhenitsyn, Alexander. *Lenin in Zurich.* Farrar, 1976, 1st U.S. ed, dj. ....$20–$25

Solzhenitsyn, Alexander. *One Day in the Life of Ivan Denisovich.* Frederick Praeger, 1963, dj. ....$20–$35

Solzhenitsyn, Alexander. *Stories and Prose Poems.* Farrar, 1971, 1st U.S. ed, dj. ....$15–$30

Sonneck, Oscar G.T. *"The Star Spangled Banner. . . ."* GPO, 1st ed, illus. ....$45–$75

Sonneck, Oscar George Theodore. *The Star Spangled Banner.* DC, 1914. ....$15–$20

Sontag, Susan. *Illness as Metaphor.* Farrar Straus Giroux, 1978, 1st ed, dj. ....$30–$35

Southwell, T. *The Seals and Whales of the British Seas.* Lon, 1881, illus. ....$175–$300

Spark, Muriel. *The Driver's Seat.* Knopf, 1970, 1st U.S. ed, dj. ....$25–$30

Spark, Muriel. *The Girls of Slender Means.* Lon, 1963, 1st ed, dj. ....$30–$50

Spark, Muriel. *The Girls of Slender Means.* Knopf, 1963, 1st U.S. ed, dj. ....$25–$30

Spark, Muriel. *The Prime of Miss Jean Brodie.* NY, 1961, 1st ed, dj. ....$30–$35

Sparks, J. *The Life of Gouverneur Morris.* Bos, 1832, 3 vols. ....$30–$55

Sparks, Jared. *The Life of George Washington.* Bos, 1839, 1st ed. ....$65–$95

Spearman, Frank. *The Daughter of the Magnate.* Scribner's, 1903. ....$5–$10

Spearman, Frank H. *Whispering Smith.* NY, 1906, 1st ed, illus by N.C. Wyeth. ....$30–$55

Spears, John R. *The American Slave-Trade.* NY, 1900, illus. ....$45–$67

Speck, F. *Masking in Eastern North America, Vol 15.* Phila, 1950, illus. ....$15–$18

Speck, Frank. *Study of Delaware Indians Big House Ceremony.* Harrisburg, 1931. ....$20–$45

Spencer, Elizabeth. *The Night Travelers.* NY, 1991, 1st American ed, sgn. ....$30–$40

Spencer, Herbert. *Genesis of Science and the Factors of Organic Evolution.* Humboldt. ....$22–$30

Spenser, Edmund. *Prothalamion: Epithalamion.* Bos/NY, 1902, illus, ltd 400 cc, folio, dj. ....$67–$85

Spillane, Mickey. *Kiss Me, Deadly.* NY, 1952, 1st ed, dj. .$45–$75

Spiller, Burton L. *Firelight.* Derrydale, 1937, illus by Lynn Bogue Hunt, ltd 950 cc. ....$180–$350

Spiller, Burton L. *Grouse Feathers.* NY, 1947, illus by Lynn Bogue Hunt. ....*$30–$35*

Spiller, Burton L. *More Grouse Feathers.* Derrydale Press, 1938, illus by L. Bogue Hunt, ltd #508/950 cc. ....*$200–$260*

Spiri, Johanna. *Heidi.* John C. Winston Co., 1927, clr plates. ....*$24–$30*

Spivak, John L. *Georgia Nigger.* Lon, 1933, 1st ed. .*$175–$250*

Splan, John. *Life with the Trotters.* 1889, presentation copy. .... *$110–$125*

Splawn, A.J. *KA-MI-AKIN, the Last Hero of the Yakimas.* Portland, 1917, 1st ed, illus, photos, lea. ....*$90–$110*

Spyri, Johanna. *Heidi.* Phila, 1922, illus by Jessie Wilcox Smith. ....*$40–$50*

St. John Roosa, D.B. *A Practical Treatise on the Diseases of the Ear.* NY, 1876, illus. ....*$42–$55*

St. John, Percy. *The Arctic Crusoe.* Bos, nd, illus. ....*$18–$25*

Stafford, Jean. *A Mother in History.* 1966. ....*$10–$14*

Stafford, Jean. *Boston Adventure.* NY, 1944, 1st ed, dj..*$25–$40*

Stanley, Dean. *Picturesque Palestine.* Lon, 1880–1884, 5 vols, plates. ....*$275–$350*

Stanley, Henry M. *In Darkest Africa.* NY, 1891, 2 vols, illus. ....*$25–$40*

Stanley, Henry M. *In Darkest Africa.* NY, 1890, 2 vols, 1st ed, illus, engr. fldg maps, ¾ mor, mar bds. ....*$75–$100*

Stanley, Henry M. *The Congo and the Founding of Its Free State.* NY, 1885, 2 vols, illus. ....*$60–$75*

Stansbury, Howard. *Exploration and Survey of the Valley of the Great Salt Lake.* Phila, 1852. ....*$225–$425*

Star Trek. *Trillions of Trillings.* Star Trek Concordance, 1976, 1st ed, pop-up. ....*$28–$35*

Starling, E. *The Fluids of the Body.* Lon, 1909. ....*$12–$15*

Starr, Chester G. *From Salerno to the Alps.* DC, 1948, 1st ed. ....*$48–$56*

Staveley, E.F. *British Spiders.* Lon, 1866. ....*$15–$25*

Stearns, Samuel. *The American Herbal. . . .* Walpole, MA, 1801, 1st American ed, lea. ....*$150–$200*

Steele, Matthew Forney. *American Campaigns.* DC, 1909, 2 vols, 1st ed. ....*$85–$125*

Stefansson, Evelyn. *Here Is Alaska.* 1943, 1st ed, photos. *$15–$20*

Stefansson, Vilhjalmur. *Arctic Manual.* NY, 1944, 1st ed. ....*$28–$65*

Stefansson, Vilhjalmur. *My Life with the Eskimo.* 1924..*$30–$45*

Stefansson, Vilhjalmur. *My Life with the Eskimo.* NY, 1922, sgn. ....*$60–$75*

Stefansson, Vilhjalmur. *Not by Bread Alone.* 1946, 1st ed. ....*$25–$30*

Stefansson, Vilhjalmur. *The Adventure of Wrangle Island.* NY, 1925, 1st ed, illus, fldg clr map, sgn. ....*$75–$100*

Stefansson, Vilhjalmur. *The Fat of the Land.* NY, 1956, 1st ed, sgn. ....*$35–$45*

Steffansson, Vilhjalmur. *The Friendly Arctic.* Macmillan, 1944. ....*$20–$25*

Stegner, Wallace. *Bibliography.* 1990, sgn. ....*$55–$60*

Stegner, Wallace. *The Sound of Mountain Water.* NY, 1969, presentation copy. ....*$35–$45*

Steichen, Edward. *A Life in Photography.* Garden City, 1963, dj. ....*$45–$65*

Stein, Gertrude. *Autobiography of Alice B. Toklas.* Harcourt, 1933, 1st ed, ltd. ....*$25–$40*

Stein, Gertrude. *Bee Time Vine and Other Pieces (1913–1927).* New Haven, 1953, 1st ed, dj. ....*$55–$65*

Stein, Gertrude. *Brewsie and Willie.* NY, 1946, 1st ed, dj. ....*$35–$75*

Stein, Gertrude. *Wars I Have Seen.* NY, 1st ed, dj. ......*$35–$45*

Stein, Gertrude. *Wars I Have Seen.* NY, 1945, dj. ....*$18–$20*

Stein, Leonard. *The Balfour Declaration.* Lon, 1961, dj. .*$18–$25*

Steinbeck, John. *Burning Bright.* NY, 1950, 1st ed, dj. .*$45–$50*

Steinbeck, John. *Cannery Row.* NY, 1945, 1st ed, dj. .*$55–$120*

Steinbeck, John. *Of Mice and Men.* Covici-Friede, 1937, 1st ed, 1st issue, dj. ....$200–$550

Steinbeck, John. *Sweet Thursday.* 1954, 1st ed, dj. ....$55–$75

Steinbeck, John. *The Grapes of Wrath.* Viking, 1939, 1st ed, dj. ....$400–$650

Steinbeck, John. *The Log from the Sea of Cortez.* NY, dj. ....$50–$100

Steinbeck, John. *The Pearl.* Viking, 1947, 1st ed, dj. ...$55–$65

Steinbeck, John. *The Red Pony.* NY, 1945, 1st ed, boxed. ....$35–$90

Steinbeck, John. *The Wayward Bus.* NY, Viking, 1947, 1st ed, dj. ....$40–$75

Steinbeck, John. *The Winter of Our Discontent.* Viking, 1961, 1st ed, dj. ....$40–$65

Steinbeck, John. *The Winter of Our Discontent.* Heinemann, 1961, 1st English ed, dj. ....$25–$65

Steinbeck, John. *Travels with Charley.* Viking, 1962, 1st ed, dj. ....$25–$40

Steiner, Jesse Frederick and Roy M. Brown. *The North Carolina Chain Gang.* . . . Chapel Hill, 1927, 1st ed. ....$100–$150

Stellman, Louis J. *Mother Lode.* 1939, photos. ....$28–$37

Stephens, James. *Crock of Gold.* Lon, 1912, 1st ed, presentation copy, sgn. ....$95–$250

Stephens, James. *The Crock of Gold.* NY, 1923, illus by Wilfred Jones. ....$14–$18

Stephens, James. *The Crock of Gold.* Lon, 1912, 1st ed, dj. ....$85–$95

Stephens, James. *The Demi-Gods.* Lon, 1914, 1st ed, 1st issue. ....$45–$50

Stephenson, William B. Jr. *The Land of Tomorrow.* NY, 1919, illus. ....$8–$15

Stern, Philip Van Doren. *Robert E. Lee, The Man and the Soldier: A Pictorial Biography.* NY, 1963, 1st ed, illus. ......$18–$25

Stetson, George R. *The Southern Negro as He Is.* Bos, 1877, 1st ed. ....*$75–$100*

Stevens, Abel. *History of the Methodist Episcopal Church.* NY, 1868, 4 vols. ....*$30–$45*

Stevens, Hazard. *The Life of Isaac Ingalls Stevens.* Bos, 1900, 2 vols, 1st ed, illus. ....*$50–$85*

Stevens, Thomas. *Around the World on a Bicycle, Vol. 1.* NY, 1889, illus. ....*$35–$50*

Stevens, Thomas A. *Old Sailing Days in Clinton.* Deep River Savings Bank, 1963, illus. ....*$14–$20*

Stevens, William Oliver. *Nantucket.* NY, 1937–39. ....*$24–$35*

Stevenson, Adlai. *Speeches.* 1st ed, folio. ....*$14–$18*

Stevenson, Robert Louis. *David Balfour.* Scribner's, 1924, illus by N.C. Wyeth. ....*$55–$60*

Stevenson, Robert Louis. *Kidnapped.* Scribner's, 1946, illus by N.C. Wyeth, rprnt. ....*$30–$45*

Stevenson, Robert Louis. *Kidnapped.* NY, Scribner's Classic, 1913, illus by N.C. Wyeth. ....*$45–$75*

Stevenson, Robert Louis. *The Strange Case of Dr. Jekyll and Mr. Hyde.* NY, 1930, illus by Beaman, S.G. Hulme, 1st thus. ..*$50–$65*

Stevenson, Robert Louis. *Treasure Island.* Scribner's, 1911, 1st ed, illus by N.C. Wyeth. ....*$40–$55*

Stevenson, William G. *Thirteen Months in the Rebel Army . . . by an Impressed New Yorker.* Lon, 1862, 1st English ed, rbnd. ....*$50–$75*

Stewart, Elinore Pruitt. *Letters of a Woman Homesteader.* Bos, 1914, 1st ed, illus by N.C. Wyeth. ....*$25–$37*

Stewart, G. *The Sowing and the Reaping.* Caxton Printers, 1970, 1st ed. ....*$18–$25*

Stewart, Henry. *The Shepherd's Manual.* NY, 1876, illus..*$27–$35*

Stickley, Gustav. *Craftsman Homes.* NY, 1909, 1st ed. .*$125–$250*

Stock, Dennis. *California Trip.* NY, 1970, 1st ed. ....*$14–$20*

Stocking, Charles E. *Thou Israel.* Chi, 1921, 1st ed. ....*$30–$40*

Stockton, Frank R. *Pomona's Travels.* Scribner's, 1894, illus by A.B. Frost. ....$25–$45

Stockton, Frank R. *The Girl at Cobhurst.* NY, 1898, 1st ed. ....$45–$50

Stoddard, Charles. *Over the Rocky Mountains to Alaska.* St. Louis, 1907. ....$30–$45

Stoddard, Charles Warren. *Cruise under the Crescent.* Chi/NY, 1898, illus, buckram. ....$10–$20

Stoddard, Eugene M. *Frances Elliott Clark. . . .* Brigham Young Univ., 1968, lea. ....$13–$17

Stoker, Bram. *Dracula.* NY, 1975, illus by Saty, dj. ......$60–$70

Stoker, Bram. *Dracula.* Limited Edition Club, 1965, illus by Felix Hoffman, sgn by Hoffman, slipcase. ....$35–$45

Stoker, Bram. *Dracula's Guest and Other Weird Stories.* Lon, 1914, rprnt. ....$35–$45

Stoker, Bram. *The Jewel of the Seven Stars.* NY, 1904, 1st U.S. ed. ....$40–$50

Stoker, Bram. *The Mystery of the Sea.* NY, 1902, 1st ed..$40–$50

Stone, I.F. *The Haunted 50s.* NY, 1963, 1st ed, dj. ....$30–$40

Stone, I.F. *Underground to Palestine.* Boni & Gaer, 1946. ....$16–$20

Stone, Lawrence. *Sculpture in Britain in the Middle Ages.* NY, 1972. ....$40–$50

Stone, W. *Bookplates of Today.* NY, 1902, 1st ed. ....$30–$40

Stone, William. *Visits to the Saratoga Battle Grounds.* Alb, 1895, 1st ed. ....$35–$40

Stoney, S.G. *Plantations of the Carolina Low Country.* Charleston, 1938, 1st ed, dj, slipcase. ....$85–$165

Story, A.T. *The Story of Wireless Telegraphy.* 1904, 1st ed, illus. ....$45–$85

Stout, Rex. *Death of a Doxy.* Viking, 1966, 1st ed, dj. .$25–$60

Stowe, Harriet Beecher. *A Key to Uncle Tom's Cabin.* Bos, 1853, 1st ed. ....$65–$150

Stowe, Harriet Beecher. *Dred: A Tale of the Great Dismal Swamp.* Bos, 1856, 2 vols, 1st ed. ....*$40–$55*

Stowe, Harriet Beecher. *Uncle Tom's Cabin, or Life among the Lowly.* Bos, 1852, 2 vols, 1st ed, Hobart & Robbins on copyright page, J.P. Jewett & Co. on foot of spine. ....*$500–$650*

Strand, Paul. *Retrospective, 1915–1968.* Large folio. ...*$90–$110*

Strange, Daniel. *Pioneer History of Eaton County, Michigan, 1833–1866.* . . . 1923, 1st ed, illus. ....*$60–$85*

Stranwold, Olaf. *Norse Inscriptions on American Stones.* NJ, 1948, dj. ....*$16–$22*

Strickland, F. *A Manual of Petrol Motors and Motorcars.* London, 1907, illus. ....*$65–$90*

Strong, Charles S. *The Story of American Sailing Ships.* NY, 1955, illus, drawings. ....*$12–$18*

Strout, Richard Lee (ed). *Maud.* NY, 1939, 1st ed, dj. .*$25–$32*

Stuart, James. *Three Years in America.* NY, 1833, 2 vols, 1st American ed. ....*$50–$90*

Stuart, Jesse. *Kentucky Is My Land.* 1952, sgn, dj. ....*$50–$80*

Stuart, Jesse. *Man with a Bull-tongue Plow.* NY, 1934, 1st ed, sgn, dj. ....*$270–$300*

Stuart, Jesse. *Taps for Private Tussie.* NY, Dutton, 1943, 1st ed, dj. ....*$50–$90*

Stuart, Ruth McEnery. *Sonny, A Christmas Guest.* Century Co., 1910. ....*$12–$20*

Stubbs, S. *Birds-eye View of the Pueblos.* Univ. of Oklahoma Press, 1950. ....*$17–$22*

Stutley, Margaret. *Ancient Indian Magic and Folklore.* Boulder, CO, 1980, illus, dj. ....*$10–$20*

Styron, William. *Lie Down in Darkness.* Ind, 1951, 1st ed, dj. ....*$90–$155*

Styron, William. *Set This House on Fire.* NY, 1960, 1st ed, sgn, dj. ....*$55–$85*

Styron, William. *Sophie's Choice.* Random House, 1979, 1st ed, sgn, dj. ....*$60–$75*

Styron, William. *The Confessions of Nat Turner.* NY, 1967, 1st ed, dj. ....$20–$50

Styron, William. *The Confessions of Nat Turner.* NY, 1967, 1st ed, 2nd prntg. ....$15–$25

Suckow, Ruth. *The Bonney Family.* NY, 1928, 1st ed, ltd #66/95 cc, sgn, dj. ....$35–$40

Sue, Eugene. *The Wandering Jew.* Lon, 1844–1845, 1st ed. ....$275–$315

Sullivan, May Kellogg. *A Woman Who Went to Alaska.* Bos, 1902, illus. ....$30–$40

Summers, Montague. *The History of Witchcraft and Demonology.* Lon, 1973, rprnt of 1926 ed, dj. ....$8–$12

Sun Chief. *The Autobiography of a Hopi Indian.* Yale, 1942, 459 pp, 1st ed, illus. ....$28–$35

Surtees, R.S. *Hawbuck Grange.* Lon, nd, illus by H.K. Browne and W.T. Maud. ....$50–$85

Surtees, R.S. *Hunts with Jorrocks.* NY, 1908, illus by G. Denholm Armour. ....$50–$85

Swain, Clara A. *Glimpse of India. . . .* NY, 1909. ....$12–$20

Swan, M.E. and K.R. Swan. *Sir Joseph Wilson Swan F.R.S.* 1929, 1st ed, illus. ....$40–$55

Swanson, W.E. *Modern Shipfitter's Handbook.* NY, 1941, illus, 2nd ed, dj. ....$25–$30

Swanton, John R. *Indian Tribes of the Lower Mississippi Valley. . . .* DC, 1911. ....$45–$60

Sweeney, J.B. *A Pictorial History of Sea Monsters. . . .* NY, 1972, illus. ....$30–$45

Swinburne, Algernon Charles. *A Century of Roundels and Other Poems.* NY, 1883, 1st American ed, dj. ....$40–$45

Swinburne, Algernon Charles. *Erechtheus.* Lon, 1876. .$40–$55

Swope, John. Camera Over Hollywood. NY, 1939, illus, dj. ....$95–$125

Sykes, Sir Percy. *Persia.* 1922, fldg map. ....$22–$30

Symons, Julian. *The End of Solomon Grundy.* Harper & Row, 1964, 1st American ed, dj. ....$14–$20

Szyk, Arthur. *The Haggadah.* Jerusalem, 1956, 1st ed, mor, boxed. ....$100–$145

Szyk, Arthur. *The New Order.* NY, 1941, dj. ....$125–$200

Taber, Gladys. *A Very Personal Cat.* NY, 1970, 1st ed, dj. ....$20–$30

Taber, Gladys. *Daisy and Dobbin: Two Little Seahorses.* Phila, 1948, illus by Kurt Wiese. ....$18–$25

Taber, Gladys. *Especially Spaniels.* Macrae-Smith, 1945, illus, 4th prntg, photos, dj. ....$10–$15

Taber, Gladys. *Flower Arranging for the American Home.* Phila, 1948, 2nd prntg, dj. ....$18–$25

Taber, Gladys. *Harvest of Yesterdays.* 1976, 1st ed, dj. .$10–$15

Taber, Gladys. *Mrs. Daffodil.* Phila, 1957, 1st ed, dj. ....$45–$55

Taber, Gladys. *Reveries at Stillmeadow.* 1970, 1st ed, dj..$22–$30

Taber, Gladys. *Stillmeadow Cook Book.* Lippincott, 1965. ....$35–$45

Taber, Gladys. *Stillmeadow Kitchen.* Phila, 1947. ....$12–$20

Taber, Gladys. *Stillmeadow Road.* 1962. ....$14–$18

Taber, Gladys. *Stillmeadow Seasons.* Phila, 1950, illus, dj. ....$15–$22

Taber, Gladys. *The First Book of Cats.* Franklin Watts, 1950, illus. ....$18–$25

Taber, Gladys. *The First Book of Dogs.* NY, 1949, dj. ..$25–$40

Taber, Gladys. *What Cooks at Stillmeadow.* Phila, 1958, 1st ed, dj. ....$37–$55

Taft, J.A. *A Practical Treatise on Operative Dentistry.* Phila, 1868, calf. ....$37–$45

Tait, L. *Diseases of Women.* NY, 1879. ....$40–$50

Talbot, Bishop Ethelbert. *My People of the Plains.* NY, 1906, 1st ed. ....$52–$65

Talbot, Edith A. *Samuel Chapman Armstrong: A Biographical Study.* NY, 1904, 1st ed, illus. ....$25–$50

Talbot, Fritz B. *Mr. Besom Starts Curling.* MA, private prntg, 1936, illus. ....$35–$45

Tanner, Z.L. *Deep-sea Exploration.* DC, GPO, 1896, illus, drawings, fldg plates. ....$50–$85

Tarbell, Ida. *The Life of Abraham Lincoln.* 1924, 4 vols, Sangamon ed. ....$60–$75

Tarbell, Ida M. *In the Footsteps of the Lincolns.* NY, 1924, illus. ....$30–$40

Tarbell, Ida M. *The Life of Abraham Lincoln.* NY, 1903, 5 vols. ....$45–$50

Targ, W. *Bibliophile in the Nursery.* Cleve, 1957, 1st ed, dj. ....$25–$35

Tarkington, Booth. *Cherry.* Harper, 1903, illus. ....$12–$25

Tate, Allen. *The Fathers.* Putnam, 1938, 1st ed, dj. ...$110–$140

Taverner, P.A. *Birds of Canada.* 1934, illus. ....$35–$40

Taylor. *Pondor, Last of the Ivory Hunters.* NY, 1955, 1st ed, dj. ....$25–$35

Taylor, Albert P. *The Complete Garden.* 1931, clr plates. .$14–$20

Taylor, Bayard. *Colorado: A Summer Trip.* NY, 1867, 1st ed. ....$40–$55

Taylor, Bayard. *Eldorado.* NY, 1860, 18th ed. ....$14–$20

Taylor, Bayard. *Eldorado or Adventures in the Path of Empire.* NY, 1850, 2 vols, 1st American ed. ....$225–$600

Taylor, Bayard. *Lands of the Saracen. . . .* NY, 1855, 1st ed. ....$35–$65

Taylor, Bayard. *Northern Travel.* NY, 1859. ....$30–$40

Taylor, Bayard (ed). *Siam: The Land of the White Elephant.* NY, 1893, illus, steel engr. ....$22–$35

Taylor, Bayard. *The Lake Regions of Central Africa, Travels in South Africa.* NY, 1873, 2 vols, illus, fldg maps. ....$40–$50

Taylor, Benjamin. *Between the Gates.* Chi, 1878, 1st ed..$24–$32

Taylor, Elizabeth A. *The Woman Suffrage Movement in Tennessee.* NY, 1957, 1st ed, dj. ....$20–$25

Taylor, Griffith. *With Scott: The Silver Lining.* Lon, 1916, 1st ed, illus, maps. ....*$195–$450*

Taylor, J. *Lives of Virginia Baptist Ministers.* Rich, 1838, 2nd ed, lea. ....*$35–$45*

Taylor, John L. *Memoir of His Honor Samuel Phillips, LL.D.* Bos, 1856, 1st ed, illus. ....*$30–$75*

Taylor, Peter. *A Summons to Memphis.* NY, 1986, dj. ...*$15–$25*

Teasdale, Sara. *Strange Victory.* NY, 1933, 1st ed, dj.....*$15–$40*

Telford, John. *The Life of John Wesley.* NY, 1887. ....*$14–$18*

Teller, Daniel W. *The History of Ridgefield, Ct.* Danbury, 1878, illus, ¾ mor. ....*$50–$75*

Tennyson, Alfred, Lord. *Locksley Hall.* . . . 1886, 1st ed. ....*$25–$40*

Terkel, Studs. *American Dreams Lost and Found.* dj. .*$12.50–$15*

Terkel, Studs. *Division Street: America.* Pantheon, 1967, 1st ed, dj. *$28 $35*

Terkel, Studs. *Working.* Pantheon, 1974, 1st ed, dj. ....*$25–$30*

Terry, Ellen. *The Story of My Life.* NY, 1908. ....*$20–$50*

Terry, Ellen. *The Story of My Life.* Lon, 1908, illus, ltd 1,000 cc, plates, teg, sgn. ....*$125–$150*

Thacher, J. *The American Revolution.* Hartford, 1861, illus. ....*$37–$55*

Thackeray, William. *Vanity Fair.* Lon, 1910, lea. ....*$20–$50*

Thatcher, James M.D. *History of the Town of Plymouth, from Its First Settlement in 1620 to the Present Time* . . . Bos, 1835, 2nd ed, illus, map. ....*$145–$175*

Thayer, M. Russell. *A Reply to Mr. Charles Ingersoll's "Letter to a Friend.* . . . " Phila, 1862, 26 pp, 1st ed, wrps. ....*$30–$50*

Theobald, W. *Defrauding the Government.* Myrtle Pub., 1908. ....*$18–$25*

Theroux, Paul. *Saint Jack.* Bos, 1973, 1st ed, dj, sgn. .*$95–$100*

Theroux, Paul. *Saint Jack.* Bos, 1973, dj. ....*$30–$40*

Theroux, Paul. *The Black House.* Houghton Mifflin, 1974, 1st ed, dj. ....*$30–$35*

Theroux, Paul. *The London Embassy.* Bos, 1983, 1st American ed, dj. ....$25–$32

Theroux, Paul. *The Mosquito Coast.* Houghton Mifflin, 1982, 1st ed, dj. ....$35–$50

Thirkell, Angela. *High Rising and Wild Strawberries.* NY, 1951, 2 vols, 1st ed, djs. ....$25–$40

Thirkell, Angela. *Love at All Ages.* NY, 1959, 1st U.S. ed. ....$18–$22.50

Thoburn, James M. *The Christian Conquest of India.* NY, 1906, 1st ed. ....$7–$14

Thomas, Dylan. *A Child's Christmas in Wales.* 1954, 1st ed, dj. ....$40–$65

Thomas, Dylan. *Adventures in the Skin Trade.* NY, New Directions, 1955, dj. ....$40–$55

Thomas, Dylan. *Adventures in the Skin Trade.* New Directions, 1953, 1st ed, dj. ....$55–$75

Thomas, Dylan. *New Poems.* Norfolk, CT, 1943, 1st ed, dj. ....$30–$50

Thomas, Dylan. *Quite Early One Morning.* NY, 1954, 1st U.S. ed, dj. ....$35–$45

Thomas, Dylan. *The Beach of Falesa.* NY, 1963, 1st ed, dj. ....$35–$45

Thomas, Dylan. *Under Milk Wood.* NY, 1954, 1st ed, dj. ....$60–$100

Thomas, Edward H. *Chinook: A Hist. and Dict. of N.W. Coast Trade Jargon.* Portland, 1935. ....$35–$50

Thomas, Isaiah. *The Holy Bible Containing the Old and New Testaments.* Worcester, 1800. ....$120–$150

Thomas, Katherine. *Women in Nazi Germany.* Lon, 1943, 1st ed. ....$25–$35

Thomas, Lowell. *Old Gimlet Eye: The Adventures of Smedley D. Butler.* NY, 1933, 1st ed, sgn by author and Butler. ....$125–$175

Thomas, Lowell. *So Long until Tomorrow.* NY, 1977, 1st ed, dj. ....$18–$25

Thomas, Will. *God Is for White Folks.* NY, 1947, 1st ed, dj.
....*$15–$20*

Thomason, John W. *Jeb Stuart.* NY, 1930. ....*$20–$25*

Thompson, Charles J. *Alchemy: Source of Chemistry and Medicine.* Sentry Press, 1974, facs of 1897 ed, dj. ....*$12–$20*

Thompson, Dorothy. *"I Saw Hitler."* NY, 1932, 1st ed. ..*$18–$25*

Thompson, E. Porter. *A Young People's History of Kentucky.* MO, 1897, illus. ....*$24–$30*

Thompson, Edward William. *Smoky Days.* NY, 1896. ..*$20–$25*

Thompson, G. *Prison Life and Reflections.* Hartford, 1854.
....*$30–$40*

Thompson, Margaret J. *Capt. Nathaniel L. Thompson and the Ships He Built, 1811–1889.* Lauriat, 1937, 1st ed. ....*$35–$45*

Thompson, Maurice. *Byways and Bird Notes.* U.S. Book Co., 1885. ....*$10–$12*

Thompson, Ruth Plumly. *The Cowardly Lion of Oz.* Reilly & Lee, illus by J.R. Neill. ....*$60–$75*

Thompson, Ruth Plumly. *The Gnome King of Oz.* Reilly & Lee, 1st ed, illus by J.R. Neill. ....*$95–$120*

Thompson, Ruth Plumly. *The Hungry Tiger of Oz.* Reilly & Lee, 1926, illus by J.R. Neill. ....*$60–$100*

Thompson, Ruth Plumly. *The Lost King of Oz.* Chi, 1925, 1st ed, illus, clr. plates. ....*$90–$100*

Thompson, Ruth Plumly. *The Purple Prince of Oz.* Reilly & Lee, illus by J.R. Neill. ....*$65–$75*

Thompson, Ruth Plumly. *The Wishing Horse of Oz.* Reilly & Lee, nd, illus by J.R. Neill. ....*$65–$75*

Thompson, Ruth Plumly. *The Yellow Knight of Oz.* Reilley & Lee, illus by J.R. Neill, dj. ....*$60–$100*

Thompson, Zadock. *Geography and Geology of Vermont . . . State and County Outline Maps.* VT, 1848, illus, maps. .*$50–$80*

Thompson, Zadock. *History of Vermont . . . in Three Parts.* Burlington, 1842, 1st ed, illus, fldg map, calf. ....*$115–$150*

Thoms, William Capt. *A New Treatise on the Practice of Navigation at Sea.* NY, 1902. ....$16–$20

Thomson, J.J. *Corpuscular Theory of Matter.* Lon, 1907, 1st ed. ....$55–$100

Thoreau, Henry David. *Cape Cod.* Bos, 1865, 1st ed. ..$300–$750

Thoreau, Henry David. *Men of Concord.* Bos, 1936, illus by N.C. Wyeth, dj. ....$45–$55

Thoreau, Henry David. *Walden.* Bos, 1854, 1st ed. ..$950–$1,600

Thoreau, Henry David. *Walden, or Life in the Woods.* Bos, The Bibliophile Society, 1909, 2 vols, illus, ltd 483 cc, vellumlike paper over brown buckram, slipcases. ....$200–$325

Thornton, Willis. *The Country Doctor.* Grosset & Dunlap, 1936, illus. ....$18–$35

Thorp, E. *Beat the Market.* NY, 1967, dj. ....$18–$28

Thorp, Raymond W. *Spirit Gun of the West.* CA, 1957, illus. ....$35–$60

Thrasher, Halsey. *The Hunter and Trapper.* 1863. ....$65–$100

Thurber, James. *Fables for Our Time.* NY, 1940, 2nd issue. ....$25–$40

Thurber, James. *The White Deer.* NY, 1945, illus. ....$8–$15

Thurman, Arnold. *The Folklore of Capitalism.* New Haven, 1937, 1st ed. ....$85–$115

Thurston, Robert. *History of the Growth of the Steam-engine.* NY, 1878. ....$45–$60

Tibbles, Thomas Henry. *Buckskin and Blanket Days.* NY, 1957. ....$20–$45

Toffler, Alvin. *Future Shock.* NY, 1970, dj. ....$15–$20

Toklas, Alice B. *Alice B. Toklas Cook Book.* Lon, 1954, 1st ed, illus. ....$150–$225

Tolkien, J.R.R. *Father Christmas Letters.* Lon, 1976, 1st ed. ....$50–$65

Tolkien, J.R.R. *Pictures.* Bos, 1979, 1st American ed, slipcase. ....$48–$65

Tolkien, J.R.R. *Smith of Wootton Major.* 1967, 1st ed, dj..$30–$45

Tolkien, J.R.R. *The Hobbitt.* Houghton Mifflin, 1966, 3rd prntg, boxed. ....*$32–$45*

Tolkien, J.R.R. *The Hobbitt.* Bos, 1938, illus by Tolkien, 1st American ed. ....*$250–$500*

Tolkien, J.R.R. *The Lord of the Rings.* Bos, 1965, 3 vols, rev. 2nd ed, dj, boxed. ....*$150–$275*

Tolkien, J.R.R. *The Silmarillion.* 1977, 1st ed, maps, dj. .*$12–$20*

Tolkien, J.R.R. *The Silmarillion.* 1977, 1st ed, dj. ....*$45–$100*

Tolley, Cyril. *The Modern Golfer.* NY, 1924, illus. ....*$30–$50*

Tolstoi, Alexis. *Vampires: Stories of the Supernatural.* NY, 1969, 1st English ed, dj. ....*$40–$50*

Tomes, Robert. *The Battles of America by Sea and Land.* NY, 1878, 3 vols, illus. ....*$145–$175*

Tomlinson, H.M. *Gallions Reach.* NY, 1927, ltd, 350 cc, sgn. ....*$14–$20*

Tompkins, W. *Santa Barbara's Royal Rancho.* CA, 1960, illus, dj. ....*$14–$18*

Tooker, William W. *The Indian Place-names on Long Island. . . .* NY, 1911. ....*$35–$40*

Torrey, Edwin C. *Early Days in Dakota.* Minn, nd. ......*$55–$65*

Tourgee, Albion. *A Fool's Errand and the Invisible Empire.* NY, 1880. ....*$15–$25*

Toynbee, Arnold. *Lectures on the Industrial Revolution of 18th Century England.* Longmans Green, 1912. ....*$18–$25*

Train, Arthur. *Yankee Lawyer—The Autobiography of Ephraim Tutt.* NY, 1943, 1st ed, illus, dj. ....*$35–$50*

Travers, P.C. *Mary Poppins Comes Back.* NY, 1935, 1st U.S. ed, dj. ....$30–$45

Travis, Joseph. *Autobiography of the Rev. Joseph Travis. . . .* Nashville, 1856. ....*$27–$38*

Treat. *National Political Manual.* NY, 1872. ....*$39–$48*

Tredgold, Thomas. *Elementary Principles of Carpentry.* Lon, 1840, illus, 3rd ed, plates. ....*$40–$50*

Tregaskis, Richard. *Guadalcanal Diary.* NY, 1943, 1st ed, dj.
....$10–$14

Tremaine, F. Dewey. *Little White Nose.* Putnam, 1953, 1st ed, illus, dj. ....$15–$20

Trevor-Roper, H. *Hermit of Peking: The Hidden Life of Sir Edmund Backhouse.* NY, 1977, 1st ed, dj. ....$30–$40

Trevor-Roper, H.R. *The Lost Days of Hitler.* NY, 1947, dj.
....$33–$45

Trilling, Lionel. *The Middle of the Journey.* NY, 1947, 1st ed, sgn.
....$45–$65

Trimble, Harvey M. *History of the 93rd Regiment Illinois Volunteer Infantry.* Chi, 1898, illus, fldg map. ....$125–$150

Triscott, C. Pette. *Golf in Six Lessons.* Phila, nd, 1st ed, illus.
....$30–$40

Trollope, A. *The West Indies and the Spanish Main.* NY, 1860, 1st American ed. ....$70–$90

Trollope, Anthony. *North America.* NY, 1862, 1st American ed.
....$60–$125

Trollope, Anthony. *North America.* Lon, 1862, 2 vols, 3rd ed.
....$125–$180

Trollope, Anthony. *The Last Chronicle of Barset.* Lon, 1867, 2 vols in one. ....$110–$125

Trotter, William. *On the Rearing and Management of Poultry.* Lon, 1852, wrps, illus. ....$28–$35

Trowbridge, J.T. *The South: A Tour of Its Battlefields and Ruined Cities....* CT, 1866, 1st ed, illus. ....$45–$55

Truman, B. *The Field of Honor: A Complete History of Duelling.* NY, 1884, 1st ed. ....$25–$35

Truman, Harry. *Memoirs by Harry S. Truman.* Garden City, 1955, 1956, 2 vols, 1st ed, sgn, dj. ....$350–$380

Truman, Margaret. *Harry S. Truman.* NY, 1973, photos.
....$35–$45

Truman, Margaret. *Murder in the White House.* 1980, dj.
....$18–$25

Truman, Nevil. *Historic Costuming.* NY/Chi, 1947, illus..$14–$22

Trumbull, James Hammond. *Natick Dictionary.* GPO, 1903. ....*$20–$60*

Tryon, T. *Harvest Home.* 1973, dj. ....*$12–$18*

Tucker, Sophie. *Some of These Days.* sgn, dj. ....*$35–$45*

Tucker, T.W. *Waifs from the Way-bills of an Old Expressman.* Bos, 1872, 1st ed, illus. ....*$45–$75*

Tuckerman, A. *A Short History of Architecture.* NY, 1887, illus, calf. ....*$75–$95*

Tuckerman, Bayard. *Life of General Lafayette.* NY, 1889, 2 vols, 1st ed. ....*$37–$45*

Tudor, Tasha. *Tasha Tudor's Favorite Christmas Carols.* McKay, 1978, illus, dj. ....*$20–$30*

Tuer, Andrew. *Old London Street Cries and the Cries of To-day.* . . . Lon, 1885, illus. ....*$20–$25*

Tullidge, Edward W. *Life of Brigham Young.* NY, 1876, 1st ed. ....*$60–$80*

Turnbull, W.P. *Chessmen in Action.* 1914, 1st ed. ....*$14–$20*

Turner, Elizabeth. *The Cowslip.* Phila, 1839, illus. ....*$30–$40*

Turner, G. *Hair Embroidery in Siberia and North America.* Ox, 1955, illus, photos, maps, drawings. ....*$20–$30*

Turner, J. *Mary Todd Lincoln: Life and Letters.* Knopf, 1972, 2nd ed, dj. ....*$12–$15*

Turner, William. *Transfer Printing on Enamels, Porcelain, and Pottery.* Lon, 1907, illus. ....*$115–$150*

Turney-High, Harry Holbert. *The Flathead Indians of Montana.* WI, 1937, dj. ....*$22–$30*

Tuttle, Charles. *An Illustrated History of the State of Wisconsin.* 1875. ....*$55–$75*

Twain, Mark. *A Dog's Tale.* NY, 1905, illus by Smedley. .*$16–$20*

Twain, Mark. *A Double Barrelled Detective Story.* NY, 1902. ....*$55–$75*

Twain, Mark. *Adventures of Tom Sawyer.* Hartford, 1876, 1st ed. ....*$2,000–$4,000*

Twain, Mark. *Adventures of Tom Sawyer.* 1876, 1st American ed, 2nd prntg. ....*$450–$1,250*

Twain, Mark. *Following the Equator.* Hartford, 1897, 1st ed, 1st issue. ....*$75–$175*

Twain, Mark. *Life on the Mississippi.* Heritage Press, 1972, slipcase. ....*$10–$15*

Twain, Mark. *Life on the Mississippi.* Bos, 1883, 1st ed, 2nd state. ....*$125–$150*

Twain, Mark. *Life on the Mississippi.* 1883, 1st American ed, 1st issue. ....*$250–$550*

Twain, Mark. *Mark Twain's Autobiography.* NY, 1924, 2 vols. ....*$20–$35*

Twain, Mark. *Pudd'nhead Wilson. . . .* Hartford, 1894, 1st U.S. ed. ....*$100–$185*

Twain, Mark. *The $30,000 Bequest and Other New Stories.* NY, 1906, 1st ed, 2nd state. ....*$45–$60*

Twain, Mark. *The Prince and the Pauper.* Bos, 1882, 1st American ed. ....*$100–$175*

Tyler, Anne. *Breathing Lessons.* 1988, 1st ed, dj. ....*$5–$12*

Tyler, Anne. *Dinner at the Homesick Restaurant.* NY, Knopf, 1982, 1st ed, dj. ....*$45–$60*

Tyler, David Budlong. *Steam Conquers the Atlantic.* NY/Lon, 1939, 1st ed, illus, dj. ....*$20–$30*

Tyler, Parker. *Magic and the Myth of the Movies.* 1947, 1st ed. ....*$15–$22*

Tyndall, John. *Hours of Exercise in the Alps.* NY, Appleton, 1875, 473 pp, illus. ....*$30–$45*

Tyree, M.C. *Housekeeping in Old Virginia.* 1965, rprnt. .*$20–$30*

U.S. Commissioner of Patents. *Report for the Year 1854: Arts and Manufacturers.* DC, 1855, 2 vols, illus. ....*$40–$65*

Ude, Louis Eustache. *The French Cook.* Phila, 1828, rbkd with lea. ....*$295–$375*

Underwood, T.H. *Our Flag.* NY, 1862. ....*$28–$35*

Updike, John. *A Month of Sundays.* NY, 1975, 1st ed, dj. .*$15–$25*

Updike, John. *Pigeon Feathers.* NY, 1962, 1st ed, dj. .*$75–$125*

Updike, John. *Rabbit Redux.* NY, 1971, 1st ed, dj. ....*$45–$75*

Updike, John. *Rabbit is Rich.* NY, 1981, 1st ed, sgn, dj..*$75–$100*

Updike, John. *Rabbit Run.* NY, 1960, 1st ed, dj. ....*$250–$400*

Updike, John. *The Witches of Eastwick.* NY, 1984, 1st ed, dj. ....*$15–$30*

Updike, John. *The Witches of Eastwick.* Franklin Library, 1984, illus, lea, sgn. ....*$65–$85*

Updike, Wilkins. *History of the Narragansett Church.* Bos, 1907, 3 vols. ....*$75–$125*

Upham, Alfred H. *Old Miami.* OH, 1947, illus, rprnt. ..*$10–$13*

Upham, Charles W. *Life, Explorations, and Public Service of John Charles Fremont.* Bos, 1856, 1st ed. ....*$20–$40*

Urban, J.W. *Battle Field and Prison Pen.* Phila, 1882. .*$32–$40*

Urban, John W. *In Defense of the Union.* DC, 1887, 1st ed, illus. ....*$35–$45*

Urban, Joseph. *Theatres.* NY, 1929, illus, ltd, plates. ..*$70–$140*

Van De Water, Fred. *In Defense of Worms.* NY, 1949, 1st ed, dj. ....*$18–$25*

Van Der Rohe. *Furniture and Furniture Drawings.* MOMA, 1977. ....*$15–$20*

Van Der Zee, Jacob. *The Hollanders of Iowa.* Iowa City, 1912, 1st ed, illus. ....*$55–$75*

Van Dine, S.S. *Scarab Murder Case.* NY, 1930, 1st ed, dj. ....*$90–$150*

Van Dine, S.S. *The Dragon Murder Case.* NY, 1933, 1st ed, dj. ....*$100–$150*

Van Dine, S.S. *The Dragon Murder Case.* NY, 1933, 1st ed. ....*$25–$50*

Van Doren, Mark. *The Country Year: Poems.* NY, 1946, 1st ed, sgn, dj. ....*$20–$50*

Van Dyke, Henry. *Fisherman's Luck.* Tor, 1899, illus. ..*$40–$50*

Van Dyke, Henry. *Out-of-Doors in the Holy Land.* Scribner's, 1908, illus. ....*$25–$30*

Van Dyke, Henry. *The Lost Boy.* Harper, 1914, 69 pp, illus by N.C. Wyeth. ....*$18–$25*

Van Dyke, Henry. *Travel Diary of an Angler.* Derrydale Press, 1929, illus, ltd, 750 cc. ....*$225–$250*

Van Dyke, Theodore S. *The Still-hunter.* NY, 1937, illus..*$12–$18*

Van Gulik, Robert. *Murder in Canton.* NY/Lon, 1967, 1st American ed, dj. ....*$30–$75*

Van Gulik, Robert. *Necklace and Calabash.* NY, 1971, 1st ed, dj. ....*$35–$45*

Van Gulik, Robert. *The Chinese Lake Murders.* NY, 1960, illus, 1st U.S. ed. ....*$45–$65*

Van Gulik, Robert. *The Willow Pattern.* Lon, 1965, illus, 1st British ed, dj. ....*$25–$35*

Van Gulik, Robert. *The Willow Pattern.* NY, 1963, dj. .*$18–$25*

Van Pelt, Daniel. *The Hollanders in Nova Zembla (1596–1597).* NY, 1884. ....*$18–$75*

Vance, A.T. *Real David Harum.* NY, 1900, illus. ....*$12–$18*

Vance, Wilson J. *Stone's River: The Turning Point of the Civil War.* NY, 1914, 1st ed. ....*$45–$75*

Vandiveer, Clarence A. *The Fur-trade and Early Western Exploration.* Cleve, 1929, 1st ed. ....*$95–$145*

Vandiver, Frank. *Rebel Brass.* Baton Rouge, 1956, illus, sgn, dj. ....*$25–$37*

Variety Inc. *Radio Directory, 1937–1938.* 1937, 1st ed..*$45–$60*

Vassall, Henry. *Football: The Rugby Game.* NY, 1890, 1st ed. ....*$65–$95*

Vaughan, B.F. *Life and Writings of Rev. Henry R. Rush, D.D. . . .* Dayton, OH, 1911, 1st ed. ....*$55–$75*

Vaughn, John. *Tales of Appalachia.* NY, 1972. ....*$19–$18*

Veblen, Thorstein. *The Higher Learning in America.* NY, 1918, 1st ed. ....*$50–$70*

Veblen, Thornstein. *The Vested Interests.* NY, 1919, 1st ed. ....*$35–$65*

Venable, Emerson (ed). *Poets of Ohio.* Cinc, 1909. ......*$15–$22*

Verne, Jules. *A Journey to the Centre of the Earth.* Bos, nd, illus by Riou. ....$18–$25

Verne, Jules. *A Winter in the Ice.* Bos, 1876. ....$25–$35

Verne, Jules. *In Search of the Castaways.* Phila, 1874, illus, 2nd U.S. ed. ....$50–$85

Verne, Jules. *The Tour of the World in 80 Days.* 1873, 1st ed. ....$45–$75

Verne, Jules. *The Wreck of the Chancellor.* Bos, 1875, 1st U.S. ed. ....$20–$30

Verne, Jules. *Their Island Home.* NY, 1924, 1st U.S. ed...$40–$50

Vernon, Grenville. *Yankee Doodle-doo.* NY, 1927, 1st ed, illus, bds. ....$30–$40

Verwyst, F.C. *Chippewa Exercises.* Harbor Springs, 1901. ....$35–$40

Vestal, Stanley. *Jim Bridger, Mountain Man.* Morrow, 1946, 1st ed, dj. ....$25–$45

Vestal, Stanley. *Warpath and Council Fire.* NY, 1948, 1st ed, dj. ....$40–$65

Victor, O. *History of the Southern Rebellion.* NY, 4 vols, illus. ....$165–$225

Vidal, Gore. *Kalki.* Random House, 1978, 1st ed, dj. ....$10–$18

Vidal, Gore. *Myra Breckinridge.* Little Brown, 1968, 1st ed, dj. ....$28–$35

Vidal, Gore. *The Season of Comfort.* NY, 1949, 1st ed, dj. ....$25–$40

Villard, Oswald Garrison. *John Brown.* NY, 1929, illus..$14–$20

Villiers, Alan. *The Cutty Sark.* Lon, 1957, illus, dj. ....$12–$20

Villiers, Alan. J. *Last of the Wind Ships.* NY, 1934, illus, photos. ....$33–$45

Vinson, Maribel Y. *Primer of Ice Skating.* NY, 1938, 1st ed, illus. ....$30–$50

Visscher, William Lightfoot. *Blue Grass Ballads and Other Verse.* Chi, 1900, presentation copy, sgn. ....$25–$35

Von Braun, Wernher. *Space Frontier.* 1967, 1st ed, sgn..$45–$55

Von Loon, Henrik. *Ancient Man.* NY, 1920, 1st ed. ......*$35–$45*

Von Mucke, Hellmuth. *The Ayesha.* Bos, 1917, illus, maps.
....*$18–$25*

Vonnegut, Kurt. *A Precautionary Letter to the Next Generation.* np, 1988. ....*$18–$30*

Vonnegut, Kurt. *Breakfast of Champions.* NY, 1973. ....*$20–$25*

Vonnegut, Kurt. *Canary in a Cat House.* NY, 1962, sgn, dj.
....*$100–$125*

Vonnegut, Kurt. *God Bless You, Mr. Rosewater.* Holt, Rinehart & Winston, 1965, 1st ed, dj. ....*$95–$125*

Vonnegut, Kurt. *Jailbird.* np, 1979, 1st ed, dj. ....*$25–$75*

Vonnegut, Kurt. *Palm Sunday.* Delacorte, 1981, 1st ed, dj.
....*$30–$45*

Vonnegut, Kurt. *Slaughterhouse Five.* NY, 1969, sgn, dj.
....*$175–$300*

Vose, George L. *Bridge Disasters in America.* Bos, 1887, 1st ed.
....*$28–$35*

Voth, H.R. *Oraibi Natal Customs and Ceremonies, Vol. VI, No 2.* Field Columbian Museum, 1905, illus. ....*$35–$50*

Voth, H.R. *The Oraibi Oaqol Ceremony, Vol. VI, No 1.* Field Columbian Museum, 1903, illus. ....*$85–$130*

Voth, H.R. *The Oraibi Summer Snake Ceremony, Vol. III.* Field Columbian Museum, 1903, illus. ....*$95–$145*

Vrooman, J.J. *Forts and Firesides of the Mohawk Valley.* Phila, 1943, 1st ed, ltd 106 cc. ....*$65–$90*

W.P.A. *A Maritime History of New York.* NY, 1941, illus, dj.
....*$45–$55*

W.P.A. *Alaska.* 1943, 1st ed, dj. ....*$30–$35*

W.P.A. *Anthology of Writers in Fed. Writer's Project, 1st book appearance.* ....*$50–$75*

W.P.A. *California.* NY, 1939, 1st ed, map. ....*$35–$45*

W.P.A. *Cape Cod.* 2nd prntg. ....*$30–$35*

W.P.A. *Cavalcade of the American Negro.* Chi, 1940. ....*$50–$75*

W.P.A. *Iowa.* NY, 1938, 1st ed, pocket map, dj. ....*$30–$40*

W.P.A. *Key West.* NY, 1949, 2nd ed, dj. ....*$14–$20*

W.P.A. *Maine.* Bos, 1937, 1st ed. ....*$25–$35*

W.P.A. *Maryland.* NY, 1940, 5th prntg. ....*$12–$15*

W.P.A. *Michigan.* Ox, 1941, 1st ed, pocket map, dj. ......*$30–$40*

W.P.A. *Minnesota.* NY, Viking Press, 1938, 1st ed, map, dj. ....*$40–$45*

W.P.A. *Montana.* 1st ed, map, dj. ....*$35–$100*

W.P.A. *New Orleans City Guide.* 1938, map. ....*$22–$30*

W.P.A. *New York City Guide.* Random House, 1940, map, dj. ....*$28–$35*

W.P.A. *New York City Guide.* 1939, pocket map. ....*$30–$40*

W.P.A. *North Dakota.* Fargo, 1938, 1st ed. ....*$37–$50*

W.P.A. *South Dakota.* NY, 1952, 2nd ed, maps, dj. ....*$40–$50*

W.P.A. *South Dakota.* 1st ed. ....*$60–$95*

W.P.A. *Texas: A Guide to the Lone Star State.* NY, 1940, 1st ed, illus, dj. ....*$24–$35*

W.P.A. *The Negroes of Nebraska.* Lincoln, NB, 1940, 1st ed. ....*$45–$60*

W.P.A. *Wyoming.* 1st ed, map, dj. ....*$60–$95*

Wack, Henry Wellington. *The Story of the Congo Free State.* NY, 1905, 1st ed, illus. ....*$125–$175*

Wagenkneckt, E. *The Movies in the Age of Innocence.* Univ. of Oklahoma Press, 1962, dj. ....*$15–$18*

Wagner, Charles L. *Seeing Stars.* NY, 1940, illus. ....*$15–$20*

Waitz, Julia Ellen. *The Journal of Julia Le Grand, New Orleans, 1862–1863.* Rich, 1911, 1st ed. ....*$68–$85*

Wakefield, J. *History of Waupaca County, Wisc.* Waupaca, WI, 1890, 1st ed. ....*$60–$85*

Wakeley, J.B. *Lost Chapters Recovered from Early Hist. of Amer. Methodism.* NY, 1858. ....*$27–$35*

Wakoski, Diane. *Love the Lizard.* Prov, 1975, sgn. ....*$20–$25*

Wakoski, Diane. *Trilogy.* Middletown, 1968, dj. ....*$18–$20*

Walford, Eric W. *Practical Motor Car Repairing.* Lon, 1909, illus, 2nd ed. ....$18–$30

Walker, Alice. *The Color Purple.* NY, 1982, sgn, dj. .$325–$450

Walker, Alice. *The Temple of My Familiar.* NY, 1989, sgn, dj. ....$40–$50

Walker, Alice. *The Temple of My Familiar.* Harcourt, 1989, ltd, 500 cc, sgn, dj, slipcase. ....$85–$100

Walker, Elizabeth. *Hawaii and the South Seas: A Guide Book.* NY, 1931, 1st ed, map, sgn, dj. ....$37–$95

Walker, Eric Anderson. *Great Trek.* Lon, 1938, illus, 2nd ed, maps. ....$10–$20

Wall, E.G. *Handbook of the State of Mississippi.* Jackson, 1882, 1st ed, illus. ....$85–$125

Wall, E.J. *The History of Three-color Photography.* Lon, 1970, illus. ....$25–$40

Wall, Robert. *Ocean Liners.* NY, 1977, illus, dj. ....$27–$40

Wallace, Dillon. *Long Labrador Trail.* Chi, McClurg. ....$10–$14

Wallace, Dillon. *The Camper's Handbook.* Fleming Revell, 1936. ....$12–$15

Wallace, Dillon. *The Lure of the Labrador Wild.* NY, 1905, illus, map. ....$20–$30

Wallace, Edgar. *Tam O' the Scoots.* Bos, 1919, 1st U.S. ed. ....$35–$55

Wallace, H.F. *Hunting Winds: Big Game Hunting....* Lon, 1949, 1st ed. ....$25–$30

Wallace, Isabel. *Life and Letters of General W.H.L. Wallace.* Chi, 1909, 1st ed, illus. ....$95–$125

Wallace, Lew. *Life of General Ben Harrison.* Phila, 1888, illus. ....$14–$20

Wallace, Lew. *The Prince of India.* NY, 1893, 2 vols, 1st ed. ....$20–$30

Wallihan, A. *Camera Shots at Big Game.* NY, 1906, illus, plates. ....$35–$50

Wallis, Mrs. *Life in Feejee.* Ridgewood, NJ, 1967, rprnt, fldg chart. ....*$25–$35*

Walsh, J. *Tea-blending as a Fine Art.* 1896. ....*$30–$40*

Walton, Evangeline. *The Cross and the Sword.* NY, 1956, 1st ed, sgn, dj. ....*$95–$125*

Walton, Evangeline. *The Virgin and the Swine.* Chi, 1936, 1st ed. ....*$40–$50*

Walton, Evangeline. *Witch House.* Arkham House, 1961, dj. ....*$45–$50*

Walton, Evangeline. *Witch House.* Sauk City, Arkham House, 1945, ltd, 3,000 cc, dj. ....*$55–$70*

Walton, Isaac. *The Compleat Angler.* Phila, nd, illus by Arthur Rackham. ....*$82–$95*

Walton, Isaac and Charles Cotton. *The Complete Angler.* NY, 1848, ¾ lea, bds. ....*$50–$60*

Walton, Isaac and Charles Cotton. *The Complete Angler, or Contemplative Man's Recreation.* Lon, 1784, illus, 4th ed, slipcase. ....*$350–$450*

Walton, Izaak. *The Compleat Angler.* Lon, J.M. Dent, 1896, illus by E.J. Sullivan. ....*$45–$55*

Warbey, William. *Vietnam: The Truth.* Lon, 1965, 1st ed..*$25–$30*

Ward, Arch. *The Green Bay Packers.* NY, 1946, 1st ed, illus. ....*$22–$25*

Ward, Austin. *Male Life among the Mormons, or The Husband in Utah.* Phila, 1863. ....*$45–$60*

Ward, James. *Naturalism and Agnosticism.* Lon, 1899, 2 vols. ....*$40–$65*

Ward, Lynd. *God's Man.* Cleve, 1966, dj. ....*$22–$30*

Ward, Lynd. *God's Man.* 1930, 1st British ed. ....*$50–$75*

Wardle, P. *Victorian Lace.* NY, 1969, dj. ....*$18–$25*

Ware, W. Porter. *Occupational Shaving Mugs.* Chi, 1949, illus. ....*$25–$30*

Warhol, Andy. *"A."* NY, 1968, 1st ed, dj. ....*$35–$45*

Waring, Janet. *Early American Wall Stencils.* nd, illus, clr and b/w, reissue. ....$22–$45

Warner, David S. *Glimpses of Palestine and Egypt.* Chi, 1914, illus, photos. ....$15–$25

Warren, John. *The Conchologist.* Bos, 1834, 1st ed, illus, presentation copy, lea, bds. ....$115–$130

Warren, Robert Penn. *Meet Me in the Green Glen.* NY, 1971, 1st ed, presentation copy, sgn. ....$100–$225

Warren, Robert Penn. *Wilderness.* Random House, 1961, 1st ed, dj. ....$50–$30

Warren, T. Robinson. *Shooting, Boating, and Fishing for Young Sportsmen.* NY, 1871, 1st ed. ....$40–$50

Washington, Booker T. *Up from Slavery.* NY, 1901, 1st ed. ....$65–$85

Washington, Booker T. *Working with the Hands.* Doubleday, 1904, 1st ed. ....$55–$75

Watanna, Onoto. *A Japanese Nightingale.* Harper, 1901, 1st ed, illus. ....$17–$24

Watanna, Onoto. *The Heart of the Hyacinth.* Harper, 1903, illus, teg. ....$18–$24

Waters, Frank. *Midas of the Rockies.* 1937. ....$22–$25

Waters, Frank. *The Man Who Killed the Deer.* American Library, 1942, 4th ed, dj. ....$12–$15

Watson, Doris. *The Handbell Choir.* NY, 1959, illus. ....$10–$15

Watson, J. *The Dog Book.* 1909, illus. ....$30–$45

Watson, Louis H. *Watson on the Play of the Hand.* NY, 1934, 1st ed, illus. ....$32–$40

Watson, Richard. *Conversations for the Young.* NY, 1849..$8–$14

Watson, Wilbur J. *Bridge Architecture.* NY, 1927, illus..$50–$75

Watson, William. *Adventures of a Blockade Runner.* Lon, 1892. ....$100–$155

Watson-Watt, Sir Robert. *Three Steps to Victory.* 1957, illus, 1st British ed. ....$45–$60

Watts, Isaac. *The Psalms of David.* Lon, 1824, lea. ......$16–$30

Waugh, F.A. *Landscape Gardening.* NY, 1899, 1st ed. ..*$32–$45*

Wayland, Francis. *Memoir of the Life and Labors of the Rev. Adoniram Judson, D.D.* Bos, 1853, 2 vols, 1st ed. ....*$25–$35*

Wayre, Philip. *A Guide to the Pheasants of the World.* Lon, 1969, plates, dj. ....*$18–$22*

Webb, Herbert Laws. *The Telephone Handbook.* 1900, 1st ed, illus. ....*$22–$30*

Webb, T. *The Freemason's Monitor, or Illustrations of Masonry.* Salem, 1816. ....*$25–$45*

Webb, Walter Prescott. *The Texas Rangers.* Houghton Mifflin, 1935, illus. ....*$30–$35*

Webb, Walter Prescott. *The Texas Rangers.* Houghton Mifflin, 1935, 1st ed, illus. ....*$52–$60*

Webb, William Seward. *Calif. and Alaska, and Over the Canadian Pacific Railway.* NY, 1890, illus, ltd 500 cc. ....*$120–$155*

Weber, Carl J. *Fore-edge Painting.* Irvington-on-Hudson, 1966, illus, dj. ....*$165–$200*

Weber, Rev. Francis J. *A Bibliography of California Bibliographies.* Ward Ritchie Press, illus, slipcase, ltd 500 cc. ......*$65–$85*

Webster, Noah. *A Dictionary for Primary Schools.* NY, 1841, lea. ....*$12–$25*

Webster, Noah. *American Spelling Book.* NY, 1804, illus, woodcuts. ....*$50–$65*

Webster, Noah. *An American Dictionary of the English Language.* NY, 1832, 10th ed, calf. ....*$20–$25*

Webster, Noah. *The American Spelling Book.* Bos, 1789, 1st ed. ....*$175–$250*

Webster, Thomas. *An Encyclopedia of Domestic Economy.* NY, 1845, 1st ed. ....*$65–$125*

Wechsberg, J. *The Glory of the Violin.* NY, 1973, 1st ed, dj. ....*$18–$25*

Wee Gee. *Naked City.* NY, 1945, 1st ed. ....*$25–$35*

Wee Gee. *Weegee's People.* NY, 1946, 1st ed, illus, photos. ....*$27–$40*

Weeden, Howard. *Songs of the Old South.* NY, 1901, 1st ed, illus, clr plates. ....*$75–$100*

Weeks, Alvin G. *Massasoit of the Wampanoags.* np, private prntg, 1920. ....*$22–$34*

Weeks, Edwin Lord. *From the Black Sea through Persia and India.* Harper & Bros., 1896, illus. ....*$35–$55*

Weems, M.L. *The Life of George Washington.* Phila, 1840. ....*$85–$150*

Weir, Mitchell S., M.D. *Fat and Blood: An Essay on the Treatment. . . .* Phila, 1902, 8th ed. ....*$30–$45*

Weise, A.J. *The History of Albany, NY.* Alb, 1884. ....*$35–$50*

Welch, Robert H. Jr. *May God Forgive Us.* Chi, 1952. ....*$10–$15*

Welles, Gideon. *Diary of Gideon Welles, Sect. of Navy under Lincoln and Johnson.* Bos/NY, 1911, 3 vols, 1st ed. ....*$85–$115*

Welles, Orson and Roger Hill. *The Mercury Shakespeare.* NY/Lon, 1934, 1939, illus. ....*$25–$35*

Wellman, Paul I. *The Trampling Herd.* NY, 1939, 1st ed, illus, dj. ....*$30–$50*

Wells, Emma M. *The History of Roane County, Tennessee, 1801–1870.* Chattanooga, 1927, 1st ed, illus. ....*$55–$75*

Wells, Frederic P. *History of Newbury, Vermont.* St. Johnsbury, VT, 1902, illus, fldg plate, ¾ mor. ....*$40–$55*

Wells, H.G. *Ann Veronica.* NY, 1909. ....*$15–$20*

Wells, H.G. *Experiment in Autobiography.* NY, 1934, illus. ....*$12–$18*

Wells, H.G. *First and Last Things.* Lon, 1908, 1st ed. ..*$18–$24*

Wells, H.G. *Men Like Gods.* Lon, 1923, 1st ed. ....*$25–$40*

Wells, H.G. *Tales of Space and Time.* NY, Doubleday & McClure, 1899, 1st American ed. ....*$45–$65*

Wells, H.G. *The Time Machine.* Lon, 1931, illus by Dwiggins. ....*$30–$55*

Wells, H.G. *The Time Machine.* NY, 1931, illus by Dwiggins. ....*$20–$30*

Welsh, R.E. and F.G. Edwards. *Romance of Psalter and Hymnal: Authors and Composers.* NY, 1889. ....$15–$22

Welty, Eudora. *Delta Wedding.* NY, 1946, 1st ed, dj. ..$100–$300

Welty, Eudora. *In Black and White.* Northridge, Lord John Press, 1985, sgn. ....$165–$250

Welty, Eudora. *The Golden Apples.* NY, 1949, 1st ed, dj. ....$75–$100

Welty, Eudora. *The Ponder Heart.* Harcourt, 1954, 1st cd, sgn, dj. ....$125–$200

Welty, Eudora. *The Wide Net and Other Stories.* NY, 1943, 1st ed, dj. ....$350–$500

Wenger, J.C. *Glimpses of Mennonite History.* PA, 1940, illus. ....$14–$18

Wenham, Edward. *Domestic Silver of Great Britain and Ireland.* NY, 1935. ....$35–$40

Werner, Carl. *A Textbook on Tobacco.* NY, 1914, illus. ..$25–$35

West, Anthony. *The Vintage.* Bos, 1950, 1st American ed, dj. ....$25–$30

West, Benjamin. *The New England Almanack for 1776.* Prov, 1775. ....$125–$150

West, James E. *The Lone Scout of the Sky.* NY, 1927, Boy Scout Book. ....$15–$18

West, Mae. *Goodness Had Nothing to Do with It.* NY, 1959, 1st ed. ....$18–$25

West, Maria. *Romance of Missions: Inside View of Life and Labor in Ararat.* NY, 1875. ....$30–$40

West, Nathaniel. *The Day of the Locust.* 1939, 1st ed. ..$40–$70

Westervelt, W.D. *Legends of Old Honolulu.* Bos/Lon, 1915, 1st ed, illus. ....$50–$85

Wetmore, Mrs. Helen C. *Last of the Great Scouts: The Life Story of Buffalo Bill.* Duluth, 1899, 1st ed, illus, plates. ....$75–$175

Weyand, A.M. *American Football: Its History and Development.* Appleton, 1926, 1st ed, dj. ....$20–$30

Whall, W.B. *Sea Songs and Shanties.* Glasgow, 1920, illus, 4th ed. ....$50–$75

Wharton, Edith. *Ethan Frome.* NY, 1911, 1st issue. ..$150–$165

Wharton, Edith. *Italian Villas and Their Gardens.* NY, 1904, 1st ed, illus by Maxfield Parrish. ....$150–$350

Wharton, Edith. *The Children.* NY, 1928, 1st ed, dj. ..$75–$125

Wharton, Edith. *The Fruit of the Tree.* NY, 1907, 1st ed..$50–$65

Wharton, Edith. *The House of Mirth.* NY, 1895, 1st ed, illus. ....$40–$85

Wharton, Edith. *Xingu and Other Stories.* NY, 1916, 1st ed. ....$60–$75

Wheeler, F.G. *Billy Whiskers at the Fair.* Akron, 1909, 1st ed, illus, plates. ....$30–$35

Wheeler, O. *Colour Photography.* Bath, 1929, 1st ed, illus. ....$22–$35

Wheelock, Irene Grosvenor. *Birds of California.* Chi, 1910, 2nd ed, presentation copy, sgn. ....$16–$22

Whistler, James McNeill. *The Paintings.* New Haven/Lon, 1980, 2 vols, illus, dj. ....$85–$150

Whitaker, Fess. *History of Corporal Fess Whitaker.* Louisville, KY, 1918, 1st ed, illus. ....$60–$75

White, Alma. *The Ku Klux Klan in Prophecy.* NJ, 1925, 1st ed. ....$150–$275

White, E.B. *Charlotte's Web.* NY, 1952, 1st ed, illus by Garth Williams, dj. ....$100–$450

White, E.B. *Charlotte's Web.* NY, 1952, dj. ....$22–$65

White, E.B. *Letters of E.B. White.* NY, 1976, 1st ed, sgn, dj. ....$30–$35

White, E.B. *Points of My Compass.* 1962, 1st ed, dj. ....$25–$40

White, E.B. *Stuart Little.* NY, 1945, dj. ....$50–$175

White, Edward L. and John E. Gould. *The Modern Harp....* Bos, 1874. ....$35–$45

White, James. *The Early Life and Later Experiences ... of Elder Joseph Bates.* Battle Creek, 1877, illus. ....$115–$150

White, Joseph J. *Cranberry Culture.* NY, 1909, illus. ...*$18–$30*

White, Owen P. *Them Was the Days.* NY, Minton, Balch & Co., 1925, 1st ed, illus. ....*$35–$55*

White, Stewart E. *The Forest.* NY, 1903, 1st ed, illus...*$14–$20*

White, Stewart Edward. *African Camp Fires.* Doubleday/Page, 1913, 1st ed, illus. ....*$22–$30*

White, Stewart Edward. *The Riverman.* Garden City, 1913.
....*$22–$35*

White, W.H. *A Manual of Naval Architecture.* Lon, 1882, illus.
....*$65–$85*

Whitehead, Alfred North. *Science and the Modern World.* NY, 1937, dj. ....*$15–$20*

Whitehead, Don. *The FBI Story.* NY, 1956, sgn by Hoover, dj.
....*$45–$50*

Whitehouse, E. *Texas Flowers in Natural Colors.* Austin, private prntg, 1936. ....*$18–$25*

Whiting, Hubert B. *Old Iron Still Banks.* 1968, 1st ed. ..*$10–$14*

Whitlock, Brand. *The Little Green Shutter.* NY, 1931, 1st ed, sgn.
....*$14–$25*

Whitman, Walt. *November Boughs.* Phila, 1888, 1st ed.
....*$90–$325*

Whitman, Walt. *Specimen Days and Collect.* Phila, 1882–83, 1st ed, 2nd issue. ....*$125–$225*

Whitney, Ada. *Mother Goose for Grown Folks.* NY, 1859, 1st ed, sgn. ....*$125–$250*

Whitney, Grinnel, Wister. *Musk-ox, Bison, Sheep, and Goat.* 1904. ....*$35–$40*

Whitney, J.D. *The Metallic Wealth of U.S.* Phila, 1854, illus.
....*$25–$30*

Whitney, Mrs. A.D.T. *Mother Goose for Grown Folks.* Loring, 1870, illus by N. Hoppin and H. Billings. ....*$18–$25*

Whittier, John Greenleaf. *Among the Hills.* Bos, 1869, 1st ed.
....*$15–$40*

Whymper, C. *Egyptian Birds for the Most Part Seen in the Nile Valley.* Lon, 1909, illus. ....$70–$85

Whymper, Frederick. *Travel and Adventure in the Territory of Alaska.* Harper & Bros., 1871, illus. ....$65–$85

Wickersham, James. *A Bibliography of Alaskan Literature, 1724–1924.* . . . Cordova, 1927. ....$225–$275

Wickson, Edward J. *The California Fruits and How to Grow Them.* CA, 1900, illus, 3rd ed. ....$14–$22

Wiesel, Elie. *Zalmen or the Madness of God.* NY, 1974, 1st ed, sgn. ....$18–$24

Wiggin, Kate Douglas. *Mother Carey's Chickens.* Bos/NY, 1911, 1st ed. ....$30–$50

Wiggin, Kate Douglas. *Penelope's Irish Experiences.* Bos, 1902, illus by C.E. Brock. ....$30–$40

Wiggin, Kate Douglas. *Romance of a Christmas Card.* 1916, 1st ed. ....$25–$35

Wiggin, Kate Douglas (ed). *The Arabian Nights.* 1909, 1st ed, illus by Maxfield Parrish. ....$33–$45

Wiggin, Kate Douglas. *The Birds' Christmas Carol.* 1912, illus. ....$18–$27

Wiggin, Kate Douglas. *The Diary of a Goose Girl.* Bos, 1902, 1st ed. ....$15–$20

Wiggin, Kate Douglas. *The Old Peabody Pew.* Bos/NY, 1907, 1st ed. ....$35–$50

Wiggin, Kate Douglas. *Timothy's Quest.* Grosset & Dunlap, 1894, illus, Photoplay ed. ....$14–$18

Wight, J.B. *Tobacco: Its Use and Abuse.* Columbia, SC, 1889. ....$20–$35

Wilbur, M.E. *Raveneau De Lusson, Bucaneer.* Cleve, 1930, 1st ed, illus. ....$40–$50

Wilcox, R. Turner. *Five Centuries of American Costume.* Scribner's, 1963, illus, dj. ....$15–$25

Wilcox, R. Turner. *The Mode in Hats and Headdress.* NY, 1945, 1st ed, sgn. ....$30–$35

Wilcox, Walter Dwight. *The Rockies of Canada.* NY/Lon, 1900.
....*$75–$100*

Wilde, Oscar. *The Poems of Oscar Wilde.* NY, 1927, illus by Jean DeBosschere. ....*$30–$65*

Wilder, Thornton. *The Angel That Troubled the Waters.* Coward McCann, 1933, sgn, dj. ....*$37–$45*

Wilder, Thornton. *The Cabala.* NY, 1926, 1st ed. ....*$65–$200*

Wilder, Thornton. *Theophilus North.* NY, 1973, 1st ed, presentation copy, sgn, dj. ....*$80–$100*

Wiley, Bell Irvin. *The Life of Johnny Reb.* Ind, 1943. ...*$28–$40*

Wiley, Bell Irvin. *The Plain People of the Confederacy.* Baton Rouge, 1944, 1st ed, dj. ....*$35–$50*

Wilkins, Capt. George H. *Flying the Arctic.* NY, 1929, illus, dj.
....*$25–$40*

Willey, G.R. *Archeology of the Florida Gulf Coast, Vol. 113.* Smithsonian, 1949, illus. ....*$87–$145*

Williams, Edward V. *The Bells of Russia.* NY, 1985, illus.
....*$50–$70*

Williams, G.F. *Bullet and Shell: War as the Soldier Saw It.* NY, 1882, illus. ....*$24–$35*

Williams, J. *The Compleat Strategist: A Primer on Theory of Games.* NY, 1954, 1st ed, illus. ....*$15–$25*

Williams, J.R. *Cowboys Out Our Way.* NY, 1951, 1st ed, dj.
....*$40–$50*

Williams, Maxcine M. *Alaska Wildflower Glimpses.* Juneau, 1953, illus, photos, drawings, sgn. ....*$18–$25*

Williams, Mentor L. (ed). *Schoolcraft's Indian Legends.* MI, 1956, 1st ed, dj. ....*$28–$40*

Williams, Mrs. *The Neutral French.* . . . Published by author, 1841. ....*$50–$75*

Williams, O.W. *Pioneer Surveyor.* El Paso, 1956, dj. ......*$25–$32*

Williams, R. *Bermudiana 1936.* 1936. ....*$15–$20*

Williams, Sherman M. *Yearbook of the Methodist Episcopal Church, Glens Falls, NY.* Glens Falls, 1893. ....*$10–$15*

Williams, Tennessee. *Cat on a Hot Tin Roof.* Secker, 1956, 1st English ed, dj. ....$75–$90

Williams, Tennessee. *Cat on a Hot Tin Roof.* NY, 1955, 1st ed, dj. ....$75–$100

Williams, Tennessee. *The Glass Menagerie.* NY, Random House, 1945, 1st ed, dj. ....$65–$80

Williams, Tennessee. *The Roman Spring of Mrs. Stone.* NY, 1950, 1st ed, dj. ....$50–$75

Williams, Tennessee. *The Rose Tattoo.* New Directions, 1951, 1st ed, dj. ....$60–$125

Williams, W. *Appleton's Northern and Eastern Traveller's Guide.* NY, 1855, illus, maps. ....$85–$130

Williams, William Carlos. *The Broken Span.* Norfolk, CT, 1941, 1st ed, dj. ....$125–$180

Willoughby, Hugh. *Across the Everglades.* . . . Lippincott, 1906, illus, fldg map, photos. ....$27–$40

Willoughby, Malcolm F. *The Coast Guard's T.R.'s* Bos, 1945, illus, dj. ....$20–$45

Wilson, Colin. *Ritual in the Dark.* Houghton Mifflin, 1960, 1st ed, dj. ....$24–$30

Wilson, Colin. *The Philosopher's Stone.* NY, 1971, 1st U.S. ed, dj. ....$40–$50

Wilson, Edward L., et al. *Mountain Climbing.* NY, Scribner's, 1897, 1st ed, illus. ....$38–$45

Wilson, Elija N. *Among the Shoshones.* Salt Lake City, 1910, 1st ed. ....$200–$250

Wilson, Eugene E. *Kitty Hawk to Sputnik to Polaris.* MA, 1960, 1st ed, sgn, dj. ....$10–$15

Wilson, Herbert Earl. *The Lore and the Lure of Yosemite.* SF, 1923, 1st ed, sgn. ....$20–$25

Wilson, J. *China: Investigations in the Middle Kingdom.* NY, 1887, 1st ed, clr map. ....$27–$35

Wilson, John. *Christopher in His Sporting Jacket.* NY, 1901, illus by Alex McLellan, ltd, 2,500 cc. ....$16–$20

Wilson, Joseph Thomas. *The Black Phalanx: A History of Negro Soldiers of the U.S.* CT, 1888, 1st ed, illus. ....$175–$250

Wilson, Rev. Edward F. *Missionary Work among the Ojebway Indians.* Lon, 1886, 1st ed, illus. ....$75–$150

Wilson, T. *The Biography of the Principal American Military and Naval Heroes.* NY, 1821, 2 vols. ....$55–$65

Wilstach, Frank. *Wild Bill Hickok, The Prince of Pistoleers.* NY, 1926, illus, dj. ....$12–$18

Wilstach, Paul. *Hudson River Landings.* Ind, 1933, 1st ed, ltd, 160 cc, boxed, sgn. ....$55–$65

Wilstach, Paul. *Tidewater Maryland.* Bobbs-Merrill, 1931, 1st ed. ....$20–$25

Wilstach, Paul. *Tidewater Virginia.* Bobbs-Merrill, 1929, photos. ....$12–$20

Wingert, P.S. *Sculpture of Negro Africa.* NY, 1950, illus..$40–$50

Wise, Winifred E. *Jane Addams of Hull House.* NY, 1935, 1st ed, 1st prntg. ....$16–$20

Wister, Owen. *Journey in Search of Christmas.* NY, 1904, 1st ed. ....$25–$30

Wister, Owen. *Roosevelt: The Story of Friendship.* NY, 1930. ....$18–$25

Wister, Owen. *The Virginian.* NY, 1902, 1st ed. ....$75–$150

Witchell, N. *The Loch Ness Story.* Suffolk, 1976, illus...$20–$45

Witt, P.N. and J.S. Rovner (eds). *Spider Communication Mechanisms and Ecological Significance.* Princeton, 1982, illus. ....$20–$30

Wodehouse, P.G. *Bill the Conqueror.* NY, 1924, 1st American ed. ....$50–$75

Wodehouse, P.G. *Carry on, Jeeves!* NY 1927, 1st U.S. ed. ....$45–$65

Wodehouse, P.G. *Golf without Tears.* NY, 1924, 1st ed. .$60–$85

Wodehouse, P.G. *Love among Chickens.* Lon, 1936. ......$35–$40

Wodehouse, P.G. *Mike at Wrykyn.* 1953, 1st ed, dj. ....$20–$25

Wodehouse, P.G. *Piccadilly Jim.* Lon, 1924. ....$30–$40

Wodehouse, P.G. *Plum Pie.* NY, 1967, dj. ....$16–$22

Wodehouse, P.G. *Sunset at Blandings.* Lon, 1977, dj. ...$28–$38

Wodehouse, P.G. *Thank You, Jeeves.* Lon, 1934, 1st ed. ..$75–$85

Wodehouse, P.G. *The Code of the Woosters.* Lon, 1938, 1st ed. ....$35–$50

Wodehouse, P.G. *The Head of Kay's.* Lon, 1924. ....$30–$40

Wodehouse, P.G. *The Inimitable Jeeves.* Lon, 1923, 1st ed. ....$40–$50

Wodehouse, P.G. *The Prince and Betty.* 1912, 1st ed. ...$50–$65

Wodehouse, P.G. *Uncle Fred in the Springtime.* NY, 1939, 1st ed, dj. ....$40–$55

Wodehouse, P.G. *Uneasy Money.* Lon, 1934. ....$30–$35

Wodehouse, P.G. *Very Good Jeeves.* NY, 1930, 1st ed. ..$30–$40

Wodehouse, P.G. *Very Good, Jeeves.* NY, 1930. ....$25–$30

Wolf, Simon. *The American Jew as Patriot, Soldier, and Citizen.* Phila, 1895, 1st ed. ....$65–$75

Wolfe, Thomas. *From Death to Morning.* NY, 1935, 1st ed, dj. ....$100–$225

Wolfe, Thomas. *Of Time and the River.* NY, Scribner's, 1935, 1st ed. ....$45–$65

Wolfe, Thomas. *The Web and the Rock.* NY, 1939, 1st ed, dj. ....$70–$120

Wolfe, Thomas. *The Web and the Rock.* NY, 1939, dj. ...$40–$70

Wolfe, Thomas. *You Can't Go Home Again.* NY, 1940, 1st ed, dj. ....$40–$125

Wolfe, Tom. *Bonfire of the Vanities.* 1987, 1st ed, dj......$40–$60

Wolfe, Tom. *The Painted Word.* 1975, dj. ....$20–$40

Wolfe, Tom. *The Right Stuff.* NY, 1979, 1st ed, dj. ....$25–$30

Wolfson, Abraham. *Spinoza, A Life of Reason.* NY, 1969, 2nd ed, sgn. ....$18–$25

Wolk, Ruth. *History of Woodbridge.* NJ, 1957, 1st ed. ..$25–$35

Wolwode, Larry. *Born Brothers.* 1988, ARC, dj. ....$22–$30

Wolwode, Larry. *The Neumiller Stories.* 1989, ARC, dj. .$22–$25

Wood. *In Heart of Old Canada.* Tor, 1913. ....*$18–$24*

Wood, Edward J. *Curiosities of Clocks and Watches from the Earliest Times.* Lon, 1866, 1st ed. ....*$150–$220*

Wood, Edward J. *Giants and Dwarfs.* Lon, 1868, 1st ed. ....*$58–$75*

Wood, Frederick. *The Turnpikes of New England and Evolution of the Same. . . .* Bos, 1919, illus. ....*$15–$25*

Wood, G. and E. Burbank. *The Art of Interior Decoration.* NY, 1917, illus. ....*$25–$50*

Wood, G.S. *Radicalism of the American Revolution.* 1992, 1st ed, dj. ....*$14–$18*

Wood, George B. *The Dispensatory of the United States of America.* Phila, 1865, 12th ed. ....*$45–$60*

Wood, The Rev. J.G. *Common Objects of the Microscope.* Lon, nd, illus. ....*$30–$40*

Wood, Robert W. *Physical Optics.* NY, 1914, illus, rev..*$25–$30*

Wood, Stanley. *Over the Range to the Golden Gate. . . .* Chi, 1905, illus. ....*$47–$75*

Wood, Stanley. *Over the Range to the Golden Gate.* Chi, 1891. ....*$35–$45*

Wood, Wales W. *A History of the Ninety-fifth Regiment Illinois Infantry Vols.* Chi, 1865, 1st ed. ....*$145–$175*

Wood, Walter. *Harvesting Machines.* NY, 1882, wrps. ...*$30–$40*

Woodward, Grace. *Pocohantas.* Univ. of Oklahoma Press, 1969, 1st ed, dj. ....*$18–$24*

Woodward, P. *The Secret Service of the Post Office Department.* Hartford, 1886, 1st ed. ....*$30–$45*

Woolf, Virginia. *Between the Acts.* NY, Harcourt, 1941, 1st American ed, dj. ....*$55–$100*

Woolf, Virginia. *Flush: A Biography.* NY, 1933, 1st ed..*$15–$25*

Woolf, Virginia. *The Waves.* Lon, 1931, 1st ed, dj. ....*$75–$225*

Woolf, Virginia. *The Years.* Harcourt, 1937, 1st U.S. ed, dj. ....*$85–$125*

Woolman, John. *A Journal. . . .* Phila, 1837, lea. ....*$25–$50*

Wordsworth, William. 1857, 6 vols, Zaehnsdorf binding.
....$175–$250

Worthington, T. *Brief History of the 46th Ohio Volunteers.* DC, 1877–1880, wrps. ....$75–$100

Wouk, Hermann. *The Caine Mutiny.* Garden City, 1951, 1st ed, dj. ....$115–$145

Wouk, Herman. *This Is My God.* 1959, 1st ed, dj. ....$20–$25

Wright. *Britain and American Frontier, 1783–1815.* Athens, GA, 1975. ....$18–$25

Wright, Frank Lloyd. *A Testament.* Horizon, 1957, dj. .$50–$110

Wright, Frank Lloyd. *Architecture: Man in Possession of His Earth.* NY, 1967, 1st ed, boxed. ....$42–$50

Wright, Frank Lloyd. *Genius and the Mobocracy.* NY, 1949, 1st ed, dj. ....$45–$75

Wright, Frank Lloyd. *The Future of Architecture.* NY, 1953, dj.
....$40–$65

Wright, Frank Lloyd. *The Japanese Print and Interpretation.* NY, 1967, 1st ed, boxed. ....$90–$250

Wright, Frank Lloyd. *The Living City.* 1958, 1st ed, dj..$55–$67

Wright, Frank Lloyd. *The Natural House.* Horizon, 1954.
....$50–$150

Wright, Frank Lloyd. *When Democracy Builds.* Univ. of California Press, 1945. ....$75–$125

Wright, G. Frederick. *The Ice Age in North America.* Appleton, 1889, 1st ed. ....$12–$20

Wright, H.B. *Shepherd of the Hills.* 1907, 1st ed. ....$45–$70

Wright, Harold B. *The Uncrowned King.* Book Supply Co., 1910.
....$30–$40

Wright, Harold Bell. *A Son of His Father.* NY, 1925, 1st ed.
....$15–$20

Wright, Harold Bell. *Mine with the Iron Door.* NY, 1923, 1st ed, dj. ....$25–$65

Wright, Henry. *History of the Sixth Iowa Infantry.* Iowa City, 1923. ....$55–$65

Wright, Richard. *Black Boy.* 1st ed, dj. ....*$25–$60*

Wright, Richard. *Black Power.* Harper, 1954. ....*$22–$25*

Wright, Richard. *Native Son.* NY, 1940, 1st ed. ....*$40–$50*

Wright, Robert. *Dodge City—The Cowboy Capital and the Great Southwest.* np, nd, 2nd ed. ....*$65–$100*

Wright, William. *The Grizzly Bear.* NY, 1913, illus. .....*$40–$75*

Wyatt, Thomas. *Manual of Conchology.* NY, 1838, 1st ed, illus, lithos. ....*$65–$85*

Wyeth, Betsy James. *Christina's World.* Bos, 1982, 1st ed, illus, oblong folio, dj. ....*$50–$75*

Wyler, Seymour B. *The Book of Old Silver.* NY, illus, 7th ed, dj. ....*$18–$28*

Wylie, Elinor. *Nets to Catch the Wind.* Harcourt, 1921, 1st ed. ....*$50–$75*

Wylie, Philip. *The Murderer Invisible.* NY, 1931, 1st ed..*$35–$50*

Wyman, Donald. *The Arboretums and Botanical Gardens of North America.* Chronica Botanica, 1947. ....*$15–$25*

Wynne, John. *The Jesuit Martyrs of North America.* NY, 1925, illus, maps. ....*$15–$30*

Wysong, Thomas Turner. *The Rocks of Deer Creek, Hartford County, Maryland.* Balt, 1879, 1st ed. ....*$65–$95*

Yallop, D. *The Day the Laughter Stopped.* NY, 1976, 1st ed. ....*$25–$35*

Yates, Helen. *Bali, Enchanted Isle.* 1933. ....*$10–$18*

Ybarra, T.R. *Caruso, the Man of Naples and the Voice of Gold.* NY, 1953. ....*$18–$30*

Yeats, W.B. *Fairy and Folk Tales of the Irish Peasantry.* Lon, 1888. ....*$95–$125*

Yeats, W.B. *Per Amica Silentia Lunae.* NY, 1918, 1st American ed. ....*$25–$35*

Yeats, William Butler. *Michael Robartes and the Dancer.* Dublin, Cuala Press, 1920, ltd 400 cc. ....*$100–$145*

Yeats, William Butler. *The Winding Stair and Other Poems.* Lon, 1933, 1st ed, dj. ....*$250–$350*

Yoder, Don. *Pennsylvania Spirituals.* PA, 1961, sgn. ......$18–$25

Yost, Nellie. *Man as Big as the West.* Boulder, 1979, 1st ed, dj. ....$18–$25

Young, A.B. Filson. *The Complete Motorist.* Lon, 1904, 1st ed, illus. ....$55–$100

Young, Albert. *Stories from the Adirondacks.* NY, 1899..$25–$30

Young, Egerton R. *My Dogs in the Northland.* NY, illus, 5th ed, sgn. ....$22–$35

Young F. *Happy Motorist.* 1906. ....$16–$20

Younger, Edward (ed). *Inside the Confederate Government.* Oxford Univ. Press, 1957, 1st ed, dj. ....$30–$40

Yount, George C. *George C. Yount and His Chronicles of the West.* Rosenstock, 1966, 1st ed, illus, fldg map. ....$50–$75

Zaharias, Babe Didrikson. *This Life I've Led.* NY, 1955, 1st ed, dj. ....$20–$27

Zangwill, Israel. *Children of the Ghetto.* Lon, 1892, 3 vols, 1st ed. ....$125–$150

Zeidler, J. and J. Lustgarten. *Electric Arc Lamps.* 1908, 1st ed, illus. ....$35–$45

Zeitlin, Ida. *Gessar Khan.* NY, 1927, 1st ed, illus. ......$95–$125

Zeitlin, Solomon. *The Rise and Fall of the Judaean State.* Phila, 1964, 3 vols, illus, 2nd prntg, maps, dj. ....$30–$50

Zevi, Bruno. *Architecture as Space.* NY, 1957, 1st U.S. ed. ....$18–$24

Ziel, Ron. *Twilight of Steam Locomotives.* Grosset & Dunlap, 1963, illus. ....$14–$20

Ziemann and Gillette. *The White House Cook Book.* Chi, 1903, illus, plates. ....$30–$35

Zolotow, Charlotte. *But Not Billy.* Harper, 1983, 1st ed, illus, sgn. ....$30–$40

Zolotow, M. *Marilyn Monroe.* NY, 1960, 1st ed, sgn, presentation copy. ....$45–$75

Zuber, Richard L. *Jonathan Worth: A Biography of a Southern Unionist.* Chapel Hill, 1965, 1st ed, dj. ....$28–$35

Zucker, A.E. *The Chinese Theatre.* Bos, 1925, illus, ltd #329/ 750 cc, slipcase. ....*$195–$250*

Zukor, Adolph. *The Public Is Never Wrong.* NY, 1953, sgn. ....*$30–$35*

Zumbo, Jim and Lois. *The Venison Cookbook.* NY, 1986, dj. ....*$18–$25*

Zworykin, V.K. and G.A. Morton. *Television: The Electronics of Image Transmission.* 1940, 1st ed, illus. ....*$30–$45*

BIBLES

American Bible. "The Eliot" or "Natick Bible." Camb, Indian language translation, scarce. ....$175,000–$250,000

American Bible. Phila, 1790, 2 vols, 1st American ed of the Douai or Roman Catholic Bible. ....$6,500–$10,000

American Bible. Trenton, 1791. ....$1,000–$1,300

American Bible. Phila, 1794, pocket size. ....$75–$100

American Bible. Windsor, VT, 1812. ....$800–$1,000

Bible. Edin, 1817, red mor, aeg. ....$25–$35

Bible. NY, American Bible Society, 1831, lea. ....$24–$35

Bible. Lon, Edward Whitechurch, 1541, 6th ed, folio, sheep binding. ....$1,900–$2,500

Bible in English. Ox, Baskett, 1717, 2 vols, large folio, many errors, called the "Vinegar Bible" because of a proofreading error in Luke XX (word "vinegar" substituted for "vineyard"). ..$600–$900

Bible in English. The Oxford Lectern Bible, Ox, 1935, designed by Bruce Rogers, large folio. ....$6,000–$8,000

Biblia Sacra Polyglotta. Lon, 2 vols, folio. ....$250–$275

Holy Bible. Phila, Bible Society of Philadelphia, 1812, lea, stereotype ed. ....$125–$225

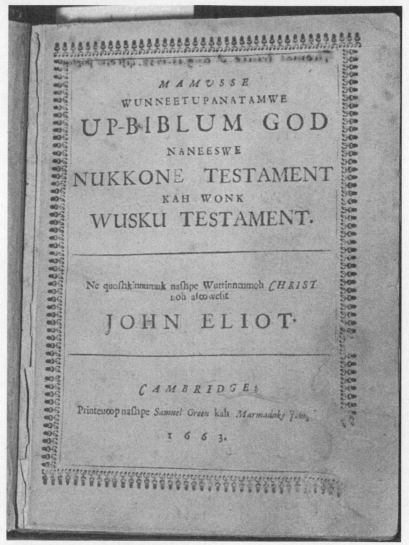

The earliest example in history of an entire bible translated into a new language by John Eliot, known as the Eliot Bible or Natick Bible, it was printed for the Natick colony of "praying Indians" west of Boston, Massachusetts, and completed 1663. (Courtesy of the Trustees of the Boston Public Library. Photographed by Marilyn Green.)

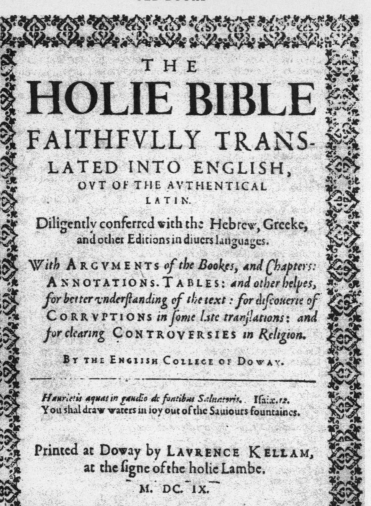

THE
HOLIE BIBLE
FAITHFVLLY TRANS-
LATED INTO ENGLISH,
OVT OF THE AVTHENTICAL
LATIN.

Diligently conferred with the Hebrew, Greeke,
and other Editions in diuers languages.

With ARGVMENTS of the Bookes, and Chapters:
ANNOTATIONS. TABLES: and other helpes,
for better vnderstanding of the text : for discouerie of
CORRVPTIONS in some late translations : and
for clearing CONTROVERSIES in Religion.

BY THE ENGLISH COLLEGE OF DOWAY.

_____

Hauritis aquas in gaudio de fontibus Saluatoris. . Isaïa. 12.
You shal draw waters in ioy out of the Sauiours fountaines.

Printed at Doway by LAVRENCE KELLAM,
at the signe of the holie Lambe.

M. DC. IX.

Title page of the first edition of the Roman Catholic Old Testament in English. It was printed at the city of Douai in France, spelled phonetically "Doway." It was considered unwise to attempt such a publication in England, where Protestantism had been adopted as the recognized state religion. The border is composed of repetitive impressions of a standard design, found in the stock of most printers of that time.

Holy Bible. Lon, 1963, 3 vols. ....$75–$95

Holy Bible, Containing the Old and New Testaments. Cooperstown, NY, 1839, lea. ....$30–$45

Holy Bible, Containing the Old and New Testaments. Phila, 1796, illus, large folio, 376 unnumbered leaves, 16 engr plates, 2 maps, full calf, gilt. ....$1,500–$2,000

Holy the Great Book, Old Testament and New Testament. Lon, 1861, Cree language, calf. ....$500–$850

New Testament. Lon, 1616, 136 pp, mor. ....$75–$100

New Testament. Lon, 1816, folio, silver hinges and clasps. ....$1,200–$1,400

Psalms, Hymns, and Spiritual Songs of the Rev. Isaac Watts. Bos, 1852. ....$10–$15

* * *

Magil, Joseph. *Magil's Linear School Bible.* The 5 Books of Moses, NY, 1905. ....$15–$24

Yates, Elizabeth. *Joseph: The King James Version of a Well-Loved Tale.* Knopf, 1947, 1st ed, dj. ....$15–$22

RECOMMENDED
PERIODICALS
AND RESEARCH BOOKS

AB Bookman's Weekly. P.O. Box AB, Clifton, NJ 07015.

This weekly magazine is arguably the most valuable single source of information currently available for the serious bookman. It includes articles and commentary on specialty markets, personalties in the business, as well as an extensive advertising section of want lists and books for sale. May be the most widely disseminated magazine in the trade, seen all over the world by more dealers and collectors than any other current publication in the field.

AB Bookman's Yearbook. P.O. Box AB, Clifton, NJ 07015.

This treasure is included in the package when subscribing to the weekly magazine, or it can be bought separately. Its features include: bookseller associations directory, geographical listings of dealers, categorical listings of dealers, dealers' permanent want lists, directories of specialty publishers, remainder houses, bookselling services, directories of auction houses, information about foreign dealers, and advertisements.

American Book Prices Current. Box 1236, Washington, CT 06793.

The annual compilation of realized prices of books sold at auction. It lists sales of $50 or more. While an excellent investment, the volumes are expensive and your best bet is to find a good library that carries the books in the reference department.

Bookman's Price Index. Gale Research Inc., Detroit, MI 48226-4094.

A pricing resource.

Carter, John. *ABC for Book Collectors.* Knopf, NY, 1991.

An excellent resource for both novice and expert. Written in the form of a glossary.

Howes, Wright. *U.S. Iana.* R.R. Bowker, NY.

A bibliography of books on the United States.

Mandeville, Mildred. *The Used Book Price Guide.* P.O. Box 82525, Kenmore, WA 98028.

"Mandeville" has been a standard for dealers for decades, offering extensive lists of books and current prices, but subject to the usual cautions as to errors or fluctuations in the markets that pertain to any regularly produced price guides.

McBride, Bill. *Identification of First Editions—A Pocket Guide.* Hartford, CT 06105.

Pointers for identifying first editions from various publishers over the years.

Membership Directory. The Antiquarian Booksellers Association of America (ABAA), 50 Rockefeller Plaza, NY 10020.

A comprehensive listing of dealers in the association. This may overlap the directories in the *AB Bookman's Yearbook* somewhat, but it is more complete and well worth the price. Lianne Wood-Thomas will send a directory to anyone who sends her a business size, self-addressed, stamped envelope and 75 cents.

Muir, P.H. *Book Collecting as a Hobby.*

Out of print, but worth finding.

Zempel, E. and L.A. Verkler (eds). *Book Prices Used and Rare.* Spoon River Press, 2319-C West Rohmann, Peoria, IL 61604-5072.

A price guide.